The Hidden-Hand
Presidency

THE
HIDDEN-HAND
PRESIDENCY

Eisenhower as Leader

FRED I. GREENSTEIN

Basic Books, Inc., Publishers

NEW YORK

WITH THIS BOOK, the Miller Center of Public Affairs at the University of Virginia inaugurates a sponsored series of analytic works on the American presidency.

These works represent the scholarship of those whose research and writing have been encouraged by the Center and who have participated as visiting scholars in the Center's Program on the Presidency. Through this program, the Center undertakes to contribute to the building of a new science of the presidency for our time. The focus is on the study of the organs and philosophies of central power and leadership in the American constitutional system; the underlying concern is how to reconcile the need for effective central leadership with the constitutional imperatives of limited government and divided but shared power—particularly under twentieth-century conditions. Three main areas of inquiry are embraced in the Center's presidency program. One is concerned with the nature and purposes of the presidency as an instrumentality of governance and of leadership in its larger institutional, political, cultural, and historical setting. A second area of inquiry concentrates on particular problems in which the presidency is deeply involved or which carry far-reaching implications for the conduct and organization of the office. A third area of inquiry concentrates on the study of individual presidencies, to learn what lessons may be drawn from the past.

In this path-finding study, Fred I. Greenstein draws a bold new portrait of a president whose approach to the leadership responsibilities of the presidency were not widely perceived during his tenure in office. At the same time, Mr. Greenstein offers a novel approach to understanding the interactions of personalities, institutions, events, and issues that commends itself to future scholars in the continuing search for better understanding of the unique office that is the American presidency.

Mr. Greenstein was visiting scholar at the Miller Center in 1979–80. Here he conducted research and commenced the writing of *The Hidden-Hand Presidency: Eisenhower as Leader*.

Kenneth W. Thompson, Director,
Miller Center of Public Affairs
James Sterling Young, Director
of the Program on the Presidency

Arthur Greenstein
(March 24, 1901 to April 26, 1982)
and Rose Greenstein

Library of Congress Cataloging in Publication Data

Greenstein, Fred I.
    The hidden-hand presidency.

    Includes bibliographical references and index.
    1. Eisenhower, Dwight D. (Dwight David), 1890–1969.
    2. United States—Politics and government—1953–1961.
    3. Leadership—Case studies.   I. Title.
    E836.G73   1982   353.03′1′0924   82–70847
    ISBN 0-465-02948-5 (cloth)
    ISBN 0-465-02951-5 (paper)

Contents

ILLUSTRATIONS   *following p. 55*

PROLOGUE AND ACKNOWLEDGMENTS   *vii*

PART I

Introduction

1   An Exemplary President?   *3*
2   What Manner of Man?   *15*

PART II

Eisenhower's Leadership Style

3   Political Strategies   *57*
4   The Two Faces of Organization   *100*

v

Contents

PART III

An Assessment of the Style and Its Uses

5 Strengths and Weaknesses of the Style:
The Joe McCarthy Case   155
6 Lessons for Other Presidents   228

KEY TO PRIMARY SOURCES AND ABBREVIATIONS   249
NOTES   251
INDEX   273

Prologue and Acknowledgments

I COULD never have imagined in the 1950s that years later I would immerse myself in the study of Dwight D. Eisenhower's leadership. I had voted Democratic as a 1952 undergraduate majoring in political science and as a 1956 graduate student learning to teach and practice it. Before the decade was over I had my own students and was teaching them to view Eisenhower in the same fashion that most of my colleagues and all of the journalists I respected viewed him—as a good-natured bumbler, who lacked the leadership qualities to be an effective president.

Events, speculations, and hard evidence changed my view. The events were the manifest difficulties Eisenhower's successors had in maintaining political effectiveness, even at the minimum levels of winning and serving out second terms. Compared to them he stands up well. The speculations were those of exceptionally perceptive journalists such as Murray Kempton[1] and Garry Wills,[2] who by the late 1960s had re-examined Eisenhower's record and seen in it evidence of shrewd uses of political art and craft, masked by a nonpolitician's façade. The hard evidence began piling up in the mid-1970s in the form of countless previously secret documents showing a fascinating leader not unlike the man Kempton and Wills claimed Eisenhower to be—a politician with apolitical protective coloration. More broadly, the archives and the testimony of numerous former associates of Eisenhower's made it clear that he employed a well-articulated, and to a considerable extent, self-conscious approach to handling certain of the built-in dilemmas of American presidential leadership. It is an approach that needs to be explicated both for the record and because it provides potential lessons for future presidents.

I have had much help in my effort to identify and assess Eisenhower's leadership style. One of my debts is to the audiences, large and small, that listened to my accounts of work in progress; they challenged my assertions, made their own suggestions, and repeatedly sent me back for new information to the archives and on to new interviews with former Eisenhower aides. Archives and interviews, however, were no help in the case of one question I often was asked: "If you knew then, what you know now, would you have shifted your 1952 and 1956 votes to Ike?"

For two reasons I have no answer. First, I have been preoccupied mainly with understanding and assessing the means of Eisenhower's leadership, not its end. His policies also clearly warrant assessment, but they are a mixed bag and would require many separate assessments; and if my aim was retrospective reinspection of my personal voting record, I would also have to re-examine my own political beliefs, both as they apply today and as they would have applied to the circumstances of 1952 and 1956. Since I have not carried out this project, I have no basis for recanting or reaffirming two votes in the 1950s that at any rate are unchangeable and even at the time would have had no effect if changed.

The "what if you knew then what you know now" question has a second, more fundamental reason for being unanswerable. As an outsider I could not then have known the centerpiece of my present knowledge—that behind Eisenhower's seeming transcendence of politics was a vast amount of indirect, carefully concealed effort to exercise influence. My account in chapter 5 of Eisenhower's covert efforts in 1954 to undermine Joe McCarthy, for example, reports exercises of presidential influence on Eisenhower's part that have never before been made public. Furthermore, if they had been made public in 1954, they would have created a congressional backlash that almost certainly would have prevented the Senate's censure of McCarthy in December of that year. In short, my representation of Eisenhower's operating procedures precludes by definition the possibility that in the 1950s I *could* have known what I now know about Eisenhower as a leader and, in particular, about one of his main sources of political effectiveness.

Just as I could not name all the people who asked me helpful questions in my public discussions of Eisenhower's leadership, it would inevitably be an incomplete list if I sought to name the Eisenhower colleagues, friends, and family members who have taken the time—in some cases, many hours, and repeated conversations and exchanges of correspondence—to comment on my interpretations and furnish me with their recollections. Roughly two dozen of them have answered my questions. It was quite clear that many others would have joined them, if I had not finally felt it appropriate to bring my research to a close and write this book. A few of my interviews produced specific information not available elsewhere. In these instances I cite the interviews in the footnotes. But all of the interviews, whether or not cited, have helped to provide me with an appreciation of Eisenhower the man and Eisenhower the leader. I have had conversations with associates of all nine of the modern presidents from Roosevelt to Reagan. None of the nine groups is more unified than Eisenhower's in its admiration of its leader. Even if this book were intended as an apologia (it emphatically is *not*), I am sure that many of the people who have told me of their recollections of Eisenhower would disagree with various of my interpretations. I do hope, however, that they recognize this as a serious exercise in nonfiction and one that at least in its broad contours is consistent with the chief executive they observed directly from their various perspectives.

I will, however, follow the tradition of naming academics and editors who helped me, by adding the customary reminder that although I drew liberally on their advice, the faults and errors in this book are my responsibility. I received valuable suggestions on the content and style of the manuscript from Kathy Antrim, John Burke, I.M. Destler, Richard Fenno, James Fleming, Alexander George, Helen Gregutt, Erwin Hargrove, Hugh Heclo, Richard Immerman, Martin Kessler, Douglas Kinnard, William K. Muir, Anna Kasten Nelson, Nelson Polsby, Gary Reichard, Aaron Wildavsky, and Robert Wright.

Prologue and Acknowledgments

Sheila Leyton, Jeanne Wiggs, Mildred Kalmus, and June Traube typed the manuscript at its various stages.

Finally the Miller Center for Public Affairs of the University of Virginia freed me from teaching for the year during which I consolidated my research and wrote a first draft. I decided upon this topic during a year of research on the evolution of the modern presidency that was supported by resources from a Guggenheim and the American Council of Learned Societies, as well as the Henry R. Luce Foundation, which provided me with an annual research fund during the eight years of my tenure as Henry Luce Professor of Politics, Law and Society at Princeton University. Princeton's Woodrow Wilson School, and in particular Dean Donald Stokes, have furnished me with a research environment and teaching opportunities that contributed substantially to my endeavors. In addition, my work in progress comparing Eisenhower's use of advisors with advisory arrangements in other presidencies, which has been supported by the Ford and Russell Sage Foundations, has inevitably helped me acquire information that I drew upon in this book.

PART I

Introduction

1

AN EXEMPLARY
PRESIDENT?

BY THE 1980s the American presidency has become conspicuously problematic, devouring its incumbents with appalling regularity. Carter and Ford were both defeated for second-term election bids. After a brief honeymoon, each experienced plunging support, largely because much of the public perceived them as ineffective in the use of their powers. By the end of Reagan's first year, his Gallup poll approval rating dipped to 49 percent and most observers foresaw further troubles ahead as a result of ill-conceived policies. Nixon and Johnson came to grief, because they seemed to carry their policy aims too far. So many Americans felt they had abused presidential power that Nixon resigned to avoid removal by Congress, and Johnson scrapped his renomination plans.

Kennedy's one thousand days, numbered by assassination rather than unpopularity, initiated a period of ephemeral presidencies. Increasingly, the chief executive has become a bird of passage. Not long after taking office, he begins to lose credibility with the domestic and foreign leaders whose cooperation he needs to be effective, because of his probable impermanence and because the polls attest to his unpopularity.

From January 1953 to January 1961, however, the United States did have a uniquely popular president, Dwight D. Eisenhower. He was the sole chief executive to serve the two terms permitted by the Constitution since ratification of the Twenty-second Amendment. He averaged 64 percent approval in Dr. Gallup's monthly soundings of how Americans rate the president's performance, exceeding all of the post–World War II presidents except Kennedy, who did not live to face the cost of such policies as his administration's increasing military involvement in Vietnam.[1]

Eisenhower's unique record in winning and holding public support provides one reason why students of American politics have begun to dissect the way this man, who in his time was widely thought of as politically inept and indifferent, carried out the tasks of presidential leadership.[2]

Eisenhower's ability to bridge contradictions built into the presidency provides another reason for the timeliness of his example. The deck of American politics is stacked against effective presidential leadership, even at the minimum level of maintaining enough public support for the president to have a chance to leave an imprint on public policy. Presidents come into office making extravagant promises, but the legal and political checks and balances in the political system (and other intractable forces such as the ups and downs of the economy) make it inevitable that they will disappoint their followers.

In the half-century since the rise of big government and the expansion of the president's role in American politics during Franklin D. Roosevelt's time in office, the presidency has seemed to grow in influence. But in doing so it has acquired disastrous potentialities for its incumbents. Presidents, for example, now have more autonomous executive powers than they had before the 1930s. But every presidential order carries with it the possibility of making enemies and disappointing followers as well as winning friends and successfully shaping policy. Presidents now propose annual legislative programs to Congress, but presidential programs often simply arouse expectations that cannot be fulfilled. And the modern president, in contrast to his pre-1930s predecessor, has come to dominate the headlines—virtually personifying the government. Here again, however, he is vulnerable. He stands out as the best available target for animus when national and international conditions turn sour.[3]

One of the most profound sources of discontent with the performance of presidents was built into the job of chief executive in 1787 by the framers of the Constitution. The American president is asked to perform two roles that in most democracies are assigned to separate individuals. He must serve both as chief of state and as the nation's highest political executive. The roles seem almost designed to collide. As chief of state—the equivalent of a constitutional monarch—the president is a symbol of unity. He is expected by Americans to represent the entire nation. However, as political head of the executive branch, he has the intrinsically divisive responsibilities of a prime minister. He is expected to prevent or prosecute wars, foster a prosperous economy, and bring about desirable social conditions. If he passively sits back and assumes the stance of a genuine constitutional monarch, the country is likely to founder from lack of central guidance. If, on the other hand, he conspicuously leads the polarizing process of welding policy-making coalitions, he loses his broad acceptance as leader of the entire nation.[4]

The unique characteristic of Eisenhower's approach to presidential leadership was his self-conscious use of political strategies that enabled him to carry out both presidential roles without allowing one to undermine the other. These strategies derived from leadership style that explicitly departed from the emphasis of most presidents since Franklin D. Roosevelt on establishing what Richard Neustadt calls professional reputation—the impression of being a skilled, tough politician.[5] On the assumption that a president who is predominantly viewed in terms of his political prowess will lose public support by not appearing to be a proper chief of state, Eisenhower went to great lengths to conceal the political side of his leadership.

He did this so well and played the part of nonpolitical chief of state so convincingly that until recently most writers on the presidency viewed him through the lens of his 1950s liberal critics as an aging hero who reigned more than he ruled and lacked the energy, motivation, and political know-how to have a significant impact on events. During Eisenhower's time in office most president watchers would have agreed with the *New Yorker*'s Richard Rovere, who saw his personality as blandly "standard American," his mind as "unschematic" and "distrustful of fine distinctions," and his performance as that of a man who "most of the time" was bored by "the whole operating side of government."[6] Nor was Rovere alone in his low estimate of Eisenhower. In 1962, Arthur Schlesinger, Sr., asked seventy-five academic authorities on the presidency to list thirty-one chief executives from Washington to Eisenhower in order of "greatness." Eisenhower ranked twenty-first, tied with Chester Arthur.[7] To these scholars, if Eisenhower served as an exemplar of anything it was of how *not* to conduct the presidency.

Some of the revival of interest in Eisenhower derives from no more than nostalgia for what in retrospect seems to have been an untroubled era presided over by a kindly, simple man. Eisenhower nostalgia, by stressing his political innocence, reinforces the impression that there is nothing to be learned from how he did his job.[8]

A more important source of new interest is appreciation of his actions and goals. At the time he left office, Republican boasts of an administration that ended the Korean War and presided over seven-and-a-half years in which not a soldier was lost in combat sounded like standard campaign rhetoric. After Vietnam, however, this could readily be viewed as an accomplishment. Eisenhower's caution in expanding domestic welfare programs seemed uncreative to the authorities Arthur Schlesinger polled in 1962, the great bulk of whom were liberals. In our present postliberal era of disillusionment with the fruits of the Great Society's programs, however, his go-slow social policy has begun to appear more attractive. Similarly, Eisenhower's horror of inflation no longer sounds quaint in light of soaring inflation in the 1970s and 1980s. And his struggle to hold down military expenditures, which in the 1950s was castigated by many liberal Democrats as contributing to bomber and missile gaps, now is open to favorable reassessment as a policy that might have averted the arms race which escalated in the Kennedy and Johnson years.

Not all policy reevaluations have endorsed Eisenhower's goals and actions. In the 1950s, his administration's covert intervention brought about the overthrow of the Mossadegh government in Iran (1953) and the Arbenz government in Guatemala (1954). The political climate of the 1970s and 1980s has not produced retrospective idealization of secretly engineered overthrows by the United States of regimes that the president views as potentially hostile to American interests.[9]

Both the positive and the negative re-evaluations of Eisenhower's policies contribute to still another source of renewed interest in him—his approach to leadership. That he not only had policies worthy of reassessment but pursued his political goals in unique ways undermines the 1950s view of his incumbency as no more than an interregnum of leaderless drift. It is not then a contradiction in terms (as contemporary critics would have said) to speak of "Eisenhower leadership." Instead, it is a challenge—the one to which this book is addressed—to unravel, characterize, and illustrate his leadership style.[10]

Even during Eisenhower's presidency some political observers sensed that there were aspects of Eisenhower's leadership, and of the man himself, that did not meet the eye. Rovere, for example, while sharing the liberal view that Eisenhower was not seriously committed to leading, acknowledged that his presence in office had helped to neutralize the poisonous internal security controversy epitomized in Senator Joseph McCarthy's allegations that domestic subversion was rampant. Moreover, in spite of powerful pressures, Eisenhower had refused to become involved in military conflict in Asia. "One hesitates to attribute political adroitness to a man who has revealed so much political ineptitude as Eisenhower," Rovere concluded, "but it happens to be a fact that he has achieved, through luck or good management, a number of things that are commonly thought to be the product of skill."[11]

The New York Times's Arthur Krock, in a 1957 article on the difference between "impressions of the President" and Eisenhower "the man," came close to identifying Eisenhower's approach of publicly displaying the warm, benign qualities of an uncontroversial head of state, while shielding his coolly detached, politically informed prime ministerial attributes. What Krock called the "outer man" exhibited all the head of state qualities, including those of personal appearance, that helped make him so appealing to the public.

> The President's stature is a happy compromise between the short and the tall. His usual complexion is ruddy under the golfing tan. His blue eyes are kindly, but penetrating. His voice has the rough grain that is accepted as the token of virility, and his accent is the kind known as "Midwestern" that is prevalent in North America.

His manner is genial; his ways and reflexes are kindly; his bearing is soldierly, yet his well-tailored civilian clothes never seem out of character. His smile is attractively pensive, his frequent grin is infectious, his laughter ready and hearty. He fairly radiates "goodness," simple faith and the honest, industrious background of his heritage.

This public Eisenhower, Krock acknowledged, seemed problematic as a presidential technician. Perhaps, Krock suggested, his "staff system make[s] him too dependent on subordinates for the choice and synthesis of public matters laid before him, and for the selection of those to be admitted to his presence." That Eisenhower's personal friends were businessmen and military men seemed to reflect "at least a mild distaste for the company of professional politicians." And Krock wondered whether his "frequent changes of scene and recreation . . . imply that he is irked by his heavy and incessant duties." Krock also reminded his readers of the well known grammatical disorders of Eisenhower's press conference prose "in which numbers and genders collide, participles hang helplessly and syntax is lost forever."

In spite of such outer appearances, Krock, whose prominence in Washington journalism won him numerous off-the-record conversations with Eisenhower, was persuaded of his political ability. "[T]he President is remarkably well informed in a vast field of government operations," Krock wrote. "[H]is occasional unawareness of a major event is merely the result of special concentration at the same time on some difficult administrative problem, and . . . while perhaps he wishes he were not the President more often than some of his predecessors did, he enjoys the power and the glory and is absorbed in his task." Moreover, Krock acknowledged that he periodically sensed in the inner Eisenhower facets not reflected in his normally visible image. There seemed to be more steel and less folksy, idiomatic warmth to the private man than to the public man. Eisenhower, at a press conference, for example, "froze at an implication that helicopters were being bought by public funds for his recreational use."

And when a reporter asked if he had been "filled in" on a large affair of government—a phrase revealing unconscious acceptance of the critical line that the President doesn't know what is going on in Washington unless someone chooses to tell him—he chillingly remarked that this was a "strange locution". . . . The instant effect . . . of the language employed was one of the many demonstrations provided by the press questioning periods that the President's mental process is penetrating and alert.[12]

Several years after Eisenhower left office, another journalist, the *New York Post*'s Murray Kempton, provided the first re-examination of Eisenhower that explicitly delineated an Eisenhower approach to leadership based on complementing the public appearance of political innocence with private toughness. Kempton concluded that he and other 1950s observers had deliberately been misled into "the underestimation of Dwight D. Eisenhower." Reading between the lines of Eisenhower's memoirs and rethinking the episodes of his presidency, Kempton was persuaded that behind the warm outward appearance there was an Eisenhower who never lost the disposition to calculate, consider options, and accept casualties as well as victories required of a supreme commander.[13]

Eisenhower's unsentimental political realism, Kempton felt, was revealed in his easy acknowledgement that in 1960 the Soviet Union had captured a U-2 spy plane and its pilot only because a mechanical failure had prevented the plane from disintegrating and therefore the pilot inadvertently survived.[14] Kempton believed that Richard Nixon was on the mark in his explanation of why Eisenhower had seemed ready to abandon him as a running mate in 1952 and 1956 for political expediency. Eisenhower, Nixon notes, "was a far more complex and devious man than most people realized."*

Since the 1970s, direct sources for reevaluating the man and his leadership have been uncovered. It is no longer necessary to speculate as to whether Eisenhower was the simple "Kansas farmer-boy"-turned soldier[16] he claimed to be, rather than a politician whose operations were deliberately shielded from contemporaries other than his immediate associates.

Mountains of unpublished documents from the Eisenhower presidency have been released for the use of scholars by such archival reposi-

---

*Adding the propitiatory qualifier "in the best sense of these words," Nixon went on to suggest why this was so. Eisenhower was "not shackled to a one-track mind." Rather, "he always applied two, three or four lines of reasoning to a single problem and he usually preferred the indirect approach where it would serve him better than the direct attack on the problem."[15]

tories as the Dwight D. Eisenhower Library, Abilene, Kan., and the John Foster Dulles Collection, Princeton University, Princeton, N. J. Eisenhower's orderly record-keeping habits and those of his associates, notably his confidential secretary, Mrs. Ann Whitman, have left us minute-by-minute records of those who entered and left his office each working day, with a careful indication of whether meetings were off the record. Eisenhower himself maintained an extensive confidential correspondence with an extraordinary range of friends and acquaintances in many walks of life at home and abroad, virtually all of it under security classification at the time it was written or marked "private and confidential." His phone conversations and official and unofficial meetings were carefully summarized by minute-takers. Even some of his one-to-one conversations in the Oval Office were recorded and transcribed. In addition, a private diary he kept intermittently from 1935 to several months before his death in 1969 is now available, as are the numerous oral histories of his associates and a still growing body of their memoirs.*

Extensive evidence is now also available on the portion of Eisenhower's prepresidential military years in which he was deeply involved in civil-military relations. The first phase of this service, extending for more than a decade before Pearl Harbor, is documented largely by his diary, oral histories, and various memoirs. The second phase, after his rapid rise to prominence, is copiously documented in the nine volumes of *The Papers of Dwight D. Eisenhower* published to date, and archives, memoirs, historical studies, and other sources.[17]

Eisenhower's prepresidential papers reveal an extraordinary continuity in his career and leadership style before and after entering the White House. His mode of politicking in the military, when he dealt

---

*The main Eisenhower Library manuscript collections I have drawn on, along with other primary sources, are listed on pp. 249–50. My account of Eisenhower and his style of leadership is also based on interviews and correspondence with twenty-eight of his former associates, including family members. For some general background, I was able to make a complete examination of the still unreleased Sherman Adams papers from the Baker Library, Dartmouth College, Hanover, N.H., which were complemented by conversations with Mr. Adams. The reader should bear in mind that most of the unpublished sources I have used provide a glimpse of Eisenhower's leadership from *his* perspective and from that of his associates or at least sometime political allies. It is outside the compass of my study to survey observations about his leadership in the archives of his critics and adversaries, except to the degree (which in Eisenhower's case is substantial) that their views were reflected in the media of the day.

with Churchill, Roosevelt, de Gaulle, or Truman, was remarkably parallel to his manner of resolving the potential role conflict built into the presidency. In both settings he denied being a "politician" or understanding politics, but in both he exercised political influence. In each case his public discourse was scrupulously nonpolitical. He made his appeals in terms of the national interest and in terms of the specialized competence he could claim by virtue of his official role, whether as a military technician before he went into politics in 1952 or as a defender of constitutional principles when he was in the White House.

Eisenhower himself felt that being president was an extension of his previous leadership experience. Reflecting on his first day in the Oval Office, he noted in a January 21, 1953, diary entry that he was encountering "plenty of worries and difficult problems." But, he continued, "such has been my portion for a long time—the result is that this seems (today) like a continuation of all I've been doing since July '41—even before that."[18]

He had good grounds for this observation. In the summer of 1941, as chief of staff of the Third Army, Eisenhower, for the first time, received national attention. The press reported that he was the strategist for the winning side in a major defense-preparedness war game. For the previous decade and a half he had been known within the army as a promising officer. He had been intensely interested in both national security and international order in the years between the wars and was convinced that the unresolved problems spawned by the First World War would lead to a new global conflict. Moreover, his career during that period had been, in a broad sense, richly political rather than strictly military.

He rose to service-wide visibility because he graduated first in a class of 275 officers, in 1926, in the army's elite Command and General Staff School; the army promptly shifted him from run-of-the-mill assignments to major civil-military responsibilities, first, in Washington, as an aide to General Pershing and then, after 1929 as deputy of the Assistant Secretary of the Army. From 1933 to 1940 he was chief aide and speech writer for the army's most colorful, politically manipulative general, Douglas MacArthur. Eisenhower worked under MacArthur in Washington from 1933 to 1935, when MacArthur was Chief of Staff, and after 1935 in the Philippines, where MacArthur was military-preparedness advisor to that then emerging nation.

Eisenhower had been in an excellent position to learn the mores of politics in the capital during his prewar service in Washington. His youngest and favorite brother, Milton, was already off to an impressive start as a career civil servant, specializing in public relations for the Department of Agriculture. Milton was a regular tutor to Dwight in the maze of national government. Moreover, the older brother was directly exposed to the massive expansion in size and responsibilities of the federal government as the Hoover administration made way for Roosevelt and the New Deal.

It was after Roosevelt's election that Eisenhower became MacArthur's aide, a position he held until 1940. "I found," Eisenhower later recollected, that MacArthur "was well acquainted with most of the people in government in almost every department. Working with him brought an additional dimension to my experience. My duties were beginning to verge on the political, even to the edge of partisan politics."[19] And after 1935, with MacArthur in the Philippines, Eisenhower took the leading part in drafting the bills presented to the Philippine legislature for military preparedness. He became well acquainted both with lawmakers and with President Manuel Quezon. As Lucius Clay, an astute observer and close friend, was to comment, Eisenhower's exposure to all dimensions of Philippine public policy making gave him a broader education in the problems of civil government than advising in a large, industrial society would have permitted.[20]

The prepresidential phase of Eisenhower's career most relevant to his performance in office began several days after Pearl Harbor, when he was transferred by Chief of Staff George C. Marshall to the Planning Division of the War Department. Only a few hours after reporting to Marshall, Eisenhower furnished the Chief of Staff with a plan, which Marshall asked him to frame, detailing the basic elements of a strategy for responding to the devastating damage the Japanese were inflicting on Allied forces. Eisenhower's analysis melded political with narrowly military considerations. Militarily he focused on the need to establish Australia as a base of operations, securing its supply lines. The political issues he raised were connected with alliance maintenance. He stressed the need to keep Russia in the war. And, even though he knew the American forces in the Philippines were doomed, he urged supplying them, because the Chinese and other allies in the area (and he could well have added the American people) "may excuse failure but will not excuse abandonment."[21]

Such analyses clearly impressed Marshall, who continued to test his new aide, pouring on increasingly demanding assignments. By February 1942, the first photograph of Eisenhower accompanied by a headline story appeared in the *New York Times*—he had just been named head of the Planning Division.[22] By the end of June, having been carefully scrutinized by Roosevelt and Churchill, he was advanced again. Leapfrogging hundreds of officers with greater seniority, he was named Commanding General, European Theater of Operations.

By the end of 1942, Eisenhower was deeply immersed in both the military and political complexities of commanding the Western Alliance. He became a globally prominent target for incessant media attention that quickly made him a "personage." His negotiations with Vichy French leaders to secure a safe landing in North Africa provoked intense controversy. They also provided him with an object lesson in the highly sensitive political requirements of supreme commandership in a war dependent on maintaining an alliance between the armed forces of fiercely independent nations and on rallying "home front" support.

The inextricably fused military-political requirements of Eisenhower's World War II job are excellently captured in Stephen Ambrose's *The Supreme Commander*.[23] During the war he dealt personally with the major leaders of the European Alliance. He came to know most of the significant figures in his own nation's government. Above all, he emerged a national hero. Without a break, serving from November 1945 to February 1948, Eisenhower returned to Washington, this time as Army Chief of Staff, and performed as a significant behind-the-scenes actor in the politics of unifying the military and seeking to maintain a defense establishment consistent with great-power status. After the war he was especially closely associated with Truman, Defense Secretary James V. Forrestal, and the leaders of both congressional parties. At the same time, he managed to maintain cordial but studiously noncommittal relations with the leaders of both parties who between 1945 and 1952 sought to persuade him to become a presidential candidate.

The archives covering Eisenhower's prepresidential years from

1948–50 as president of Columbia University (and frequent Defense Department consultant) and 1951–52 as North Atlantic Treaty Alliance Organization (NATO) commander show that he continued to exercise a major, if largely unpublicized, political influence, seeking to shape and maintain the postwar Western Alliance. During his university presidency he also undertook to express in rather general terms his enthusiasm for "free enterprise," asserting a commitment to domestic economic conservatism that stimulated more Republican than Democratic efforts to draft him as a presidential nominee. At this time he vastly extended his personal acquaintances among nationally prominent figures, including a network of prosperous business friends who later were to finance his presidential candidacy.

When Eisenhower resigned his NATO command in June 1952 to run for the Republican nomination, he brought with him an unusual mind-set for an ostensibly nonpolitical national hero. He knew most of the major international leaders and had just been closely involved with what was to be a major concern of his administration— maintaining the Western Alliance. He realized that those politicians and business leaders in his own country whom he did not know personally knew who he was and took him seriously as a political force. He had a well-developed sense of the workings of national government and a conception he was gradually to reveal of how they might be improved.

Although Eisenhower's presidential style evolved from his prepresidential style, his conduct of the presidency was not a simple extension of his military experience and training. Rather, both his military and his political performance reflected his personal qualities. Some of the qualities of Eisenhower the man are so closely tied to his approach to presidential leadership that they must be examined both to understand that approach and to establish whether any aspects of it could be employed by someone other than Dwight D. Eisenhower.

2

WHAT MANNER OF MAN?

EISENHOWER'S vice-president, Richard Nixon, was not the only one to remark on his complexity; many others acquainted with the nonpublic man, made similar observations. What most of them appear to have recognized was the obvious intricacy of the political psychology of a leader who in many respects displayed antithetical qualities in public and in private. The testimonies of three such observers—a journalist, a congressman, and a presidential advisor—point to an array of Eisenhower's personal qualities, each differing in its public and private manifestations, that shaped his leadership style.

Journalist Theodore White reports that in the course of covering Eisenhower at NATO in 1951 and observing him closely he was forced to reverse the impression he had formed on the basis of Eisenhower's public persona. "I made the mistake," White confessed, "so many observers did of considering Ike a simple man, a good straightforward soldier."

Yet Ike's mind was not flaccid; and gradually, reporting him as he performed, I found his mind was tough, his manner deceptive; that the rosy private smile could give way, in private, to furious outbursts of temper; that the tangled rambling rhetoric of his off-the-record remarks could, when he wished, be disciplined by his own pencil into clean hard prose.[1]

Congressman Stuyvesant Wainwright, an Eisenhower Republican, discovered a world of difference between the impression left by the *New York Times,* which "always made him out to be a mediocre, fumbling, ignorant boob," and the informed, issue-involved president with whom he had periodic conferences. Moreover, his bond as an Eisenhower loyalist was strengthened by his awareness of the president's depth of knowledge about public affairs:

> When I went in there to talk with him, I used to come away on cloud nine, I was so impressed. And not just by the man. I was impressed because he knew exactly what he was talking about. I'd read about how he had been out in the morning taking putting practice, but when we went there he knew his business. He would ask us about paragraph three of section 4B. And I used to say, "Mr. President, someone must have briefed you pretty well five minutes ago," and he would say, "No, I looked it over last night." He knew what was in the bill, and he knew what to ask. It was just the opposite from what the papers said![2]

It was Henry Kissinger, however, whose perception of Eisenhower changed most dramatically. He first met the former president during the last months of his life. Though physically enfeebled, Eisenhower nevertheless still exhibited a vividly forceful personality and great political sophistication and interest. Kissinger met Eisenhower in Walter Reed Hospital shortly after Nixon's election and again, with Nixon, soon after his inauguration, only seven weeks before Eisenhower's death. On the first visit Kissinger's purpose was to seek advice on how to coordinate national foreign policy-making machinery. Eisenhower's practice had been to coordinate agencies responsible for making foreign policy in the Executive Office of the President, but Kennedy had abolished this procedure and Johnson had experimented with a State Department-led interdepartmental group that promptly became the object of rivalry among agencies competing for foreign policy-making primacy. Kissinger recalls that Eisenhower was emaciated by his illness and largely immobilized by a heart pacemaker. I had never met him before, and held about him the conventional academic opinion that he was a genial but inarticulate war hero who had been a rather ineffective President. Two of my books and several articles deplored the vacuum of leadership of his Administration—a view I have since changed. Successive heart attacks had left little doubt that he had not long to live. Despite this, his forcefulness was surprising. His syntax, which seemed so awkward in print, became much more graphic when enlivened by his cold, deep blue, extraordinarily penetrating eyes and when given emphasis by his still commanding voice.[3]

Eisenhower promptly displayed his sensitivity to the realities of Washington politics, warning Kissinger that bureaucratic competition would doom the Johnson-initiated arrangements. The Defense Department would not "accept State Department domination of the national security process. It would either attempt end-runs or counterattack by leaking."

Kissinger's second meeting with Eisenhower was on February 2, 1969. He and Nixon told Eisenhower of a State Department proposal that the United States take a direct part in international negotiations designed to force Israeli concessions in the interest of achieving détente in the Middle East. They discussed this and other national security issues with Eisenhower, who "seemed even more emaciated" than the last time Kissinger had seen him.

He spent much of the time warning Nixon against leaks of NSC proceedings. Nixon told him about our Middle East discussion. Eisenhower argued against major American involvement in the negotiations. Probably reflecting the agony he went through over Suez in 1956, he thought the best course was to let the parties work it out themselves. If we became active we would be forced in the end to become an arbiter and then offer the parties our own guarantee of whatever final arrangement emerged. This would keep us embroiled in Middle East difficulties forever. The next day, I had not been in my office many minutes before an irate Eisenhower was on the phone. He had just read a *New York Times* story reporting that the NSC meeting had determined that the United States would not pursue a more active policy in the Middle East. With a vigor that belied my memory of his frailty—and a graphic vocabulary at variance with his sunny smile—he berated me for letting down the President by not restricting the number of participants.[4]

17

These accounts reveal apparent contradictions in Eisenhower's personal qualities that I will illustrate and analyze in this chapter. My illustrations of the man, however, also often illuminate his leadership style, which is the topic of chapters three and four. Taken together, therefore, chapters two through four provide insight into the influence of Eisenhower's personality on his leadership.[5] Both White's and Kissinger's accounts capture a particularly striking dichotomy between the public man whose "tangled, rambling rhetoric" made him seem on first impression to be a vague thinker, and the private one who expressed himself with clear incisiveness, reflecting a keen analytic mind. Eisenhower channeled both the public vagueness and the private precision into his style of leadership.

Wainwright and Kissinger detected a second apparent contradiction in Eisenhower's political psychology: he professed and appeared to be nonpolitical but clearly understood and sought seriously to influence politics and policy.

Wainwright's implication that leaving meetings with Eisenhower "on cloud nine" strengthened his attachment to him points to a third aspect of the man: his extraordinary capacity to win the support of other political leaders. This "trait" paralleled the truly distinctive capacity Eisenhower had for winning support from the American public. Both in winning and sustaining this support Eisenhower *seemed* totally artless, in White's phrase "a simple man." However, underlying his capacity to win support was a dimension he did not make public, that of self-conscious artfulness. An Eisenhower whose strong temper and emotions contrasted with the beaming visage on the campaign buttons emerges in White's and Kissinger's remarks. This raises yet another consideration—that of the nature of his feelings and energies and the ways he expressed and channeled them in his leadership. Finally, there is the matter of his specifically political feelings—his beliefs and convictions. Only an awareness of them makes possible an understanding of certain of his political actions, which, notably in domestic policy, differed from his publicly stated policy positions.

Public Vagueness and Private Precision

Since Eisenhower's press conference transcripts were the single most influential source of his reputation for vague expressions and muddled thinking, it is well to keep in mind Kissinger's observation that, even when Eisenhower's sentences did not parse, his meaning was hammered home by the force and vividness of his personality. Compare the transcript of an Eisenhower press conference with a recording of it. In the recording, the muddled syntax recedes and his voice emphatically and persuasively conveys his message. The films of Eisenhower, which became regular fare for the television viewers—who by the mid-1950s included virtually the entire electorate—are even more effective. His mobile, expressive face and dignified but comfortable comportment, emerge as the expression of a manifestly warm human being who speaks earnestly of his and the nation's ideals.[6] He comes across as solid and full of common sense—a reassuring figure who lived up to his own premise that, as the visible symbol of the nation, the president should exhibit a "respectable image of American life before the world."[7]

By no stretch of the imagination, however, could the bulk of his press conference discourse be said to reveal sharply honed reasoning. Even when he dealt with some of the complexities of an issue, he usually did so through broad simplifications and in a colloquial manner. And asserting that he was not informed about them, he often refused to discuss complexities. He conveyed the impression of a leader who took it for granted that much of the detailed content of contemporary issues was "non-presidential," frequently referring questioners to cabinet secretaries for answers to issues that he said were in their domain, not his, or had not yet been sufficiently studied by subordinates to come to his attention.

The intellectual thinness and syntactical flaws in press conference texts, Eisenhower would later write, resulted from caution. With press conferences open to quotation and broadcast, "an inadvertent misstatement in public would be a calamity." But, he continued, realizing that "it is far better to stumble or speak guardedly than to move ahead smoothly and risk imperilling the country," by consistently focusing on ideas rather than on phrasing, he "was able to avoid causing the

19

nation a serious setback through anything I said in many hours, over eight years of intensive questioning." Then, in the understated mode he used when he chose to draw attention to one of his strengths, he went on to add, "I soon learned that ungrammatical sentences in the transcripts caused many to believe I was incapable of using good English: indeed, several people who have my private papers, many in my handwriting, have expressed outright astonishment that in my writings syntax and grammatical structure were at least adequate."[8]

They were, as he well knew, more than adequate. The Eisenhower Library files contain many letters and memoranda he composed, some marked "private and confidential," others classified for security purposes, reflecting the clean, hard writing, and, by extension, thinking, to which White refers. They include dispassionate, closely reasoned assessments of contemporary issues and personalities that belie the amiable, informal, and often vague usages of his press conference discourse. Startlingly, for a man who seemed, to as acute an observer as Richard Rovere, to have an "unschematic" mind, many of his confidential writings display geometric precision in stating the basic conditions shaping a problem, deducing their implications, and weighing the costs and benefits of alternative possible responses.[9]

Eisenhower's reasoning ability and method are best revealed in one of his confidential analyses of a particularly complex, controversial issue, a six-page single-spaced letter to his one-time chief of staff, then NATO Commander Alfred Gruenther, on the "offshore islands" dispute. This dispute, a legacy of the Chinese civil war, mainly concerned Quemoy and Matsu, which are immediately adjacent to the Chinese coast. When the mainland became the People's Republic of China (PRC), the defeated Nationalist regime had established itself roughly 150 miles from the mainland on Formosa and the neighboring Pescadores, but it also retained islands virtually in sight of the shore. Sharing the belief of Chiang Kai-Shek that Quemoy and Matsu could serve as springboards for a Nationalist return to the mainland, powerful forces within Eisenhower's party were deeply committed to the Nationalist cause. The PRC viewed Nationalist occupation of the islands as a provocation and wanted Quemoy and Matsu as its own stepping-stones—to Formosa.

Eisenhower wrote to Gruenther on February 1, 1955, shortly after securing a congressional resolution authorizing the president to defend Formosa, the Pescadores, and, in phrase that was conspicuously vague, "such related positions and territories of that area now in friendly hands . . . as he judges to be appropriate in assuring the defense of Formosa and the Pescadores." In his long letter Eisenhower carefully laid out the official and unofficial rationale behind his deliberately ambiguous public position. The letter deals with strategy but is of importance here for what it shows about how Eisenhower's mind worked when he was not expressing himself for publication. His statement to Gruenther of his reasoning is carefully elaborated and tightly organized; he approaches this emotional issue with analytic detachment; and his use of language reveals both experience with political analysis and a jaundiced view of Chiang Kai-shek and his friends and enemies which, if publicized, would have undermined the image of simple Ike Eisenhower, incapable of seeing flaws in his contemporaries.

Eisenhower begins by listing and characterizing the foreign and domestic actors implicated in any possible action that might be taken on the offshore islands, in effect positing axioms from which his analysis follows:

> We have a Europe that, speaking generally, is fearful of what some Europeans consider American recklessness, impulsiveness and immaturity in the foreign field. In Red China we have a dictatorial regime which seeks every opportunity to develop among its own people and all other Asiatics a deeper and deeper hatred of the West, particularly of the United States. In Formosa we have the remnants* of the Chinese Nationalists who are suspicious of any move in the Far East that does not involve an "immediate direct and destructive attack on Red China."

"At home," he went on, using language that would have antagonized Asia-oriented Republicans, who were prepared to fight for Quemoy and Matsu, and liberal Democrats, who saw no reason to defend even Formosa and the Pescadores, "we have the truculent and the timid, the jingoists and the pacifists."

---

*A pejorative usage that would have offended the "return to the Mainland" Republican right.

21

To these initial premises he added a further axiom. Like "any military man," he and Gruenther could readily

> make clear distinction between the defense of Formosa and the defense of the so-called offshore islands. Not only are two different military problems presented, but in the one case [Formosa] we are talking about territories the control of which has passed from nation to nation through the years—and in the other case [Quemoy-Matsu], about territories that have always been a part of the Chinese mainland both politically and, in effect, geographically. If there were no other factors than the military to consider, you and I, for example, would study the problem and would very quickly reach a decision that we would permit *no* advance by the Communists beyond the offshore islands, but that in any struggle involving only the territory of those islands, we would see no reason for American intervention.

But the problem was not simply military. Eisenhower went on to infer the likely responses of the domestic and foreign actors, to a declaration committing the United States to defend Formosa but not the offshore islands. A policy of "no advance beyond the offshore islands" would "infuriate the Chinese Communists," whose real interest was Formosa; a policy of no intervention in the case of an attack only on those islands "would infuriate the Chinese Nationalists." Both commitments "would more or less please our European friends": not defending the islands "implies to them a moderate attitude on our part," while agreeing to defend Formosa would be approved by "responsible officials in those countries" who would fear domino effects that could lead to eventual loss of Japan, the Philippines, and Indonesia.

"At home," Eisenhower continued, the hypothetical solution of defending only Formosa and letting it be known that the offshore islands were not to be defended, "would be accepted by most merely because it is simple to describe," though, of course, he knew it would not be accepted by the powerful bloc of congressional Republicans who backed Chiang Kai-shek. Abroad, he continued, the Nationalists' morale and hence "their hope that some day they will go back to their homeland" would have to be maintained to keep the West from losing "the island barrier in the Western Pacific."

Eisenhower then turned to the likely consequences of the solution that Chiang and his American supporters urged—that the United States "state flatly" that it would defend Quemoy and Matsu. This solution, he concluded, "would frighten Europe and of course . . . infuriate the Chinese Communists." Moreover, it would pose a major geopolitical problem:

> By announcing this as a policy we would be compelled to maintain in the area, at great cost, forces that could *assure* the defense of islands that are almost within wading distance of the mainland. This defensive problem could be extremely difficult over the long term, and I think the world in general, including some of our friends, would believe us unreasonable and practically goading the Chinese Communists into a fight. We could get badly tied down by any such inflexible attitude.

Given this delicate balance of pros, cons, and contingencies, Eisenhower had retained personal control over whether to commit American forces, if the PRC attacked Quemoy and Matsu. He explained to Gruenther that in "the Resolution . . . passed by the Congress, at my request . . . , [the] wording, as to areas outside Formosa and the Pescadores, is vague. In view of what I have just said, you can understand why this is so." He would, Eisenhower continued, defend the offshore islands if and only if an invasion of them were "primarily a preliminary movement to an all-out attack on Formosa." And although he did not tell Gruenther how he would decide whether this was the case, as a military man Gruenther would have been aware of two factors that protected Eisenhower from having to make a hair-trigger decision: an attack truly bent on reaching Formosa would have called for more amphibious equipment than the PRC had at its disposal; and, through aerial reconnaissance, the president could establish whether a PRC threat to invade the offshore islands was accompanied by sufficient equipment to be taken seriously.

Anchoring his analysis, Eisenhower stressed, was the root premise "that nothing could be worse than global war" and a parallel assumption that the Soviet Union did not want

> war at this time—in fact, I do not believe that if we became engaged in rather a bitter fight along the coast of China, Russia would want to inter-

23

vene with her own forces. She would, of course, pour supplies into China in the effort to exhaust us and certainly would exploit the opportunity to separate us from our major allies. But I am convinced that Russia does not want . . . to experiment with the means of defense against the bombing that we *could* conduct against her mainland. At the same time, I assume that Russia's treaty with Red China comprehends a true military alliance, which she would either have to repudiate or take the plunge. As a consequence of this kind of thinking, she would probably be in a considerable dilemma if we got into a real shooting war with China. It would not be an easy decision for the men in the Kremlin, in my opinion.

The letter to Gruenther reflects a far more carefully articulated line of reasoning than domestic critics of the "provocative" offshore island policy would have credited to Eisenhower. It reveals that he had deeply skeptical views both of Chiang and of "truculent" domestic politicians, which his public comportment never revealed. It also displays an ability rarely detected in the utterances of leaders. Eisenhower describes *how* he reasons his way to policies. "More and more," he reflected,

> I find myself, in this type of situation—and perhaps it is because of my advancing years—tending to strip each problem down to its simplest possible form. Having gotten the issue well defined in my mind, I try in the next step to determine what answer would best serve the *long term* advantage and welfare of the United States and the free world. I then consider the *immediate problem* and what solutions we can get that will best conform to the long term interests of the country and at the same time *can command a sufficient approval in this country so as to secure the necessary Congressional action.* [10] (Emphasis in the original.)

"Command a sufficient approval," "necessary Congressional action"—these phrases and his value judgments about "jingoists" and "pacifists" suggest the second personal quality that bears on Eisenhower's political leadership—the capacity of this ostensibly nonpolitical man to think in political terms.

The "Nonpolitician" as a Political Man

The letter to Gruenther reveals more than Eisenhower's rhetorical and cognitive style; it indicates that he had a capacity for practical political thought. He assessed the political motivations of others, anticipating their likely responses to alternative courses of action, and had an explicit decision-making criterion—a decision must be in the long-term public interest *and* must be acceptable domestically so that congressional support can be assured. In short, the Eisenhower who was widely thought of as nonpolitical, who himself insisted that he was not a politician, and who in private used the words "politics" and "politician" pejoratively, employed reasoning processes that bespoke political skill and sensitivity.

Eisenhower's inclination and capacity to analyze the behavior of others in terms of their political motives became apparent immediately after his rise to public visibility. During his 1942 dealings with the Vichy France commander in North Africa, Admiral Jean Darlan, Eisenhower explained to Marshall what it was about the behavior of Darlan and the other Vichy leaders that led him to work with the admiral and to shape his own action in ways that would best maintain Darlan's cooperation. Acknowledging that he had "some appreciation of all the political problems created by the necessity we have met of dealing with Darlan," he noted that nevertheless "the source of all practical help here has been Darlan."

> All the others . . . await his lead and will do nothing definitive unless he speaks. So far he has refused us nothing. If he is playing a crooked game with us locally it is so deep that he can afford to give away initial advantages of every kind, even those upon which our existence depends in our present attenuated condition.

Given this, Eisenhower felt it essential to "preserve the attitude that we are dealing with a friend rather than an enemy."

> I feel it is a mistake to demand cooperation and a friendly attitude on the one hand and on the other to act here like we have a conquering Army which enforces its will by threat and views with intense suspicion every pro-

posal of these people. This explanation is submitted to you personally so you may understand why in certain details that appear to us relatively unimportant we attempt to be magnanimous and ostentatiously trustful.[11]

The reference to Darlan's "game" fits perfectly with an account of Eisenhower's analytic bent by a long-time aide, General Andrew J. Goodpaster, who was present at many of Eisenhower's strategy conferences at NATO and in the White House. Pointing out that Eisenhower's apprenticeship during a 1922–24 tour of duty as executive officer in Panama with the legendary military intellectual, General Fox Conner, and his work at the Command and General Staff College had instilled in him "the orderly process of reasoning and analysis that is represented in the commander's estimate of the situation," Goodpaster observed that this called for thinking of collective activities in terms of the options open to the various parties. Goodpaster perceived a parallel between Eisenhower's political (as well as military) reasoning and game theory, the formal, mathematical, decision-making mode developed in the 1940s and 1950s and extensively used in cold war nuclear deterrence calculations. "Anything that's based on the theory of games, or a doctrine or technique that conforms to that," Goodpaster commented, "fits well into . . . the way that General Eisenhower's mind works."

He's a great poker player, and extremely good bridge player. He plays bridge very much in poker style and he's a tremendous man for analyzing the other fellow's mind, what options are open to the other fellow, and what line he can best take to capitalize or exploit the possibilities, having figured the options open to the other man. Under Fox Conner . . . he became keenly interested in the command process, not just the mechanics of it so much as the analysis of what was in the commander's mind—what was in Lee's mind, for example, at Gettysburg.

In analyzing "the other fellow's mind" Eisenhower used the reasoning process he described to Gruenther: stripping a problem "down to its simplest possible form." He did not dwell on the sources or subtleties of personalities. Rather, he parsimoniously identified principal traits, focusing on those that bore directly on public performance. As he stressed in conversations with Goodpaster, he formed in his mind explicit sketches of what he called the "personal equations" of his counterparts.[12]

An example is Eisenhower's effort to unravel President Lyndon B. Johnson's motives for announcing after the Tet offensive in Vietnam that he would cease bombing the North "in the hope that this would lead to a satisfactory peace" and that he would not accept renomination. "This abrupt change in policy, without any *quid pro quo* from Hanoi, will," Eisenhower reflected, "of course, further bewilder the United States." As far as he could see, Johnson's shift lacked a cogent rationale.

It appears to be not only contrary to the President's announced determination in the matter, but a partial capitulation, at least, to the "peace at any price" people in our country. . . . The final and most puzzling feature of his talk was his declaration that he would not seek and would not accept the nomination of his Party for the Presidency of the United States. . . . To me it seems obvious that the President is at war with himself and while trying vigorously to defend the actions and decisions he has made in the past, and urging the nation to pursue those purposes regardless of cost, he wants to be excused from the burden of office to which he was elected. He made no mention of the leader from his own Party who should now, in his stead, carry forward the effort. Indeed, I was left with the conclusion that the President had not truly analyzed the implications of his speech. . . .

A. One possible interpretation would be that the speech should be taken at its face value, with the President believing that he was doing a service to the nation by trying thus to keep the Presidency out of partisan and divisive politics. If taken in this way . . . I believe it shows some very confused thinking.

B. Another possibility is that the President, who has always been sensitive to public and private polls, has come to the conclusion that he cannot win in the coming political campaign and is therefore taking the occasion, before the Wisconsin Primary, to remove himself from the political scene. . . .

C. Another possibility is that the President may have hoped by this speech to re-establish the trust in him which has been lacking among our people. . . .

D. The purpose of this talk may have been to discredit McCarthy and Kennedy. By picturing himself as a self-sacrificing patriot, concerned only in his country, he may have hoped to show up these two men—one as a sheer opportunist, the other a visionary.

27

I am besieged by papers and others to "make a statement." I am . . . refusing to say anything until I can convince myself of the true motivation of this performance.[13]

Johnson's "equation," Eisenhower felt, revolved around extreme readiness to be opportunistic about policies. He also was aware that Johnson as a congressional leader had been a pragmatic analyst of political consequences. Since even an opportunistic motive for the announcement was difficult for Eisenhower to infer, he was suspending judgment.

Eisenhower's diagnosis of Johnson, with whom he had worked closely in the past, was exceedingly negative. He imparted his view of Johnson to his friend William E. Robinson, while the two were watching the 1960 convention the morning Kennedy was to announce his choice for vice-president. "At that moment," Robinson recorded, "any gambler would have got 20-to-1 that Lyndon Johnson would not be a candidate. Yet the President was positive about it and didn't even want to make a second guess," Robinson reports:

I remonstrated with him, saying "How could Lyndon Johnson—having said all the things he did about Kennedy, having said over and over again he wouldn't be a Vice Presidential candidate, having said he would much rather be the Senate leader of the majority party where he would have more power and influence—could he possibly consider what would be, under Kennedy, a very obscure job (not like Nixon under Eisenhower)?"

Dwight D. Eisenhower said to me, "Of course, that's very sound thinking and fairly good deduction, unless you know Johnson. He is not a big man. He is a small man. He hasn't got the depth of mind nor the breadth of vision to carry great responsibility. Any floor leader of a Senate majority party looks good, no matter how incompetent he may be. Johnson is superficial and opportunistic."[14]

Eisenhower, however, would have considered it politically unwise to make public his distaste for Johnson. He managed, in fact, to maintain the affection of that thin-skinned man. Arthur Krock describes a conversation he had with President Johnson in May 1965. The occasion was one of Johnson's long rambling White House lawn walks accompanied by newspaper reporters. Johnson went to considerable lengths to praise Dwight Eisenhower as a man and as a mind. He said the satiric descriptions of Ike as a do-nothing bumbler were dead wrong, that Eisenhower remained today one of the sharpest men in any conference on a critical problem. He said every time he conferred with Ike that Ike said, "Have you taken steps against these contingencies and plugged these holes" and that they were always acute points overlooked by most whiz kids. Johnson appeared to be very, very sincere in all this and to hope historians would not misunderstand the man.[15]

Eisenhower's impulse to avoid personal disagreements with other political figures was established in his long years in Washington. A vignette from his first term as Chief of Staff is especially telling, because it establishes a link between his personal feelings about politics and his leadership style.

Eisenhower prevented what might have been an ugly dispute between the War Department and the vociferous Mississippi Congressman John Rankin, who usually confined his efforts to assailing blacks, Jews, and Reds. Early in 1945, Rankin had called for an investigation of one of Eisenhower's chief wartime officers, General Mark Clark, who had commanded a World War II engagement in which the casualties were great, the Rapido River crossing. Rankin was echoing the demand by backers of the National Guard division that participated in the action that the army take "the necessary steps to correct a military system that will permit an inefficient and inexperienced officer, such as General Mark Clark, in a high command to destroy the young manhood of the country."[16]

In response, Eisenhower dealt first with Clark and then with Congress. Urging Clark to ignore Rankin, he predicted that a reply would "initiate unnecessarily a public quarrel" which would have

many unfortunate effects, among these being a tendency to drag forward as a volunteer witness every single individual who may through venom, spite, or mere love of personal publicity, see a chance of doing a bit of damage. You must remember that on our side we have only facts and honest conclusions to combat arguments based largely on sentiment and emotional appeal.[17]

Fearing the unruly emotions that would be unloosed in a public exchange, he arranged that a formal report be forwarded to Congress. The high casualty river crossing, the army reported, was a diversion drawing German troops from the Anzio landing site. The congressional military affairs leaders quietly accepted the army's explanation.[18]

The issue threatened to emerge again later in the year when Clark's promotion to permanent major general went to the Senate, but his promotion went through without public outcry. Eisenhower explained his rationale to Clark: it was that nonconfrontation, lubricated by informal negotiations on the Hill is the best way to get results in such a situation. "I wanted," he stressed, "very much to avoid a name-calling campaign." This was why he had urged Clark to ignore Rankin. But Eisenhower had not remained passive. He noted,

> I did talk personally to several members of the committee and they knew I was prepared to go down and do my stuff if it became necessary. What I was going to do was dwell upon Grant's second charge at Cold Harbor and Pickett's charge at Gettysburg, directed by Lee. I'd figured that the proper treatment of these two incidents would do more than to argue about the specific tactical situation existing on the Rapido.[19]

The testimony that never occurred not only illuminates Eisenhower's conflict-avoiding approach to potentially ugly rows, it also shows how he could manipulate situations to his own ends while still maintaining the personal image of a neutral spokesman for the national interest. His plan after all had been to defuse an attempt to examine a specific wartime episode by changing the topic. He proposed not to discuss the Rapido battle at all except by analogy to nineteenth-century events. It is unlikely that the lawmakers would have cared to debate with a popularly acclaimed, recently victorious supreme commander about technical problems of assault tactics and the fine points of Civil War military engagements. Moreover, his ploy probably would have succeeded, even if he were not a national hero, because he had the personal confidence and support of the bulk of Congress, who like other leaders he met face to face, found him admirable and compellingly attractive.

Artlessness and Art in Winning the Support of Other Leaders

Every World War II buff knows that a crucial part of Eisenhower's contribution to the Axis defeat was holding together the strong-minded, diverse leaders of the Western alliance. When asked to explain how Eisenhower managed this, his associates often sought recourse in such ambiguities as "the mystery of leadership." The biographer of Eisenhower's war years, Stephen Ambrose, gets closer to the heart of the matter in his own response to a question posed to Secretary of War Henry Stimson by a group of American senators visiting Eisenhower's North African headquarters: "Cunningham commands the naval forces, Tedder commands the air forces, and Alexander commands the ground forces. What in hell does Eisenhower command?" Ambrose retorts, "He commanded Cunningham, Alexander, and Tedder. Eisenhower brought this about not through any structural change, but by holding weekly meetings with the three British officers, by having frequent casual conversations with them individually, by acting as referee to settle their inter-service disputes, and above all by the force of his personality."[20]

Clearly this personal force in face-to-face leadership was palpable to those who worked with him even though they had difficulty finding precise words to express the experience of working with Eisenhower. One cabinet aide, for example, characterizes Eisenhower's presence in meetings as "electric."[21] Harvard law and political science professor Robert Bowie, an observer whose accounts of events usually subordinate personal feelings to analytic interpretation, recounts his first meeting with Eisenhower (in 1945, during Eisenhower's brief stint as military governor of Germany) not in terms of its content, but of the emotions induced in him and others by Eisenhower's manner. "What struck me," Bowie recalls, "was the vibrant personality, the very magnetic appeal which he had, even in dealing with people that he hadn't met or known before." Although he had just defeated them, he even "created an immediate sense of friendliness with the Germans and avoided any memory or recollection of prior relationships which could have made it awkward."[22]

31

Whatever the elements in Eisenhower's "electricity," they had been longstanding, even if they were dormant during his many desk-bound years as a staff officer. Eisenhower's secretary, Mrs. Whitman, discovered a letter dated 1918, when Eisenhower led an army training unit. The author, a junior officer under his command, though describing times and circumstances far removed from presidential demands, picturesquely captures Eisenhower's ease in whipping up subordinates' enthusiasm, his appealing mixture of humor and seriousness, and the other outgoing, personable qualities that encouraged spontaneous identification with him.

> Our new captain, Eisenhower by name, is, I believe one of the most efficient and best Army officers in the country. He is a . . . corker and has put more into us in three days than we got in all the previous time we were here. He is a giant for build and at West Point was a noted football and physical culture fiend. He knows his job, is enthusiastic, can tell us what he wants us to do and is pretty human, though wickedly harsh and abrupt. . . . He gets the fellows' imaginations worked up and hollers and yells and makes us shout and stamp until we go tearing into the air as if we mean business. . . . Every now and then Eisenhower would jump on us and say we were having too good a time, call us to attention and put us through the manual for five minutes, but you could see that he enjoyed it all too.[23]

Later accounts describe similar, quite tangible sources of Eisenhower's effectiveness in face-to-face leadership conferences. One source, his capacity for earnest, forceful exhortations was especially effective with associates, such as his cabinet members who had joined the administration because of their admiration for him.* His cabinet included a number of strong personalities who ranged in viewpoint from deep conservatism to middle-of-the-road Republicanism, but who nevertheless all accepted him as an appropriate spokesman for the national interest.

Speech writer Emmet Hughes provides an action portrait of how Eisenhower would rally the cabinet members during their regular meetings. His "ears never seemed to leave the discourse around him." Eisen-

---

*No one asked to serve in his cabinet "declined an invitation from the great World War II leader—a statistic unique in the modern presidency."[24]

hower's "interjections" in the discussions "were sudden, sometimes sharp or even explosive."

> Again and again the President would seize on some particular matter of legislation or administration as spark for a warm homily on his personal views—the world need for free trade, or the practical necessity (and "cheapness") of programs of mutual security, or the need to temper austere "businesslike administration with signs of concern for "the little fellow," or the "unthinkable" dimensions of nuclear war. For almost all the persons present these fervent sermons carried an authority almost scriptural.[25]

Eisenhower's comments impressed his colleagues not simply because they were made with intensity, but also because they reflected his extensive personal knowledge of governmental affairs. The cabinet members, Hughes sensed, were especially impressed by his personal acquaintance with other world leaders—for example, "the warmth of his friendship for Harold Macmillan or his tolerance of the idiosyncracies of Charles de Gaulle." Especially to those members of the cabinet with limited experience in national and international affairs, "such a range of acquaintanceship with things and with people seemed no less than dazzling."[26]

Robert Bowie did not confine his explanation of Eisenhower's effectiveness to "vibrancy." Eisenhower also impressed him in settings such as National Security Council meetings because he displayed two precisely definable qualities. One, which many other observers remark on, was his ability to make decisions, "to face the issues . . . and resolve them." The other was his ability to cut through complex discussions and make persuasive, though unpretentious sounding, judgments.

> Often the discussion would be marked by impressive analysis by various individuals who, as intellectuals, struck you as sometimes more articulate than he. But at the end, I felt that he frequently came out with a commonsense appraisal . . . which was wiser than the input which he'd received from the separate advisors. Somehow, almost in an intuitive way, in a way which quite clearly wasn't a one, two, three lawyer's type of analysis, nevertheless he came out with a net judgment which often struck me

as wiser or more sensible than the specific positions taken by any individual.*[27]

Eisenhower's ability to win support in group settings may have seemed artless, but it actually represented a conscious application of what he realized were proven tactics for effective leadership, although his use of such tactics no doubt became second nature to him, requiring little conscious forethought. One of the closest observers of Eisenhower's practices over an extended period of demanding leadership, his World War II Chief of Staff, Walter Bedell Smith, explained that Eisenhower consulted subordinates as much to win them over as to canvass their views:

> His personality is such that it impresses itself immediately upon senior subordinates as completely frank, completely honest, very human and very considerate. . . . He has great patience, and he disdains no advice regardless of source. One of his most successful methods in dealing with individuals is to assume that he himself is lacking in detailed knowledge and liable to make an error and is seeking advice. This is by no means a pose, because he actually values the recommendations and suggestions he receives, although his own better information and sounder judgment might cause them to be disregarded.[28]

Subordinates so consulted, Smith observed, tended to be highly loyal and to accept Eisenhower's policies readily, presumably because they were flattered to be taken seriously and to feel that whatever line of action Eisenhower embarked upon had been informed by consultation with them.

C. D. Jackson, the Time Inc. executive who in 1953 and early 1954 worked closely with Eisenhower as a national security consultant and speech writer, also noted Eisenhower's habitual close attentiveness to others, by observing that "the only time his features seem to sag is when he is bored." But it was clear to Jackson that Eisenhower took pains

---

*We have seen that Eisenhower's letter to Gruenther did in fact follow a "one, two, three" reasoning mode. This explicitly deductive reasoning style is especially evident in Eisenhower's written communications. In discussions, he presented his main points and his conclusion, giving his rationale in a comfortably conversational, less formal way.

to master this appearance. Even the sag in his features, Jackson commented, "is only momentary, because his almost fantastically patient courtesy comes into play almost instantly in order to give the bore the impression that he is being listened to with interest."[29]

Appointments Secretary Robert Gray also noted that Eisenhower's skill and ease in dealing with visitors to his office was built on experience and technique. Eisenhower's meetings with visitors were "never stiff," Gray reported, though he "could manage a near complete schedule of important appointments at quarter-hour intervals, clear his mind in the seconds it took me to escort out his old visitor and bring in the new, and be locked on the fresh subject in full concentration by the time I withdrew." If the visitor became tongue-tied in Eisenhower's presence, "the President could carry the conversation single-handedly," finding common ground through small talk until "the visitor had settled back on his chair prepared to discuss the . . . business that had brought him."[30]

The artfulness that Eisenhower applied to what he called "leadership in conference"[31] is revealed in his ability to advise others on how to win over groups and individuals. Evidence of what Goodpaster described as Eisenhower's keen "interest in the command process" appears in a lengthy 1948 memorandum to Defense Secretary James Forrestal discussing how the secretary should go about seeking to harmonize the centrifugal demands of the members of the Joint Chiefs of Staff. The methods suggested were those that Eisenhower was often to employ in meetings when he was president. Whenever a member shows "a tendency to become a special pleader," he wrote, "the subject should be skillfully changed and a constant effort made to achieve unanimity of conclusion, first upon broad generalities and these gradually brought closer to concrete application to particular problems."[32]

In a wartime letter to his son, Eisenhower commented, "The one quality that can be developed by studious reflection and practice is the leadership of men."[33] Eisenhower undoubtedly overestimated the transferability of his leadership qualities. Nevertheless as a leader of other leaders he did more than effortlessly exude charm and warmth. He worked at the job.

35

Artlessness and Art in Winning Public Support

Eisenhower's equal success in rallying and sustaining public support also was not arrived at without effort, though it was based on a personal public attractiveness to people with which few leaders are endowed. Films of Eisenhower's public appearances reveal an animated, enthusiastic man inspiring in the public a reciprocal enthusiasm. This is evident in the wartime newsreels showing a smiling, confident, unpretentious general, easily making his way through formations of troops; in the ticker-tape parades celebrating his return to the United States in 1945; and finally in films showing the motorcades with Eisenhower, both as a candidate and president, standing in open cars, beaming, waving, and signaling the familiar V for victory as he entered the cheering communities where he was making appearances.

The sober Bradley and staid Marshall never could have elicited a comparable response. And the other World War II general to win national popularity, MacArthur, seemed to reinforce his long association with political conservatives by his austere martial air. Numerous public opinion polls at that time reveal that, although both MacArthur and Eisenhower received strong support as "most-admired American," MacArthur's support was parochial, concentrated largely among conservative Republicans, while Eisenhower's crossed partisan and ideological lines.[34]

Striking evidence that Eisenhower took the buoyant displays that won over first troops and later electorates as still another part of his responsibility—an appearance to be cultivated if necessary—can be found in an introductory chapter he did not use in *Crusade in Europe*, but which is preserved in draft form in the Eisenhower Library. The published book deals predominantly with events, not emotions and perceptions. The omitted introduction addresses itself to suppressing and countering feelings of despondency when faced by setbacks, stalemates, or stasis.

Eisenhower recalls the tense weeks he spent in the dank tunnels of Gibraltar immediately before the North African invasion in 1942 when following upon many months of work and planning, conducted sometimes at almost hysterical intensity, a great Allied amphibious force had sailed from its ports to attack North Africa and my staff and I were condemned to days of almost complete passivity . . . as we awaited the outcome. During those anxious hours I first realized, I think, how inexorably and inescapably strain and tension wear away at the leader's endurance, his judgment and his confidence. The pressure becomes more acute because of the duty of a staff constantly to present to the commander the worst side of an eventuality . . . and the commander inherits an additional load in preserving optimism in himself and in his command. Without confidence, enthusiasm and optimism in the command, victory is scarcely obtainable.

Realizing that "optimism and pessimism are infectious and they spread more rapidly from the head downward than in any other direction," Eisenhower "clearly saw the dual advantages to be obtained from a commander's cheerful demeanor and constant outward optimism." One was that "the habit . . . tends to minimize potentialities within the individual himself" to become demoralized. The other was that it

has a most extraordinary effect upon all with whom he comes in contact. With this clear realization, I firmly determined that my mannerisms and speech in public would always reflect the cheerful certainty of victory—that any pessimism and discouragement I might ever feel would be reserved for my pillow. To translate this conviction into tangible results . . . I adopted a policy of circulating through the whole force to the full limit imposed by physical considerations . . . I did my best to meet everyone from general to private with a smile, a pat on the back and a definite interest in his problems.[35]

Eisenhower realized that a leader must inspire confidence and support, no matter how he feels. Describing his 1952 campaign in *Mandate for Change,* Eisenhower speaks of "the candidate's stepping blithely out to face the crowd, doing his best to conceal with a big grin the ache in his bones and the exhaustion in his mind."[36] Yet he insisted on appearing in motorcades, which was a grueling physical ordeal. And he urged politicians to follow his own practice of projecting a sense of warm enthusiasm. As one aide remembers, "I moved around with him a great deal and I've heard him tell professional politicians: 'Now here's what you do. Get out there. Don't look so serious. Smile. When the people are waving at you wave your arms and move your lips, so you look like you're talking to them. It doesn't matter what you say. Let them see you're reacting to them.' "[37]

The smiling, confident exterior often concealed more than "pessimism and discouragement." It concealed the hard-driving side of this complex man as well as a fiery temper that he kept in check out of a deep commitment to subordinate personal feelings to the duties of leadership. The Democratic jibe that Eisenhower's was an era in which the bland led the bland is contradicted by a multitude of firsthand observations.

The Easygoing Leader as Dynamo, The Smile and the Temper

In wartime letters reflecting on the demands of his job, Eisenhower observed that an "inexhaustible fund of nervous energy" is needed to carry out the responsibilities of a higher commander.[38] Ambrose discloses that as supreme commander Eisenhower normally slept only five hours a day. He never napped, he rarely missed work because of illness, and he regularly worked seven-day weeks, taking holidays only when ordered by Marshall to do so. And he chain-smoked—a four-pack-a-day habit.[39]

This intense work and the smoking habit neither began nor ended with his World War II duty. As he later reminisced, "My immoderate use of tobacco was matched by immoderate working hours whenever a big job was to be done. I was, when working, driven by the need to go at top speed, day after day, starting early and continuing past midnight."[40] In March 1949, while on leave from Columbia University to help weld the new Defense Department, he was seized with severe gastrointestinal disorder (one he first experienced in the Philippines and which later was diagnosed as ileitis and was successfully treated by surgery in 1956). When told that he would have to cut back on smoking, he was as forceful as he had been in the relentless workaholic routines his smoking accompanied. In an act of will that can be best understood by an ex-tobacco addict, he simply stopped cold turkey.[41]

As a national figure in constant demand for public appearances, a regularly consulted statesman, *and* a university president, Eisenhower was less successful in finding respite from a relentlessly full schedule of activities than in abandoning cigarettes. His physicians and his own sense of his health reached parallel conclusions. His blood pressure and susceptibility to digestive-tract disorder were high. His sense of well-being was low. The prescription—imperfectly adhered to but nevertheless helpful—was for him to block out time every several weeks for genuine rest, if possible physically removing himself from town.[42]

By the time he entered the presidency at age 62, Eisenhower had already attacked his life's work with an intensity that would have broken the constitution of a man who did not have a fundamentally sound and resilient physical and emotional makeup. Physically he was helped by the hard manual work and exposure to the outdoors made possible by his rural upbringing, by the early years of his military career when he was not constantly deskbound, and by the stamina he had built up as an athlete. Emotionally, he had a capacity to turn from worries to congenial, typically gregarious entertainment; although, except for his hobbies of painting and cooking, his preferred distractions were less relaxations than shifts from intense work to intense play. Golfing companions describe the stubborn determination he would pour into replaying an unsatisfactory shot. And what he liked about bridge was the opportunity it gave him to focus sharply on the solution to a logical problem and at the same time master the psychology of effective cooperation with his partner and competition with his opponents.[43]

In his White House years, he continued the regimens he and his friend and longtime personal physician, Dr. Howard Snyder, had established to put periodic dampers on his restless energy. The much publicized golfing trips, the working vacations, and even the Wild West stories he read at bedtime, which many critics suggested were the outward signs of a passive president with a flaccid mind, paradoxically were prescriptions for winding down a man whose drive and intensity needed to be kept in check. This was even more the case after his three major illnesses, all typical of the "immoderate" worker—a heart attack in

1955, an ileitis episode in 1956, and a slight stroke in 1957. Despite the remonstrances of some critics and political advisors to abjure golf or at least conceal his participation in it,[44] Eisenhower let the relaxations become part of the image, perhaps recognizing that a golfing Ike was a more reassuring symbol than a harried chief executive presiding over circumstances so unsettled that the fairways were off limits. And the Gallup Poll, in support, found that the majority of the public had no objection to the time he spent on golf courses.[45]

The eyewitness accounts of his behavior at meetings uniformly point to an energetic, restless temperament. Though he subjected himself to the passive context of regular long meetings and more tightly packed, longer work schedules than he chose to publicize, his physical comportment in meetings revealed his force and drive. His concentration was intense: his excess energy spilled over as he would doodle, finger his glasses, swivel in his chair, and look at other speakers with piercing bright blue eyes that innumerable observers sensed as windows to an inner dynamism.

National Security Advisor Dillon Anderson was one of many people who described the way Eisenhower would get up and pace the floor in an informal meeting as his enthusiasm mounted. "He was a man of a lot of native animal energy, which came out when a subject stirred him up, and he used to get up and walk the floor." Anderson, a dignified Texas banker who chaired Eisenhower's National Security Council staff briefly in 1955 and 1956, found himself nonplussed to be looking up at a striding president. "When he would get up, I would get up, and he would say, 'God damn it, sit down' and I would sit back down. Finally I got to where I could be comfortable sitting down in a room where the President of the United States was not seated." Visiting Eisenhower in 1960, his last year in office, Anderson noted the same energy and restless stride. His several illnesses and the approach of his seventieth birthday had not made him placid.[46]

In earlier years Eisenhower's dynamism was even more visible. When William Robinson initiated negotiations with Eisenhower after the war about writing a memoir, Eisenhower seemed "to get on fire" as Robinson talked about how an account of Eisenhower's wartime leadership would make a fundamental contribution to maintaining postwar allied unity. Robinson reported to his boss,

He would, every few minutes, arise from the chair in which he was sitting and stride up and down the office, talking about his limitations at one moment and in the next outlining the manner in which he would like to be of service, the things he would like to say, the guidance he would like to give historians in setting forth the facts of his mission in Europe. He was completely free, unguarded to the point even of indiscretion. There was no pose, no pretence, no attempt to establish anything for the record, no attempt to build an impression of any kind. He was natural, alive, alert, spirited, and gave the impression of having an intense amount of unloosened energy, both intellectual and physical. . . . His high spirit and his great emotional potentiality might conceivably develop a highly unbalanced entity in a person of lesser intellectual capacity.[47]

White House appointment lists carefully document everyone with whom the president met and state whether these meetings were on or off the record. They cover his official weekday working hours— usually from 8 A.M. to 5 or 5:30 P.M.—and often record Saturday and Sunday work, as well as evening activities, including entertainment of state guests and "stag dinners" for prominent citizens. They show a steady level of activity (excluding periods when he was ill or on a real rather than working vacation) through the end of his second term.

The official lists fail to record his informal workday.[48] Most days he had business breakfasts at 7:30, often with confidants such as his brother Milton or Lucius Clay. By then he had read several newspapers, even examining items tucked away on the business pages. Both his press secretary and the men who briefed him on intelligence reports recognized that, although Eisenhower often chided his associates for wasting time reading the newspapers, he frequently tripped them up by mentioning information they had not noticed in the morning's news.

Even before rising his mind often was at work. Eisenhower told his boyhood friend "Swede" Hazlett that he had never wholly been able to overcome the annoyance of a wartime habit of waking very early in the morning, but he felt that the abbreviated sleep was a healthy sign.

Ever since the hectic days of the North African campaign, I find that when I have weighty matters on my mind I wake up extremely early, apparently because a rested mind is anxious to begin grappling with knotty questions.

Incidentally, I never worry about what I did the day before. Likewise, I spend no time fretting about what enemies or critics have said about me. I have never indulged in useless regrets. Always I find, when I have come awake sufficiently to figure out what may be then engaging my attention, that I am pondering the same question that is still unanswered.

So I think it is fair to say that it is not worry about the past, but a desire to attack the future, that gets me into this annoying habit.[49]

At the end of the workdays when he had no evening obligations, Eisenhower often continued to conduct presidential business informally over drinks in the residential quarters of the White House. Sometimes his cocktail time was purely social, but frequently he used it for such purposes as culling information or mending fences. It was in this setting that he and one or two of his legislative liaison aides would meet with Democratic House and Senate leaders, Sam Rayburn and Lyndon Johnson, so that neither his partisans nor those of the Democratic leaders could complain that party purity was being undermined by bipartisan conniving.

Eisenhower preferred to avoid evening work, but he frequently edited speeches, read government reports, and did other homework. He chose not to publicize these nocturnal activities, just as he chose not to make available a complete listing of his daily meetings for the appointment calendars published in the newspaper each day. Publicity of his nighttime work (like complete lists of all his appointments) would have been discordant with the impression he conveyed of being a president who so successfully maintained national and international order that he did not have to work intensively around-the-clock.

In fact, however, like other presidents, he had associates who were empowered to "re-open the day" after he retired for the evening. "One evening in 1958, around midnight," Eisenhower's legislative liaison chief Bryce Harlow remembers,

Speaker Sam Rayburn telephoned me about an urgent requirement on an important bill then in intense controversy in the House of Representatives. He needed a Presidential decision at once, but Eisenhower had retired for the night. I told him to stand by, went to the President's rooms, had him awakened, explained the problem, got his decision, and reported back to the Speaker, well within 20 minutes.[50]

Anyone in regular, informal contact with Eisenhower knew that his energy was not always manifested in a dulcet mood. Accounts of his proclivity to flare up in red-faced anger go back to his preteen years in Abilene. Without attempting to psychoanalyze the diverse sources of what Harlow called his "Bessemer furnace" personality[51] we can note that he himself suggested a role model, referring to the awesome temper of his patriarchal Pennsylvania Dutch father, David Eisenhower.[52] He also claimed he learned to control his temper from his gentle, pacifistic mother, but one aide commented, "I thought to myself what a poor job she had done."[53] Childhood models notwithstanding, the very energy he poured into problem solving needed outlet when nevertheless things went wrong—often his anger was not directed at a person but at an impersonal obstacle.

Eisenhower erupting was by all accounts impressive. As he remarked in an early 1960s CBS interview,

> I told my staff . . . once in a while you people have just got to be my safety-valve. So I'll get you in here and I will let go, but this is for you and your knowledge, and your knowledge only. Now I've seen these people going out, and I've gotten a little bit extreme, a little white, but pretty soon one of them comes in and laughs and says, "Well, you were in good form this morning, Mr. President," or "General," or whatever it was at the time.[54]

Former staff members who witnessed it agreed that although his temper was formidable it was also short-lived—summer thunderstorms followed by balmy good humor.

Eisenhower's capacity to fly into towering rages was not unique among modern presidents. Both Lyndon Johnson and Richard Nixon were known for their tempers. Unlike Johnson, Eisenhower did not smolder and bear long-term grudges. If he believed someone to have grave character defects and there were no reasons of state for dealing with him, Eisenhower would simply cut off his association with that person. Also unlike Johnson, he did not bully subordinates.

Eisenhower's awareness and attempts to control his temper distinguished him from Richard Nixon. For Eisenhower, there was no denial of angry impulses. Nixon appears sometimes to have repressed anger, driving it from consciousness, only to have it surface in outbursts that conveyed the impression of meanness of spirit.[55] Eisenhower's practice was suppression, not repression, and suppression for practical reasons. Public loss of temper was inconsistent, he felt, with a leader's duties. "I learned a long time ago," he told his CBS interviewer, "that . . . anybody that aspired to a position of leadership of any kind . . . must learn to control his temper."[56]

In the internecine conflicts within the World War II alliance, Eisenhower showed this ability to control his temper in the face of extreme provocation in order to realize his policy aims. The most striking example is his forbearance in dealing with the caustic, self-centered Field Marshall Bernard Montgomery, who, though Eisenhower's subordinate, refused ever to visit his headquarters. He repeatedly criticized Eisenhower's performance as a general, urging that he himself be named to replace him. Because of Montgomery's great popularity in Britain, it was impossible either to relieve him of his position or publicly chastise him.[57] Eisenhower curbed expression of animus toward Montgomery by analyzing that bantam cock, thus mentally putting him in his place rather than allowing conflict with Montgomery to surface. As he told Marshall, while he did not voluntarily choose Montgomery as a subordinate, "I have his personal equation and have no lack of confidence in my ability to handle him."[58] Drawing on his reading of Montgomery's character, Eisenhower reasoned with the Field Marshall when necessary, gave him his way when he felt it appropriate, but had no hesitation about overruling him.

Although Eisenhower viewed his bad temper as a special curse, his awareness of it and his capacity to control it enabled him to turn it to practical use on occasion. Vernon A. ("Dick") Walters, Eisenhower's translator in NATO negotiations, recounts a time when Eisenhower deliberately indulged himself in a blowup in order to terminate a disagreement he felt was not worth negotiating through to a conclusion.

We stopped in Italy to see Defense Minister Pacciardi. He had insisted that the Greek and Turkish forces be under an Italian commander. Both, however, had told Eisenhower that this was out of the question. During the discussion Eisenhower suddenly appeared to misunderstand something that Pacciardi had just said and I had translated. Pacciardi, after a few feeble attempts to explain that he had been misunderstood, gave in and accepted a U.S. commander for the Greek and Turkish sector of NATO. I was greatly crestfallen as it appeared to Pacciardi that I had mistranslated what he had said and that this had provoked Eisenhower's anger. . . . The matter of the command settled, we returned to Naples airport and took off for Paris. I was sitting in the forward cabin feeling quite glum when General Eisenhower came forward, tapped me on the shoulder and said, "Dick, if I sometimes appear to misunderstand what you say, it is just that I need a hook on which to hang my anger." He added with a grin, "It worked, too."[59]

Eisenhower's quick reference in the CBS interview to temper and the need for a successful leader to control it does, however, show that he knew his own "equation" and factored it into his leadership. One reason why he controlled his temper so successfully was that he had an even more powerful conviction that leaders are charged with responsibilities and must suppress personal impulse if duty so dictated.

Eisenhower's capacity for controlling outward manifestations of his feelings also undoubtedly stemmed from his conviction that a leader's *duty* is to keep his impulses in check and act rationally. Barber is correct in emphasizing the centrality of feeling of duty to Eisenhower's political psychology.[60] These feelings, captured in the old fashioned-sounding abstract nouns of the West Point motto—"duty, honor, country"—resonated with the verities of his rural turn-of-the-century background and surely were strengthened by his immersion as a child in a pietist tradition revolving around the principle that the individual is ultimately responsible to a Supreme Being and to values higher than self-interest.[61]

Eisenhower reminisced in *At Ease* that his early military career had included a frustrating sequence of unchallenging assignments. What kept him going was his resolution "to perform every duty given me . . . to the best of my ability . . . no matter what [its] . . . nature."[62] This sense of duty eventually extended to becoming President of the United States. His diary entries for 1950 leave little doubt that he was profoundly ambivalent about adding the burden of a presidency (it seemed certain that he *could* be nominated and elected) to an already full career. He reflected irritably on how to respond to the constant demands of politicians and business friends, among others, that he become a candidate. His efforts to think aloud on paper revolved around the issue of where his duty lay. Even if he did not want to run, he asked himself, was he morally obliged to do so if it were the only way of achieving the public policies to which he was committed?[63]

Perhaps the most influential single man in forcing him to a decision, his old friend Lucius Clay mercilessly pressed him on this ground. Reflecting in 1954 on how he could best retire at the end of his first term, Eisenhower returned to his diary. Clay had been pressing him anew, striking at what Eisenhower knew to be his most vulnerable point: "All that a person has to say to me is 'the good of the country'," he wrote, "and . . . I probably yield far too easily to generalizations instead of demanding proof."[64]

Ironically, Eisenhower's heart attack, which incapacitated him for much of the fall of 1955, may have insured that he would feel duty bound to run again. He evidently had been disposed—with Milton's aid—to groom a candidate or field of candidates to replace him, but his illness prevented him from doing so in time. When he finally had medical approval to complete his first term and run again, it was clear there was no other Republican candidate in the wings who would both satisfy Eisenhower's aims and be assured of election.[65]

Beliefs—as Held and as Expressed

Political convictions—more precisely a core of convictions concerning war and peace, international community, and broad domestic policy principles—were intensely important to Eisenhower. For most people political beliefs are peripheral personality structures, a combination of habitual assumptions and short-lived responses to immediate circumstances and events. To an issue oriented political leader like Eisenhower, however, beliefs are usually stable and can have a profound impact on feeling and action. Clear beliefs and policy positions founded on them are powerful instruments for leadership, since the leader who possesses them is better able to set priorities, communicate a public stance, and delegate specifics to associates by giving them clear guidelines for making detailed decisions.

Eisenhower's most deeply felt concern—the preoccupation that led him to take on the presidency at an age when he was giving thought to reducing his involvement in public service—was with the state of world order. Foreign and international politics clearly were his prime focus, though he recognized their integral link to domestic politics and policy.

The phrase "collective security" best describes his major short-run policy aim—that of welding a sturdy cold war coalition of Western and other non-Communist nations. This coalition, he was convinced, could not merely be military. It needed a solid political, economic, and ideological framework. He believed that if such a coalition could be achieved, there would be a greater likelihood of attaining the most fundamental long-run need of mankind, international harmony. Given time and Western steadfastness, "world communism" might lose its monolithic expansionistic qualities, and a strong, resourceful West could then take the lead in dissipating the cold war. And détente, he was convinced, would have to occur eventually to prevent the ultimate catastrophe—global nuclear war.

Eisenhower recurrently sought to bring home to Republican conservatives the awful significance of nuclear weaponry. Senior Republican Senator Styles Bridges of New Hampshire, for example, in 1957 rumbled publicly that the administration's foreign policy proposals were not true to cold war orthodoxy. The recording machine that from time to time was used to monitor conversations in the Oval Office captured an extended, impassioned Eisenhower exercise in setting Bridges straight. In response to Bridges's concern about "this atomic treaty"—reference to the administration's disarmament proposals—Eisenhower stressed, "this is part of a great program we have to pursue if we are going to save us from some catastrophe."

EISENHOWER: Even assuming that we could emerge from a global war today as the acknowledged victor, there would be a destruction in the country [such] that there would be no possibility of our exercising a representative free government for, I would say, two decades at the minimum.

... Did you ever see one of those net evaluation studies given to me every year?

BRIDGES: No.

EISENHOWER: I will give you just one figure. ... On a single attack ... [one in which] we had enough warning for some preparation with our people and weapons ... we figure something like 25 million killed, 60 million had to go to hospitals, and there were not enough hospitals. When you begin to think of things like that you know there must not be war.[66]

As he put it to one correspondent in a 1958 letter, nuclear weapons had changed the character of war more in the twenty-one years since 1945 than any change between the beginning of the sixteenth century and Hiroshima. The usual notion of war was now obsolete; the new weaponry of extermination would leave no winner. There remained no alternative to finding means of East-West accommodation.[67]

Eisenhower viewed his attempts as president to assure collective security in the West and bargain from strength to begin building a peaceful East-West relationship as a direct extension of his activities in the postwar years that culminated in his NATO leadership. And he thought of his efforts as a coalition builder after 1945 as a continuation of his allied leadership in the war. In his postwar prepresidential years Eisenhower harnessed his long-standing but never publicly expressed or sharply defined conservatism on domestic policy to his views on collective security. Although he felt that the American defense establishment was underfunded and precipitously demobilized in the immediate postwar years, he also was acutely sensitive to the possibility that high taxes and governmental expenditures—whether for military or domestic purposes—would weaken economic productivity through excessive federal regulation and reduction of incentives to invest. And he was preoccupied with the potential costs of an inflation that might be spurred by government spending, including "unproductive" spending on arms.*

Eisenhower was conservative enough to view the nomination of the

*He appears to have done much of this thinking about the need to balance adequate spending for collective security and the requirements of a sound economy when he was chief of staff under Defense Secretary Forrestal. In his diary as early as January 1949 he notes his agreement with Forrestal on the central national security premise that "we must hold our position of strength without bankrupting ourselves."[68] This prepresidential reflection prepared the way for his presidential "New Look" defense policy, which relied on high retaliatory power in order to restrain national security costs.

man widely held to personify standpat Republicanism—Robert A. Taft—with equanimity in terms of domestic policy. The problem, however, was that Taft seemed prepared to lead the Republican party to abandon the Atlantic Alliance and the other internationalist policies that Eisenhower deemed essential for national survival.

Just before leaving to command NATO in January 1951, Eisenhower met with Taft privately in the Pentagon. Eisenhower brought to this meeting a prepared statement in which Taft was to commit himself broadly to internationalist foreign policy principles and Eisenhower would renounce a candidacy. But when he and Taft could not agree, Eisenhower destroyed the statement and left himself in a position to accept the Republican nomination on the grounds that keeping open the option of seeking nomination was his only weapon against choice by the Republicans in 1952 of an isolationist candidate.[69] As he put it in a 1967 interview:

> I wasn't going to remove the threat of possibly becoming a candidate, although I had no idea of ever doing it, I assure you. But I just didn't want to let these people nail me down, neutralize me completely, and then still go their own happy way, one I thought was wrong.[70]

Once Eisenhower was president and Taft was Senate Republican leader, it became clear that Eisenhower's private domestic political convictions were *more* conservative than Taft's, even though throughout the convention and campaign Eisenhower was judged further to the left on the political spectrum than either Taft or the bulk of senior Republicans.*

Eisenhower's conservatism is documented in a diary entry for the years when he was president of Columbia University. A January 1950 passage bemoans the demise of the New York *Sun,* a bastion of standpat doctrine. Eisenhower pasted in the diary a *Sun* editorial and car-

---

*In fact, during the six months before Taft's death when the two worked together, Eisenhower resisted such Taft proposals as an aid to education bill, which he explained several years after Taft's death to Ohio Congressman Clarence Brown, was "far more 'liberal and radical' than anything to which I could ever agree."[71] Shortly after Taft died, Eisenhower wrote in his diary, "In some things, I found him extraordinarily 'leftish.' This applied specifically to his attitude toward old-age pensions. He told me he believed every individual in the United States, upon reaching the age of 65, should automatically go on a minimum pension basis, paid by the Federal government."[72]

toon decrying the "welfare state" and the "gravy train" and indicated his accord with a series of catchwords of conservative orthodoxy listed by the editorial writer in the form of evils the paper had long sought to thwart: "Socialism, Communism, governmental extravagance, the encroachments of bureaucracy and that form of governmental paternalism which eats into the marrow of private initiative and industry."[73]

Why, then, was Eisenhower, when he returned from NATO in June 1952 to seek the Republican nomination, universally considered a representative of the party's liberal to moderate wing? This was in part because liberal Democrats had sought to draft Eisenhower for their party's nomination in 1948, and in part because Republicans with that reputation—notably Eastern industrial state leaders such as New York Governor Thomas E. Dewey—were behind the draft Eisenhower movement in 1952. But it was also because of the "Taft can't win" slogan used to persuade office-hungry Republicans to back Ike. Taft-style Republicanism, as typified by Taft's high-button-shoes appearance and blunt attacks on liberalism, would, the argument went, frighten an electorate that had come to rely on New Deal social welfare policies. Circumstances required a reassuringly moderate Eisenhower.

Eisenhower obliged these supporters, both in the campaign and in the presidency. Moreover, his assessment of what political realism required if the Republicans were to prosper led him deliberately to temper his private conservatism. In justifying the maintenance of New Deal social welfare reforms to his fervently right-wing brother Edgar, he bluntly admonished: "Should any political party attempt to abolish social security and eliminate labor laws and farm programs, you would not hear of that party again in our political history."* He therefore sought to keep the public from perceiving the Republicans as the party of big business while at the same time thwarting passage of "radical" Democratic programs by initiating moderate Republican alternatives.

This domestic policy is reflected in communications such as the fol-

---

*"There is," he added, "a tiny splinter group, of course, that believes that you can do these things. Among them are H. L. Hunt, . . . a few other Texas oil millionaires and an occasional politician and businessman from other areas." But "their number is negligible and they are stupid."[74]

lowing to Budget Director Joseph Dodge who had objected to a program for medical aid to public assistance recipients proposed by Health, Education and Welfare Secretary Oveta Culp Hobby:

> On balance I believe we should go ahead with Secretary Hobby's program, but limit this year's expenditure to 20 million dollars. I recognize clearly the dangers that are outlined in your memorandum, but I am quite certain that the pressures to do something of this nature will eventually be irresistible. . . . It seems to me it would be best to try to establish a moderate program in this field while there is still in the Executive Department a clear comprehension of the dangers as well as the anticipated advantages and a determination to oppose, and even veto, any project that to us would seem to be in reckless disregard of correct principles.[75]

Following the same logic that a Republican domestic program should be fiscally conservative but convey a commitment to social betterment, he instructed Dodge during the 1953 budget preparation process that he wanted to hold down requests for appropriations, but that nevertheless it was vital to include measures in the administration program that would proclaim "broad and liberal objectives in certain fields that affect the whole country directly and indirectly." The measures needed to be advanced not only on their merits, but also "to fix in the public mind the character of our political thinking."

> So in (a) slum clearance and public housing, (b) utilization of America's water resources, (c) extension of social security and old age benefits, I should like to put ourselves on record as being forward looking. . . . In addition, to give substance to our words, I should like to see *no* reduction—possibly even a slight increase—in housing appropriations. The same applies to a few *small* public work projects—and also I would like to see initiated one of the planned and project[ed] major conservation projects, even though we would plan for a very modest appropriation for the first two or three years in such a project.[76]

Eisenhower hoped that by enunciating "broad and liberal objectives," advancing moderate improvements in social programs, and establishing a reputation (and above all a record) for fostering a thriving economy, he could (if he could preserve an untroubled international environment) reconstitute the electoral base of his party. "Twentieth Century Republicanism," he hoped, would deprive the Democrats of their corner on "the common man," especially if his own "broad and liberal" Republican programs (and his personal appeal) helped bring young, attractive leaders into the party—leaders who would modernize the party's organizational procedures as well as its policy stance.

Thus, in the interest of building a stable Republican majority, he was prepared to moderate his fundamental conservatism. Voicing political sentiments that were more liberal than his private credo made sense to him in domestic policy. Similarly, in foreign policy he would sometimes modulate Secretary of State Dulles's strident cold war rhetoric (the two men held virtually identical beliefs about the "Soviet threat") in order to underscore the fundamental commitment of his administration to international peace. This was exemplified in his highly publicized personal promulgation of the Atoms for Peace and Open Skies proposals.

Eisenhower did not depart from his own foreign policy convictions in enunciating his pro-détente programs. However, he did temper his beliefs concerning domestic policy in the interest of appealing to the Democratic party's constituency. In making such compromises he did not simply acknowledge the requirements of expediency, but rather defended the need for compromise itself on principled grounds, with the studied rationalism that marks so many of his private communications. He once even invoked, as a reason for moderation, the formal statistical properties of the bell-shaped normal distribution curve in which the bulk of cases converge at the center and only a smattering are at the far left or right. "The noticeable fact," he wrote, "is that under what has been called 'nature's curve,' the extreme comprise small percentages of the whole."

> What might be called the compatible group is about two-thirds of the aggregate. Most people believe that in a general way they belong to the "middle of the road" group. . . . While in the field of moral truth or basic principle the statement tends to be black or white, the task of the political leader is to devise plans among which humans can make constructive progress. This means that the plan or program itself tends to fall in the "gray" category. This is not because there is any challenge to the principle or the moral truth, but because human nature itself is far from perfect.[77]

The Eisenhower Dichotomies

Eisenhower the man shaped the distinctive Eisenhower leadership style. His personal makeup was permeated by contrasts. Each element in his makeup has the same duality between what the public saw in him and the private man. As a thinker, the public saw a folksy, common-sense replica of the man on the street. The confidential records show a man with extraordinary capacities for detached, orderly examination of problems and personalities. In public he seemed to be removed from the political arena. But the inner Eisenhower reasoned about political contingencies with greater rigor and readiness than many political professionals and drew on a long-standing acquaintance with the labyrinths of national and international governance. His ability to win friends and influence people—both face to face and in the mass—seemed to result simply from the magnetism of his sunny personality. But he worked at his apparent artlessness, consciously choosing strategies that made people want to support him. And on occasion the sunny personality masked anger or despondency, since he viewed it as a duty of the responsible leader to exude optimism.

As president, he conveyed a warm, reassuring presence and presided over a peaceful and reasonably prosperous decade while seeming not to work at it. In fact, he pushed and disciplined himself relentlessly. Finally, his political convictions were more intense than those of many who spend their entire careers in party or elective office. But he curbed his strongly felt conservatism to profess the extent of domestic liberalism that seemed necessary to win his party middle-of-the-road support. And he moderated the harsh side of his cold war world view by taking the lead in making peace initiatives.

This was a man with a striking propensity to establish "space" between his private and public self. While this propensity also characterizes hypocrites, Eisenhower, in no letter, conversation, or diary entry reveals the mark of a hypocrite, if that term is taken to connote contradictory public and private behavior informed by cynicism. Responding to a war correspondent's description of Eisenhower's use of profanity, one letter writer suggested that a supreme commander's language ought to reflect his dependence on divine guidance. Eisenhower expostulated: "Why, dammit, I *am* a religious man!"[78] His private political comments show a similar impatiently intense idealism, as he chafed at politicians and business and labor leaders whom he viewed as too shortsighted to act in the national interest.

Compartmentalizing public and private elements of his personal makeup required considerable effort, self-discipline, and a conception of his duties in which eschewing expression of impolitic impulses was taken for granted as an obligation of responsible leadership. Many of the Eisenhower dichotomies reflect a reassuringly benign-seeming public self and a private one with a well-developed capacity for tough-minded political realism. A personality capable of maintaining this division is perfectly suited for adapting to the contradictory public expectations that the president serve both as uncontroversial chief of state and potentially divisive prime minister. Such a person is also well suited to carry out the organizational procedures necessary to rationalize the official routines of public leadership while maintaining a capacity to develop flexible unofficial means for adapting organizational leadership to the complexities and idiosyncracies of the people he is leading.

PART II

*Eisenhower's
Leadership Style*

The Political Education of a General

Eisenhower's years in the War Department during the 1920s and 1930s gave him a keen insight into the realities of Washington politics. He is shown here as an aide to Chief of Staff Douglas MacArthur during the Veterans' Bonus March. *United Press International Photo.*

The spontaneous warmth, optimism, and informality he displayed as wartime commander became the trademark of the Presidential Ike. He is shown here on one of his innumerable encounters with the troops. *United Press International Photo.*

Managing the Image

Eisenhower's press conferences were carefully orchestrated to project a public image and convey *his* perceptions of policy. As the author documents, even the evasiveness and garbled syntax were often deliberate. *United Press International Photo.*

With James Hagerty, Eisenhower gave a new importance to the political role of press secretary. *Dwight D. Eisenhower Library.*

Eisenhower frequently used his brothers as sounding boards. Shown here are his brothers Earl E. and Milton. Milton was his most trusted confidant. *Dwight D. Eisenhower Library.*

Contrary to what was widely believed at the time, both Sherman Adams, Eisenhower's domestic chief of staff, and John Foster Dulles, secretary of state, were implementers of Eisenhower's policies and not prime movers. *Dwight D. Eisenhower Library.*

Presidential Moods: Private and Public

In private, Eisenhower was well known for his temper, only rarely revealed (as in this instance) in public press conferences. *United Press International Photo.*

Much more characteristic was the shrewd, pensive Eisenhower captured in this photograph. *United Press International Photo.*

But it was the smiling Ike whom the American public saw.
United Press International Photo

Containment without Confrontation: The full extent of Eisenhower's behind-the-scenes efforts to stop Senator Joseph McCarthy (R-Wis.) are revealed in this book for the first time. *Wide World Photos.*

Defusing the Opposition: Eisenhower's dealings with California's William Knowland epitomizes his unique ability to keep the support of a leader whose views he deplored. *Dwight D. Eisenhower Library.*

In the final analysis, the success of the hidden-hand presidency rested on the very real rapport between Ike and the American people. *United Press International Photo.*

3

POLITICAL STRATEGIES

EISENHOWER, like Truman, had a desk ornament bearing a motto epitomizing his view of leadership. Rather than "The buck stops here," Eisenhower's declared *"Suaviter in modo, fortiter in re"* (Gently in manner, strong in deed). The motto nicely captures the essence of Eisenhower's approach to leadership, a repertoire of six strategies that enabled him to exercise power without seeming to flex his muscles. The strategies, which were characteristic of Eisenhower the man, enabled him to balance the contradictory expectations that a president be a national unifier yet nevertheless engage in the divisive exercise of political leadership.

For covertly exercising the prime-ministerial side of the chief executive's job Eisenhower employed five strategies: hidden-hand leadership; instrumental use of language; the complementary strategies of refusing in public to "engage in personalities" but nevertheless privately basing actions on personality analyses; and the selective practice of delegation. Together these enabled him to use a sixth strategy that helped make him a credible chief of state—building a public support that transcended many of the nation's social and political divisions.

The individual strategies were not uniquely Eisenhower's. Any single act or utterance of Eisenhower was likely to include more than one strategy, and the six strategies did not exhaust his repertoire. But he fit them together in a way that made his presidential leadership distinctive.*

Hidden-Hand Leadership

Presidents often find it necessary to maneuver in secrecy. Presidents who seek to establish a professional reputation with other leaders as skilled, tough operators, and who want to be recognized by historians as "presidential activists," however, sometimes deliberately stimulate accounts of their tour de force exercises of personal influence. Kennedy used this tactic in his bravura 1962 assault on the steel industry that forced a price increase recision.[1] In 1964 Johnson encouraged publicity about his personal mediation of an impending railroad strike, an around-the-clock exercise in which he virtually locked union and management negotiators in the White House cabinet room.[2] Carter's intense personal participation in negotiation in the Camp David accords between Egypt and Israel is another example of publicized presidential activism.[3]

Although Eisenhower cultivated the reputation of being above political machination, he was an activist. However, in part because he chose not to publicize his activities and in part because his activities did not always fit the popular conception of an activist, he was not considered one. Commentators usually associate activism with efforts to effect major innovations (usually liberal) in public policy. Eisenhower sought, at least in domestic policy, to restrain policy change, but he was active in doing so.[4] He worked hard, considered it his responsi-

*In elucidating Eisenhower's leadership style, I inevitably present a somewhat idealized impression of its efficacy and of Eisenhower's skill. Before concluding that Eisenhower offers a panacea to the enduring dilemmas of presidential leadership, the reader should consider my evaluations in chapters five and six of his approach and of its applicability to other presidents

bility to shape public policy, and followed through on his initiatives.

A president who seeks influence and cultivates a reputation for not intervening in day-to-day policy-making will necessarily hide his hand more often than one who seeks recognition as an effective political operator. Eisenhower often camouflaged his participation not only in political activity generally falling outside popularly conceived bounds of presidential leadership, but also in more commonplace political leadership. In either case sometimes he used hidden-hand strategy to conceal his activities from all nonassociates; sometimes it suited his purposes to target his hidden-hand leadership so that selective nonassociates would be made aware of his actions.

An example of simple hidden-hand leadership—one that is a paradigm of Eisenhower influence attempts and has been kept completely secret—was his 1954 effort to influence Senate Democratic Leader Lyndon Johnson, an act which, if exposed, would have been controversial in any administration. Believing that Johnson was straying from the course of "fine conservative government," the president used a wealthy Johnson supporter to coerce him. Employing an intermediary, who concealed from the Johnson backer that Eisenhower had initiated the scheme to influence Johnson, Eisenhower "laundered" his own participation in the exercise. Mrs. Whitman took notes on Eisenhower's telephone conversation to Treasury Secretary George Humphrey, during which he told Humphrey to call Texas oil multi-millionaire Sid Richardson, who Eisenhower noted "was really the angel for Johnson when he came in." The telephone log summarizing their conversation records these instructions:

> Ask [Richardson] . . . what it is that Tex wants. We help out in drought, take tidelands matter on their side, and tax bill. But question is, how much influence has Sid got with Johnson? He tells Sid he's supporting us, then comes up here and disproves it (yesterday for instance). Perhaps Sid could get him on the right channel, or threaten to get [Texas Governor Allen] Shivers in a primary and beat him for Senate.[5]

Because Richardson was an old friend of Eisenhower's—they met in 1941—Eisenhower and Humphrey agreed that the latter should talk to Richardson so "it can't be said that DDE is taking advantage of a longtime friendship."[6]

Clearly Eisenhower's efforts to influence Johnson required such discretion. Eisenhower, however, also concealed his involvement in conventional politicking that would not have been controversial if he had been prepared to be viewed as a political professional. In 1957, for example, he sent a letter to Secretary of the Treasury Robert Anderson. Anderson, a Texas lawyer, whom Eisenhower frequently mentioned to associates as the man he felt best equipped to succeed him, had served as Secretary of the Navy, and Deputy Assistant Secretary of Defense, and had just assumed the Treasury secretaryship. Throughout this period, although ostensibly not a political operative, at Eisenhower's behest, Anderson drew on his long personal friendship with Lyndon Johnson to serve as private administration conduit to and pulse taker of the mercurial Senate Democratic leader by maintaining virtually daily contact with Johnson. This role extended into that of a general behind-the-scenes political aide.[7]

Eisenhower's letter to Anderson contained a detailed set of procedural suggestions for managing congressional relations. The suggestions were originally drafted by Henry Cabot Lodge, who had been a two-term senator and an active figure in securing Eisenhower's nomination. From his post as United Nations ambassador, Lodge regularly and also without publicity advised Eisenhower on strategy and tactics for domestic politics. Eisenhower had originally offered Lodge the job that Sherman Adams was to fill. When Lodge stated his preference for the United Nations position, Eisenhower agreed but stipulated that Lodge should advise him privately on domestic matters. (The two exchanged about 150 letters on this topic during Eisenhower's presidency.)[8]

In his letter to Anderson, the "apolitical" Eisenhower passed on Lodge's suggestions. They included such standard fare as insisting that department secretaries establish personal friendships with the congressional chairmen whose committees supervised agency operations and also ingratiate themselves with the chairmen's wives; that they grant all favors requested by friendly congressmen immediately if possible, and if not possible, explain why, stressing their desire to be helpful wherever feasible; and that they pay verbal deference to congressional authority when testifying on Capitol Hill but frame their approach to Congress on the premise that congressmen would prefer to be led than to lead.

This not very novel codification of ways to influence Congress would have elicited only modest interest had it leaked from the Kennedy or Johnson White House. In the Jimmy Carter years its release might even have been a reassuring sign that the president was learning the rules of the Washington game. But such directives were inappropriate for a president who avoided being linked with political operations. Consequently, in sending the Lodge memorandum, along with a comment on it by General Persons, Eisenhower instructed Anderson to study the documents carefully, and after doing so, "I request that you personally destroy them both. I am particularly anxious that no word of any concerted effort along this line ever reach the outside because a leak would tend to destroy the value of the effort." Eisenhower noted, however, that Anderson was free to communicate the contents to his staff, but with a key qualification, "[A]s your own ideas."[9]

Eisenhower used the targeted variant of hidden-hand leadership in which he and his team concealed his maneuvers from only some outsiders (in this case the general public, but not from the person he wished to influence) in a 1953 exchange with South Carolina Governor James Byrnes, a 1952 Eisenhower supporter who had protested an administration executive order instituting racial integration in Southern federal facilities. In a letter to Byrnes Eisenhower stressed that he was acting out of a conviction about what was constitutionally required of him and not because he was insensitive to Southern mores or because his high personal regard for Byrnes had weakened.[10]

Eisenhower discussed with a White House aide the possible impact his message would have if made public. He decided to have the letter marked "personal and confidential." "After all," he pointed out, "we are not after publicity for this particular letter; what we want is the governor to go along with us completely in the enforcement of federal regulations." The concluding sentence of his interoffice memorandum to the aide perfectly captures Eisenhower's predilection to defuse conflicts rather than bring them to a head: "Our job is to convince; not to publicize."[11]

Eisenhower himself believed that this kind of hidden-hand strategy had been responsible for termination of the Korean conflict. When Eisenhower entered the White House, he was convinced that the Chinese forces were so well entrenched on the current truce line that a negotiated settlement was the best course of action. The alternative possibilities of bloody fighting for limited gains or a major assault on the mainland that at worst could escalate into a global war and at best might unify Korea, thus leaving the United States with unwanted control of North Korea, seemed to him to be wholly inappropriate. But the truce talks were stalled, and no obvious Chinese advantage was to be gained in reopening them. After considering the possibility of using tactical nuclear weapons on North Korean troop concentrations and being persuaded that such a course of action would be repugnant to the NATO allies,[12] Eisenhower records that he conveyed an unpublicized message to the Chinese through indirect channels. Proceeding on the premise that China would not relish nuclear devastation of its industrial and military concentrations and would expect a new American regime led by a general to be more bellicose than Truman's, he acted in a way calculated not to arouse NATO fears of an expanded war, but even so to create among the Chinese the expectation that if they did not negotiate a settlement they would bear unacceptable costs. As he put it:

> In India and in the Formosa Straits area, and at the truce negotiations at Panmunjom, we dropped the word, discreetly, of our intention . . . to move decisively without inhibition in our use of weapons, and . . . no longer be responsible for confining hostilities to the Korean Peninsula. . . . We felt sure that it would reach Soviet and Communist ears.[13]

There is no way short of examining Communist sources to prove that this strategy was effective. Eisenhower felt it had been, since, almost immediately after the signals were issued in February 1953, the Chinese became more open to negotiations. A truce settlement was agreed upon by the summer of 1953.

Hidden-hand tactics also helped Eisenhower to conceal his part (indeed the part of the United States) in the overthrow of the Mossadegh government in Iran in 1953 and of the Arbenz government in Guatemala in 1954.[14] In neither instance did the mainstream American media even suggest that these operations were initiated by America, much less by Eisenhower.

Hidden-hand leadership, whether simple or targeted, by an ostensibly nonpolitical president can, however, cut two ways. While it may permit the president to achieve what would be a controversial outcome without backlash, it also has intrinsic limitations in situations where the object of influence can best be persuaded if he thinks the action urged on him is one the president wants him to take.

The strategy failed on two occasions when Eisenhower attempted to exercise influence indirectly within his official family. His efforts in one instance were merely unsuccessful and in the other contributed to prolonging a state of affairs that was not in the administration's tactical interest. In the first Eisenhower tried indirectly to dissuade Nixon from running for vice-president in 1956; in the second—also involving Nixon—the president sought, in 1958, to persuade Sherman Adams to resign.

In February 1956, before Eisenhower had announced his own candidacy, he suggested to Nixon that his chance of becoming a winning Republican presidential candidate in 1960 would be greater if, rather than running for a second vice-presidential term, he establish independent status as secretary of a major cabinet department, adding with matter-of-fact detachment, "if we can count on my living five years." Recapping this conversation to party chairman Leonard Hall, Eisenhower talked about another reason for removing Nixon from the ticket: to get a stronger running mate and groom an alternate 1960 candidate for the presidency. Robert Anderson, as usual, was his first choice. He also was fascinated with the notion that it might be possible to crack the New Deal coalition by enlisting a conservative Democrat and Roman Catholic, Ohio Senator Frank Lausche.[15]

Although Eisenhower preferred an alternative to Nixon as a running mate, he made clear to an aide that he felt "there is nothing to be gained politically by ditching him."[16] Hall, in a massive underestimation of Nixon's tenacity, assured Eisenhower that it would be "the easiest thing to get Nixon out of the picture willingly." Eisenhower replied, "Well, all right, you see him and talk to him, but be very, very gentle."[17] Hall's mission, of course, failed.

Unwilling to depart from his strategic rule of avoiding visible wirepulling within the party and, unwilling to instruct Nixon not to run, Eisenhower succumbed to the pressures of Nixon's many party supporters and to the impact of the write-in votes Nixon garnered in the early primaries. He announced in March that the team would again be "Ike and Dick." Eisenhower deliberately traded one desired result, dropping Nixon, for others, such as preserving his politics-free image and avoiding a factional squabble. And in doing so, he failed to accomplish his goal of obtaining a preferable second-term running mate.

In the second episode, Nixon in turn acted as Eisenhower's tacit agent in a 1958 conversation designed to encourage Adams to conclude that he would best serve the administration by resigning. In June, Adams had acknowledged to the committee investigating attempts to influence federal regulatory agencies that he realized he had been indiscreet in phoning the Federal Trade Commission to inquire about the status of charges against his old friend, textile manufacturer Bernard Goldfine. Adams explained that Goldfine's gifts were part of a pattern of gift giving between the two families. Eisenhower, taking it for granted that a chief of staff was invariably subject to political heat and realizing that Adams frequently served as a foil for indirect attacks on Eisenhower's own leadership, promptly announced his support for the former New Hampshire Governor. But by early August, Goldfine seemed to fit the Truman-era mold of the influence buyer. His gifts had been not only to Adams but also to other public figures, and the gifts had been written off by Goldfine as business expenses. Eisenhower's businessmen friends and the bulk of Republican congressmen up for reelection that year publicly and privately bombarded him with pleas for Adams's resignation.

Eisenhower breakfasted with Nixon the morning of July 15th. Mrs. Whitman summarized the breakfast agenda as a discussion of "the pros and cons of Governor Adams staying or leaving" by noting that "as a result of that breakfast, the Vice President had, at five o'clock, made an appointment with Governor Adams. The Vice President reported, in full, to me. . . . He had made it very clear that the President had not asked him to have the talk with Governor Adams." Nixon, in the recapitulation of the meeting he dictated to Mrs. Whitman for Eisenhower's attention, reported that he told Adams, "I have been weighing the factors and that I had, this morning, had breakfast with the President, who for the first time, had discussed the matter with me." He explained to Adams that Eisenhower's loyalty to his chief of staff made him unwilling to discuss the possibility of a resignation. "I made it clear, in other words, that the President had not indicated the course of action he believed Governor Adams should follow."

"Then," Nixon continued, "I proceeded to weigh the various pros and cons of staying and leaving, most of which I had discussed with the President this morning." The pros and cons Nixon and Eisenhower had discussed pointed compellingly to the desirability of a resignation, including "the fact that the overwhelming majority of Republicans in the House and Senate believe that he should resign," the liability he would be to the president who "would be asked in press conferences from now on . . . about the standard of ethics as applied in Adams's case and whether or not there was a double standard," and the certainty that any Republican congressional losses would be blamed on Adams. To the half-dozen strong pro reasons there were only two weak cons: that Adams was an effective worker and that Eisenhower would have trouble replacing him.[18]

Adams simply said he would wait for word from the president. Finally on September 17, Adams resigned but only after Eisenhower had staged still another meeting, this time between Adams and the new Republican Chairman Meade Alcorn, who pointedly told Adams that by staying on he was damaging the party's electoral chances and Eisenhower's program, and that Eisenhower shared Alcorn's view even though he would not request Adams to resign. Taking Adams's resignation phone call, Eisenhower stressed his anxiety "that we not do anything that can be interpreted as pressure," adding that he wanted to protect Adams "from anything that looks cold or indifferent."[19] At the same time he encouraged Adams to consummate his resignation promptly. Eisenhower had, of course, also protected *himself* from appearing cold or indifferent and had enabled Adams to say in the passage in his memoirs on his resignation that the decision about whether to resign was left "entirely up to me."[20] But Eisenhower's refusal personally to press the issue delayed Adams's departure and possibly contributed to the substantial Republican losses in 1958.

Instrumental Use of Language

Eisenhower found it natural to express himself straightforwardly and incisively, arraying facts and rigorously justifying his policies and actions. He could do this by using precisely etched prose and he took pride in his capacity to do so. He was, however, also willing to replace clear, reasoned discourse with alternative ways of expressing himself when they better served his purposes. Neither pride in ability nor his natural predilection for clarity kept him from deliberately turning to language that was emotive and inspirational or purposely ambiguous. Verbal expression was his instrument; he refused to indulge his obvious pleasure in analytic thought and clear expression as an end in itself.

I say that clear expression was natural to him because it is the manner he adopted in private circumstances. The personal diary passages he used for self-clarification and that he never released for publication are lucidly written, as are his innumerable prepresidential and presidential memoranda to aides and associates, as well as his letters to his most confidential correspondents. His penchant for clarity also is evident in the many drafts that have been preserved of reports, letters, and speeches that he personally edited to hone the prose.

His dictated list of editorial changes on the first draft of his 1954 State of the Union message shows Eisenhower's work as a word clarifier and also as a stylist striving for public effect. As one of the rare editing efforts in which he explained the reasons for his changes, the list illustrates how in his writing, as in other endeavors, he formulated abstract rules for many of his operating procedures. In the course of transmitting four general and thirty-eight specific instructions for change, he tightened the prose by telling the speech writer that "sections need to be more distinctly marked" and admonished: "Do not be afraid to say 'I come to so-and-so'. . . . You cannot take the human mind from subject to subject . . . quickly!" And, almost nigglingly, he had the assertion "confidence had developed" changed to "constantly developing confidence" to indicate "continuing action."[21]

Eisenhower also conveyed instructions designed, in a latter-day phrase, to make the speech play better in Peoria. He instructed the speech writer to eliminate such technical language as "substantial reductions in the size and cost of Federal Government" and "deficit spending" on the grounds that the "man we are trying to reach" better understands the phrases "purchasing power of the dollar" and stability "in the size of his market basket."[22] The changes advanced his aim of expanding his party's base to encompass the upper blue-collar and lower white-collar nucleus of the Democratic party's coalition.

In addition to using words as instruments for communicating substance and emotions, Eisenhower also sometimes employed them in a fashion similar to his hidden-hand strategy—to create smoke screens for his actions in his role as covert prime minister. Some of his utterances served to obscure sensitive subjects from public view; others conveyed deliberately ambiguous messages that left him freedom of action. Deliberate use of ambiguity and evasiveness were, of course, not unique to Eisenhower. What distinguished him from other politicians was the ability to leave the impression that such utterances were guileless.

His press conferences furnish a good perspective on his use of language to convey ambiguity. The most instructive are those for which transcripts have been kept of the preliminary briefings so that a record is available of what he chose to say and why. But the entire body of his official exchanges with the press reveals his use of ambiguity and other verbal strategies. Some of his press conference practices contributed to the impression that he simply was uninformed, when in fact he was choosing to be ambiguous. He was more disposed than other presidents simply to say that he was not aware of certain issues, including some that had received wide press attention. He also often directed questioners to one of his associates for an answer, suggesting that the issue on which he was being queried was not of sufficient magnitude or "ripeness" to warrant presidential attention: "Well, this is the first I've heard of that," and "You'd better take that up with Secretary X" are common assertions in his press conferences.

The texts of the preliminary briefings make it clear, however, that in claiming ignorance he often was following a practice he used as early as his first press conference on becoming European theater commander in June 1942, which the *New York Times* described as an "excellent demonstration of the art of being jovially outspoken without saying much of anything."[23] Even then he was sufficiently self-conscious about ways that a leader can use his mode of expression as a tactic to advise others—such as his embarrassingly outspoken subordinate commander, George S. Patton, Jr.—on verbal comportment. Quoting "an old proverb...:'Keep silent and appear stupid; open your mouth and remove all doubt,'" he advised Patton that "a certain sphynx-like quality will do a lot toward enhancing one's reputations."[24]

Eisenhower's strategy of remaining silent is illustrated in the summary of the briefing before his July 31, 1957, press conference. Aides reminded Eisenhower that Egyptian President Nasser had been making speeches criticizing the United States and that the "Egyptians are trying to say [they] have disturbed us." Eisenhower told his briefers that if the question came up, he would say he had not read Nasser's speeches.[25] On that occasion the question did not come up.

Earlier that month, however, his briefers did correctly anticipate a question. On July 17 Eisenhower and his aides discussed an issue that was likely to be on the reporters' agenda, because Secretary of State John Foster Dulles had raised it in his news conference the previous day: the disposition of American missiles in Europe. Eisenhower expressed annoyance that Dulles had "wandered" into a topic he felt should have been a matter for "no comment" on national security grounds. Phoning Dulles to be reminded in detail of what he had said, Eisenhower hung up and told his associates that if the question came up at the press conference, he would "be evasive."[26]

It did and he was. Quoting Dulles, Peter Lisagor of the *Chicago Daily News* noted that the Secretary of State "yesterday disclosed that consideration is being given to a plan for establishing nuclear stockpiles of weapons and fissionable materials for NATO powers." How did the president stand on this matter? Lisagor asked. In his reply Eisenhower denied knowledge of the very information he had just confirmed in his conversation with Dulles. "Now I don't know what he told you about a plan," he said. "What we have just been doing is studying means and methods of making NATO effective as a defensive organization. . . . Now that is all there is to that."[27]

Such intentional evasiveness was a standard Eisenhower press conference tactic.* Sometimes, as in a March 16, 1955, press conference,

---

*The views of Augustine and Kant (and, in a more qualified way, Sissela Bok in her recent work *Lying: Moral Choice in Public and Private Life*)[28] that untruths are rarely if ever justified

he mixed vagueness with ambiguity studiously designed to have different effects on different audiences. The issue was whether, under what
circumstances, and with what kinds of weapons the United States
would defend Quemoy and Matsu. In his previous news conference,
Eisenhower had warned that in the event of a "general war" in Asia
the United States was prepared to use tactical nuclear weapons. Just
before the following week's conference, the State Department conveyed through Hagerty the urgent request that the president not discuss this delicate matter further. Eisenhower reports that he replied,
"Don't worry, Jim, if that question comes up, I'll just confuse them."[29]

Joseph C. Harsch of the *Christian Science Monitor* raised the question, asking, "If we got into an issue with the Chinese, say, over Matsu
and Quemoy, that we wanted to keep limited, do you conceive us using
[atomic weapons] in that situation or not?" Eisenhower responded:

> Well, Mr. Harsch, I must confess I cannot answer that question in advance.
> The only thing I know about war are two things: the most unpredictable
> factor in war is human nature in its day-by-day manifestation; but the only
> unchanging factor in war is human nature. And the next thing is that every
> war is going to astonish you in the way it occurred, and in the way it is
> carried out. So that for a man to predict, particularly if he has the responsi-
> bility for making the decision, to predict what he is going to use, how he
> is going to do it, would I think exhibit his ignorance of war; that is what
> I believe. So I think you just have to wait; and that is the kind of prayerful
> decision that may some day face a president.[30]

The vagueness and ambiguity in this response was contrived to serve
several ends. It allowed Eisenhower to sidestep a potentially divisive
encounter with right wing "China Firster" Republicans, which would
have destroyed his ability to pass such high priority programs as the
annual foreign aid appropriation. It also conveyed an ambiguous warning message to the PRC, which would have been delighted to occupy
Quemoy and Matsu, a matter alluded to in his letter to Gruenther a

---

in human discourse would strike Eisenhower as visionary. He was no Machiavellian; he recognized
the importance of honesty and intellectual clarity in private deliberations but took it as an unspo-
ken axiom that public language was to be adapted to the circumstances at hand and toward the
best possible consequences.

month earlier. Finally, for the American public, the message was a reassuring reminder that any decision taken would reflect the professional judgment of a president who understood the nature of war. Eisenhower and Hagerty recognized that Eisenhower's style in press conferences was well received by the general public, even if it left the impression among Washington cognoscenti that he was obtuse. They, after all, introduced the practice of releasing tapes and kinescopes of presidential news conferences to the public.

Eisenhower preferred to persuade other leaders through reasoned discourse, but did so only with those of his counterparts who he thought had the capacity and motivation to be influenced by rational argument.

He summoned his persuasive powers—sometimes carefully setting forth his reasoning, but other times arguing from premises he knew to be simplistic, but persuasive—more than once to steer the Republican right toward the middle of the road. In the April 30, 1953, Legislative Leadership meeting, Eisenhower gave an extended, closely reasoned, factual presentation of his administration's review of Truman's outgoing budget and its proposed cuts. The analysis included a lengthy report introducing the New Look defense policy, which was designed to weigh defense costs against the goal of avoiding burdening the economy with taxes or deficits that might reduce productivity or foster inflation. On the basis of this exercise in balancing "the external threat of Communism and the internal threat of a weakened economy," Eisenhower reported that Truman's request for funds for the next year would be reduced by $8.6 billion and that there would be additional cuts in spending during the remainder of the current fiscal year. After extensive discussion of the report by Eisenhower and other administration spokesmen and legislators, the response of his erstwhile nomination adversary, Senator Taft, as reported in the antiseptic prose of the official minutes (witnesses say he angrily pounded his fist on the cabinet table), was that,

> he could not possibly express the deepness of his disappointment at the program the administration presented today. The net result of it, he thought would be to spend as much as Mr. Truman spent. Either there would be a large deficit or Congress would have to levy new taxes. . . . Sen.

Taft asserted with all due respect for the NSC [National Security Council], he didn't believe the members knew anything more than he. . . . The NSC has relied on the same JCS [Joint Chiefs of Staff] people who have been here and they can't change their positions. He said he could not defend this program.

Eisenhower knew from his private discussions with Taft that the Ohioan was open to reason. The official meeting minutes note that "The President then quietly began to review the essentials of U. S. global strategy, which he termed 'not too difficult to understand.' " The review had the well-ordered quality of his private letters and memoranda outlining policies.

He noted first that "all agreed that Europe must not be allowed to fall to Russia, that there was no desire on the part of the United States to take over political control of Europe, and that our policy must therefore be founded upon making the free countries of Europe stronger both physically and in spirit." Moreover, it was necessary to prevent "the Middle East, in possession of half the oil resources of the globe, from falling to Russia." "Going further around the globe," he called attention to the "alarming news of the invasion of Laos by the Communists and the resultant increased peril to all of Southeast Asia," stressing "the need for maintaining a position of strength in all these areas or facing the danger of Russia taking them over gradually without having to fight." The overall military problem "was to take hold of the upward trend of expenditures and bend it down," but in doing so he could not "endanger the security of the country by agreeing to any less than adequate program."[31]

Eisenhower's inward response to Taft's outburst had been distinctly unantiseptic and not at all calm. As he noted in a diary entry the next day, he first had to curb his own temper before "quietly" proceeding.

The ludicrous part of the affair came about when several of my close friends around the table saw my temper was getting a little out of hand at the demagogic proceeding, and of course they did not want any breach to be brought about that would be completely unbridgeable. So [Treasury Secretary] George Humphrey and [Budget Bureau Director] Joe Dodge in turn jumped into the conversation as quickly as there was the slightest chance to interrupt and held the floor until I had cooled down somewhat.

71

After regaining composure,

> I simply laid out the general basis of our global strategy, its inescapable re-
> quirements in terms of vital areas, the obvious truth that protection cost
> a mint of money, and defended the individuals on the Security Council
> who had worked so long and so earnestly to bring about the projected sav-
> ings. . . . By the time the Senator had seen the reaction to his own talk
> and heard the general comment about the table, he was to a very consider-
> able amount backing up; before the meeting was over he had the appear-
> ance of being a jolly good fellow who had merely expressed himself emphati-
> cally.[32]

In the next leadership meeting Eisenhower joked easily with Taft about
the exchange.[33]

If Taft would listen to reason, this was not true of certain other right-
wing Republican legislators. In ironing out differences of opinion with
the deeply emotional conservatives and nationalists in his own party,
Eisenhower often met them on their own narrowly defined terms
rather than seeking to convert them to his more comprehensive view
of contemporary issues. When, for example, referring to the planned
trial of an American soldier who had killed a Japanese woman, Taft's
successor, William Knowland rumbled in the Legislative Leadership
meeting that he would not want a son of his to be tried by a Japanese
court, Eisenhower did not take the time to discuss the importance of
adhering to the Status of Forces Treaty. He allowed the aide conducting the briefing to placate Knowland by simply noting that in such cases
Japanese courts settled for a fine and an apology: an army court martial
would yield a long prison sentence.[34]

Needless to say there is nothing unique, in or out of politics, about
adjusting one's discourse to circumstances. What distinguishes Eisenhower's is its remarkably wide range—from highly cognitive, to emotional, through deliberately obfuscated uses of language—the self-
consciousness with which he changed gears, and, above all, his ability
to keep discrepancies in his expressive modes from coming across as
inconsistency. He accomplished this largely by using cool reasoning in
private contexts and benign, if not bumbling sounding, discourse in
public.

"I Do Not Engage in Personalities"

This was Eisenhower's curiously phrased way of asserting his strategy of not criticizing others personally, no matter how strong the provocation. He enunciated his rationale to Bryce Harlow after editing a public statement Harlow drafted for him on a currently hot issue. Harlow recalls that Eisenhower

> picked up his pen, leaned forward, and struck out a word. He sat back and said, "Now, Bryce, that's a fine statement. . . . Go ahead and issue it. I made one little change." And I said, "Well, sir, what's that?" He said, "I struck out the word 'deliberate.' " He said, "This is an attack on a person. When you said it was deliberate, what he had done, you were attacking his motives. Never, ever, attack a person's motives, Bryce."[35]

Eisenhower's sensitivity to the costs of handling personalities indelicately is illustrated repeatedly in his statements and actions throughout his public career. The tasks he faced as Supreme Commander Allied Forces Europe were so thoroughly steeped in personality management that, only two months after returning to the United States and becoming army Chief of Staff, he advised West Point Superintendent Maxwell Taylor to introduce a course in "practical or applied psychology" to the military academy curriculum. The course was needed, he said, because

> [t]oo frequently we find young officers trying to use empirical and ritualistic methods in the handling of individuals—I think that both theoretical and practical instruction along this line could, at the very least, awaken the majority of Cadets to the necessity of handling human problems on a human basis and do much to improve leadership and personnel handling in the Army at large.[36]

Although wartime leadership was plagued by personality conflicts, Eisenhower made clear many years later, that he had deliberately omitted reference to them in his VE-Day Victory Order which declared, "Let us have no part in the profitless quarrels on which other men will engage as to what country, what service, won the European War."[37] Drawing attention to the reference to "quarrels," he noted in a 1959 letter that the passage "might just as well have contained the word 'individual' as well as 'country' and service.' " He stressed that, "So far as I know I have not, myself, consciously violated the exhortation I then delivered the command." Thus, for example, in spite of the many personal recriminations and invidious comments others introduced into their World War II memoirs, in Eisenhower's own *Crusade in Europe,* "wherever there is given . . . any impression of mine concerning an individual, it invariably winds up with an expression of respect and even admiration."[38]

Eisenhower's fullest statement of the reasons for his rule not to engage in personalities and its basic rationale is in a March 9, 1954, letter to his businessman friend, Paul Helms.

> For the past thirteen years I have occupied posts around which there focused sufficient public interest that they were considered news sources of greater or lesser importance. . . . Out of all those experiences, I developed a practice which, so far as I know, I have never violated. That practice is to avoid public mention of any name *unless it can be done with favorable intent and connotation;* reserve all criticism for the private conference; speak only good in public. (Eisenhower's emphasis)

Then, stating the psychological basis for the practice, he observed:

> This is not namby-pamby. It certainly is not Pollyanna-ish. It is just sheer common sense. A leader's job is to get others to go along with him in the promotion of something. To do this he needs their goodwill. To destroy goodwill, it is only necessary to criticize publicly. This creates in the criticized one a subconscious desire to "get even." Such effects can last for a very long period.[39]

When Eisenhower told Helms he reserved personality "criticism for the private conference," he did not go on to suggest the almost clinical objectivity with which he could analyze and think about the problems of dealing with people who hampered him but whom he refused publicly to criticize. There is no better illustration of how his private and public assertions diverged than the contrast between a 1953 exchange with persistent journalists who sought to foster a confrontation between Eisenhower and Senator Taft and a diary entry he made a month later. Taft, in a speech of May 26, 1953, concerning the stalemated Korean truce negotiations, asserted that if the negotiating team meeting in Korea could not agree on a militarily secure truce line, the United States should "let England and our allies know that we are withdrawing from all further peace negotiations in Korea" because we "might as well . . . reserve to ourselves a completely free hand."[40]

This was typical of the kind of emotional statement by Taft that Eisenhower deplored. He noted in the diary entry that

> [i]n the foreign field, Senator Taft never disagrees with me when we discuss such matters academically or theoretically. . . . However, when we take up each individual problem or case, he easily loses his temper and makes extravagant statements. He always does this when he starts making a public speech—he seems to work himself into a storm of resentment and irritation. The result of all this is that our allies fear him and all he influences. They think he gives McCarthy ideas and McCarthy, with his readiness to go to the extremes in calling names and making false accusations, simply terrifies the ordinary European statesman.[41]

The White House withheld comment on Taft's speech, but Senator John Sparkman, the 1952 Democratic vice-presidential candidate, called the speech a "diametric contradiction" of Eisenhower's policy, and the senior Democratic foreign policy spokesman, Senator Walter George, said that Taft was advocating "the road that leads directly to complete isolation and a third world war."[42] In Eisenhower's May 28 press conference, Richard Wilson of Cowles Publications, attempted in an extended colloquy to smoke Eisenhower out. Did he, or did he not agree with the senator? Eisenhower avoided "engaging in personalities" with Taft by being persistently elusive, insisting that Taft's remarks had been misinterpreted by the reporters.

> Wilson: As I read Senator Taft's speech . . . if the present truce negotiations fail, that then we should go it alone.
> Eisenhower: Well now, I am not going to put words in Senator Taft's mouth because I did not read the speech in detail.* But I do believe this: when he says go it alone, he *must* mean that we insist on following our

*In his press conference briefing papers, Hagerty forewarned Eisenhower that he should be prepared to answer questions on Taft's speech, including, "Do you agree on go it alone?"[43]

own beliefs and convictions in the situation. He certainly doesn't mean we just would throw everybody out. [emphasis added]

Wilson persisted, "if I read his speech correctly—in fact, that is what he said exactly." No doubt Taft was referring to the possibility that lack of cooperation by the *Chinese* could force the United States to withdraw from negotiations, Eisenhower speculated. Yes, Wilson replied, but he took Taft's position to be that disagreement between the United States and Great Britain might also be cause for withdrawing.

> Eisenhower: There is something confusing here. I don't believe I had better answer it. I don't understand what could be meant by such a thing. Look— suppose all of us here are friends, and we are trying to get somebody out on the street to agree to something and he disagrees, does that mean we all suddenly here become enemies and break up? I don't understand that!

Straining for precision, Wilson received permission to read directly from Taft's speech, which contained the blanket assertion, "I think we should do our best now to negotiate this truce, and if we fail, then let England and our other allies know that we are withdrawing from all further peace negotiations in Korea." Eisenhower again offered an interpretation of Taft's meaning: it might be that the United States *and* its allies would at some point agree that the negotiations had become fruitless and withdraw from them. "As I say," Eisenhower concluded, "there is some idea there that I am not grasping, and I don't think it is fair to ask me to try to comment on it when I don't."

Eisenhower relentlessly refused to grasp an idea that would force him to disagree publicly with Taft. Later in the news conference when Texas newspaperwoman Sarah McClendon asked if he would read Taft's speech in detail and comment, he replied, "If I had to read all the speeches that are in the papers in detail, I would be pretty badly off," thus terminating the discussion and, as usual, fostering his "above the fray" appearance.[44]

Action Based on Personality Analysis

World War II presented Eisenhower with a classic leadership dilemma: how to maximize the effectiveness of subordinates who have some personal qualities that make them well suited for the tasks that need to be performed, but who also have flaws that can undermine their performance. The man who was in the best position to evaluate Eisenhower's wartime leadership, European command Chief of Staff, General W. Bedell Smith, once described how Eisenhower dealt with this complication by assessing each subordinate's qualities in terms of assets and liabilities and shaping his job so that it exploited the former and minimized the impact of the latter. Smith explained that Eisenhower

> considers his commanders and senior staff officers the tools with which he works and he uses them in accordance with their particular capacity. For example, General Patton, the typical cavalryman with all the ideals and traditions of mobile action and with the dash and flamboyancy of a Custer, was invariably selected as the commander of forces engaged in wide maneuver aggressive action and deep penetration which required great initiative, boldness and a certain disregard of consequences. Other commanders with slightly different qualifications were used on equally important, though less conspicuous assignments which were in keeping with their temperaments.[45]

Personality assessment was virtually a reflexive act for Eisenhower. This propensity is most extensively documented during the war years when he kept up a regular flow of letters to his immediate superior, General George Marshall, explaining his thinking and actions. The comments on Patton alone are voluminous: For example,

> I doubt that I would ever consider Patton for an army group commander or for any higher position, but as an army commander under a man who is sound and solid, and who has enough sense to use Patton's good qualities without becoming blinded by his love of showmanship and histrionics, he should do as fine a job as he did in Sicily.[46]

Of the problems of Patton's predecessor as II Corps Commander, General Lloyd R. Fredendall, Eisenhower reflected (shortly before returning him to the United States to command a training unit):

Fredendall . . . is tops—except for one thing. He has difficulty in picking good men and, even worse, in getting the best out of subordinates. . . . I must either find a good substitute for Fredendall or must place in his command a number of assistants who are so stable and sound they will not be disturbed by his idiosyncracies.[47]

Without a Marshall to report to while president, examples of Eisenhower's use of personality analysis in determining how to respond to people and how to employ them tend to be preserved only in fragmentary form. These include his diary notes on Taft; a comment warning his press aide Hagerty that it would be difficult to persuade Agriculture Secretary Ezra Taft Benson to retract an error because he is a "stubborn man and I don't suppose we can get him to do that;"[48] and his warning to the Republican party chairman to be "very, very gentle" with Nixon in discussing his political ambitions.[49]

Nevertheless, from time to time during his presidency Eisenhower devoted a full communication to a personality analysis and how he wanted his associates to act on it. An illustration is his instruction to Dulles that John Sherman Cooper, the new ambassador to India, should "do everything possible to win the personal confidence and friendship" of Prime Minister Nehru because of "the amount of evidence we have that Nehru seems to be often more swayed by personality than by logical argument." Cooper, he stressed, should be protected from any "chores . . . that would almost compel him to show an unsympathetic attitude toward the Premier" on the grounds that if Cooper pursued the "one single *general* objective" of winning over Nehru personally, "that could possibly pay off in big terms."[50] (Eisenhower's emphasis.)

In congressional relations, because the committee and leadership way stations are controlled by semiautonomous individuals, each with his own idiosyncracies, personality analysis played a particularly key role. Personal relations based as much on art as spontaneity, for example, were crucial in Eisenhower's establishment of unexpectedly amiable relations with Taft. During the period from which the quotation on pp. 75–76 was taken, Eisenhower regularly consulted with Taft, even insisting that the Majority Leader feel free to enter the Oval Office unannounced.

Eisenhower's sensitivity to personalities enabled him to identify and therefore bypass blocks in his channels for influencing Congress. One frequent block was Taft's successor as Senate Republican leader, William F. Knowland. Eisenhower recorded in a diary reflection on how great a loss Taft's death in the summer of 1953 had been: "Knowland means to be helpful and loyal, but he is cumbersome. He does not have the sharp mind and the great experience that Taft did. Consequently, he does not command the respect in the Senate that Taft enjoyed."[51] He was regularly irritated by Knowland's simplistic views as well as clumsy leadership. (He told a friend that "Knowland has no foreign policy except to develop high blood pressure whenever he mentions the words 'Red China.' "[52]) But he successfully concealed his distaste from Knowland, who in his Columbia Oral History interview made only the conventional observations that Eisenhower was a nonpolitical leader, "sincere" and "without guile."[53]

A week before Taft's death, Eisenhower had made an arrangement intended to circumvent a cumbersome Senate party leader. After a breakfast meeting with Senator Everett Dirksen, Eisenhower recorded that

I asked him to be "verbal leader" of the middle-of-the-road philosophy (my philosophy) in the Senate. Regardless of the formal leadership, he would be the man to take on all attackers, the champion who would put on armor and get on the white horse and take on the fight.[54]

Dirksen could be especially useful as an ally because his widely publicized tirade against Eisenhower's nomination at the 1952 convention had established his *bona fides* with conservative Republicans. When a strong Taft backer spoke out for Eisenhower's policies, it was persuasive testimony to his congressional colleagues that the administration was acting consistently with the principles of the man who had personified traditional Republican principles. On the House side, Eisenhower also established an informal working relationship with a leader he had sized up as being more effective than the aging official party head, Joseph Martin. His choice was the second-ranking Republican, Indiana Congressman Charles Halleck, who in Eisenhower's diary is warmly described as a selfless, "highly intelligent and mentally alert . . . team player."[55]

Eisenhower's analyses of the personalities of members of his official family also were of the greatest importance, particularly in determining the extent and nature of the authority he delegated to subordinates. The thumbnail sketches he made in his private diary four months after taking office of two occupants of major cabinet posts, the secretary of state and the secretary of defense, not only illustrate his characterizations of subordinates but also provide insight into his practice of selective delegation.

Of John Foster Dulles, Eisenhower wrote,

> I still think of him, as I always have, as an intensive student of foreign affairs. He is well informed and, in this subject at least, is deserving, I think of his reputation as a "wise" man. . . . [But] he is not particularly persuasive in presentation and, at times, seems to have a curious lack of understanding as to how his words and manner may affect another personality.[56]

Of Charles Wilson, whose confirmation hearings had been flawed by the first of many verbal faux pas, he observed, "Mr. Wilson is prone to lecture, rather than to answer, when asked a question. This not only annoys many members of Congress, but it gives them unlooked for opportunities to discover flaws in reasoning and argument."[57] But neither man's defects incapacitated him from Eisenhower's standpoint, because he was able to devise ways to use their strengths and neutralize their weaknesses.

Delegation Selectively Practiced

Eisenhower's wartime experience of commanding a vast intricate organization and his extensive staff experience in the army, an institution with an explicitly elaborate organizational structure, undoubtedly account for the self-consciousness and subtlety with which he approached delegation of authority. First, he was highly attentive to the general need for delegation, if the head of a complex organization is not to be inundated with details. Secondly, he took care not to delegate in a fashion that would dilute his own ability to keep the actions of his associates in line with his own policies, adjusting the degree of his supervision both to the abilities of his associates and to the extent he believed his own participation in a policy area was necessary. Finally, he was highly sensitive to a side effect of delegation, that of sharing credit with subordinates for popular policies, but also (especially important for a president who emphasized his role as chief of state) diffusing blame for unpopular policies throughout the administration rather than allowing himself as chief executive to be the main recipient of blame.

Taking stock of the leadership principles he had practiced and commenting on a *Life* editorial praising his presidency but asking whether he had sometimes been "too easy a boss," Eisenhower stated his view on the general need to delegate in a 1960 letter to Henry Luce. Eisenhower's comments were straightforward extensions of his prepresidential administrative rhetoric and action, exemplified both by his tribute in *Crusade in Europe* to General Marshall's advancement of subordinates who had the capacity to make decisions without constantly referring back to higher authority,[58] and the instruction he gave to his principal aides in June 1942 on assuming American command in Europe that they were "free to solve their own problems wherever possible and not to get in the habit of passing the buck up."[59] Eisenhower pointed out to Luce that "the government of the United States has become too big, too complex, and too pervasive in its influence on all our lives for one individual to pretend to direct the details of its important and critical programming. Competent assistants are mandatory: without them the executive branch would bog down." Moreover, wholehearted support of subordinates could not be won by "desk pounding":

> To command the loyalties and dedication and best efforts of capable and outstanding individuals requires patience, understanding, a readiness to delegate, and an acceptance of responsibility for any honest errors—real or apparent—those associates and subordinates might make. . . . Principal subordinates must have confidence that they and their positions are widely respected, and the chief must do his part in assuring that this is so.[60]

81

Eisenhower handled delegation selectively to be sure his policies were satisfactorily carried out. One kind of selective delegation he practiced before and during his presidency consisted of assigning a clearly defined mission to an able subordinate who, in effect, would become more of a deputy than a delegate. The discussion of Sherman Adams in chapter 4 considers in depth this approach to devolving power. The deputy approach is one that Eisenhower used with his first Budget Bureau director, Joseph Dodge. Eisenhower admired Dodge greatly but also had well-developed personal views about how to reshape the budgetary legacy of the Truman administration. Therefore, he sought to establish precise guidelines for Dodge so that when the budget director made decisions, Dodge in effect would be a simple extension of Eisenhower in dealing with the inevitable departmental appeals that follow reductions in budget requests. As Eisenhower wrote to Dodge in 1954,

> It is essential that we understand each other very clearly, because necessarily you must act as my authoritative agent in working on these problems. While, of course, each Department head always has direct access to me, I think it vastly important that if any appeal from your decisions is made, that you must be present at the time—and even more important that you and I approach these problems so definitely from the same viewpoint that the occasions for such appeals will be minimized.[61]

Robert Anderson, as we may infer from Eisenhower's willingness to support him as a successor, also fell in the category of a deeply respected subordinate. During the time he was Treasury secretary, beginning in 1957, Anderson was used as a delegate rather than a deputy and presided over issues of great complexity about which Eisenhower was not minutely informed; he felt as though Eisenhower had given him virtual carte blanche. Anderson, who was also closely associated with Lyndon Johnson during his presidency, compares the two presidents:

> President Eisenhower's background in history was a military one. He came up through all of his life in the atmosphere of having staffs, delegating large amounts of responsibility, assuming large responsibility delegated to him, but having a very tight staff operation. For example, when I was in the Treasury, I have no recollection of the President ever calling me to suggest a policy or anything of the sort. It was always the other way around. . . . On the other hand . . . President Johnson . . . grew up as a congressman.

. . . He was not surrounded by either large staffs or where he could say, "I'm going to delegate these responsibilities," because *he* was the congressman, *he* was the senator, *he* was the majority leader. . . . So I think, in President Johnson's administration, there was more of a personalized presidency, a president who by his very nature became more involved in more details, in more operations, and in more procedural matters, than in the days of President Eisenhower.[62]

Not all of Eisenhower's subordinates, however, were extended the same freedom of action that Anderson enjoyed. Although some were left largely to their own devices, others would periodically experience Eisenhower's direct intervention in their activities. As one might expect both from Eisenhower's expert knowledge of national security issues and from his private characterization of Charles Wilson, the first Eisenhower defense secretary had little policy-making leeway. Much of the time Eisenhower treated Wilson neither as a deputy nor as a delegate, but rather as little more than an expediter of detailed presidential instructions.

In his diary entry on the former General Motors chief, Eisenhower observed: "In his field, he is a really competent man. He is careful and positive, and I have no slightest doubt that, assisted by the team of civilian and military men he has selected, he will produce the maximum security for this country at minimum or near minimum cost."[63] The last six words indicate the principal reason the top executive of the nation's largest corporation had been chosen for the Defense Department. Eisenhower did not need a military expert to head a department he knew inside out and to determine overall policy: in this sphere, the president's own background and skills scarcely could be equaled. Thus, following the approach described by Bedell Smith, the "tool" Eisenhower chose to head the largest government department was a man with a record for efficiently managing the nation's largest corporation. Wilson's duties, however, were limited mainly to internal management—making the department function in a businesslike manner—while Eisenhower and those closest to him in the national security policy-making community were responsible for establishing defense policy.

Eisenhower is often quoted as having expressed impatience at Wilson's proclivity to bring problems to the White House that might have been settled by Wilson himself: "Charlie, you run defense. We both can't do it, and I won't do it. I was elected to worry about a lot of other things than the day-to-day operations of a department."[64] It may be true that Eisenhower had to press Wilson to be more independent in the managerial aspects of Defense Department leadership, but it is clear that on major policy issues—ranging from levels of funding to overall strategic stance—Eisenhower personally made defense policy and in doing so entered deeply into organizational and managerial issues. The Eisenhower Library files contain countless communications to Wilson. They commonly are in the form of directives, often defining in minute detail a Defense Department policy as when, on November 30, 1953, he expressed "shock" at recently having received information "that we now have a proportion of general and flag officers in the Services approximately three times as great as it was in the wartime year of 1944."

> The ratio of colonels and captains to overall service strength likewise appears high. This level of rank must also be considered in the executive or overhead category since there are far more captains in the Navy than there are ships and far more colonels in the Army than there are regiments. I am told that the present proportion of colonels and captains in the Armed Services is approximately four times what it was during 1944.

Noting that if the statistics he cited were incorrect he should be informed, Eisenhower pointed out that although personnel costs were small "compared with the gigantic sums involved in the procurement of equipment . . . nevertheless these examples are extremely important as symbols."

> Please take a good look at the manning situation in these higher ranks. I'd like to talk to you further about the matter because I'm seriously considering the adoption of an executive policy of limiting nominations in the higher grades to a percentage of those legally authorized.[65]

Considerably more important than Eisenhower's close attention to the ratios of officers in varying ranks, however, were his communications explicitly enunciating major strategic policies in his capacity as commander in chief. On December 21, 1955, for example, after policies concerning ballistic missiles had been promulgated in the National Security Council (NSC) and listed in the actions of the December 1 NSC meeting, Eisenhower sent Wilson a memorandum simply announcing that he had, on further consideration, amended the Record of Action to include an additional item in which the NSC

> noted the President's statement that the political and psychological impact upon the world of the early development of an effective ballistic missile with a range in the 1,000–1,700 mile range would be so great that the early development of such a missile would be of critical importance to the national security interests of the United States

and another item stating that

> the President directed that the IRBM and ICBM* programs should both be research and development programs of the highest priority above others. Mutual interference between these programs should be avoided so far as practicable, but if a conflict should occur . . . [which] would in the opinion of the Secretary of Defense, cause major damage to the security interests of the United States, then the matter will be promptly referred to the President.[66]

The mere ministerial function sometimes played by Wilson as head of a major cabinet department is perhaps best conveyed in the language Eisenhower used in informing NSC staff chief Robert Cutler in 1953 of the steps that would be taken to carry out the strategic and budgetary planning for implementing the New Look—if possible in time for the 1955 budget. Enumerating with his customary planner's logic a six-step sequence of what should be done, Eisenhower simply began the memorandum by saying, "I *instructed* Mr. Wilson as follows on the budget matters."[67] (Emphasis added.)

Unlike Wilson, whose authority was so clearly limited, Attorney General Herbert Brownell found that he had far more leeway in policy making than he had expected, although Eisenhower made clear in their first conversation that the attorney general would hear from the president if he felt Brownell's actions were inappropriate. Eisenhower rarely corrected Brownell. When he did, the correction was not likely to be

*Intermediate range and intercontinental ballistic missiles

on a legal matter, but rather in another capacity for which he often used this experienced party politician, that of a wise judge of how to proceed in decisions which involved careful balancing of political considerations. When in his capacity as a political operative Brownell was reproved, it was with the greatest of tact, as is evident in a note from Eisenhower written early in 1954 during a period of intense bargaining over possible ways to rephrase the Bricker Amendment so it would be acceptable to the administration.

Eisenhower had signed a letter to Senator Knowland that Brownell drafted. Knowland made the letter public. Eisenhower felt that if he had known in advance the letter was for publication, he would have reworded it to sharpen the message. His understated reproof was as strong a signal as Brownell ever would get when his actions were out of line with Eisenhower's desires:

> When you asked me to sign the letter . . . did you know that he intended to publish it this evening? . . . While I have no particular objection to this action, I do think I should have been carefully informed as to the ultimate purpose of the letter when I signed it. . . . Please do not do anything about the matter—I was just wondering whether I stupidly missed something this morning that I should have picked up from the conversation.[68]

This is not to say that on legal matters Brownell operated independently of Eisenhower. The president once used his own legislative drafting background in editing the Justice Department's brief in the second *Brown* v. *Board of Education* case.[69] He often dispatched legal questions to Brownell, frequently inquiring pointedly into the substance of the underlying issues and suggesting his own preferences. Often the topics that concerned him arose out of his extensive communications with the many businessmen among his close friends and acquaintances. In April 1956, for example, Eisenhower wrote Brownell inquiring about a 1950 Justice Department ruling affecting the relationship between the larger automobile companies and their dealers—a ruling that some one of the many businessmen he knew seems to have informed him created inequities making it easier for large companies to sell cars. "As you know," he observed, "I am not sufficiently familiar with legal matters to know whether the ruling . . . is a fair and just interpretation of the law," but I am informed that under prior and different interpretation, the law had been working well for thirty years and had preserved order and equity in a business which has since become chaotic and inequitable. . . . I request that you make a personal investigation in this matter and give me your opinion as soon as possible. If the law permits no interpretation except that now existing, I should like your further recommendations as to whether we should seek a change in the law.[70]

Eisenhower concluded by indicating that he was sure the law should be changed if the allegations presented to him were correct. But if Brownell had come forth with persuasive evidence to counter the president's information or the policy to which he was inclined, Brownell's views would have received far more serious consideration than would Wilson's suggestions in connection with defense policy.

Eisenhower also delegated to Secretary of State Dulles substantial power, but with Dulles, unlike any other cabinet member, he entered into a collegial working relationship. Although most accounts of United States foreign policy between 1953 and 1958 take it for granted that Dulles was the senior colleague,[71] the reverse was true. The two men were in daily touch even when Dulles was out of the country on his many missions as presidential emissary. If they could not talk by telephone because Dulles was overseas, they exchanged coded cables. Eisenhower often accepted Dulles's advice. They jointly perfected policies, but Eisenhower made the final decisions and Dulles executed them.

This is firmly documented, as Richard Immerman has shown, by the record of personal communication between the two—including telephone conversation transcripts and memoranda—and by the reports of those aides who personally observed them at work.[72] Their response to the downing of a British plane and two American search planes off Hainan in June 1954 illustrates the dynamics of the collaboration. Dulles, on learning of these events, called the White House. Eisenhower asked Dulles how he suggested handling the matter. Dulles's reply was that if the president approved, he would issue "a protest against further barbarities in attempting to shoot down rescue-type planes." Eisenhower not only already knew of the incident but also had already discussed making a protest with the congressional leaders who agreed that this should be done. He told Dulles he had asked the leaders to keep the information secret until there had been consultation within the administration and instructed him to send a message to British Foreign Secretary Anthony Eden urging that the British simultaneously release a strong statement. This would increase the impact of the American statement and avoid possible Anglo-American friction. Dulles agreed with this tactic. The two concluded that Dulles, after clearing the policy with Eden, would make the public statement and Eisenhower would delay any comments of his own.[73]

This episode reveals genuine consultation. It also shows that before hearing from Dulles, Eisenhower had already established a course of diplomatic action. Moreover, Eisenhower determined the tactic that was pursued, but Dulles, in implementing Eisenhower's instructions, was the publicly visible actor.

A number of Eisenhower's practices inadvertently or deliberately fostered the impression that Dulles had nearly complete autonomy in foreign policy making and that he was the more skilled and informed of the two with respect to foreign affairs. Much of the detailed content of foreign policy was announced in Dulles's Tuesday press conferences. Eisenhower, who met the press on Wednesdays, explained foreign policy in broad, colloquially stated common-sense terms. He referred questioners to Dulles's remarks of the previous day for elaboration. In fact, however, Dulles's utterances had been cleared in detail with Eisenhower in the course of intense consultation. And if they strayed from Eisenhower's views, Eisenhower "reinterpreted" them in his own Wednesday meetings with the press.[74]

Eisenhower felt so strongly that Dulles should be recognized as an authoritative spokesman of the administration that on one occasion he arranged to take the blame for a Dulles slipup in diplomatic practice. He recounts the event in his diary. He discovered the error in a February 1953 meeting with the retiring ambassador to the Court of St. James, "my good friend, Walter Gifford."

While Eisenhower was still at Supreme Headquarters Allied Powers Europe (SHAPE), he had learned of Gifford's plan to retire as soon as the next administration was in office.

With this knowledge, I of course was interested in the task of selecting a completely acceptable and useful successor. We started this job shortly after election in early November and it was not long before we determined that all things considered Winthrop Aldrich would be our best bet. This selection was made on the most confidential basis, but to our consternation it was soon public knowledge.

Because Dulles felt the situation embarrassing, he believed a public explanation was in order. Eisenhower authorized him to do this but "put in my word of caution that Walter Gifford would have to be protected and in every possible way."

In the haste to act quickly, Gifford's planned resignation and Aldrich's intended appointment were announced promptly, without clearing the matter with the British. Eisenhower continues:

> This upset the British government very badly—and I must say most understandably. As Anthony Eden pointed out in his informal protest to Walter Gifford, this meant that Britain was being subjected to pretty rough treatment when there was no effort made to get the usual "agreement." He said that with this precedent, any small nation could pursue the same tactics and if Britain should protest, they could argue that since the United States had done this and Britain had accepted it, no real objection could be made. . . . To guard against any such development as this, I am going to advise Anthony, when I see him next month, to lay the blame for this whole unfortunate occurrence squarely on me. He will have the logical explanation that my lack of formal experience in the political world was the reason for the blunder. Actually, I was the one who cautioned against anything like this happening, but manifestly I can take the blame without hurting anything or anybody, whereas if the Secretary of State would have to shoulder it, his position would be badly damaged.[75]

Eisenhower's private communications to Dulles about policy—in contrast to his public rhetoric, which was more broadly humanitarian than Dulles's—also contradict the standard view that Eisenhower was the more conciliatory of the two men. In a March 1958 memorandum, for example, Eisenhower warned Dulles of a "potentially dangerous" situation.

> This is the credence, even respect, that the world is beginning to give . . . spurious Soviet protestations and pronouncements. As their propaganda promotes this world confusion the tone of Soviet notes and statements

89

grows more strident. The more the men in the Kremlin come to believe that their domestic propaganda is swallowed by their own people and the populations of other countries, including some we have counted upon as allies, the greater the risk of American isolation. . . . I personally believe that one of the main objectives of our own efforts should be to encourage our entire people to see, with clear eyes, the changing character of our difficulties and to convince them that we must be vigilant, energetic, imaginative and incapable of surrender through fatigue or lack of courage.[76]

Eisenhower, then, was not more accommodating to the Soviet Union than was Dulles. Nevertheless, Eisenhower recognized that Dulles's demeanor and mode of expression conveyed an impression of harshness and intractability. His 1953 comment that Dulles "is not particularly persuasive in presentation and, at times, seems to have a curious lack of understanding as to how his words and manner may affect another personality," was paralleled by a remark he made to Goodpaster in January 1958: "I sense a difference with Foster Dulles. . . . His is a lawyer's mind," and he tends to proceed like "a sort of international prosecuting attorney," indicting the Soviet Union for its policies and actions. Eisenhower preferred to present the American position more positively: "Of course, we have got to have a concern and respect for fact and reiteration of official position, but [we] are likewise trying to 'seek friends and influence people.' "[77] In these remarks Eisenhower seems explicitly to have accepted the implicit division of labor in his and Dulles's public utterances. Dulles appeared to be the austere cold warrior; Eisenhower, the warm champion of peace. It was Dulles who issued the bulk of the "get tough" foreign policy statements (placating domestic anti-Communists as well as presenting a firm international position), while amiable Ike could be more effective in his gestures towards international humanitarianism and détente—for example, Atoms for Peace, Open Skies, goodwill trips, and summitry.

The difference in the public images conveyed by Eisenhower and Dulles raises the general issue of how credit and blame were shared in Eisenhower's practice of selective delegation. Stephen Hess views Eisenhower's delegations of authority as an "artfully constructed . . . elaborate maze of buffer zones," adding that "Eisenhower gave himself considerable freedom of action by giving his subordinates considerable leeway to act."[78] The image of a "lightning rod" captures Hess's point even better than "buffer zone."[79]

Dulles was only one object of animosity that in another presidency would have been directed toward the chief executive. Other Eisenhower associates performed the same function—consciously or unconsciously—in their own spheres. Farmers who rankled at the moves toward decreasing subsidization of agriculture blamed the zealous Mormon elder, Ezra Taft Benson, who served as Agriculture secretary for eight years—not Eisenhower. Many of the inevitable irritations produced by White House nay-saying found their target in the staff chief, Sherman Adams. There is no evidence that Eisenhower chose these people because they would be ready targets for critics. Adams and Dulles in fact were succeeded by men of gentle personality. Nevertheless, Eisenhower's underlining in the following passage describing Lyndon Johnson's presidential style in Arthur Krock's memoirs, shows his awareness of how a subordinate's tendency to garner criticism could protect his leader's public support:

> *Partly because of his incessant ubiquity, Johnson, as much as any president in our history, has closely identified himself and his office with the disasters, foreign and domestic, economic and social, into which the United States has become more and more deeply involved in his time.* This . . . is to a considerable degree the consequence of his innate trait of craftiness. But it also is the product of an evasive or soaring loquacity which induces him to utter and write paragraphs when sentences would cover the point or event, and to allow his promises to run far beyond the clear limits of attainment. *Another source of this close identification with all acts, policies and thorny situations is a passion to control every function of government, though subordinates are always available in profusion to take the gaff*, or, without diminishing him, the credit.[80] (Eisenhower's underlining)

The strong personal loyalty engendered in Eisenhower's team players accounted for their willingness to accept criticism for policies that were in fact the president's and that did not arise from their own delegated authority. As Press Secretary James Hagerty recollected,

> President Eisenhower would say, "Do it this way." I would say, "If I go to that press conference and say what you want me to say, I would get hell."

91

With that he would smile, get up and walk around the desk, pat me on the back and say, "My boy, better you than me."[81]

Building Public Support

In examining Eisenhower's strategies it is no surprise to find him underscoring Arthur Krock's diagnosis that Lyndon Johnson's presidency had ended so painfully because Johnson dissipated public support, among other ways, by identifying "himself and his office with . . . disasters" and "with all acts, policies and thorny situations" despite the availability of subordinates "to take the gaff." In his own presidency, Eisenhower had been helped by gaff-taking subordinates and had even occasionally simulated acts of delegation to deflect controversy. More generally, by keeping the controversial political side of the presidential role largely covert (without, however, abdicating it) and casting himself as an uncontroversial head of state, he maintained an extraordinary level of public support.

This high level is well known: his 64 percent average approval rate in the Gallup polls throughout his eight years; always more approval than disapproval in the monthly Gallup polls asking, "How good a job do you think President X is doing?"; and his two landslide elections.[82] The nature of this support—why people liked him—is less precisely documented. One valuable source of evidence, however, is available in the reports that citizens gave of why they liked or disliked each candidate in the pioneering 1952 and 1956 electoral surveys conducted by Angus Campbell and his University of Michigan associates.

In 1952 Eisenhower, who had been wooed by both parties since World War II because of a powerful public appeal that regularly put him at or near the top of Gallup's annual "most admired American" poll, was mentioned far more often for his human qualities (for example, warmth and sincerity) than for his experience, beliefs, or leadership skills. In 1956, after four years of acquiring governing experience and giving the public an opportunity to reach conclusions about the merits (or lack thereof) of his policies and skills, he was again mentioned more often for what he was as a person than for what he had done or could do as a president. But there was a difference between public responses to him in the 1952 and 1956 polls that puzzled the Michigan voting analysts: references to why Eisenhower was liked were even *more* lopsidedly personal and less political and governmental in 1956 than in 1952.[83] While this difference might have seemed to belie common sense, we can readily see that it follows from his leadership style of refusing to be identified with "disasters" and "thorny situations."

Partisan Democrats would have had less difficulty explaining the findings than did the studiously nonpartisan University of Michigan scholars. They would readily have granted that Eisenhower had maintained his popularity by accentuating the chief of state role. Liberal columnist Marquis Childs, for example, described him as a "captive hero," a term borrowed from an ancient practice in which the powers that be in a country legitimized their political control by capturing a king who served as a reassuring but impotent figurehead.[84]

As we have seen Eisenhower *did* exercise political leadership. If his economics tended to be laissez-faire, his politics were decidedly though covertly interventionist. Much of his intervention, however, was geared to preventing conflicts before they occurred, or resolving them without associating the mechanics of their resolution with the president and presidency. Two examples of Eisenhower's hidden-hand interventions bear directly on why it was possible for him to remain popular and to accentuate his apolitical image while in office. The first is the 1953 leak directed to the Chinese Communists to stimulate them to reach a truce agreement. An Eisenhower who was still presiding over a stalemated war of attrition in Korea would neither have been popular nor viewed so often as "good" on purely personal grounds.

The second example is his part in quelling Senator Joseph McCarthy. As will be shown in chapter 5, Eisenhower was far from passive in the McCarthy episode, although his action was so carefully disguised there has been no previous published account of it as of 1982. If Joe McCarthy had remained on the scene in 1956, gnawing at the Republican party from within, and charging the Executive branch with harboring subversion, the positive, issue-free image of an apolitical president would have been undermined, since McCarthy would inevitably have given currency to the view that Eisenhower was "soft" on subversives in the government.

Apart from maintaining support by quietly eliminating irritants that eventually would have tarnished his popularity, Eisenhower was intensely preoccupied with and worked intensely at "public relations," a phrase he used freely to describe actions not only during his nominating campaign and presidency,[85] but also during his prepresidential years.

Eisenhower's personal qualities became a staple for journalists virtually as soon as he assumed the European command in 1942. He promptly began to receive mention as a potential candidate for public office, a prospect he was quick to deprecate whenever friends mentioned it. Yet he could not escape awareness of his growing visibility, popularity, and reputation for refreshing informality and openness. Shortly after the invasion of North Africa in the fall of 1942, his portrait appeared on the cover of *Time*. [86] Increasingly, journalists portrayed "Ike Eisenhower" as tough as nails, but delightfully warm; determined to win, but impatient with martial postures; and a modest, all-American leader.[87] In spite of his assertions that he did not want to call personal attention to himself and his policy of encouraging press coverage of his subordinates, laudatory reports of him seemed perversely to increase rather than diminish. Moreover, though he made light of his personal popularity, he also acknowledged that he needed it to carry out his military leadership.

The Eisenhower who disclaims an interest in being publicized, but nevertheless makes it clear that his modus operandi brings him press attention, which he uses in his leadership, is evident in the wartime years. Eisenhower expresses these contradictions in a 1944 letter to his brother Edgar:

> To the extent possible in a position such as mine, I have constantly shunned the headlines. This has not been entirely due merely to a sense of modesty, but because of the nature of an Allied Command. Any "glory grabbing" on the part of the top man would quickly wreck an institution such as this. Happily the official requirement has coincided exactly with my personal desire.

At this point, however, his observations undergo a seemingly uncharacteristic derailment. His efforts had *not* kept him out of the headlines. Rather,

> one result is that, almost without exception, the 500 newspaper and radio men accredited to this organization are my friends. Quite frequently they seem to be moved by a desire to see that I get "full credit" and so they write special articles and even books.

Journalists, he explains to Edgar, will

> eventually turn upon a man who shows any indication of courting them in his own self interest, no matter how "colorful" they may deem him at first. What I am trying to say is that some publicity is mandatory—otherwise, American soldiers would not know they had an American commander, interested in their welfare. The problem is to take it and use it in the amount required by the job; but to avoid distortion and self-glorification.[88]

The importance of publicity used appropriately did not dawn on Eisenhower as late in the war as 1944. On taking his assignment in Europe, Eisenhower arranged that Columbia Broadcasting System executive Harry Butcher be assigned to his headquarters as naval aide. There was no pretense that Butcher, who was in constant touch with the press corps, would have nautical obligations. Butcher even helped prepare the draft of a letter rejecting a suggestion that Eisenhower should appoint a press relations officer to "humanize" himself. "My habit," the letter read, "is to keep my name out of the papers," but there was his usual qualification: personal publicity was acceptable "when military or public relations dictate that I should speak."*

Professional public relations men were among the first civilians to gather in the loyal network of businessmen that formed around Eisenhower and participated actively in drafting him to run for the presiden-

---

*Eisenhower added an autobiographical note. He knew how to handle public relations from "my many years in Washington" better than a "press agent" would. "I believe I . . . learned the tricks of the trade sufficiently well so that if I desired, particularly in my present position, to seek publicity, I could get it very easily."[89]

95

cy. Notable among them were William E. Robinson who, after years as an advertising and sales executive at the *New York Herald Tribune*, went on to head his own public relations firm, and Sigurd S. Larmon of Young & Rubicam. When Eisenhower acceded to a presidential candidacy, his campaign for nomination and election made innovative use of spot radio and television commercials. He and his associates also made a consistent effort to improve his ability to "come across" to the American people. His whistle-stop campaign covered more miles than Adlai Stevenson's. And he flexibly experimented with prepared and outlined speeches delivered informally from notes, submitting himself to the guidance of professionals.[90] He used actor and television producer Robert Montgomery to advise him on the mechanics of delivering speeches and experimenting with other ways of reaching the public.

Eisenhower prepared his speeches with an understanding of his public image and endeavored to enhance and maintain it. As president of Columbia University, he had been carefully briefed on the specific content of his admirers' images of him. In 1948 he received 20,000 letters, virtually all urging him to run for president that year. In the summer of 1949 Eisenhower turned these over to the prominent Columbia sociologist, Robert Merton, for analysis by the university's Bureau of Applied Social Research. The bureau report revealed that the letter writers admired Eisenhower for his sincerity and humanity and viewed him as a general who had demonstrated great military competence but who was nonmilitaristic and therefore well suited for civil leadership. Many writers stressed simply that they would be comforted to know he was president, and others talked about him as a "born leader" in terms that led Merton to advise Eisenhower that he fit the classic definition of a charismatic leader. Merton went over the report "with the General almost line by line in two or three sessions" during which Eisenhower evinced keen interest in the findings.[91]

Many of Eisenhower's presidential utterances directly play on the public image of the military hero who is a soldier of peace. On one occasion he compared the primitive rifle in use when he was a lieutenant before America's entry in World War I with the devastating weapons that had emerged from World War II in order to dramatize the overriding urgency of avoiding nuclear war. He went on, using the homely language of a sincere, humane soldier of peace, to reassure his audience. Granting that the problems of nuclear stalemate have no "easy answer" and that many contemporary problems "have no answer at all, at least in the complete sense," he compared the government's responsibility of "doing our best" with "what the ordinary American family does."

> It has the problems of meeting the payments on the mortgage, paying for the family car, educating the children, laying aside some money for use in case of unexpected illness. It meets these problems courageously. It doesn't get panicky. It solves these problems with what I would call courage and faith, but above all by cooperation, by discussing the problem among the different members of the family and then saying: this is what we can do, this is what we will do, and reaching a satisfactory answer.

These homilies served to introduce a plain speaking but thoughtful exposition of the basic lines of foreign and domestic policy, including warnings against excessive fears of internal Communist subversion and a penultimate pitch for his legislative program. His concluding remarks voiced the sturdy patriotism and piety of a turn-of-the-century mid-western family, using a figure of speech that echoed the daily Bible readings of his own childhood:

> I don't mean to say, and no one can say to you, that there are no dangers. Of course there are risks, if we are not vigilant. But we do not have to be hysterical. We can be vigilant. We can be Americans. We can stand up and hold up our heads and say: America is the greatest force that God has ever allowed to exist on his footstool.[92]

None of this was calculated to appeal to an Adlai Stevenson egghead supporter, but this was not "the man we are trying to reach." The 1956 University of Michigan Survey Research Center election study tabulates reports of the number of people interviewed who mentioned the speaking style of the two candidates. While more people mentioned the rhetoric-loving Stevenson, a substantial majority of the references to his style were unfavorable ("too high fallutin"), and the fewer references to Eisenhower's style were predominantly positive.[93]

Eisenhower's press conferences consistently reinforced the 1948 let-

97

ters' characterization of him—sincere, warm, and the distinguished general who always worked for peace. The unpretentiousness of his give-and-take with reporters and his seemingly offhanded reassuring references to his prepresidential experiences are illustrated in this exchange.

Q: Mr. President, there has been some recent interest in the subject of dependents of our military men joining them overseas, sometimes in potential trouble spots around the world; and I wondered if you, as an old soldier, shall we say, believe—[laughter]

THE PRESIDENT: Make no mistake. I am proud of the title [laughter]

Q: It is the "old" I was questioning—[laughter]—believe that there is a military asset in having the wives and children of the servicemen with them overseas: and in the event of a sudden enemy attack, what would their presence mean?

THE PRESIDENT: Of course, to take your last part first, if there is a sudden enemy attack, their presence would cause very acute problems. But let us not forget this: we are in a cold war; we want to present our best foot, let us say; we want people of high morale; we want to look confident.

If every place we sent our soldiers in the world we broke our old custom of letting dependents go along, it would look like we were frightened to death and expecting an attack momentarily.

Some of you here probably may have been in Europe in January 1951, when I went over there; and you will recall, possibly, also that my wife went with me. The tension was so great at that moment—and you may have forgotten—the tension was so great that a few, 2 or 3 months later the head of one of the principal travel agencies of the United States came to me and said that the mere fact that my wife went over there, took a season where there was going to be no travel at all and made it one of the finest travel seasons of their whole career. In other words, the showing of confidence on the part of the leaders and people of a nation—as long as it is not truculent, if you are not being, you might say, bombastic and truculent and ill-mannered—I think that such things as that really encourage confidence.[94]

Whatever intellectuals may have thought of such remarks, they were unquestionably reassuring to the bulk of citizens. After, as before taking office, Eisenhower's seemingly effortless facility in winning public confidence never stopped him from also working to find additional ways to enhance his support. This accounts for the great care he took in preparing speeches, planning campaigns, and working at the task of exhibiting the buoyant, optimistic side of his personality. Nor did he let his team approach to leadership vitiate his attention to maintaining personal support. He was fully aware that his popularity was essential to his ability to exercise influence over other leaders. As he once noted, "one man can do a lot . . . he can especially do a lot at any particular given moment, if at that moment he happens to be ranking high in public estimation. By this I mean he is dwelling in the ivory tower and not in the dog house."[95]

4

THE TWO FACES OF ORGANIZATION

HERE WAS a major parallel between Eisenhower's political strategies and the organization of his day-to-day working procedures. In each case the visible side of how he worked was complemented by an equally significant unpublicized side. His strategies involved making the chief of state aspect of the president's job evident, while veiling much of his political leadership. His organizational style drew attention to the formal face of his policy machinery and did not publicize his flexible use of informal organization.

There are both formal and informal components in any entity sufficiently institutionalized to warrant being called an organization. Formal organization consists of rules and regulations, power relationships outlined in organization charts, and officially sanctioned operating procedures. But organizations do not operate by formal means alone. Members' personalities are too complex to mesh with official job descriptions, and the subtle choices posed by each new decision cannot be anticipated by regulations, no matter how detailed. Invariably any formal organization is intertwined with an informal network of personalities, practices, and relationships. The informal will sometimes impair the formal organization, but it can also provide the lubricants that make it work.[1]

Eisenhower ran organizations by deliberately making simultaneous use of both formal and informal organization. This style of organizational leadership is underrepresented in the standard analyses of statecraft. In fact, one well-recognized classification of how presidents organize their aides distinguishes between "formalistic" organization of the presidency and various informal methods, taking no account of the organizer who simultaneously turns both ingredients to effective use.[2]

Eisenhower was, as all accounts of the organization of his presidency recognize, highly attentive to finding orderly formal procedures for insuring that routine or repetitive tasks were carried out reliably, consistently, and systematically. Yet as president, and in his prepresidential thought and practice, he placed at least equal emphasis on informal aspects of organizational leadership.

Undoubtedly Eisenhower's binocular perspective on leadership accounts for the universal recognition of his prowess as an organizer during his pre-White House years. From his West Point graduation in 1915, through World War II to NATO, his assignments either required organizational management or gave him vantage points from which to view and reflect on the problems of guiding large-scale collective endeavors. With this preparation he proved superlative as wartime supreme commander, a role that demanded supervision of the largest invasion force ever assembled; alliance management; mediation among fractious personalities; and maintainance of the morale of fellow leaders, troops, and the civilians on the home front. Ironically, for a man whose presidency gave the contemporary impression of reflecting narrow, militarily derived formalism, he was universally recognized in his military capacities (even by critics of his skill as a soldier) as outstandingly gifted in "political generalship"—that is, management of the personal (and by this token informal) component of leadership.

Given Eisenhower's many tours of duty in Washington holding positions that enabled him to observe the presidency, it is not surprising that he assumed that office with a strong sense of how he would set it up. When he arrived in Washington in the late 1920s, the White House was so unbureaucratized that the term "organization" was not applicable. Herbert Hoover had conducted business with the aid of a few clerks. In that simpler era, the president still held periodic public receptions and shook hands with any citizen willing to wait in the line that trailed from the Corcoran Gallery to the White House. The park-like White House grounds were surrounded by a low fence rather than the present electronically wired barrier. Open gates permitted Eisenhower to stroll from his office in the State, War and Navy Department building across the White House grounds when he visited his brother at the Department of Agriculture.[3]

Before Eisenhower left Washington in 1935 for his tour of duty in the Philippines, however, the presidential office had become a beehive. Franklin Roosevelt employed a host of advisors, using them informally and flexibly. Some received their paychecks as nominal employees of executive branch agencies and others served without remuneration. By the time Eisenhower returned to Washington shortly after Pearl Harbor, Roosevelt, while still exercising his informal and improvisatory approach to using aides and conducting his leadership, had initiated the process of giving the presidency a formal organization with an official staff. A much enlarged and activated Bureau of the Budget (now the Office of Management and Budget) was by then ensconced in the building in which Eisenhower previously worked, providing the president with a cadre of career civil servants. The West Wing by then housed a new entity called the White House Office, composed of politically appointed middle-management aides officially assigned to help the president advance his program.

During his two postwar years as Truman's chief of staff, Eisenhower saw the Budget Bureau and the White House Office grow in size and importance and the Council of Economic Advisors and National Security Council become part of the new Executive Office of the President (EOP). Truman paid more attention than Roosevelt to using orderly, official procedure, but even his more formalized presidency had the aura of a conclave of Missouri politicians conducting their business in a casual manner rather than that of an orderly staff of disciplined policy analysts.

Reflecting on his own experience as an administrator and what he had seen of the presidency, Eisenhower described in his memoirs the cast of mind he brought to organizing the presidency:

> For years I had been in frequent contact with the Executive Office of the White House and I had certain ideas about the system, or lack of system, under which it operated. With my training in problems involving organizations it was inconceivable to me that the work of the White House could not be better systemized than had been the case during the years I observed it.[4]

To this he added a more general observation about organizational planning: although "organization cannot make a genius out of an incompetent," nor "make the decisions which are necessary to trigger action, disorganization can scarcely fail to result in inefficiency and can easily lead to disaster."[5]

President watchers in the 1950s were fully aware of Eisenhower's preoccupation with organizing the presidency.[6] Many of them argued that he overorganized and overformalized a position which by virtue of being political required informal flexibility. In their view his years of training in the hierarchies of the military had led him to fall into the trap of seeking to run the presidency as if the chief executive's tasks could be mechanically codified, after the fashion of a field manual.

The evidence seemed plain. In the White House, rather than following Roosevelt's and Truman's practices of setting themselves astride their own advisory networks, Eisenhower introduced a staff chief. To his critics it seemed clear that this patently military practice would reduce the quantity and quality of information and advice the president received. Their impression was that Eisenhower was fed predigested information, largely through "channels." This surmise appeared to be confirmed by the press conference exchanges in which he claimed ignorance of currently publicized events and issues.

In discussing his relations with cabinet members, Eisenhower and his aides stressed that he was delegating significant authority to them. Such a practice again seemed to fit the military model—a supreme commander necessarily would be accustomed to relying on his many field commanders to use their knowledge of local conditions and make their own tactical and strategic decisions. Critics felt he was misapply-

103

ing a principle of military organization to government. This impression was corroborated by Eisenhower's practice at press conferences, of directing questions concerning the specifics of a policy or event to the appropriate cabinet secretary.

Finally, Eisenhower's approach toward his cabinet as a collective entity appeared unlike those of a skilled politician. Roosevelt, for example was famous for trivializing the cabinet meeting. Those who have followed American politics have read the many accounts of how an FDR cabinet meeting was the last place a department secretary would consider raising an important issue. After each haphazard, unfocused meeting, individual members crowded in the "Amen corner" to speak to Roosevelt alone and raise the matters they considered significant. The prevailing view held that part of Roosevelt's genius was to foster competition among his aides and to reach out informally to a great diversity of people in many walks of life for advice, thus maximizing his information and his options. Truman took his cabinet meetings more seriously than Roosevelt did, but he too acted on the assumption that in the United States, cabinet secretaries battled for their departments' programs and constituencies, while resisting being encroached upon by the programs of other departments and even by the president. So he too conducted serious business outside the formal cabinet meetings, and he also made extensive use of unofficial advisors.[7]

Eisenhower, on the other hand, met regularly with his cabinet, thus conveying the impression both that these sessions were central for conducting the business of his administration and that he had departed from his predecessors' practice of making decisions in informal contexts. His reliance on official meetings seemed, like his use of a staff chief and his extensive delegation of authority, to have military roots—in this case in the planning conferences of top military commanders.

The likely outcome of these procedures when transferred to politics, his critics argued, was "government by committee," which in turn would surely smother creativity by fostering compromises that reduce policies to the lowest denominator acceptable to the committee members. Moreover, the cabinet was not the only committee meeting Eisenhower regularly held. His week began with a session with Republican congressional leaders; Thursdays he met at length with the NSC;

Friday was cabinet meeting day. These formal routines, however, were the outward face of his organizational leadership. While their significance was far from trivial, they did not begin to represent the full texture of his organizational practices. This can best be illustrated by three examples: an instance of his team leadership; a review of how his formal and informal procedures for operating the cabinet and National Security Council related to his overall approach to domestic and foreign policy making; and finally a sketch of his formal White House organization and the informal organization in which it was intertwined.

Eisenhower Organizes His Presidency: The Hotel Commodore Meeting

Shortly after noon on January 12, 1953, at his campaign and transition headquarters in New York's Hotel Commodore, Eisenhower presided over a rare if not unprecedented gathering in the history of the presidency, a preinauguration cabinet meeting. He used the meeting for three purposes: to brief the cabinet, the vice-president-elect, and key White House aides on changes he planned in formal operating procedures; to solicit advice on the immediate issues of what to cover in his inaugural address and how to deal with a potential political conflict with senior congressional Republicans; and, most importantly, to build rapport and cohesion. In so doing, he was organizing the informal even more than the formal side of his organizational changes.

Early in the session Eisenhower stressed that he planned to operate his cabinet differently from those of his predecessors. Even at this stage Eisenhower's cabinet meeting was more formalized than cabinet meetings of other presidents. There was a written agenda, minutes were kept, and digression was kept to a minimum. Noting that "I have attended in the past a number of Cabinet meetings . . . as a specialist to talk about the European problem or a military problem of some kind," Eisenhower said that the preinaugural meeting gave him

105

a good chance to express a very definite opinion in front of all of you. Sometimes I have had to sit while the Cabinet, so called, went through its gyrations, and there is certainly no more charitable word that you could use with respect to what I have seen. My hope will be to make this a policy body, to bring before you and for you to bring up subjects that are worthy of this body as a whole.[8]

Eisenhower described another step he was taking to systematize the organization of his presidency. He was strengthening the White House staff by adding aides who were to have the ability and stature of department secretaries. These aides, who also attended the meeting, were assigned to jobs "I have filled on the theory that those positions are equally important with any Cabinet position that we have." While some were assigned to new staff positions, others were in old positions, which required better-qualified personnel and demanded more responsibility than had previously been the case. Noting that holding comparable "positions down in Washington now [are] men who are, at least in one or two instances that I know of, scarcely above the clerical level," Eisenhower observed that if a president's staff aides are not given substantial status and stature they "cannot bring . . . problems to the attention of Cabinet officers and get something done on them." Therefore his own aides were to be sufficiently elevated so that "people . . . can walk into the offices of any one of [them] and say, 'Bill, this thing is wrong. We have got to do something.' "

The most prominent new position was assigned to former New Hampshire Governor Sherman Adams. He was chief of staff, but bore the deliberately nonmilitary title the assistant to the president. Another Eisenhower innovation was to introduce a special assistant to the president for national security. This new position was occupied by Robert Cutler, a Boston banker with extensive experience as a wartime aide to Marshall and senior advisor to Truman's NSC. When his turn came to brief the cabinet, Cutler explained that, like the cabinet itself, the NSC was to become a significant element in the new administration's operating procedures. Cutler's job was to reorganize the NSC so that it could meet its new responsibilities and to manage its operations.*

*This position, augmented to include many more responsibilities than Cutler was assigned, became highly visible in later presidencies where it served as a base for advocating and enunciating

Eisenhower's old friend, longtime War Department congressional liaison worker, Wilton ("Jerry") Persons, presided over still another increment in formal organization. He headed the newly established White House congressional relations unit. Persons, who had risen to major general as army congressional liaison specialist, left retirement first to manage Eisenhower's NATO congressional relations and then, enlisting several other veterans of the legislative corridors, he set up and ran Eisenhower's White House congressional lobbying operation.

Cutler, Persons, and Adams were much more experienced than most of the cabinet members, a number of whom, like former General Motors president Charles Wilson, were political neophytes. It was consistent with Eisenhower's Washington-wise mode of conducting the less visible side of official business to put political insiders in the White House Office and Executive Office of the President to back up those of the cabinet members who were politically inexperienced.

Another presidential aide with substantial political savvy was Joseph Dodge, who had worked with Eisenhower in overseeing occupied Germany and, like Cutler, was a banker with considerable experience in the foreign policy-making community. Eisenhower had made up his mind before the election that he wanted Dodge to head the most important agency in the EOP. He invited Dodge to spend election night with him, and immediately signed him up for the Budget Bureau job. Dodge was instructed to spend the preinauguration period observing the preparation of Truman's outgoing budget and to become acquainted with Budget Bureau career officials, so that Truman's budget request could quickly be reduced to proportions consistent with Eisenhower's commitment to lower expenditures. Still another political veteran sitting among the staff aides at the Hotel Commodore meeting was Press Secretary James Hagerty, who had been New York Governor Thomas Dewey's press chief and had managed media relations in Dewey's 1940 nomination bid and the 1944, 1948, and 1952 Republican election campaigns.

Eisenhower explained to his incoming cabinet that the disciplined

---

foreign policy, when filled by such men as McGeorge Bundy, Walt Rostow, Henry Kissinger, and Zbigniew Brzezinski. Eisenhower's principle, however, was that staff aides had the job of compiling information and coordinating and clarifying options, but that recommending, deciding, and, especially, publicly discussing decisions was the job of the cabinet secretaries, other line officials, and ultimately the president.

cabinet and NSC meetings he would hold, coupled with the strengthened White House staff, would help the team coordinate its activities, because most significant policy issues overlapped departmental jurisdictions. The changes in the formal organization of the presidency were designed to help make certain that a secretary proposing an activity could be sure that his "group is properly coordinated with Labor, with Agriculture, with Defense and State, and all the way around."

At this meeting he also urged the members to practice what he had long ago concluded was essential for effective organization—spontaneous mutual coordination. "I hope," he preached, "that before we have gone very long each one of you will consider the rest of you here your very best friends in the world so that you can call up and do your own coordinating. That is the perfect way." By "friendship" he did not mean that his colleagues had to be bosom companions; his aim was that they develop comfortable, compatible working relationships. To this end he had chosen some associates already well-connected with one another: Attorney General Herbert Brownell, Press Secretary Hagerty, and Appointments Secretary Thomas Stephens were longtime co-workers in the Dewey organization. General Persons, too, chose as staff aides men he had worked with in the past, such as former House Armed Services Committee staff chief Bryce Harlow.

Eisenhower had already started to put the cabinet to work as a unit in early December. Fulfilling his campaign promise to visit Korea, he took along several of his designees. Together they planned the new administration as well as inspected the military situation. On the return trip, they met many of Eisenhower's remaining associates flown to Wake Island at his request. The uninterrupted sea voyage to the United States gave the president-elect's party a chance to ponder policy and learn each other's ways.

On concluding the January 12 session, Eisenhower gave the group another nudge toward learning to practice friendly, spontaneous coordination. He asked his associates to get together for small dinner meetings to discuss mutual interests, rather than convening them for a formal banquet. In general he staged a meeting that was remarkable in tone and content. He managed both to convey that routines would be more orderly than in other presidencies and yet to induce a lively camaraderie. In spite of the formal innovations announced at the meeting, the discussion was if anything more flexible, relaxed, and constructive than it was in Truman and Roosevelt cabinet meetings.

Eisenhower began discussion of his inaugural address by reading its most recent draft. After cutting short the applause that followed, he explained that

> I read it far more for your blue pencils than I did for your applause. At first in our attempt to state a philosophy of government and of intent we were not close enough down to our daily living. So we have been gradually rewriting it, but it is very difficult to abandon in our own thinking and your own writing an original conception. One reason I wanted to read it now is so that you can think it over and be ready to tear it to pieces.

He stressed he did not want to be as colloquial as a campaign address, rather, "I deliberately tried to stay on the level of talk that would make as good reading as possible at the Quai d'Orsay or at No. 10 Downing." Nevertheless, in establishing a high tone, "I particularly tried to make the words that would sound good to the fellow digging the ditch in Kansas."

The group was enthusiastic about the speech but was quick to offer suggestions. There were comments on both its phrasing and content. When Eisenhower agreed with them, he passed them on to speech writer Emmet Hughes to be incorporated into the next draft. When he disagreed, he said so and explained his objections. Thus in responding to comments on speech rhetoric, he was also able to make certain that the group understood his policy objectives and the reasoning behind them.

Defense Secretary-designate Charles Wilson, for example, was distressed at the implication that the United States might begin trade in nonstrategic goods with Iron Curtain countries. Wilson grumbled that he had never liked the idea of selling "firearms to the Indians." "Remember this," Eisenhower replied,

> You are trying to set up out of Moscow what you might call a series of centrifugal forces. The last thing you can do is to begin to do things that force all these peripheral countries—the Baltic states, Poland, Czechoslovakia and the rest of them—to depend on Moscow for the rest of their lives.

How are you going to keep them interested in you? If you trade with them, Charlie, you have got something pulling their interest your way. . . . You just can't preach abstraction to a man who has to turn for his daily living in some other direction.

Not convinced, Wilson announced, "I think I am going to be on the tough side of this one." Eisenhower settled the issue agreeably but decisively, remarking, "Charlie, I am talking common sense." The final speech read, "We shall strive to foster everywhere, and to practice ourselves, policies that encourage productivity and profitable trade."

The speech markup was lively, but a rolled-up-sleeves sense that this was a group of working politicians planning strategy was more evident when they tackled the potential conflict with Republican congressmen. At stake was another formal innovation, the President's Advisory Commission for Governmental Organization (PACGO), which Eisenhower set up in the Executive Office of the President. This was designed to be a continuing unit to propose ways of organizing executive branch operations more efficiently, which the president could then submit to Congress for approval. Under prevailing procedures, reorganization plans would go into effect unless Congress voted otherwise. Eisenhower demonstrated his commitment to PACGO by announcing its existence and membership at the same time that he announced his cabinet and key White House staff appointments and by including his closest advisor, Milton Eisenhower, as one of the three members of the panel. (The others were Nelson Rockefeller as chairman, and Arthur Flemming.)

But two influential Republican congressmen, Representative Clarence Brown of Ohio and Senator Homer Ferguson of Michigan, were already on record favoring an instrument for proposing reorganizations that could readily have clashed with PACGO proposals, a "second Hoover Commission," modeled on the independent study group Truman had instituted under the chairmanship of ex-president Herbert Hoover. From the standpoint of Eisenhower and his associates, a Hoover II would have the disadvantage of being independent of administration control. Moreover, by having to recruit staff and hold hearings it would delay the reorganization procedures Eisenhower wanted to put into effect as soon as possible.

The Commodore meeting participants considered two options: they could either override Brown and Ferguson or they could placate them by devising an outcome that would give the congressmen a nominal victory but would not impede the activities of PACGO. As the discussion came to a head, Eisenhower joined those who favored the second approach, and revealed that he had already taken steps that were consistent with initiating it. That morning he had met with Brown and Ferguson. Since the two had traveled from Washington to New York with Dodge, who as a Detroit civic leader knew Ferguson well and also happened to know Brown slightly, the congressmen were aware of the potential conflict and assured Eisenhower that they did not want a "dog fight."

Stating to the group his strategy for calming this political minitempest he began with his customary disclaimer: "I am no politician as you well know." Then, in effect contradicting the disclaimer, he outlined his proposal for defusing the issue, following the approach he favored to resolve conflict—yield on symbolism, win on substance—and a basic assumption for dealing with Congress—defer to its coordinate constitutional status, but seek to lead it. No matter how misguided or unnecessary Brown and Ferguson's proposal was, he did not doubt the intensity and sincerity of the views of these men whose support would be essential in the narrowly Republican Eighty-third Congress.

"Those two men have both introduced their resolutions," he observed, "and they just act like they are newborn children." Eisenhower's recommended solution was to constitute Hoover II well after the start of the legislative session, assign it intractable problems, and insure that it not report until late in the legislative session, meanwhile expeditiously dispatching PACGO-initiated resolutions to Congress. The members of the new Hoover Commission were not named until July. They included Brown and Ferguson as well as the Republican ex-president whose special merit as a diagnostician of executive branch inefficiency they so much admired. The commission reports were deeply conservative. In contrast to PACGO recommendations, most of which were accepted by Congress, few Hoover II recommendations were adopted.

Turning to the general issue of working with congressional Republicans, the president-elect went on to refute the widespread impression (one he cultivated) that he did not intend to seek legislative influence.

He planned a reeducation program to encourage Capitol Hill Republicans to "reverse their philosophy that they are the opposition group" and learn that with a Republican president their job "is to hold up the hands of the Executive departments." "They have not learned that yet," Eisenhower explained.

> There is no Republican in Congress today who was ever there under a Republican President, with the result that anything the Executive proposes is almost automatically opposed by the Republican Congress. . . . [Therefore] we must come at it on the basis of nurturing and carrying along these people until they understand that we . . . are their friends, that we are the guys they have to help, not kick in the teeth.

Eisenhower then described still another innovation he was adding to the formal organization of his presidency. He would meet weekly with the Republican congressional leadership. Unlike Truman's personal conferences with the Big Four—the two top Democrats in each House—Eisenhower's legislative meetings would comprise a larger, more varied group of his party's congressional leaders and would also include the newly instituted legislative liaison aides as well as cabinet members responsible for legislative issues to be discussed at a particular meeting. The meetings would help provide an early warning system, minimizing occasions for Republicans in the two branches to collide because of sheer lack of coordination or over disagreements that could be straightened out in advance. "I think," the president explained, "we can gradually sell them some way under which we don't have to suddenly say 'Here, that is wrong.' "

Late in the first day's session of the preinauguration meeting Adams announced that a transcript of the discussion would be at everyone's place at the table in the morning. "Someone has got to edit the transcript very carefully," Eisenhower warned. "We talked about Senator Ferguson and some of the others," he reminded the group. "I don't want anything in the transcript here to look like it is critical of anybody or anything when we talk about our problems." Pressing the matter, Eisenhower added that he saw no need to circulate a transcript "unless you people want it." None did.

What then should Hagerty tell the press about the day's meeting, Adams asked? Eisenhower suggested blandly uninformative wording:

"I would say we are having discussions about our future duties. We are getting acquainted with each other and so on." Hagerty, he added, should put this noncommittal announcement "in nice words."

The Cabinet and Domestic Policy Making

In many administrations the cabinet would meet so rarely that the term referred mainly to the collective department heads, not to a functioning collegial body. The importance Eisenhower attached to cabinet meetings is evident from their profusion—ten in eighty days—during the formative, policy and team-shaping period immediately after he took office. (Kennedy, in contrast, held only three in his first eighty days.) Eisenhower held an average of thirty-four cabinet meetings a year over his two terms, never pulling back from the commitment he made at the Hotel Commodore meeting to use the cabinet as a "policy body."

Indeed, in seeking to live up to his promise "to bring up subjects that are worthy of this body as a whole," he evolved more systematic formal machinery than that used in any other presidency to shape cabinet agendas, to insure that the participants had advance briefings, and to record and implement the decisions he announced in the meetings. He instituted the new machinery, a cabinet secretariat, in the fall of 1954, by drawing on a study he commissioned by Carter Burgess,[9] an organization planner who had designed the staff procedures for several wartime and postwar governmental agencies, and Bradley Patterson, a civil servant in the State Department's secretariat.

Late in the previous year Eisenhower had begun systematizing cabinet deliberations and had given White House aide Maxwell Rabb, the added job of cabinet secretary. The Burgess-Patterson study specified the operating procedures Rabb and his successor, Robert Gray, were to use and provided them with a deputy in the form of Patterson, whom Rabb and Adams invited to transfer to the White House staff.

It is one thing to have a cabinet secretariat, however, and another to curb the powerful impulse of department secretaries to avoid jeopardizing valued projects by airing them in meetings. The department heads, Patterson notes, were indisposed to "hasten to suggest items for discussion." Rather, it was up to the cabinet secretary "to dig, wheedle, persuade and finesse Cabinet members to bring to the common table what were clearly common matters, but which department heads . . . would much prefer to bring privately to the Oval Office." But how could a mere White House aide force department secretaries to go public with programs that might then be rejected because of a colleague's criticisms, or be turned over to other departments? The cabinet secretary was able to overcome departments' reticence because cabinet members "knew that Eisenhower wanted it this way and no other."[10]

The secretariat saw to it that departments with business on the agenda prepared background papers explaining their proposals in advance of the meetings and circulated the papers and agenda to all members in time for them to arrive briefed at the Friday meeting. Bringing in the secretaries' executive assistants immediately following each cabinet session, it conducted virtual replicas of each meeting to initiate implementation of the proposals and to review the cabinet discussion. The secretariat further insured implementation of administration policies by preparing a Record of Actions—a summary of the decisions Eisenhower approved at each meeting—and followed that up with a Status of Actions report every three months. Sherman Adams's task was to needle departments with "significant delinquencies, bringing them back on schedule."[11]

Note, however, that Eisenhower had said that the cabinet would serve only as a "policy body," not a policy-*making* or policy-*initiating* body, much less the *only* source of domestic policy. (The NSC was the main formal forum for foreign policy.) This leads to a number of observations about the overall domestic policy-making process and the relationship between the formal cabinet meetings (which were well publicized especially among audiences likely to approve of businesslike efficiency) and Eisenhower's unpublicized informal means of policy shaping and making. (1) The Record of Actions was of Eisenhower's actions, not the cabinet's. There was no voting in the cabinet. After listening to discussion, Eisenhower would make his decisions, including decisions to let an issue ripen while awaiting further information. He was scrupulous about explaining the rationale behind his decisions, but he did not make them on the basis of nose counts. (2) Much cabinet activity was advisory in nature; the cabinet served more as a sounding-board than as a policy-considering body—that is, it functioned much as it did in the Hotel Commodore discussions, where at least as much of the significance of the meeting was in its give-and-take discussions and their contribution to solidifying the administration team as in its influence on Eisenhower's own decisions. (3) Many of the issues that came before the cabinet had already been decided upon by Eisenhower, though he was often prepared to reopen an issue, change his mind, or modify details if discussion (in or outside of the formal cabinet meeting) seemed to him persuasive enough to do so. Thus, these meetings often functioned to brief the cabinet members on and discuss ways of implementing policies already worked out by Eisenhower. In his December 22, 1953, memorandum to Budget Director Dodge, for example, Eisenhower tells Dodge not to cut and if possible to increase certain welfare and public works programs in order to signal to the public the administration's progressive philosophy (see chapter 2). Had such a presidential domestic policy decision made its way to the cabinet and been registered in that meeting's Record of Action, the record, though seemingly of a cabinet action, would have been of a decision announced in cabinet but not made there. (4) The cabinet minutes show that not all meeting time was devoted to policy discussions. Some time was spent briefing members on matters of broad concern, such as the vice-president's findings on his trips abroad. (5) Finally, certain issues were too sensitive, or divisive, or in need of tactical day-by-day management to be suitable for cabinet discussion. (One such issue, Eisenhower's covert battle with Senator McCarthy, will be discussed in chapter 5.)

Why should Eisenhower have insisted on devoting so much time to carefully planned conferences with a group that was not the nexus of policy making? Part of the answer can be found in Bedell Smith's comment concerning Eisenhower's longstanding use of consultation as a means of exercising leadership. Eisenhower knew that advice seeking was an effective tool for winning the willing support of those he consulted, even though he might not take their advice.

By being consulted, particularly by someone displaying open eagerness, Eisenhower's associates were encouraged to think of themselves as part of a collective enterprise rather than as individual entrepreneurs.

They believed the president respected them sufficiently to consider their recommendations when making final policy decisions, although as loyal team members they recognized that many factors influenced Eisenhower's final decisions. Therefore, it was incumbent on them to fall in line, even if their particular recommendation was not followed.

When Eisenhower asked advice in the cabinet meeting, he could contribute in still further ways to what plainly was the primary function of the formal component of his domestic policy machinery— administration consolidator. By knowing what their colleagues were doing, members could coordinate their activities. The attorney general, for example, on finding proposals requiring legal back-up in the form of precedents and orders, could immediately set his staff to work. Members who attended the briefings and read briefing papers were in a position to defend aspects of administration policy falling outside their immediate areas. Being privy to high-level information outside their own departmental domains added to their feeling that their opinions were valued and that the consultation was not perfunctory. This reinforced Eisenhower's explicit message that in the cabinet the members were to view themselves as general statesmen, not simply defenders of departmental positions. So viewing themselves the cabinet members had still another reason (whatever their private disagreements) to unite behind Eisenhower's program. His administration suffered remarkably few cabinet-level leaks, feuds, or reports initiated by members indicating that they were at variance with Eisenhower's policies.

Above all, the meeting was his bully pulpit. It was here that he personally conveyed the general principles behind his policies, giving them added force by displaying his strength of conviction and "force of personality." Bradley Patterson, although impressed with the Eisenhower cabinet procedures, considering them superior to the option papers and employment of White House intermediaries that replaced Eisenhower's approach in later presidencies, stresses that no impersonal procedure or staff aide

can equal the impact, on a group of Cabinet officers, of hearing the President, in person, deliver private remarks about his own decisions and priorities, his disappointments of the past, his hopes for the future. Coming from an emphatic and articulate man . . . often with some purple language added, Cabinet remarks by the Chief Executive carry a strength and an indelibility which the senior most White House aide cannot duplicate.[12]

Because cabinet meetings had functions other than that of debate, Eisenhower never expressed to the cabinet or the secretariat his feeling that "in some instances . . . to fill out an agenda . . . items are not of the caliber that should come before the Cabinet,"[13] a view of his that Mrs. Whitman transmitted to Milton Eisenhower. An example of this might have been a meeting that Under Secretary of State Douglas Dillon remembered where "we sat around looking at plans for Dulles airport. They had a model and everything, and we would say why don't you put a door there, and they would say why they didn't."[14] Neither this nor any other item in Patterson's seven years of preparing the agenda produced a single Eisenhower complaint "that the agenda contained an item he didn't want to discuss at the table."[15]

His reason for not complaining is contained in a private diary entry in which he evaluated the cabinet after his first year in office. (By this time the one member who was ideologically and temperamentally unsuited to function with his colleagues, the former union president who served as his first labor secretary, Martin Durkin, had resigned.) He judged his cabinet members, and by extension their regular meetings, in terms of the degree to which they had come to fit together, in their informal as much as their formal capacities, as a harmonious team.

[A]s now constituted, I cannot think of a single position that I could strengthen by removal of the present incumbent and appointment of another. By no means do I mean to imply that any one of my associates . . . is perfect in his job—any more than I deem myself to be perfectly suited to my own! I merely mean to say that I have had a good many years of experience in selecting people for positions of heavy responsibility, and I think the results so far achieved by this Cabinet and by other close associates, justify my conviction that we have an extraordinarily good combination of personalities. . . . I think the individuals in the Cabinet and other offices like each other. At least, I can detect no sign of mutual dislike among the group. I know that I like them all; I like to be with them; I like to converse with them; I like their attitude toward their duty and toward governmental service.[16]

Long before he was president, Eisenhower's thinking about how a body formally constituted as a policy council could be informally guided in a manner designed to foster its members' cohesion had taken shape. Eisenhower dispatched a lengthy memorandum to Defense Secretary James Forrestal on February 7, 1948, his final day as army Chief of Staff, containing a remarkable discussion of the practical aspects combining formal and informal organization. His particular concern in the memorandum paralleled his concern as president with mitigating departmental "parochialism." He was advising the defense secretary on how to win the support of the service chiefs for a coherent, overall defense program, discouraging the impulse of each chief to attempt to centralize maximum resources in his own branch.

"The old saying 'centralization is the refuge of fear,' " Eisenhower observed, "is partially rooted in the natural human feeling that every man wants under his own hand complete control and authority over every factor or unit that has a possible function in the discharge of his responsibilities." Eisenhower's suggestions to Forrestal on how to wean the service chiefs away from acting on this feeling were, like his means of running the cabinet, grounded on a formal secretariatlike procedure that relied on informal leadership for its dynamics.

He urged Forrestal to employ a neutral formal body—the Defense Department Research and Development Board—as the instrument for framing the agenda of discussions between the secretary and the Joint Chiefs of Staff. This body was to use the most recent Defense Department "concept of war" formulation of the nation's overall military requirements and to identify exactly which department was doing what with how much expense and overlap in function. "In this way," he explained, "the matter will be taken out of the realm of generality and brought down to specific recommendation."

He then sketched the politics and persuasive techniques that could be used to encourage genuine cooperation among the chiefs. First, although the secretary was "not expected to interfere in detailed administration of the several services," nevertheless he should work to insure the appointment of the "right type" of men in terms of intellectual commitments—that is, "officials who he has determined in advance to be completely sold on the idea of achieving greater efficiency and economy through maximum interdependence among the services."

Secondly, the men chosen should be psychologically suited to working in groups. This was no idle homily for Eisenhower. It was at the core of his principles of leadership: "In organizing teams, personality is equally important with ability. . . . Leadership is as vital in conference as it is in battle."

Underscoring the word he used both in his preinauguration meeting to advise his cabinet members how to regard one another and in his description of the cabinet after its first year, Eisenhower then emphasized that "the work of the Secretary will never be successful unless the principal members of his team are *friends.*"

> In dealing with problems, friends develop among themselves a natural selflessness that is the outgrowth of their regard for the other. Personal antagonism enjoys the defeat of the opponent—consequently objectivity and selflessness cannot be attained when it is present.

Finally, he discussed how the man conducting a council of organization chiefs should seek to encourage them to transcend the impulse simply to advance their departments. Exercising "patience and a sense of humor," the man in charge should "habitually and assiduously" bring "into the open in informal meetings major controversial issues in the attitude of one seeking *general* professional assistance so that he may make decisions on the basis of the national welfare." (Eisenhower's emphasis) To this end, Eisenhower advised that "whenever . . . any individual showed a tendency to become a special pleader," the subject should be "skillfully changed and a constant effort made to achieve unanimity of conclusion, first upon broad generalities and these gradually brought closer to concrete application.[17]

Although Chief of Staff Eisenhower's 1948 memorandum to the Secretary of Defense foreshadows how President Eisenhower was to make informal use of an official policy advising body to promote cohesion among its members, Eisenhower's formal meetings were only one of the vehicles he used for making team players of his associates. Consider the case of one of the most independent-minded—and in Eisenhower's view, valuable—cabinet members, Treasury Secretary George Humphrey. (As former president of Hanna Steel, he was one of the most conspicuous sources of the somewhat inaccurate aphorism that the cabinet consisted of nine millionaires and a plumber.) Humphrey was the only cabinet member who joined Eisenhower's personal circle of bluff, hearty, intelligent-but-not-intellectual golf and bridge friends. Humphrey's economic conservatism undoubtedly helped Eisenhower buttress his own somewhat inchoate similar views, but Eisenhower did not accept Humphrey's most conservative views, especially those bearing on international activity. Since it was an article of faith of both men not to publicize their disagreements, and since Eisenhower's many social visits to Humphrey's Georgia plantation were a matter of record, observers who thought of Eisenhower as a liberal in the captivity of conservatives, typically saw Humphrey as his principal "mind guard." In fact, however, membership on the Eisenhower team was profoundly liberalizing for Humphrey.

Eisenhower did not rely on Humphrey alone for economic advice. He frequently gathered and acted on dissenting views, for example, those of Council of Economic Advisors Chairman Arthur Burns.[18] And he frequently pressed Humphrey to change his views. Humphrey became a strong defender of foreign aid, for example, and he was a firm opponent to the restraints on presidential foreign policy making power in the various versions of the Bricker Amendment. Had he remained with Hanna Steel from 1953 to 1957, he surely would have taken a businessman's stance on the opposing side of these issues. (He seems to have told Bricker as much in connection with the Ohio senator's proposed curb on presidential treaty-making powers.)[19] Moreover, when Humphrey did disagree with an administration policy, his loyalty prevailed. On one occasion, Milton Eisenhower informed the president he had just learned that Humphrey did not approve of a program for liberalizing aid and loan terms to Latin America, which Milton and Humphrey had been assigned to propose at a forthcoming meeting of the Western Hemisphere nations. The president replied:

> So long as he is the good soldier that I believe him to be, I must say that I don't see that anything is hurt by the presence in the highest councils of different kinds of thinking. It is in the combination of these various attitudes that we hammer out acceptable policies; enthusiasts for anything go too far.[20]

Shortly thereafter Milton wrote back describing a conversation with Humphrey in which the latter said that, having been told by the president that he was "a general in the cold war," he would be a "good general" and "support the State Department Program."[21]

Humphrey's behavior, however, did not invariably comport with his intentions. Through inadvertence rather than through insubordination, he provoked the most widely publicized seeming breach of cabinet unity during Eisenhower's presidency. In 1957, on the day that the administration's budget was released, the press reported that Humphrey had claimed the budget was too large and that such budgets would lead to a "depression that will curl your hair." The report was a misrepresentation of Humphrey's public statement, since in using the phrase he was not referring to the current budget. When in a preliminary cabinet meeting Humphrey had expressed his desire to release a statement warning against *future* big budgets, several members advised against making an announcement that might be viewed "as a break within the Administration."[22] Thus, Humphrey issued to the press a carefully worded letter that in no way undermined the current year's budget request.[23] Two minutes before the close of the press conference that began with his release of the letter, however, Humphrey used the "hair curling" phrase in a reference to long-run spending.[24] The story in the *New York Times* elided it with a remark Humphrey had made early in the conference about the possibility that savings could be made in the present budget. This created an account that gave precisely the impression Humphrey had been warned to avoid. Humphrey had no sooner used the picturesque phrase than the reporters asked that the stenotype be read back for quotation.[25] A professional politician no doubt would have seized upon that signal to withdraw the remark or to qualify it even more carefully. But Eisenhower had to pay a price for taking into his cabinet several corporate leaders who, though they had the technical knowledge and administrative experience, often were not politically astute.*

*Richard Neustadt's use of the episode as evidence of Eisenhower's nonprofessionalism in Washington politics captures a complaint that Eisenhower himself occasionally voiced about the businessmen he appointed to executive branch positions. They had special virtues gained in their private sector experience, but they often could be outmaneuvered by the professional politicians with whom they dealt.[26]

Although the cabinet, as a so-called policy body, was largely concerned with team building, Eisenhower clearly also valued it as one of the many forums in which he could hear and take part in debate over policy. The cabinet minutes show that there was indeed genuine debate, though it did not take the form of heated exchanges or cutting repartee, but rather the good-natured discourse one might expect in a cabinet of friends. The exchanges were consistent with Patterson's view (formed in the course of attending virtually all of the meetings after the summer of 1954) that "discussions at Eisenhower's Cabinet table were candid and lively, reflecting . . . the basic divergence in the Republican Party which was evident in the convention of 1952 itself: between conservatives and moderates."[27]

The greatest intensity reached in a cabinet debate is reflected in the January 19, 1959, discussion of aid to education, which so impressed Patterson that he transcribed rather than summarized his shorthand notes. That meeting, which clearly brought out the conservative-moderate division in the cabinet, was the occasion for a defense by Secretary of Health, Education and Welfare Arthur Flemming of his proposal that the administration request legislation authorizing poor school districts to finance the building of classrooms by issuing federally guaranteed bonds.

Eisenhower prefaced Flemming's presentation by acknowledging his own resistance in principle to federal aid to education, a basic attitude the members knew he held even though he had allowed school-aid legislative proposals to be part of the official administration legislative program under both of Flemming's predecessors in the HEW post, Oveta Culp Hobby and Marion Folsom. Nodding as it were to his conservative colleagues, Eisenhower remarked "the principle . . . still shocks me," but putting Flemming's proposal in a favorable context, he noted that it was "peanuts" compared with the sweeping aid to education package being advanced by liberals in the heavily Democratic Eighty-sixth Congress that had just convened. Then amiably saying, "having put that much of a noose around your head . . . Arthur," he asked Flemming to make his presentation.

Flemming's defense of the program—it transcended principles of fiscal conservatism and avoidance of federal involvement in education, he argued, because facilities to accommodate the population-bulge of post-World War II children were a national necessity—met with a conservative barrage. Treasury Secretary Robert Anderson argued at length that subsidized bonds were economically unsound and would compete unfairly with Treasury borrowing, while the arch-conservatives, Commerce Secretary Lewis Strauss,* Agriculture Secretary Ezra Taft Benson, and Budget Bureau Director Maurice Stans, based their arguments largely on ideology.

Flemming held his own, stressing "national need," the argument most likely to sway Eisenhower from conservative principles. Another cabinet moderate, Labor Secretary James Mitchell, backed Flemming, using the rhetoric of "investing in human resources." Flemming's strongest supporter was Vice-President Nixon, who, as in many other controversies, examined the political side of the question. Nixon remarked that, although he knew conservative opposition to aid to education extended to the Republican party's own congressional leaders, the group the cabinet should be concerned about was not the leaders, but rather those moderate Republicans who had to run against liberal Democrats in closely divided congressional districts. They would suffer if they had no alternative to the Democratic school-aid program to offer their constituents. "Nothing hits people more directly than their kids in school," Nixon observed. Whatever the views of the congressional leaders, he thought "the ultimate majority of people will say there is a need." Anticipating what was to be Eisenhower's resolution of the debate, Nixon concluded that "We cannot win on this issue by saying 'there is no need' or that 'the need will soon be met.' "

Wrapping up the discussion, Eisenhower told Flemming to present his proposal at the next White House Legislative Leadership meeting. In effect ruling against the conservative positions taken by a majority of the cabinet members, he indicated that he was sure "we are going to put up some kind of program," granting that "I do not know of anything I *hate* as much."† Having encouraged debate between the cabinet moderates and conservatives, Eisenhower made a final remark

---

*Strauss had been appointed as Commerce Secretary in November 1958 when Congress was not in session and served in that position until the Senate refused to confirm him in June 1959.

†Later in the year, Flemming forwarded a proposed administration bill to Congress. Like other school-aid proposals, it was not acted upon because of the stalemate on domestic policy making caused by the collision of the liberal Eighty-sixth Congress with Eisenhower conservatism, and the preoccupation in both parties with position taking rather than policy resolution as the 1960 nominations and election campaigns loomed.

123

which seemed to satisfy everyone: "We have had a good growl."[28]

Closely joined discussion and analysis were less important to Eisenhower in domestic than in foreign and national security policy making. He had been prepared to go along with a Taft candidacy, if Taft were disposed to accept Eisenhower's general stance on foreign affairs. The urgency of advancing collective security policy had been decisive in Eisenhower's decision to run for president. Foreign policy concerned him more deeply than domestic policy. Moreover, foreign policy decisions called for close reasoning and weighing of alternatives that hinged on complex judgments of cause and effect, and therefore required a particularly intense investment in staff work and consultation. While a federally funded health program could simply be ruled out by virtue of Eisenhower's ideology, his ideology of resisting territorial expansion by Communist nations did not yield easy answers to such questions as whether to settle for one or another proposed truce line in Korea or whether to object to Japanese trade with the PRC.

The National Security Council and National Security Policy Making

The Thursday NSC meetings absorbed more of Eisenhower's time and had a higher priority in his allocation of effort and intellectual and emotional energy than did cabinet meetings. In Eisenhower's formative first year in office, the NSC met 51 times—the previous high had been 34 meetings in one year. There was an average of ten more NSC than cabinet meetings each year—44 in contrast to 34. Over his two terms the NSC met 366 times, including meetings that were held without him because he was traveling or incapacitated by his 1955 heart attack and other lesser physical mishaps. Nevertheless, in spite of personal impediments and other demands on his schedule, Eisenhower attended and presided over 339 of these sessions.[29]

Unlike the cabinet, which is mentioned in neither the Constitution nor statute, the NSC is legally constituted. It was established by the Republican-controlled Eightieth Congress "to advise the President in respect to the integration of defense, foreign and military policy,"[30] with the president as formal head. Truman, however, chose not to attend NSC meetings in the years before the Korean War, evidently in part to make clear his refusal to accept the assertions of some supporters of the 1947 legislation that the council's function should be to limit presidential autonomy as commander in chief. Even after 1950, Truman did not always attend NSC meetings. And, although in 1950 he did authorize efforts to establish the Psychological Strategy Board to advance the NSC mission of integrating policy advice, perfecting advisory machinery was not a Truman administration priority.

Eisenhower, who as supreme commander, Chief of Staff, Pentagon advisor, and NATO military head, had been intimately familiar with national security advising and often frustrated by its defects, in two 1952 campaign speeches asserted his intention to revamp and rationalize the NSC's operations. Both speeches were drafted by Robert Cutler, a sometime NSC consultant in the Truman years,[31] who became Eisenhower's first and longest incumbent in the new position of Special Assistant for National Security. Cutler worked intensively in the post-election transition period on a task force to study ways of reorganizing the NSC. His blueprint was basically completed by the week of the preinauguration cabinet meeting. After a trial run in 1953, the plan, modified in the light of a year's experience, was institutionalized for the life of the administration.

In general structure and purpose the Eisenhower NSC paralleled (and anticipated) his cabinet machinery, but it was far more fully developed and highly articulated in its formal operating procedures. The centerpiece of the new arrangement was the regular council meeting. The core working group (expanded whenever appropriate) was deliberately kept to about a dozen members. A group of this size could easily fit around a table, thus permitting a comfortable exchange that had what Cutler called a "pow wow" quality.[32] Although conversation-sized, the group had been enlarged from the Truman era NSC to include (in addition to Cutler and his deputy) not only statutory members—the president, vice-president, secretaries of State and Defense, and director of the Office of Civil and Defense Mobilization—but also the heads of the other major agencies with national responsibilities: those in charge of intelligence, foreign aid, and overseas information, as well as the chairmen of the Joint Chiefs of Staff and the Atomic Energy Commission. In addition, Eisenhower's insistence that national security issues always be examined in terms of their economic implications led him to designate the secretary of the treasury and director of the Bureau of the Budget as NSC members. (A number of specialized aides sat along the walls rather than at the table and did not participate in discussions unless called upon, although they did help note and implement actions.)

In Eisenhower's cabinet, the liveliness of discussion depended on the ability of the cabinet secretary and the assistant to the president to cajole secretaries into putting important issues on the agenda and on Eisenhower's personal skill at bringing out diverse views in a meeting. Moreover, the agenda papers usually were prepared by the department or interdepartmental committees advancing views they themselves were recommending. In his NSC, however, the operating procedures for framing and conducting discussion were at once more formally elaborated and more conducive to fostering pointed discussion of disagreements over genuinely consequential issues. The success of these sessions refutes the premise of Eisenhower's critics that formalized advisory procedures necessarily stultify vigorous exchanges of views among advisors.[33]

The NSC agenda and above all the papers on which agenda items were based derived not from the activities of a small secretariat and departments or groups of departments working on their own, but rather from intensive discussions by the key policy planners in each of the constituent departments meeting in the twice-a-week, three-hour-long working sessions of the NSC Planning Board. A major strength of the Planning Board was that its members were the senior policy advising officers in each of the constituent departments represented in the NSC. Each board member had the entire policy planning process of his department at his disposal—indeed, each had a presidential commission *entitling* him to any information he might want from his department. Eisenhower, whose previous career had sensitized him to the bureaucratic verity that formal rank is often a necessary (though rarely a sufficient) condition to command respect in a large organization, insisted that each of the board members be assistant or under departmental secretaries. They were their superiors' principal policy planning officers. Therefore they were at once immersed in planning department policy and in generating the sharply focused NSC-meeting briefing papers that stimulated intense, clearly focused policy debate.

Cutler and his successors as special assistant for national security chaired the Planning Board sessions. The special assistant was expected by Eisenhower to use all of his informal persuasive powers to see that the detailed, carefully reasoned summaries and analyses of facts and recommendations in the board's many agenda papers lived up to the official requirement stated in the administration's written Planning Board guidelines. These specified that the board

> facilitate the formulation of policies, during the process of drafting policy recommendations, by marshalling the resources of the respective departments and agencies; by identifying the possible alternatives; by endeavoring to achieve acceptable agreements; *by discussing differences; by avoiding undesirable compromises which conceal or gloss over real differences;* and by reducing differences to as *clearly defined and narrow an area as possible* prior to reference to the Council.[34] (Italics added.)

Taken literally the criteria of maximizing both clear definition and narrowness of differences are contradictory. Critics of the Planning Board assumed that, because it concentrated on narrowing, it "papered over" disagreements. Since only a handful of NSC minutes from the 1950s have been declassified, we must turn to the testimony of participants to evaluate the accuracy of this criticism. Cutler's account and the large number of splits (specifications of disagreements) that were presented to the NSC indicate that the Board served to sharpen disagreements and force debate, not to smother them.

Cutler's 1960, closed-session testimony in Senator Henry Jackson's hearings on foreign policy machinery provides an especially detailed account of why and how the Planning Board's papers served as a debate-forcing procedure.[35] It was the special assistant, as the president's representative, and not representatives of the departments who ran the Planning Board and directed its small staff of policy analysts. And it was the special assistant's mandate from Eisenhower to make sure that differences be brought into the open and clearly stated.

Cutler described to the Jackson subcommittee the steps through which, in as many as five or six meetings over several weeks or months when time allowed, the Planning Board would go on examining the topic of each major agenda paper, drawing on "the brains and experience of the operations personnel who work day after day in the particular area" covered by each paper, identifying disagreements, consulting official intelligence estimates, and calling in key agency officials, who would be "questioned and cross-questioned about the factual subject matter and policy recommendations" of the NSC policy recommendation paper the board was preparing. By collecting the best available information from agency specialists, "the Board," Cutler explained, "seeks to squeeze out of the material all the juice that it contains."

From the board's initial investigation a draft paper would be prepared summarizing the "general considerations" (facts), proposed "general objectives" (broad policy aims), and recommendations for "policy guidance" (detailed operational suggestions), and appending a financial estimate of past and projected costs for whatever policy might be adopted. Cutler explained,

> At as many Planning Board meetings as are required this draft statement is discussed, torn apart, and revised. In the intervals between such meetings, a revised text based on these revisions and on further information is drafted by the Planning Board assistants . . . and circulated at the next following Planning Board meeting. . . . In [the intervals] the Planning Board members are able to confer with their principals, the NSC members, as to the department or agency's position on the developing issues. I used to call this procedure, Mr. Chairman, when I was chairman of 504 meetings in less than 4 years an "acid bath."
>
> Finally, through this arduous process, there results either agreement on clarity and accuracy of text, correctness of facts, and validity of policy recommendations or, as is often the case, sharp differences of opinion on basic major recommendations or statements.

The debate-forcing "splits" were set forth "clearly and succinctly . . . often in parallel columns." Cutler and his successors reported that about two-thirds of the NSC papers contained splits, often several in a paper. Time permitting, the papers, with or without splits, were circulated at least ten days before coming up in the NSC, and each NSC member was therefore able to absorb a thorough briefing on the core of the paper, to consult with his own planning body, and to be prepared to defend his agency's position on a split.

Although all participants had the documents well in advance of NSC meetings and had discussed them with their representative on the Planning Board, the special assistant had the responsibility of initiating discussion by summarizing each paper. He would bring explicit attention to the splits, labeling them by the agencies that had advocated various positions, and a free-flowing discussion would ensue, with each agency representative defending his side of each disagreement.

Commenting on Eisenhower's participation in the discussions, Cutler stressed that, as in the cabinet, decisions were made solely by the president. (The few NSC minutes that became available through Freedom of Information Act declassification appeals by 1982 are consistent with this report.) This should not imply, however, that Eisenhower ignored his colleagues—he sometimes expressed an opinion and later modified this view after hearing their arguments. Describing the part the president played in discussing papers, Cutler commented:

> The President is an active participant in the Council discussions. Sometimes issues which are in conflict are decided by him in the course of the discussion. He has to be very careful not too early in the discussion to intervene. If you are an affirmative person and you intervene early in the discussion, and you have intelligent Council members, they inevitably tend to feel a wind blowing from one direction or the other.

Of the few NSC meeting minutes now available,* the way the body's formal procedures could stimulate debate, thus providing opportunities for the president to participate in discussion and ultimately make decisions, is best reflected in the minutes for the discussion at the August 30, 1956, NSC meeting concerned with the Policy Board document "NSC 5612: U.S. Policy in Mainland Southeast Asia." This document was a revision of previous papers with such titles as "U.S. Policy in the Event of Renewal of Aggression in Vietnam, September 16, 1955." At the time, Dillon Anderson was special assistant for national security and had the responsibility of summarizing Policy Board papers and identifying points of disagreement.

*The draconian confidentiality rules currently governing national security policy documents make this entire analysis necessarily provisional. Fewer than ten NSC meeting minutes for the Eisenhower years have been released by 1982. No Planning Board papers with parallel column splits have yet been released. And the minutes Goodpaster kept of actual operational decisions made by small groups in Eisenhower's office also remain classified.

The minutes indicate that eight disagreements were resolved in the course of an extended discussion of NSC 5612 and the overall revised paper was accepted by the president. As might be expected, some of the disagreements were settled by quickly arrived at alterations in shadings of wording. Others, however, elicited sharp debate, which Eisenhower listened to and then resolved.

One split in the Planning Board document summarized by Anderson which evoked a sharp exchange was over United States economic and military assistance to neutral nations. The Burmese government had been showing disenchantment with the Soviet Union and signs of wanting to strengthen its ties to the West. Unlike neighboring Thailand, Burma was not a part of the Southeast Asia Treaty Organization. The State and the Defense departments were divided over whether the United States should give military aid to neutrals or reserve it for allies. Dulles spoke for the State Department position of permitting aid to neutrals if it was in the national interest. The allies-first position was defended by Undersecretary of Defense Reuben Robertson, who was attending the meeting as acting defense secretary and, more aggressively, by Joint Chiefs of Staff Chairman Admiral Arthur Radford.

> Secretary Dulles . . . made the point that if the United States failed to provide military assistance for neutrals like India or Burma, they would almost certainly seek such assistance and obtain it from the USSR. We wished to be able to prevent such a development. Admiral Radford replied that he could only say that we would never be able to retain our allies in Southeast Asia if our allies felt that other countries were in a position to obtain U.S. assistance without ever joining any kind of an alliance with the United States. . . . Secretary Dulles then observed that we had better begin getting rid of our allies if having such allies was going to prevent us from doing what is in the best interests of the United States. For example, said Secretary Dulles, he would rather see us lose Thailand, an ally, than lose India, a neutral.
>
> Admiral Radford pointed out that if we followed the line laid down by Secretary Dulles we would soon have to face precisely this decision. He added that the loss of Thailand would just about finish off the U.S. position in Southeast Asia.

Eisenhower, who had earlier said he understood "Secretary Dulles's desire to avoid making preferential treatment to allies an ironclad rule," but also agreed that other things being equal, "the United States should extend preferential treatment to allies over neutrals," ended the discussion by accepting a suggestion Dulles made after his exchange with Radford—that the Defense Department's pro-allies phrasing be accepted but with the amendment that this was the "general rule" and "when exceptions were in the strategic interests of the United States" they would be made.*

Another exchange over a split was occasioned by the JCS recommendation that the requirement of congressional approval of military action in response to a Communist resort to force in Mainland Southeast Asia be loosened. The original passage had justified

> military or other action to assist any Mainland Southeast Asia state or dependent territory willing to resist, "provided, that the taking of military action shall be subject to prior submission to and approval by Congress unless the emergency is so great that immediate action is necessary to save a vital interest of the United States."

The JCS-proposed revision involved deleting

> the last sentence of the text, beginning with the words "provided, that," and substitute for the deleted sentence a new sentence to read, "The Congress should be requested to give the President advance authority to act quickly in times of crises, including the use of armed forces. The grant of such authority should be publicized."

In this instance, Eisenhower had no compunction about entering early in the discussion.

> . . . the President said he could not go along with the change proposed by the Joint Chiefs of Staff. . . . [He] also expressed some concern lest the wording . . . commit the United States to military intervention in mainland Southeast Asia too readily. He thought that our intervention should be further qualified [as in the State Department drafts] by the insertion of the phrase "where American vital interests are involved." For example, he said,

---

*Translated, this banal sounding resolution of a split *is* meaningful. Dulles and Radford both had stated positions that were congenial with administration policy, but in intrinsic tension with one another in the specific instance. Eisenhower's "resolution" was to find a formula that legitimized both general positions and allowed him to judge the tradeoff and make the decision.

the United States might not deem it wise to intervene in certain instances where a Communist takeover was very far advanced.

Radford continued to argue his point but Eisenhower remained unswayed by Radford, and the original "provided" clause appeared in the final paper.[36]

Eisenhower's active participation in an NSC that met regularly served many functions, one of which was that of keeping his colleagues attuned to his criteria for deciding what would or would not be an acceptable foreign policy decision, as in his observation in the August 30, 1956, meeting that the national interest might sometimes call for *not* resisting "Communist takeovers" that were far advanced. He also was able to use his well developed capacity that had impressed Robert Bowie so much for devising common-sense resolutions of tangled group disagreements. At one point the August 30, 1956, NSC discussion seemed about to reach an impasse on the question of how Burma might be given a loan rather than formal foreign aid, since it was well known Burma would not be able to repay a loan. Eisenhower settled the matter simply by asking rhetorically: "Was it not possible to put an aid program technically on a reimburseable basis, even though we knew perfectly well that we would never be repaid for the assistances we had given?" This cut the Gordian knot.[37]

A Record of Action was prepared immediately after each meeting and cleared with the participants. Eisenhower added afterthoughts and clarifications, thus further demonstrating that *he* was making the administration's policy plans after consulting with the NSC and not using the NSC itself as the final authority.

In the case of the records of cabinet action, Eisenhower left it to the cabinet secretariat to check periodically with the departments on whether they had been implemented by asking for status reports. Eisenhower's NSC, however, had a body specifically commissioned to shape the steps for implementing each action. This was the Operations Coordinating Board (OCB), which had been drastically reshaped from Truman's Psychological Strategy Board. The OCB, like the Planning Board, was established to harness the major governmental bodies and personnel in an effective planning process that covered the entire policy cycle from agenda setting, through discussion and decision, to implementation.[38]

The OCB's job was to see that decisions did not just go into files in the form of re-edited policy papers, but actually resulted in plans for carrying out the decided policies. Cutler was fond of describing the OCB as the downward slope of a "policy hill." The image was misleading, however, in that the NSC and its extension the OCB were involved in conceptualizing policy and the procedures for implementing it, not in making concrete operating decisions.[39]

NSC sessions, like those of the cabinet, served informally to foster coordination, cohesion, and common thinking. Eisenhower clearly took greater pains with the NSC than with the cabinet to encourage debate and the exchange of information and ideas, even though he was often already familiar with the matters under review. Mrs. Whitman told Milton Eisenhower in a 1956 memorandum discussing the president's work schedule: "He himself complains that [in many cases] he knows every word of the presentations as they are to be made." However, she went on to explain, "he feels that to maintain the interest and attention of every member of the NSC, he must sit through each meeting—despite the fact that he knows the presentations so well."[40]

When the time came for Eisenhower to make an operational decision, he acted on the axiom that concrete decision making involves choices the details of which cannot always be fully anticipated. The most elaborately planned event he ever presided over was the Normandy invasion in June 1944. An intricate framing of options and coordination of activities had preceded his famous command to initiate the invasion despite a storm raging in the English Channel. But he personally made the decision at the latest possible time that would still permit its implementation, since he could not have anticipated the last minute report by his meteorological team that the storm would abate just long enough for the beachhead to be established. (The procedure of supplying him with the most up-to-date meteorological intelligence had been carefully planned and repeatedly rehearsed.) Small wonder that Eisenhower often reminded his associates of the aphorism: "Rely on planning, but never trust plans."

Eisenhower would summon small groups of key policy makers into

133

his office (often immediately after an NSC meeting) for informal discussions during which he made operational decisions. The notes of these meetings have not yet been released. One scholar, Douglas Kinnard, however, has worked with General Goodpaster's "Memoranda of Conferences with the President," which summarizes these informal meetings. Kinnard concludes that the informal meetings accomplished precisely what contemporary critics of Eisenhower's foreign policy making took the NSC to task for not accomplishing—rapid, flexible decision making by the president himself.

> Certainly the NSC planning process, especially of lesser papers, promoted a healthy interaction among the agencies and departments concerned with strategic policy. It forced appropriate officials to confront major issues of national security and to evaluate the options. Whether the procedures were too elaborate or there was too much paper, as is frequently alleged, is not of much importance. Eisenhower had a use for the NSC, but it was not the use that his critics thought. The NSC they wanted was, in effect, already in action in the Oval Room.[41]

Goodpaster was not just the note taker in the informal policy making meetings in Eisenhower's office: his role was like a combined Planning Board and OCB. He saw that critical participants were not frozen out of discussion and that Eisenhower's decisions were carried out. In this sense, his duties paralleled Cutler's. Indeed, their two positions came to be combined in later presidencies. It was this combined position that McGeorge Bundy filled as special assistant under Kennedy as did the special assistants thereafter, some of whom also took on the role of administration policy spokesman.[42]

Eisenhower came equipped to the policy-making meetings in his office with information gleaned not only from NSC papers and his own extensive background, but from many other sources as well. These included his daily exchanges with the secretary of state (especially when Dulles held that position), his daily briefings on intelligence community findings by Goodpaster (later John Eisenhower), and—in spite of his occasional claims that he paid little attention to newspapers—his close attention to press reports. He found, as have other presidents, that journalists sometimes could come up with observations or clues that might not otherwise reach him through official channels.

In a June 1959 memo to his defense secretary, Eisenhower refers to "press reports about Soviet objections to our deploying intermediate range ballistic missiles [IRBMs] in Greece." Noting that in the December 1957 NATO meetings, "we made it absolutely clear that we would not try to induce any NATO nation to accept IRBMs" but "made it clear also that we would be ready to make these available . . . where we believed their deployment would be useful as a deterrent and for defense," Eisenhower fired off a sequence of eight questions and a warning about the sensitivity of the issue, questions that illustrate his insistence on personally controlling and monitoring policy making and execution.

I should like the following questions answered:
a. Do we in fact have a firm plan for stationing IRBMs in Greece?
b. Did the Greek government initiate a firm request for these weapons?
c. Assuming the answer is "yes," did the appropriate NATO authority concur?
d. What additional numbers of uniformed services would be stationed in Greece?
e. What would be the total number of such American strength in that country?
f. What particular advantage do you expect to gain from putting these weapons in Greece in view of the fact that country is both small and exposed?
g. Does the State Department see any great advantage in stationing these weapons in this particular country?
h. Finally, what additional sums for defense support and economic assistance would be requested of the Congress as a result of any such action?

I do not want this memorandum widely circulated or worked on by junior staffs . . . these matters involve high policy and so I should like this paper handled by the fewest possible people.[43]

Eisenhower's direct forays into military policy planning were frequent and therefore provided for him an especially rich source of information. Military affairs, Mrs. Whitman commented to Milton Eisenhower, constituted "a great time-consuming area"—more than she thought reasonable.

I can't always see why some of the inter-Service problems cannot be re-solved before they come to the president, but apparently, as matters stand, they cannot. Budget, manpower, etc. take an enormous length of time, ei-ther with the Chiefs of Staff, or with the Chiefs and their civilian supe-riors.[44]

Her puzzlement reflects her failure to appreciate the degree to which Eisenhower had chosen to be his own defense secretary. His insis-tence on keeping abreast of military policy making was particularly evident in his meeting of January 30, 1958, with the JCS and the ci-vilian secretaries. Commenting on his desire to be called upon at key decision periods, he remarked that he had no criticism of the JCS, but, he said, "Don't forget that things happen afterwards. . . . To be sure, the JCS can have 872 agreements and only 3 disagree-ments . . . [but] these might well be the only readily fundamental matters."[45]

A telephone log shows Eisenhower's intimate participation in deci-sions bearing on the rapidly collapsing French military effort in Indo-China during late April 1954, shortly before the fall of the Dien Bien Phu bastion, providing a sense of how extraordinarily informal immedi-ate decision making could be. The telephone conversations were with Undersecretary of State General Walter Bedell Smith. (Smith, Eisen-hower's former SHAEF chief of staff, served as undersecretary of state in 1953 and 1954.)

On April 24, Smith had been in touch with NATO military head Alfred Gruenther, who from his headquarters outside of Paris was relay-ing reports to the State Department of developments in French poli-tics. The situation in France was "very unstable," according to Gruen-ther. The morale of French policy makers was lower than he had ever seen it, especially in regard to maintaining a commitment to fight in Indo-China. Smith reported that the "French military view is that the whole thing is washed out unless we can intervene." Eisenhower re-plied "that the French want us to come in as junior partners and pro-vide materials, etc., while they themselves retain the authority in that region." He would not "go along with them on such a notion," and he asked Smith "to have someone work on a draft for him when Dien Bien Phu falls."

Meanwhile, Eisenhower sought to encourage the British to join the United States in a coalition of nations that would take over the conduct of the war. But, as Smith told Eisenhower, British Foreign Minister Anthony Eden, "has grave doubts that Britain would cooperate in any activity" in Southeast Asia. Eisenhower, invoking "domino theory" logic, suggested that Eden be asked to "talk to his own military people." They, like Eisenhower, would recognize that the West was better off fighting in Indo-China, where 200,000 French troops were already engaged "than in some place like Burma or Thailand" without the aid of the troops currently in Indo-China.

Two days later the conversation resumed. Eisenhower had briefed the Republican leaders on the situation. He asked Smith to convene a bipartisan briefing. The two also discussed how Smith had explained to Republican Senator Styles Bridges that there would be no action in the planned moves against the leftist regime in Guatemala at the moment (the Arbenz government, which was overthrown in a CIA-aided coup that June) "because that was not a matter we wanted to make an explosion on just now."

The following day, Smith called Eisenhower to report that the British almost certainly would not join in united action. The Dien Bien Phu garrison was still holding out, and there had been a French request that the United States help supply it, using American aircraft and pilots. Eisenhower agreed that this should be done to give the French "a little hope," but only if the risk of exposure were minimal. He also warned Smith that "we still have to produce collective security in the world"; therefore, the government was publicly not to "exhibit impatience and frustrations at the British."[46]

These passages convey a process so fluid that even the term "informal organization" is stretched. They are drawn from one of the few documents recounting the detailed flow of decision making at the time when there was intense consideration within the Eisenhower administration of whether to intervene militarily in a conflict that the nation finally entered a decade later—with dire results.

Most of the primary sources bearing on United States response to the collapse of the French effort in Indo-China, like those relating to other foreign policy crises of his administration, remain classified. That even the fragmentary account of Eisenhower's personal participation

137

in these events became available only in the 1970s helps us understand why he has so often been viewed more as a constitutional monarch who relied on formal machinery to reign over his administration than as its central decision maker.

The Formal and Informal White House

The impression that Eisenhower reigned more than he ruled and was insulated by the formal arrangements he had instituted stemmed more from his use of a White House chief of staff than from any single other aspect of the organization of his presidency. Press accounts of the operating style of the man who from 1953 to 1958 held this job, the crusty, hard-driving Sherman Adams, reinforced this impression. But Eisenhower's use of a staff chief was part of a larger notion of organizational leadership and did not depend on the chief's having Adams's abrupt, no-nonsense traits. He used Adams as a deputy rather than as a delegate, and he additionally insured that Adams was only one of many sources of information and recommendations.

The "training in problems involving organization" that led Eisenhower to reorganize the White House included familiarity with the standard operating arrangement of many large-scale organizations (not just of the military)—an arrangement in which the top executive has a carefully articulated staff of aides who have been delegated explicit responsibilities. In World War II, when Eisenhower took command in Europe, his first command after having served for two decades in staff assignments, he immediately, and seemingly effortlessly, organized a vast headquarters, by making extensive use of a staff chief but devising ways to keep that aide's actions in line with the supreme commander's policies. He believed his own experience as a staff chief enabled him to know how best to use one; he once mused that he may well have headed staffs for a longer period of time than anyone else in the Army.[47]

Eisenhower originally offered the job of chief of staff to Henry Cabot

Lodge, an urbane, easy-going Bostonian whose personal impact on other public figures and portrayal by the media would have been substantially different from Adams's. When he instead chose Sherman Adams, he simply told the former New Hampshire governor that Adams "would be associated with me more closely than anyone else in the government."[48] But Eisenhower surprised Adams because he "never specifically defined my responsibilities or outlined their limits."[49] Adams's job evolved, as did the media assertions about his influence. Press coverage stressing Adams's abruptly decisive image sharply contrasted with portrayals of Eisenhower as smiling, unruffled, and free to take time off for golf. News stories emanating from the White House and magazine articles emphasizing the new president's businesslike predilection for order, delegation, and division of labor, seemed to confirm the impression that it was Adams who bore the burden of the presidential job. This interpretation became standard partisan fare; it was far easier to attack the procedures of so popular a leader than to attack the man himself.

Adlai Stevenson's remarks at a February 1958 banquet in honor of Truman were typical. Brandishing a newspaper clipping headlined "Adams Insists Ike is Really President," Stevenson quipped that "no newspaper ever had to write this kind of headline about the man we honor here."[50] Academic writing of the period, much of which was by Stevenson Democrats, supported the partisan polemic. An essay by political scientist Marian Irish in the *Journal of Politics* is an excellent illustration. Drawing freely on then current press reports, she characterized Eisenhower as a presidential version of the faceless, conformist bureaucrat described in William Whyte's pop sociology treatise *The Organization Man*. She informed her readers,

Eisenhower rarely meets with his staff. Sherman Adams does it for him. The president insists that conflicts be resolved before they reach his desk; he wants only to hear the consensus, not the discussion, of the staff. He will not be bothered with a lot of paper work. He expects communications to him to be in the form of neatly drafted, one-page memos—which is probably one reason why he often shows little insight into the complex issues of the day. Eisenhower likes best a paper that ends, "OK, SA"; this he can initial "DDE": such is his confidence in Adams and his staff.[51]

Her remarks reflect the contemporary stereotype, and provide a useful vehicle for reexamining Adams's role, using the now available information directly documenting Eisenhower's leadership. It is important first to consider both Eisenhower's own views about the nature and inevitable problems of the chief of staff in a large organization and his customary way of adapting his aides' tasks to their particular abilities.

His lengthy 1948 memorandum advising James Forrestal on how to manage the sprawling Defense Department reveals Eisenhower's already set judgment of the importance of a staff chief to a complex organization and his recognition of the inevitable criticism to which an executive employing a chief of staff and, by extension, the staff chief himself will be subject. Noting that "the top man in any organization has tremendous duties that force him continually to face outward to represent the interests of his organization in all kinds of conferences and frequently viz a viz (*sic*) other segments of government," Eisenhower stresses that "this applies with particular force to Cabinet members in Washington,"*

> In policy matters only the Secretary can do this effectively, yet the time, thought, and effort consumed, leave him no chance to be a detailed coordinator of his own team. As a result the details fall into confusion; policy cannot be effectively applied. Moreover, if there is no integrated staff, all principal *operating* subordinates . . . are compelled to decide which of the chief's various "assistants" takes cognizance of a particular subject—and more frequently than not a problem involves the functions of more than one of these [specialists].[52]

Although Eisenhower emphasized as reasons for having a top assistant the need for staff coordination and for a designated staff aide to whom line officials could communicate, his own chiefs of staff also consistently had another major responsibility—that of being a deputy. In this status, an aide was supposed to be fully aware of his superior's policies or be able immediately to get clarification and further instructions. Eisenhower, stating this rationale in 1942 to his then staff chief, General Walter Bedell Smith, told Smith that he was "particularly anxious that you always understand [basic policies] so you can enlarge and elab-

---

*By the same logic it applies most strongly, of course, to the president because of his foreign relations responsibilities.

orate on them when the occasion demands."[53] The aide, in short, was to extend his superior's impact, making decisions of his own "within . . . limits of previously made larger decisions by the boss."[54]

Such a deputy would inevitably come under fire, because he would be held responsible for many unpopular decisions—for example, decisions his boss had made about which people he would or would not see. Referring in the Forrestal memorandum to the head of a cabinet department, in a comment equally applicable to the presidency, Eisenhower explains why principal associates would resent a staff chief. "Assistants who are personally close to the secretary of a government department always oppose the formation of any advisory and coordinating staff group under a single head, since this development they feel thrusts them one step away from the throne." His description of the kind of criticism to which they are vulnerable explains why Eisenhower was not surprised in the 1950s when he was taken to task for employing an articulated staff and a staff chief and why he was so ready to come to Adams's defense in 1958: "Such words as 'over-organization,' 'red-tape,' and 'duplication' are used to condemn the idea of staff integration," he remarks, in an observation that bespeaks his years of experience with organizational politics.[55]

By not specifically defining Adams's responsibilities and their limits, Eisenhower applied the principle Marshall employed in 1941 when he asked Eisenhower to outline a strategy of response to the war that had just begun. Marshall's instructions were completely open-ended.[56] In responding to the ambiguities of his mandate, Eisenhower revealed to Marshall that he had a clear incisive mind and a high degree of sensitivity to the fusion of military and political requirements in any effective strategy for fighting the war. Adams, in carrying out his open-ended assignment, showed that he was an effective, relentlessly hardworking deputy. He served well as a point of outside access to the White House. He also conducted morning White House staff briefings. But he threw himself so vigorously into a demanding schedule of personal activity, fighting day-to-day brush fires through innumerable conferences and his fabled phone conversations which neither began with "hello" nor terminated with "good-bye," that he found little time to be a staff coordinator.[57]

In the case of Adams, as in the case of the other alleged "real power" behind Eisenhower, John Foster Dulles, who requested that he not be made to handle administrative responsibilities, Eisenhower made accommodations that showed his readiness to adapt formal procedures to the personal strengths and weaknesses of those who had to execute the procedures. In response to Dulles's request, Eisenhower devolved administrative responsibilities that would normally engage at least some of Dulles's attention as secretary to an assistant secretary, and also freed Dulles from the task of administering the United States Information Agency (USIA).*

Because Adams's strength was not in organizational coordination, Eisenhower assigned this task to General Paul Carroll, a former NATO aide whom he had transferred to the White House to handle military liaison. Goodpaster, who assumed this job after Carroll's unexpected death, describes how Eisenhower informally reassigned the coordination task from his staff chief to his military liaison aide:

> The President, on one occasion, when some paperwork got crossed up—someone had done something unaware that another line of activity had begun—said, "I look to my staff to keep such things straightened out. I should not have to be my own sergeant major. . . ." About ten days later the same thing happened again, and he called the chief people of the staff and said, "I told you I don't plan to be my own sergeant major, and I don't, I want to have a staff secretary and General Paul Carroll, you're going to be the staff secretary right now."[59]

If Adams had different strengths, a staff secretary would not have been necessary. But Adams quickly demonstrated that he could spend a superhuman amount of time acting as Eisenhower's deputy. It involved not only long hours spent in his own office but also being present at a large number of Eisenhower's meetings, including regularly scheduled ones, such as cabinet and Legislative Leadership meetings, as well as ad hoc presidential conferences. By spending so much time in Eisenhower's presence, and by being filled in by whatever aide was assigned to

*When, after Dulles's death, the USIA devolution was reversed, Eisenhower made a comment that nicely shows his sensitivity to the interplay of formal and informal organization, remarking that he "found this situation somewhat amusing because of the way organizations must be juggled to fit personalities." Pointing out that in 1953 he had attempted to consolidate all activities related to foreign policy under Dulles, but that Dulles showed "a strong antipathy to operational matters," Eisenhower noted that for such personal reasons it was necessary for operations to "go back and forth from independent status to State control like a shuttlecock."[58]

make a summary of a meeting he had missed,* Adams was able to keep abreast of Eisenhower's views. He also was at liberty to enter the Oval Office for a decision without knocking, when he deemed it necessary.

By the same token, Adams was always on call when Eisenhower needed his services. And Adams did not require detailed instructions to act. When, for example, early in 1953, Wesley Roberts, the Republican national chairman, became the object of a controversial investigation into his state legislative lobbying activities, Milton Eisenhower wrote the president a letter warning that a scandal was brewing. Eisenhower passed it on to his staff chief, jotting at the bottom: "Personal and Confidential—Adams: sounds serious."[60] Roberts resigned by the end of March in response to stern queries from party leaders initiated by Adams about the propriety of his activities.[61]

The best documentation of Adams as deputy comes from times when Eisenhower was out of town and Adams remained in Washington or visited Eisenhower briefly. On those occasions notes were kept on their conversations or they corresponded. A longer than usual meeting between Eisenhower and Adams took place in Denver eighteen days after Eisenhower's heart attack. On October 12, 1955, Adams briefed Eisenhower on a series of issues that had arisen during Eisenhower's incapacity and received instructions as to how to proceed on them. Eisenhower in turn initiated a project. Following up a conversation he had had with his brother Milton about agricultural problems, the bedridden president told Adams that "some investment now in our farming areas could be cheaper than to risk farming collapse." Eisenhower went on to sketch the rationale of the soil bank program, which was to deal with "certain things, among them water and soil conservation . . . that are in the national interest. We have previously considered that every man's land, as well as his home, was his castle. . . . [H]e was permitted to ruin it. . . . But a nation cannot divest itself of interest in its own soil." Apprised that Eisenhower wanted a program that would begin the following summer in which farm income support was tied to soil conservation, Adams was in a position to initiate planning within the administration.[62]

---

*Adams sometimes did not attend NSC meetings because of other demands on his time (and when he did, it was as an observer). The classified minutes of these meetings were not available to him, since his responsibilities were domestic.

A telegram Eisenhower sent Adams from Denver the previous year explicitly specifies Adams's role as presidential deputy and sheds light on how Eisenhower expected him to perform this responsibility. The telegram discussed newspaper publisher Roy Howard's suggestions to Eisenhower of ways in which the administration's controversial farm policy might be more effectively promoted and also, Eisenhower's discovery that there had been no action on his instructions that the Defense Department's annual spending be expedited in the preelection half of that fiscal year. Eisenhower wired Adams on September 25:

> It seems to me that there is a tremendous amount of material [in the How-ard suggestions] that will be helpful in selling the farm program properly. I shall speak to Ezra [Taft Benson] on Monday, but I hope you will see that his department puts the full force of their leadership behind this busi-ness.
> [Eisenhower then shifted to the second topic]. This morning you and I talked briefly about the program for starting up expenditures to stimulate industrial activity. You stated you would soon see [Labor] Secretary Mitch-ell. Please ask him to show you the memorandum he wrote me under the date of September 16, which came to my attention this morning. I should very much like to push in the direction he advocates. For six months I have been urging the Defense Department to do the major portion of its buying now and not wait until the last half of the fiscal year. This does not seem to be happening and I think it is time that it was. Do not hesitate to use any legal authority I have to get this going and be sure to notify everybody of my personal anxiety.[63]

It is scarcely surprising that a staff aide who was instructed not to "hesitate to use any legal authority I have to get this going" would sometimes be described as "the assistant president," nor that such an aide would come to be perceived as what Professor Irish inferred Adams to be—an all-powerful gatekeeper who controlled the flow of information and recommendations to the president, and forwarded to him merely for ratification, consensus policy recommendations. Even the evidence from the 1950s documents the existence of procedures that prevented any monopoly of access to the president, however.

A 1956 article in *Time* entitled "O.K., S.A.," although mainly em-phasizing Adams's putative influence, concludes by acknowledging that Adams in fact was one of many associates in direct contact with the president. The article describes an operating procedure through which any proposal to Eisenhower had to be submitted in writing. It then would be logged by Staff Secretary Goodpaster, and would be "staffed out" so that Eisenhower would receive not only the original proposal, but also comments by White House aides and department officials who had a specialized perspective on each issue.

A key Adams duty is that of ironing—or if necessary, stomping—out the scores of differences that must arise within any Administration . . . to bring together for negotiation any department or agency heads who may have an interest in a specific problem. He can and does hold over their heads the fact that if they do not arrive at a reasonable solution he will write the recommendation himself—and his is the one that goes to the President with the all important scrawl: "O.K., S.A." . . . The papers carrying that notation are the ones that President Eisenhower is least likely to question.[64]

This *Time* account was one that Washington insiders could easily assimilate to other impressions—for example, that conveyed by comparing the *United States Organization Manual* entry for the White House office for Truman's last year in office and the Eisenhower White House entry for the year Adams resigned, or by simply noting the seemingly increased functional specialization of Eisenhower's aides over those of Truman. The *Organization Manual* lists for Truman's final period in office a mere sixteen White House aides, including holders of such nonpolitical positions as executive clerk, chief usher, White House physician, and secretary to the president's wife, and their names appear in virtually random order. The Eisenhower volume identifies fifty-seven aides, starting with Adams and indicating his exalted title— the assistant to the president. Formally arrayed under Adams, the other functionaries are listed in a fashion that clearly conveys the impression of hierarchy: beneath the assistant to the president, for example, is a deputy assistant to the president and under him are two assistants to the deputy assistant to the president.*[65]

---

*Although Truman aide John R. Steelman did have the title of assistant to the president, neither his actual duties nor the way he was portrayed resembled Adams's responsibilities and image. Steelman worked in the East Wing rather than the policymaking West Wing of the White House and served Truman largely as a personal troubleshooter on cabinet affairs and as a labor negotiator.[66]

As Stephen Hess notes, Truman's aides appeared to be politically attuned generalists who had the president as their sole constituent, but Eisenhower's seemed compartmentalized:

> Whereas the staffs under Roosevelt and Truman were composed largely of people whose talents were to be found in their finely tuned political antennae, or their overarching loyalty, or high creativity, the top-echelon Eisenhower staff was noted for its functional professionalism. James Hagerty was a *professional* press secretary. . . . General Persons . . . was a *professional* congressional lobbyist. . . . Special Counsel Bernard Shanley was hired as a lawyer, not a ghostwriter in mufti. The writing was to be done by Emmet Hughes of *Time* and *Life* magazines—a sharp break with the past, where the distinction between policy-making and word production was left deliberately fuzzy. . . . Eisenhower added a personal economist to the staff, Gabriel Hauge. Robert Montgomery, the actor-producer, was on call to advise the President on the use of television.[67]

Despite the impression of hierarchy and air-tight specialization of White House aides in Hess's portrait of Eisenhower's staff, the *U.S. Government Organization Manual* and the text of the *Time* article on Adams, a side-bar in the *Time* article conveyed a quite different impression. The facing page of the article's title, "O.K., S.A.," presents an organization chart showing the major White House staff aides with a caption stating that "the men who work under Sherman Adams are no mere spear-carrying extras; they include some of the key men in Government" and "staff channels are not so rigid as to prevent any staffer from going straight to the President." Dotted lines leading from certain associates to Eisenhower indicate those aides whose contacts with the president did not need to be "cleared with Sherm." They include Press Secretary Hagerty, the special assistant for national security, Staff Secretary Goodpaster, Special Counsel Gerald Morgan, the secretaries of the ten cabinet departments, and the directors of three major non-White House EOP agencies, the Council of Economic Advisors, the Budget Bureau, and the Office of Defense Mobilization—a sizeable (and as later evidence shows), by no means complete list.[68]

Indeed, documents in the Eisenhower Library consisting of messages, routing slips, notes on White House communications, as well as contemporary diaries and the recollections of Eisenhower's associates, clearly show that Eisenhower drew on plentiful rather than few sources for information and advice. Even within the White House the informal realities contradicted the impression of a formalistic hierarchy. The man listed in the *Organization Manual* as Adams's deputy, for example, was Wilton Persons, Eisenhower's congressional liaison chief not only in the White House, but also when he was Chief of Staff, from 1945 to 1948 and when he was NATO chief. Moreover, he was a personal friend from Eisenhower's pre-World War II years in Washington, and his ties to Eisenhower were stronger as well as older than Adams's. While Persons did coordinate with Adams to prevent organizational confusion and out of courtesy, he worked for and reported directly to Eisenhower.

Evidence of the behavior of Eisenhower's aides also undermines the entire notion that a neat division of labor was central to Eisenhower's staff organization, or at least to its informal realities. Persons, for example, gave general political advice, Hagerty made recommendations on foreign policy, and his economics advisor, Hauge, commented on political strategy.

Further proof that Adams was not an omnipotent palace guardian is that despite the impression given by Adams that Eisenhower rarely used the telephone, the logs for some days document as many as a dozen calls in which the president sought information, gave instructions, rallied support, and made policy decisions. He was also a prolific correspondent as well as a close reader of the major newspapers.

The belief that Eisenhower made significant decisions simply by ratifying memoranda that were initiated by Adams turns out to be of interest not because it is correct but rather because it illuminates the way Adams's services could provide the same lightning-rod effect for Eisenhower as did some of the actions of his other controversial associates. Major policy papers and correspondence that went to the president did *not* bear the inscription "O.K., S.A." Rather, it is largely to be found on matters such as recommendations for minor patronage positions. Apart from being time-consuming, however, decisions on these matters are a notorious source of recrimination. This therefore became one of the ways that Adams's reputation as "abominable no man" helped preserve Eisenhower's image as a benevolent national and international leader.

147

Adams's resignation and his replacement with the more easy going Wilton Persons coincides with the period of the so-called New Eisenhower. One close inside observer, Elmer Staats, who was deputy director of the Bureau of the Budget and executive secretary of the Operations Coordinating Board, holds that this White House staff substitution, combined with Dulles's departure, produced a livelier, better informed Eisenhower. Staats noted that in contrast to Adams, Persons would not say "I will talk to the President about this matter and let you know," but rather "Let's have a discussion." Then, Staats continued, "there was the opportunity for everyone to argue their position directly before the President."[69]

Persons himself reports that he brought more people into Eisenhower's office than Adams had and provided the president with details of information Adams would not have brought to his attention. He attributes this, however, to his own political style, derived from a lifetime of congressional lobbying. He felt that visitors whose loyalty and morale would be boosted by a personal meeting with Eisenhower should get to see the president if time permitted. And he felt that by providing Eisenhower with information beyond that required for decision making he could add to Eisenhower's political credibility by reducing the number of his "don't know" replies at press conferences.[70]

Even with Adams serving him, however, Eisenhower drew for advice on many White House aides, other administration members, and friends and acquaintances for what appears to have been as rich—if not as palpably contrived—a flow of face-to-face conversation, questioning, and thinking out loud as occurred under Roosevelt. By the same token the key aides freely exchanged tactical and substantive ideas with each other and not only at Adams's behest.

Press Secretary Hagerty had particularly close access to Eisenhower, because Eisenhower valued his views and appreciated his many sources of off-the-record information. Moreover, Hagerty traveled with Eisenhower to the president's public appearances, and in the course of doing so, had numerous opportunities to chat informally with him. Hagerty's diary provides many illustrations of how the president continually sought his and other aides' ideas and mined them for information. His reports accord with the Nixon observation that Eisenhower frequently engaged in "mindstretching" ruminations, tossing out ideas he did not necessarily plan to act on:

> With people he knew well and trusted, Eisenhower liked to think out loud. He would sometimes make what would seem to be completely outlandish and politically naive remarks, just to test them, perhaps even believing in some of them momentarily. He was very bold, imaginative and uninhibited in suggesting and discussing new and completely unconventional approaches to problems. Yet he probably was one of the most deliberate and careful Presidents the country had ever had where action was concerned.*[71]

Milton Eisenhower was probably the single most important influence in the informal organization of the Eisenhower White House. Since he could be completely trusted, he served as a superlative sounding board. During the 1950s as president first of Pennsylvania State University and then of Johns Hopkins University, Milton arranged with the trustees of both institutions to devote four days a week to university business, and the remaining to serving three days as aide to his brother. When in Washington, he often met with his brother at times not covered by the appointment log—at breakfast and in the evenings or by a back door to the Oval Office. He wrote numerous advisory letters to Eisenhower, typing them himself when he felt they were too sensitive to pass through a secretary. And the two brothers were connected by a secure direct telephone line, insuring that their conversations would not be monitored.†[72]

Informal, regularly-held stag dinners constituted another of Eisenhower's advisory resources. Guest lists of dozens of such events are available and reveal the close attention paid to the choice of guests and even to seating arrangements. Those best represented at these dinners

---

*The passage continues: "Because of his military experience, he was always thinking in terms of alternatives, attack and counter-attack. This was true of every problem he handled. I cannot, for instance, imagine him countenancing the plan for the 1961 rebel attack against Cuba without air power before asking: 'What is our position if the landings fail? . . .' (But) he could be very enthusiastic about half-baked ideas in the discussion."

†Milton Eisenhower was at least as important to his brother as Robert Kennedy was to John F. Kennedy. The contrast between the tactful, low visibility modus operandi of the Eisenhower brothers and the controversial public approach and teamwork of the Kennedys epitomizes the differences between the Eisenhower mode of seeking results without apparent controversy and the Kennedy emphasis on establishing the president and his team as visibly tough, "hard ball" political operators.

were the well-established or rising businessmen, usually in prominent positions of responsibility. Guests also included executive branch officials, party leaders, celebrities, leading clergymen, academics (especially natural scientists), and a few labor leaders, usually craft unionists who had supported Eisenhower's candidacy.

Typically, those invited would meet the president at 7:30 P.M. for drinks followed by dinner, and would then gather for conversation in the White House residential quarters. Although the tone was easygoing, Eisenhower would consistently direct the conversation to discussion of immediate and long-run problems about which he wanted information, insight, and advice. The meetings inevitably had a rallying as well as informative function. Not surprisingly, those favored with invitations usually left these gatherings as enthusiastic Eisenhower supporters, stimulated both by the distinction of being invited to the White House and by Eisenhower's compelling presence.

The stag dinners were the most formal manifestation of what might be called Eisenhower's "White House behind the White House," a wholly informal institution, operating as much in the living as in the working quarters of 1600 Pennsylvania Avenue, and extending to Camp David, Augusta, and Eisenhower's other favorite sites outside of Washington. He had an extraordinarily broad network of acquaintances and friends with whom he corresponded and met. Some of these friends were people with whom he could simply relax, while others, such as publisher and public-relations man William Robinson and General Clay were men whose views, breadth of acquaintance, and support he had long found valuable. In all, unofficial and official associates combined to provide Eisenhower with at least as diverse a flow of information and advice as any of the other modern presidents.

The Eisenhower Parallels

The man, his strategies, and his organizational style provide a lens for re-examining specific episodes in Eisenhower's presidential leadership; the congruence of organizational style, strategies, and man is striking. His organizational style seemed from public evidence to be highly formalistic, but its unpublicized face was directed to the informal subtleties of administrative politics. He left a public impression that he was not a political strategist, but rather a head of state who was above politics. Looked at from the inside, however, he revealed himself as a self-conscious practitioner of a leadership style that enabled him to maintain the popular support needed by a successful head of state without foregoing direct participation in the controversial politics of leadership. And at the personal level he showed a striking capacity to think in politically astute ways but presented himself as a guileless folk hero. He also worked hard at carrying off his distinctive style of leadership, but left the impression that it was all effortless.

PART III

*An Assessment
of the Style
and Its Uses*

5

STRENGTHS AND WEAKNESSES OF THE STYLE: THE JOE McCARTHY CASE

MY DESCRIPTION of Eisenhower's leadership style draws for illustration on events that occurred at diverse times in his career. To evaluate the style it is more instructive to examine a historically linked set of events. A case study provides the necessary depth and continuity of context to provide examples of circumstances in which the style is effective and not effective; to consider its long-run as well as short-run consequences; and to identify trade-offs inherent in it—that is, ways in which its strengths are also the source of weaknesses.[1]

An especially suitable historical sequence for evaluating the Eisenhower leadership is the chain of activity during his first two years in office that culminated with the Senate vote condemning Wisconsin Senator Joseph R. McCarthy.

Eisenhower's actions during the McCarthy affair are of special interest, since in the twenty-three-and-a-half months from his inauguration to McCarthy's downfall Eisenhower was sometimes successful and sometimes unsuccessful in accomplishing his aims by using each element of his leadership style. Therefore the case reveals pros and cons of each of his strategies and of his approach to organization. Moreover, the case can be assessed in terms not only of its principal outcome, the termination of McCarthy's political effectiveness, but also in terms of a corollary outcome, the negative effects of Eisenhower's indirect, unpublicized approach to combatting McCarthy on the morale and effectiveness of federal employees.

Contemporary accounts treated Eisenhower's relationship with McCarthy not as a president's exercise of leadership but rather as his failure to respond to a challenge to his influence and authority. Even in the early 1970s, when scholars uncovered many primary sources revealing important aspects of McCarthy's rise, heyday, and fall not publicly known in the 1950s, the original impression remained. One of the most extensively documented "second stratum" accounts of McCarthy echoes the conclusion of the 1950s that Eisenhower lacked the skill and will to respond to McCarthy:

> The new president was a decent man but he possessed neither the ability nor the inclination to deal with a political problem of this complexity. Urged by friends and advisers to speak out against McCarthy, he often replied: "I just will not—I refuse—to get into the gutter with that guy." The real alternatives, of course, were not limited to either standing aloof or gutter brawling. A more Machiavellian or manipulative President, a Franklin Roosevelt or a Lyndon Johnson, might have operated effectively against McCarthy while avoiding either extreme. But Eisenhower was President, and he was elected to office for reasons quite inseparable from his political naiveté.[2]

Finally, in the late 1970s—an appropriate delay for reports of the actions of a devotee of hidden-hand leadership—a third level of still more deeply buried evidence was uncovered that documented Eisenhower's direct involvement in eliminating McCarthy's influence. This is the stratum of evidence on the dynamics of Eisenhower's leadership that has made possible the re-evaluation and codification of Eisenhower's political personality set forth in chapters 2, 3, and 4.

Though Eisenhower was far from being the only (or even the decisive) agent of McCarthy's political demise, upon taking office he quickly recognized the importance of defusing the senator. He formulated and even summarized in his private diary a basic strategy for accomplishing this, a strategy he continued to use, but adjusted and supplemented during the periods of McCarthy's seemingly unchallenged sovereignty in 1953 and his precipitous decline in 1954. Throughout, Eisenhower rejected courses of action urged upon him by some of his closest allies that, it can plausibly be argued, would have perpetuated McCarthy's influence.

Since my aim is to examine instruments of Eisenhower's leadership such as selective delegation, action based on personality, and fusion of formal and informal organization, and the focus of this chapter is on the strong and weak application of these elements, my discussion of the McCarthy episode will be highly selective. In some cases events that transpired over a period of several months are summarized in only a few summary paragraphs, whereas a period of only one month in 1954 gets day-by-day attention. Moreover, it will be necessary to examine certain Eisenhower administration actions that do not appear in the usual accounts of McCarthy, because although not directed at him, they helped relegate him to the sidelines. These included Eisenhower's development of the first Republican legislative program, his loyalty and security program, and certain highly visible foreign policy actions that contributed to his great personal popularity and ability to preempt national attention at times when McCarthy was striving to dominate the front pages.

McCarthy and Eisenhower Before 1953

Three years before Eisenhower took office, McCarthy had suddenly established himself on the political scene. This lackluster product of the 1946 Republican landslide unexpectedly and almost overnight became a headline figure after giving a speech on February 9, 1950, to a small audience of Republican women in Wheeling, West Virginia. His address included a grandiose claim, which he never went on to substantiate, that he knew the names of 205 Communists working in the State Department who were busily subverting foreign policy. McCarthy said this during the traditional February Lincoln's birthday congressional recess, when Republican leaders leave Washington to deliver orations to grass-roots groups. Many other Republicans belabored the Democrats that week for being "soft on communism," yet it was McCarthy who stole the headlines. What had made *him* so newsworthy? The most plausible answer, an axiom from which Eisenhower deduced his own approach to dealing with McCarthy, was that by being outrageously brazen and extreme in his accusations and insisting that he had firm proof of them he goaded other national leaders to taking him seriously and hence engaging in attention-getting debates with him.[3]

The day after the Wheeling speech McCarthy (who by this time had adjusted his statistics to 207 State Department "bad risks" and 57 "card-carrying Communists," (numbers he was never to mention again) fired off public telegrams to Truman and the State Department. He offered to give them his list, adding a proviso he knew would be refused: the administration would have to reverse its long-established confidentiality rule and give him its loyalty files. The State Department issued a denial of McCarthy's charges, which only served further to excite public interest in them. Indeed the State Department denial of McCarthy's Wheeling charges was the basis for the first *New York Times* story—not published until two days after McCarthy's speech—on the senator's premier performance as a crusader against communism in government. On February 16 Truman let himself be drawn into McCarthy's burgeoning career as a headliner. Asked about McCarthy's charges, Truman snapped that the State Department had answered them "by saying there was not a word of truth in what the Senator said."[4] In his March 20 news conference Truman provided the colorful headline phrase for that day's McCarthy story, calling him "the Kremlin's best asset."[5] Eighty-five percent of a Gallup national sample had heard of McCarthy's charges by May 1950 and of those with opinions, 57 percent thought he was doing more good than harm.[6]

McCarthy's rise from media eminence to political potency in the course of 1950* coincided with the second "Eisenhower-for-President" boom. The first was in 1948 when liberal Democrats sought to draft Eisenhower as a candidate. Eventually he put a halt to it by renouncing any presidential aspirations. The second began in 1950 when internationalist Republicans—the most prominent of them New York Governor Thomas Dewey—and businessmen of similar leanings began urging him to become the 1952 Republican nominee.

Eisenhower's 1950 diary entries show his overextended schedule as he alternated between the fund raising required of him as president of Columbia University and consultations with Truman and his military chiefs on national security, especially after the outbreak that June of hostilities in Korea. He notes his awareness of his own popularity by wondering in April whether the president will be offended by a "60-to-30 report against him" in a Gallup poll showing that the public preferred Eisenhower over Truman as president.[8] His diary and the reports of people who talked to him during this period make it clear Eisenhower was closely following developments within the Republican party, which inevitably included the rise of McCarthy.† One entry shows he made it known as early as April 1950 to "my Republican connections in Kansas . . . that I believe we must have a Republican victory in 1952";[9] others refer to his Republican enthusiasts continually urging his candidacy.[10] Eisenhower was spared either announcing or renouncing interest in the presidency when he accepted Truman's request on October 28, 1950[11] that he become NATO commander. He estab-

---

*A number of important Democrats who were leaders in the counterattack against McCarthy were defeated in that year's mid-term election, and (on insufficient evidence) they were widely assumed to have succumbed to McCarthy's campaigns against them.[7]

†Herbert Brownell first met Eisenhower during his Columbia University presidency and then spent a day with him at his NATO headquarters when briefing Eisenhower on his prospects as a presidential candidate. On both occasions he found Eisenhower impressively informed about and intensely interested in the Republican Party, politics in general, and current issues. (Personal interview)

159

lished himself at NATO headquarters in France early in 1951. As an officer returned to active duty as well as organizer of the North Atlantic Treaty Organization he was obliged to refrain from public involvement in partisan politics.

The leaders who favored his candidacy, however, were not deterred either by Eisenhower's uniform or overseas residency and argued with him in frequent visits to NATO headquarters. And from Europe he continued to survey the American political landscape in which McCarthy was rising in prominence. Eisenhower's appeal to his party's moderate internationalists and McCarthy's to the truculent members of its radical right inevitably led politicians and political commentators to assume the two men were natural opponents. The first mention of McCarthy in Eisenhower's diary captures this. In a March 13, 1951, entry that commented on the daily news summary he received from the United States, he indicated his annoyance that the media continued to view him as a presidential contender and referred to reports by Drew Pearson that "Senator McCarthy is digging up alleged dirt with which to smear me if I run for president."[12]

On June 14, 1951, McCarthy treated the Senate to a seventy-two-thousand-word tirade against Eisenhower's mentor George Marshall for "losing China," adding in passing a blast at Eisenhower for not taking Berlin at the close of World War II. With the vitriolic hyperbole that was his trademark, McCarthy claimed Marshall had been party to "a conspiracy so immense and an infamy so black as to dwarf any previous such venture in the history of man."[13] Eisenhower's diary entry of the same day, obviously written before he had word of McCarthy's speech, describes the senator as one of the chief congressional "disciples of hate" and an obstacle to selfless bipartisan cooperation in making national security policy.[14]

Not surprisingly, in his first encounter with the press on June 5, 1952, just after resigning his NATO commission and returning to the United States to campaign for the presidency, Eisenhower was asked to take a position on McCarthy. His reply wedded two strategies: "no personalities" and "instrumental use of language," thus anticipating the way he would answer questions about McCarthy once he was president. He introduced to the public his phrase, "I am not going in any manner or means to indulge in personalities." Then he went on to use what he later described as the "indirect approach" of reply—criticism of an adversary's policies or actions phrased as an abstract statement of his own views, while studiously avoiding derogatory personal reference. Thus, without mentioning McCarthy's recurrent undocumented charges, Eisenhower stated he was determined to uproot any government subversion but would do so "without besmirching the reputation of any innocent man or condemning by loose association."[15]

Once the campaign was underway and Eisenhower and his staff were feverishly canvassing the country for every possible Republican presidential and congressional vote, Eisenhower had to deal with the problem of trying to differentiate himself from McCarthy, while at the same time trying to unite a party riven by a bitter nominating convention. When asked, therefore, about his support for McCarthy's senatorial candidacy, he fell back on allusions to his duty as a candidate to back his party's ticket. Nevertheless, he did seek to show his contempt for McCarthy's assault on Marshall by going out of his way on August 22 to pay impassioned tribute to his former chief in one of his first campaign press conferences.[16]

Eisenhower's dual emphases on keeping party unity and distinguishing himself from McCarthy collided, to his intense anger and chagrin, when against his instructions, the campaign organization scheduled him to make a September campaign stop in Wisconsin, where he found himself sharing the rear platform of the campaign train with McCarthy. Upon learning of the Wisconsin schedule, he had acceded to the suggestion of his more liberal advisors that he include in his Milwaukee speech a defense of Marshall. However, when the advance text of that speech reached Wisconsin, the state's Republican governor and Eisenhower's more politically pragmatic aides extracted from him an angry go-ahead to withdraw the Marshall passage rather than risk losing a critical state. The episode, which became known to the press, has stood ever since as the most highly publicized piece of evidence for the thesis that Eisenhower was unwilling to come to grips with McCarthy.[17]

Early Skirmishes and Accommodation Attempts

McCarthy's willingness to attack Truman was limitless. It was unclear whether he would turn his combative instincts on a chief executive of his own party, one who carried into office a Republican Congress, who pledged to sanitize the "mess in Washington," and who had been conciliatory to McCarthy personally and to his party's conservative wing. At first McCarthy's signals were mixed and gave Eisenhower some grounds for attempting to domesticate him.

The Republican-controlled Congress appointed McCarthy chairman of the Committee on Government Operations and of a body with a wholly open-ended title and jurisdiction, the Committee's Permanent Investigations Subcommittee, soon to be dubbed the "McCarthy Committee."* Armed with committee resources to augment his normal powers as a member of the upper chamber, McCarthy promptly resumed his search for Communist influence in the executive branch. He began his investigation with the International Information Agency (IIA), the body that administered the State Department's overseas information programs. In this as in other agencies he was quickly able to establish what he called his "loyal underground" consisting both of disgruntled former and current agency employees. McCarthy took aim first at the Voice of America (VOA) and the overseas information libraries. The VOA was subject to attack on its choice of sites for transmitters. In a typical hearing a witness would claim that a VOA decision on where to set up a transmitter had failed to enable American overseas broadcasts to reach the widest possible audience. McCarthy would then ask leading questions to insinuate that the choice was deliberate and intended to help the Soviet Union.

The question of the locations of transmitters is arcane; McCarthy found better headline material by investigating the government's overseas libraries, since their thousands of books inevitably included a few by alleged Communist sympathizers. These sympathizers constituted a broad, ill-defined category in that era when conservatives often

---

*I will refer to this body as a committee, since in 1953–54 the entire Committee on Government Operations for all public purposes was synonymous with the Permanent Investigation Subcommittee.

viewed Communist and liberal objectives as indistinguishable, and when in the not distant Popular Front phases of the Spanish Civil War and World War II many liberal writers had in fact sympathized with the American Communist party and the Soviet Union. Although a good number of them had subsequently renounced communism, they were still stigmatized by McCarthy for their earlier sympathies. Others who had not publicly renounced their allegiances were especially suited for bringing McCarthy attention, since he was able to subpoena them, knowing they would refuse to testify and he therefore could brand them "Fifth Amendment Communists."

Eisenhower and Dulles did not rise to defend the IIA, perhaps in part because they viewed it as an agency staffed with many liberal Democratic holdovers. When asked his reactions to McCarthy's attack on the agency, Dulles on February 27, 1953 said he welcomed "disclosures from Congressional inquiries that will help make [the State Department] more competent, loyal and secure,"[18] and Eisenhower, on March 5, after expressing his customary refusal to engage in personalities, reminded reporters of the constitutional "right of Congress to conduct such investigations as it sees fit," adding, "I don't believe it is really a proper thing for me to be discussing publicly a coordinate branch of government."*[19] He then remarked, "If ever I find that necessary, it will be through some changes of views."[20]

The *New York Times* took this watery caveat sufficiently seriously to headline a front-page story "President May Take Hand If Inquiries Imperil Amity," continuing that if McCarthy's hearings "reached a point of inviting international misunderstandings and difficulty," Eisenhower "might intervene." The wish, however, was only father to the act of interpretation in this case: the *Times*, in an editorial the previous day, had deplored McCarthy's "spectacular, free-wheeling assault" on the VOA and described it as more of an "inquisition than an investigation." (Later in the McCarthy affair Eisenhower, by giving

---

*Nevertheless, the president was discussing that coordinate branch in private, but he avoided publicly showing his hand. Following up the preinauguration Hotel Commodore meeting, in which he advised the cabinet of the need to wean congressional Republicans away from automatic opposition to the president,[21] Eisenhower used cabinet sessions and other meetings to press his team members to cultivate comfortable informal relations with the committees that oversaw and funded their operations.[22] And he personally used his formal weekly congressional leadership meetings, and informal personal contacts, to link the White House with congressional Republicans.

the press far more explicit signals, deliberately caused his "no-personalities" statements to be rephrased by the press as criticism of McCarthy.)

Although McCarthy eventually lost interest in the VOA investigation, neither this nor his more general attack on the State Department information program was without effect. By spring, numerous VOA employees had resigned or been reprimanded. Morale throughout the State Department was low. The IIA director, an Eisenhower loyalist and appointee, resigned, reportedly because of acute high blood pressure, a condition that could only have been aggravated by McCarthy's assaults. The director's chief deputy also resigned and wrote a bitter memoir[23] describing the indignity the agency suffered by exposure not only to McCarthy but also to his aides, Roy Cohn and G. David Schine. Both were in their mid-twenties and, uninhibited by lack of experience, they aped their boss's methods and arrogance. They would continue to be a problem only, however, if McCarthy refused to begin cooperating with the administration.

Eisenhower's official family was sharply split on whether it would be feasible to work with McCarthy. There were two slightly overlapping informal factions: those favoring accommodation and those advocating direct counterattack.[24] Foremost among the accommodationists was General Persons; as a career legislative liaison specialist, he was accustomed to working with Capitol Hill conservatives. Persons's main ally was an ex-Senator, Vice-President Nixon, whose career like McCarthy's had been sparked by Communist hunting. Those favoring counterattack included former members of New York Governor Dewey's staff, among them Hagerty and Appointments Secretary Thomas Stephens, and other Eastern internationalists such as Time Inc. executive C. D. Jackson.[25]

In the opening days of Eisenhower's administration, the efforts of his accommodationist aides seemed to bear fruit. Although he took on the IIA, McCarthy did yield to Nixon's entreaties that he not oppose former Harvard President James B. Conant's appointment as United States High Commissioner to Germany. On February 3, 1953, McCarthy wrote to Eisenhower explaining that although he opposed the nomination because Conant had made "innocent statements about Communist activities in education and about the presence of communism in his own [Harvard] faculty,"[26] he would not object to the appointment, because the ensuing controversy would serve Communist propaganda. General Persons passed a copy of McCarthy's letter to Appointments Secretary Stephens with a note that read "The President replied to the attached letter in a personal telephone conversation with Senator McCarthy. No further action is necessary."[27]

McCarthy's letter on Conant included the statement that he did not want an "all out fight" with Eisenhower. Before the end of March, however, he seemed about to belie this in two conflicts with the administration. One was over a nomination, and the other was over the constitutional issue of whether he was impinging on executive branch powers by negotiating himself with foreign powers. He was defeated on the nomination issue and arrived at a modus vivendi on the other.

The nomination in question was that of Charles E. ("Chip") Bohlen, Eisenhower's choice as ambassador to the Soviet Union. During the ratification process, McCarthy, for the first time since Eisenhower took office, in effect personally criticized him, by arguing that the president had sent to the Hill a key nomination without making himself aware of his nominee's background.[28] Bohlen, a distinguished Soviet specialist who entered the foreign service in 1929, had achieved sufficient eminence by World War II to be chosen as Roosevelt's interpreter and advisor on Soviet affairs at the Yalta conference. Eisenhower was well acquainted with him, since Bohlen served in the American Embassy in France when Eisenhower was NATO military commander.

McCarthy argued that as an aide to Eisenhower's Democratic predecessors, Bohlen was one of the "architects of disaster" who had blindly advanced Soviet power and that he was not an innocent architect—his loyalty file showed him to be a security risk. In impugning Bohlen's loyalty McCarthy made much of Dulles's acknowledgment, when he presented the nomination to the Foreign Relations Committee, that he, rather than the new State Department loyalty and security officer, Scott McLeod, had certified Bohlen's loyalty. Dulles explained that any file containing "derogatory" information had to be passed by the security officer to him—and, since the files often contained a hodgepodge of gossip, most did come before Dulles. McLeod's job was only to screen files, not to make final judgments about the credibility of their contents. McCarthy responded that the file contained such potent evidence against Bohlen that calling him a security risk was "putting it too weak." He went on to say he was sure that if Eisenhower would only take the time to examine the file, he would certainly withdraw the appointment.

Security files were not officially accessible to legislators, but it was plausible to believe that McCarthy had covert access to Bohlen's file, because McLeod was a close McCarthy friend. Without the knowledge of either Dulles or Eisenhower, this McCarthy ally had naïvely been appointed State Department loyalty and security officer by Donald Lourie, a former Quaker Oats president whom Dulles named to administer the department.

Eisenhower, convinced that McLeod had leaked an account of Bohlen's personnel file to McCarthy and acting in his typical behind-the-scenes fashion, urged Dulles to fire the insubordinate McLeod.[29] He relented, however, when Dulles, who was intensely interested in avoiding a clash with McCarthy, guaranteed to keep his loyalty and security officer in check. Dulles barred McLeod from testifying on the Bohlen nomination. Instead, he certified Bohlen's loyalty by arranging for Taft and Stevenson's running mate, John Sparkman, to examine summaries of Bohlen's file. The senators attested that Bohlen's record was unblemished. Asked in a press conference about Bohlen's qualifications, Eisenhower turned a very generally worded question to his purposes by countering McCarthy's implication that he was unfamiliar with the nominee and his record. The Bohlen nomination, he went out of his way to say, was an appointment "in which I was very deeply and personally concerned."

> I have known Mr. Bohlen for some years. I was once, at least, a guest in his home, and with his very charming family. I have played golf with him. I have listened to his philosophy. So far as I can see, he is the best qualified man for that post that I could find. That is the reason his name was sent to the Senate and the reason it stays there, because I believe, still, that he is the best qualified man we could find today.[30]

The next day Bohlen was confirmed—74 to 13—with Taft mustering the support of many conservative Republicans who otherwise would no doubt have voted with McCarthy. Four days later in a diary note

Eisenhower took a moment to reflect on his success in building an alliance with Taft:

I think it is scarcely too much to say that Senator Taft and I are becoming right good friends. This applies, also, to the mass of Republican senators, who in general will follow Taft's lead. In the contest on Bohlen's confirmation, eleven Republican senators voted against us. There were only two or three who surprised me by their actions; the others are the most stubborn and essentially small-minded examples of the extreme isolationist group in the party. I was surprised by the vote of Bricker and Goldwater. These two seemed to me a little more intelligent than the others, who seek to defend their position with the most specious kind of excuse and the most misleading kind of argument. In spite of this, Taft held the mass of Republicans squarely in line, and the Democrats, with the exception of two only voted solidly with us.[31]

McCarthy in this instance had been defeated rather than accommodated. Immediately after the Bohlen nomination was confirmed, when McCarthy again encroached on executive turf, Eisenhower returned, with some success, to the conciliatory mode.

On March 27, sounding as if he took it for granted that senators rather than the president initiated treaties and international agreements, McCarthy announced that he had negotiated an agreement with a Greek ship owners' group not to carry goods to Communist China. He had done this in secret, he blithely explained, because he did not want "interference" from the State and Defense departments.[32]

In short order McCarthy was in a televised exchange with State Department Mutual Security Administration Chief Harold Stassen, whose agency had been engaged in an extended series of country-to-country negotiations to curb trade between the European allies and China. Stassen charged that McCarthy had "undermined" the State Department's efforts to achieve agreements which by virtue of being between nations rather than between a senator and a private group would be enforceable.

Dulles was assigned to mediate the conflict. He met with McCarthy and after the session announced that he had explained to him "the dangers that would result if Congressional Committees entered in the field of foreign relations which is the exclusive jurisdiction of the Chief Executive." McCarthy acknowledged that he had not intended to interfere with executive power and that in the future he would report any information he had that might be useful in reaching international agreements to the "proper authorities." Dulles then conceded that since McCarthy's actions had only been efforts at persuasion, not attempts to exercise negotiating powers, they were in the public interest.

In response to queries about the status of McCarthy's "negotiations" and Stassen's charges, Eisenhower generated a veritable fogbank of legalisms and semantic niceties. McCarthy could not be faulted for "negotiating" with a foreign power, he told the reporters. McCarthy after all had not negotiated, because as a senator he did not have the *power* to negotiate. Q.E.D.

Not satisfied with this reply by syllogism, the newsmen pressed Eisenhower to take a position on Stassen's charge. Eisenhower turned to the lexicon. He was sure that Stassen had meant to use the word "infringe," since that would be what the senator had attempted if, in ignorance of the division of power between branches of the government, he had attempted a negotiation. If, however, McCarthy was (as he now claimed) only seeking to persuade the Greek shippers, he was exercising the right of all citizens to let their views be known.[33] This verbal legerdemain was a convenient way to treat a near confrontation as if it never had occurred. Stassen dutifully agreed he had meant to use the word "infringe." Editorials and headlines of the day, however, show that Eisenhower also had left the impression that he would not defend a leading associate such as Stassen against McCarthy, much less the many lowly State Department officials McCarthy had maligned. Eisenhower's language had been a double-edged instrument— one blade had cut off a controversy with McCarthy, the other had undercut an articulate Eisenhower supporter.[34] This, however, was the last negotiated agreement between McCarthy and the administration, apart from minor instances of give-and-take between Persons and McCarthy to seek the latter's vote on occasional roll calls.

Strategy, Organization, and Program Planning

Eisenhower's prime preoccupations during his first months in office included seeking to live up to such campaign pledges as ending the Korean conflict, cutting the budget, and cleaning up the "Washington mess." During this time he also framed a strategy for dealing with McCarthy, which he enunciated in his diary and in letters to friends. It was a strategy he later modified and augmented, but to which he basically remained true until McCarthy's influence crumbled. And it was a much tougher strategy than is implied in the passive, genteel-sounding phrase attributed to him: "I will not—I refuse—to get into the gutter" with McCarthy.

Before the Greek ships episode reached its conclusion, in the same April 1 private diary entry expressing his satisfaction with Taft's co-operation in the Bohlen affair, Eisenhower briefly states his view of McCarthy's prime motivation and acknowledges the mischief McCarthy was causing. "Senator McCarthy," he wrote, "is, of course, so anxious for headlines that he is prepared to go to any extreme in order to secure some mention of his name in the public press. His actions create trouble on the Hill with members of his party; they irritate, frustrate, and infuriate members of the Executive Department." He goes on to state in positive terms his policy of non-confrontation, an approach in diametrical opposition to that of the Truman administration's mode of responding to McCarthy's charges: *"I really believe that nothing will be so effective in combating this particular kind of trouble-making as to ignore him. This he cannot stand."*[35] (Emphasis added.)

Eisenhower was consistently challenged by Democrats and by liberal and middle-of-the-road editorialists to come directly and publicly to grips with McCarthy. The same demand was made by more and more of his closest personal supporters and even by his brother Milton.[36] He replied by expatiating further on his strategy of seeking to impede McCarthy by denying him the kind of publicity that personal exchange with the president would provide and indicating how he proposed to advance that strategy.

Writing his boyhood friend Everett Hazlett, he elaborated on the point in his April 11 private diary entry about McCarthy's need for publicity with a general discussion of how agitators thrive on publicity.

I think that the average honorable individual cannot understand to what lengths certain politicians would go for publicity. They have learned a simple truth of American life. This is that the most vicious kind of attack from one element always creates a very great popularity, amounting to almost hero worship, in an opposite fringe of society. Because of this, as you well know, Huey Long had his idolators. Every attack on him increased their number (an expression of the under-dog complex) and enhanced the fervor of his avowed supporters.[37]

This did not mean he believed McCarthy's challenge had to be ignored. Rather, Eisenhower continued, it would be possible to defeat a McCarthy by using "the positive approach." One "positive" tack, which became a regular Eisenhower procedure as the McCarthy affair unfolded, was to use "the indirect defense accomplished through condemnation of unfair methods." A second was to frame and execute policies that would make McCarthy's activities unnecessary and would otherwise diminish his importance. His specific reference was to follow the policy of adhering to "American principles in trials and investigations." But increasingly Eisenhower was able to use a broader range of his policies in employing "the positive approach" to deflating McCarthy, drawing on the public acclaim he received for his foreign policy actions and on the need of members of his party to get behind his general domestic program as a means of making the strongest possible appeal to the electorate in the 1954 mid-term election and to link other Republican leaders to him rather than McCarthy.

In a letter to General Electric Board Chairman Philip Reed he adds a further twist to his explanation of why as president he should not attack McCarthy by name. Leaving no doubt that he wants to see McCarthy's influence ended and does not seek to discourage others from criticizing McCarthy, he stresses that his own status makes personal reply inappropriate: "The President of the United States has a position that gives his name a terrific headline value. Therefore if he points his finger at any particular individual—meaning to name anyone specifically—he automatically gives to that individual an increased publicity value." But he explains, he could respond by persisting "in my support of a sane, decent presentation of America's case both to our own people and in every country of the globe."[38] Eisenhower provides details of this latter approach in a letter to Harry Bullis of General Mills, another of his correspondents from the business world who lamented McCarthy's influence. The letter specifies continuing "to pursue a steady, positive policy in foreign relations, in legal procedures in cleaning out the insecure and the disloyal, and in all other areas where McCarthy seems to take such a specific and personal interest."[39]

Eisenhower's comment to Bullis that an appropriate counterforce to McCarthy would be the establishment of effective procedures in the "areas where McCarthy seems to take such a specific and personal interest" reflected actions he had made known to his colleagues in his first cabinet meeting after taking office. Under the heading "security," the minutes (which at that stage were kept in the form of very brief summaries) record that "A discussion on security standards for Government personnel centered on the need for simplifying present procedures, protection of the rights of employees, personnel of security board, emphasis on the term security rather than loyalty, and confidence of Congress and the country in the effectiveness of the Administration's actions."[40]

The security-loyalty distinction was central to Eisenhower's program. Framing this program rather than planning anti-McCarthy strategy was the principal way Eisenhower used the formal face of his organizational leadership to eliminate McCarthy's influence. To Truman's criterion that public servants must not be *loyalty* risks, Eisenhower added that they not possess personal qualities that might endanger national *security*. Grounds for refusing or terminating federal employment included homosexuality (an invitation to blackmail), heavy drinking (a possible cause of loquaciousness), and indiscriminate talkativeness (in the argot of the day, "blabbermouthing"). The point was further hammered home in his first Legislative Leadership meeting. Explaining his shift from the litmus of loyalty to that of security, he added a point that he returned to repeatedly in stressing that McCarthy's ostensible goals were being well met by his administration, that working for the government is a privilege rather than a right.

Eisenhower told the legislative leaders that he would proceed vigor-

171

ously to establish an adequate security program.[41] By April 27 he promulgated the program. McCarthy was one of the participants in the White House briefing and pronounced that the procedure was "pretty darn good . . . a tremendous improvement over the old procedure."[42]

The procedure was an "improvement" over Truman's in a narrowly strategic sense. It enabled the new administration to provide "evidence" that it *was* cleaning up Washington as it had promised and was doing so without McCarthy's assistance. The new program did not turn up many alleged Communist sympathizers, but lumping them with homosexuals, alcoholics, and other "unreliables" enabled the administration periodically to cite statistics on increasing numbers of "security risks" who had been denied government employment. Eisenhower took care not to say that the people enumerated were disloyal, but on a number of occasions his associates quoted the new security risk statistics in ways suggesting that an Augean stable of subversives had been swept out of government.

The security program had not been instituted simply to serve as a counterforce to McCarthy. The bulk of administration officials—and certainly Eisenhower himself—felt that internal security measures had been inadequate in the previous administration. Preoccupation with internal security was in the air. Few Americans doubted that domestic Communists and their fellow travelers were potential agents of the Soviet Union or that Communist agents would fail to exploit "perverts" or "blabbermouths" in order to learn government secrets.[43]

In cabinet discussions, many of Eisenhower's aides gradually showed that the consequences of the new program were problematic. They spent much time seeking ways to disprove the critics' charges that they were merely playing a "numbers game." Eisenhower warned his colleagues not to treat employees who had been discharged for other reasons as security risks. Several of his department heads indicated that their agencies were suffering from the overload created by the requirement that the records of all federal personnel be reviewed. Members of the administration, notably Dulles, began to report what critics of the security program had been predicting all along—that it would produce severe costs in terms of the morale of public servants and even their continuing willingness to serve in government.[44]

As with his security program, but less directly, Eisenhower's foreign and domestic policy programs (though not designed for that purpose) were also instrumental in contributing to the senator's downfall. Immediately after the election, Eisenhower had ordered his Budget Bureau Chief-designate, Joseph Dodge, to begin work on plans for reducing Truman's planned and proposed expenditures. By the spring of 1953 he had committed key members of his congressional party to back the cuts and the foreign and domestic policy legislation he and his aides framed as part of the budget review process. By the end of his first year in office, he had an entire 1954 legislative program that could be defended in the upcoming mid-term elections as the party's and his.[45] In 1954, when McCarthy himself became the object of investigation, Eisenhower (even while insisting that judging McCarthy was the legislative branch's affair) argued for responsible hearing procedures, thus disadvantaging McCarthy, who was expert at defending himself through disruptive action in hearings. Eisenhower advanced his argument not in terms of the need to combat McCarthy, however, but rather in terms of the need to resolve the hearings on McCarthy in order to get on with the business of passing the program.

At a cabinet meeting on March 27, 1953, Eisenhower made his first and only general utterance that appears in that body's minutes on administration policy toward McCarthy. He made clear, to any of those who were in doubt, his unfavorable personal view of McCarthy; however, he reinforced his emphasis on building up his own center of strength in Congress. He preceded the official meeting by remarking on a letter that illustrated the substantial correspondence he was receiving "on the attitude he should take toward Senator McCarthy," and the minutes note, "The President added his own thoughts on the matter to the effect that he should not attack an individual but that he and the cabinet should use their influence to strengthen the position of Congressional leaders vis-a-vis extremist minorities."[46]

These observations left room for those who wanted to speak against McCarthy to do so but tended to discourage cabinet-based rather than congressionally mediated anti-McCarthy activity. They *did* in effect bar cabinet members from *supporting* McCarthy, if any were so inclined. These brief remarks were as far as Eisenhower was prepared to go in the formal context of the cabinet meeting in discussing anti-McCarthy strategy. Moreover, when later he shifted to covert battle against McCarthy, it emphatically was not in his interest to risk leaks of his secret actions, even in a normally leak-free cabinet. Thus the formal side of Eisenhower-style organization had its impact on McCarthy largely through the "positive" presidential program. It was the informal face of his style of organization that came into play when he finally shifted to framing an assault on McCarthy that went beyond avoiding giving the senator the aura of a brave underdog.

The Lines Are Drawn: Early Skirmishes

No sooner had Eisenhower committed to his diary on April 1 the observation that not mentioning McCarthy would deny him publicity than McCarthy began demonstrating his ability to remain in the limelight without such assistance from Eisenhower. Cohn and Schine departed on a notorious two-and-a-half-week jaunt through Europe, delivering off-the-cuff statements on subversive books in Information Service libraries, tangling with various overseas information officials, and eliciting derisory news stories from American and European journalists who covered their mini-grand tour. They also helped force the resignation of State Department information officials, such as Theodore Kaghan, an ex-radical who, although now an effective anti-Communist, had called Cohn and Schine "junketeering gumshoes."[47]

The State Department's response to McCarthy's inquiries into its information program exceeded mere accommodation. During the winter and spring of 1953 the department issued to its information libraries a bewildering array of orders about what books should be on the shelves. The July 10 cabinet meeting produced as many ideas as there were discussants, ranging from Defense Secretary Wilson's suggestion to eliminate the libraries to Dulles and Stassen's recommendation that the libraries contain books that an American domestic library might hold, but avoid acquiring new works that were Communist propaganda tracts.[48] The formal cabinet meeting often was a good occasion for clarifying issues, but Eisenhower's colleagues were not up to the subtleties of clarifying the matter of "subversive books," perhaps because the issue had already become profoundly muddled by recent events.*

By mid-summer, journalists who canvassed efforts in the field by State Department librarians to comply with the changing guidelines, found not only that books had been removed from shelves, but also that with consummate insensitivity to the symbolism of free and open expression, some librarians had even burned offending books. Some of the books removed more or less loosely reflected the Popular Front intellectual currents that prevailed in many writings of the 1930s and 1940s. But inevitably there were anomalies. An author alleged to be a Communist had compiled a humor anthology which was banned. The wholly nonpolitical detective classics of Dashiel Hammett *(The Maltese Falcon, The Thin Man)* had been expunged because Hammett was a "Fifth Amendment Communist." One library simply removed all works critical of Nationalist China.[50]

On June 14, Eisenhower, well aware that the book policy was the subject of international derision, finally struck back, interjecting in his remarks to a Dartmouth College commencement audience a statement unmistakably directed at McCarthy, though as usual not mentioning his name:

Don't join the book burners. Don't think you are going to conceal faults by concealing evidence that they ever existed. Don't be afraid to go in your library and read every book, as long as that document does not offend our ideas of decency. That should be the only censorship.[51]

The location, a venerable institution of higher learning, was appropriate, as was the day of the week, Sunday, the traditional occasion for public remarks designed to get headlines.†

---

*As early as April the department had changed its instructions to libraries three times and so incoherently that sensible discourse seemed impossible. One directive prohibited use of books by "Communists, fellow travelers *et cetera.*" An outraged field worker wired back in defiant mockery that he planned to continue the practice of quoting "words of Communists, fellow travelers, *et cetera,* to expose them or make them eat their own words or in furtherance of the American national interest."[49] Shortly thereafter, *"et cetera"* was deleted from the directive as a class of book writers.

†Sundays produce little "hard news" and therefore the week's press coverage often is framed by utterances made to catch Monday's front pages.

Monday papers everywhere reported this presidential call for intellectual freedom. Four days earlier in his tour, also choosing his location carefully, Eisenhower had addressed a Young Republican's convention at Mount Rushmore, listing ten major administration achievements to date, including reduction in the size of the federal government, greater efficiency, a more realistic defense posture, and an attack on "the problem of internal security with a vigor long overdue."[52] With this preparation, enunciated at a shrine of American patriotic symbolism, it was timely to use the Dartmouth forum for attacking McCarthy's excesses.

But the effect of Monday's headlines was virtually obliterated in the haze of Eisenhower's Wednesday press conference. His thoughts seemed to be no more clearly organized than the cabinet's debate had proved to be at the July 10 meeting. The conference began with a question from the senior White House correspondent, the Associated Press's Merriman Smith, who noted that many people took his Dartmouth speech "as being critical of a school of thought represented by Senator McCarthy." Eisenhower chided, "Now Merriman, you have been around me long enough to know I never talk personalities." He then went on to make a series of strong assertions about the inappropriateness of censoring "extreme" viewpoints: "I believe the United States is strong enough to expose the world to its differing viewpoints." And, to a follow-up question, he replied: "Let's educate ourselves if we are going to run a free government, and let's don't be afraid of its weaknesses as well as its strength." He argued that the failure before World War II of many Americans to read *Mein Kampf* and take it seriously had contributed to inattentiveness to the menace of nazism and asked the reporters whether they had taken the pains to inform themselves about Soviet strategy and purposes by reading Stalin's *Problems of Leninism.*

But seemingly almost at random he interspersed anti-Communist qualifications in his remarks. Many of them were completely consistent with the cold war axioms shared by almost everyone in American public life at the time. Nevertheless in allowing himself such digressions he put the intent of his Dartmouth remarks in doubt. He stressed that in talking about the "right of dissemination of knowledge" he was not referring to "any document or other kind of thing that attempts to persuade or propagandize Americans into Communism." He took the press conference as an occasion to support court decisions sentencing American Communists to prison because "they took orders from a foreign government." And he said of overseas library procurement policy that he did not want to "propagate Communist belief by using governmental money to do it." He even said that his reference in the Dartmouth speech to book burning did not preclude consigning books to fire—the term "book burning" was a metaphor for fear of knowledge.[53]

To the degree that Eisenhower's habitual caution and qualification in press conferences had been instrumental in this case, the effect was, as the Americans for Democratic Action chairman later put it, to "half retract" the original statement.[54] Monday's headlines were vitiated by those in the Wednesday evening and Thursday morning papers, including a story in Eisenhower's own favorite, the New York *Herald Tribune*, suggesting that he had withdrawn his objection to book burning.

Because combat with McCarthy was neither Eisenhower's only nor even prime preoccupation during the two years that ended with the December 2, 1954, vote of condemnation, his increasingly frequent anti-McCarthy forays were dependent on a quite delicate approach to selective delegation to pro- and anti-accommodationist aides. It was to hold back from personally initiating actions, but rather to monitor the activities of each faction and lend his own support to one or the other when he found it propitious to do so.

In July 1953 McCarthy provided the kind of opening that permitted direct counterattack, and several of Eisenhower's accommodationist aides paved the way. McCarthy hired as a committee aide publicist J.B. Matthews who had recently committed to print the view that "the largest single group supporting the Communist apparatus today is Protestant clergymen." Unlike State Department personnel, Protestant clergymen were not fair game for indiscriminate allegations. Moreover, they were scarcely without public supporters and for that matter could speak for themselves. (The charge provided the theme for many anti-McCarthy sermons the next Sunday.)

McCarthy first defended Matthews's appointment but, sensing the intensity of response, quickly showed signs of backing off. There followed something of a Mack Sennett chase scene, in which Sherman

177

Adams, anti-McCarthy speech writer Emmet Hughes, and Deputy Attorney General William Rogers (until then an accommodationist but by this time prepared to see McCarthy taken down a peg) arranged to have the National Conference of Christians and Jews dispatch to Eisenhower a protest condemning attacks on the clergy and drafted a reply for him agreeing with the conference's statement. Eisenhower edited the draft, releasing it just in time to make the wire service ticker before McCarthy's announcement of Matthews's resignation, leaving the impression that Matthews had been fired as a result of the president's intervention.[55] This episode, in which hidden-hand wire-pulling was coordinated with an instrumental statement framed in a way to undermine McCarthy but without "engaging in personalities," anticipates the strategic logic Eisenhower would use extensively in 1954 when McCarthy again put himself in a position of vulnerability.

Seizing the National Security Initiative: A Thwarted Foray

Later in the year the administration sought to counter McCarthy with another kind of initiative, but the effort backfired. On November 6, 1953, Attorney General Brownell told an audience of Chicago executives that the administration had uncovered an extreme case of laxness in national security during the Truman administration. President Truman, he claimed, had been reliably informed that Treasury Department aide Harry Dexter White was a sometime participant in a spy ring of government officials who provided information to the Soviet Union. Truman nevertheless had allowed White to be appointed to a position with the International Monetary Fund (IMF) and took no action against him. White held this position until 1946 when, three days after having been accused by the House Un-American Activities Committee of having Communist connections, he died of a heart attack.

Truman replied, "As soon as we found White was wrong, we fired him." The Democratic national chairman followed, arguing that, since McCarthy had blamed Republican losses in a number of 1953 election races on the administration's failure to establish a conspicuous program of uncovering domestic subversion, Brownell clearly was now seeking to remedy this "defect" by his own exercise in McCarthyism, stooping to release "a five year old story about a dead person."*[56]

Brownell's decision to publicize the White-Truman matter *was* an attempt to counter McCarthy, if not to draw attention from the recent election losses. Brownell's aides had turned up 1945 and 1946 Justice Department files from FBI Director J. Edgar Hoover warning Truman that White was a Communist, but Truman nevertheless had appointed him to the IMF. Brownell discussed the finding with Adams and Hagerty, arguing that he should make it public, and then received Eisenhower's approval to do so.

Sherman Adams, in his memoirs, describes Eisenhower as having accepted Brownell's rationale that his announcement would "take away some of the glamor of the McCarthy stage play."[58] Brownell, interviewed in 1981, remembers his motivation as a desire to show that in contrast to McCarthy's practice of issuing undocumented charges, the administration could uncover and correct reliably documented abuses. But, he quickly adds, "I underestimated the explosiveness of the Communist issue."[59]

At his November 11 press conference, a session almost totally devoted to the White case, Eisenhower said Brownell had told him no more than that he had information about "a man named White" that would illustrate the laxity of past security procedures, and he had not mentioned Truman. Brownell remembers that he had informed Eisenhower of Truman's involvement, but also that he and Eisenhower shared the view that the president "was most effective if he kept tremendous public support and didn't get beaten down by the day-to-day fights. He wanted the Cabinet members to be in the front line and take the blows."[60] Brownell accepted the blame when the case backfired, as it quickly did.

It backfired in two ways: Truman and his allies turned the tables effectively by getting thorough news coverage for their charge that the administration was seeking to outdo McCarthy; and McCarthy himself

---

*Brownell and his chief associate have since said that the discovery of 1945 and 1946 FBI correspondence to Truman on White, which provided the basis for Brownell's speech, was inadvertent. White's file had turned up in the course of putting the department's central file in order by recalling files, a number of which had been checked out for many years.[57]

managed to make the headlines by describing the former president as "a liar." In addition, another of the professional anti-Communists, the chairman of the House Un-American Activities Committee, threatened to subpoena Truman, an act that would have been unprecedented in the annals of former presidents and fatal for Eisenhower's relations with the Democrats, whose support he relied on frequently.

Eisenhower was less than composed at the November 11 press conference. In contrast to his usual good cheer, he seemed on the verge of losing his temper. Brownell, he maintained, had not indicated to him that Truman was responsible for the case he planned to disclose. When the reporters asked why the Chicago Executives Club had been the forum for releasing this information, Eisenhower conveyed the impression that he knew little about the matter, telling them to ask Brownell. (Brownell had been lying low, refusing to see the press.) In a response that was more a profession of patriotic faith in the presidency than a personal vote of confidence in Truman, Eisenhower added that he was sure that no American President knowingly would act against the national interest and that he did not favor attempts to subpoena Truman.*[61]

Truman received free national air time to reply to Brownell. It is "now evident," Truman declared, "that the present Administration has fully embraced for political advantage McCarthyism," a term he went on to explain that had come to mean "the use of the 'big lie' . . . in the name of Americanism and security."[63]

McCarthy moved faster than the administration, getting air time to respond to Truman, but he used the opportunity to criticize Eisenhower as well. While Eisenhower's record on communism was better than Truman's, McCarthy granted, the president had erred in a recent press conference when he said that Communists in government would not be a 1954 campaign issue, because by then his administration's successful loyalty and security procedures would have made the issue moot. McCarthy also took issue with Eisenhower for not coming to grips with

*The morning of his news conference Eisenhower telephoned Brownell to coordinate his statement to the press. Thinking out loud, he considered the possibility of saying he had known the FBI reports went to the White House, but not whether Truman had seen them. He was now sure that Truman *had*, he acknowledged, but made it evident that he disapproved of subpoenaing Truman. Therefore he would (in Mrs. Whitman's paraphrase of the phone call) "simply state he thinks the country should be disposed to take Truman's word for whatever his memory is, and that he sees no point in putting him before [an] investigation."[62]

the Chinese Communists. In not securing the release of nine hundred American soldiers alleged still to be in Communist hands, Eisenhower had failed to "liquidate the foulest bankruptcy of the Democratic Administration." What he claimed was needed was a stronger version of McCarthy's own agreement with the Greek shippers: a blockade of China, barring the trade by other nations with the PRC.[64]

Eisenhower and Dulles then came forth on December 1 and 2 with a pair of closely coordinated statements billed by the newspapers as "replies to McCarthy." Dulles attacked attempts to persuade the government to use "threats and intimidation to compel" American allies "to do our bidding. . . . We do not want weak or subservient allies."[65] The next day Eisenhower endorsed Dulles's remarks. Communism in government would not be a 1954 campaign issue, Eisenhower reiterated, because "the public . . . will wish to commend the efficiency of the Administration in eliminating this menace," an accomplishment that would be made without cost to civil liberties.[66]

More than his oblique rejoinder to McCarthy, it was a foreign policy action Eisenhower took in December that most effectively nullified the effects of McCarthy's attack. In an exceptionally well-received speech of December 8 to the United Nations General Assembly, Eisenhower offered to join the Soviet Union in making resources available for research on peaceful uses for atomic energy. This Atoms for Peace speech—one of the rhetorical landmarks of Eisenhower's eight years in office—reflected his conviction that international control of atomic power eventually would have to be established, a conviction that is even more evident in Eisenhower's private than in his public utterances.

Reflecting on the effect of Eisenhower's message, Arthur Krock wrote in the *New York Times* on December 10 that McCarthy's critique of administration foreign policy no longer seemed of any consequence. "If that challenge and its maker entered the thoughts of some who saw and listened to the President yesterday," Krock commented, "both must have shrunk to their true proportions which are nothing like what fear, indignation and shrewd publicity have made them appear to be."[67] Later that month the Gallup polls showed Eisenhower's popularity ratings to have risen to 66 percent approval, 20 percent disapproval, and 14 percent no opinion from a 58–25–17 rating of late November.[68]

181

McCarthy Becomes Vulnerable to Hidden-Hand Leadership

By the end of 1953, Eisenhower still had not deprived McCarthy of headlines. Eisenhower had studiously avoided following Truman's precedents of acting in ways that proved to bolster McCarthy's appeal. He abjured statements that by directly maligning McCarthy would give him an underdog sympathy or would add to his credibility by fostering the assumption that if McCarthy warranted presidential attention, his charges could not be without foundation. And by avoiding a direct break with McCarthy, Eisenhower maintained his party's control of an essentially evenly divided Senate.* Nevertheless, McCarthy was so capable of stirring supporters to his defense and stimulating public figures other than Eisenhower to engage in personalities with him that a presidential strategy of seeking to neutralize McCarthy by denying him the dignity of direct replies from the White House was not sufficient unless supplemented.

In 1954 Eisenhower went beyond his indirect critiques and no-personalities approach. He held his fire until McCarthy became open to attack by *any* right-thinking American. McCarthy recklessly opened himself to such an attack when, in effect replaying the 1953 controversy over the loyalty of Protestant ministers, he took on another pillar of national virtue and respectability, the United States Army. He was especially vulnerable because he struck at the army in a way that seemed to involve a self-interested game of extortion.

In the summer of 1953 Eisenhower learned from Army Secretary Robert Stevens that McCarthy's next target was subversion in the army. He advised Stevens to be sure not to allow McCarthy's investigators to interfere with the functioning of the army. If abuses were discovered, it would be necessary to correct them and apologize for them, but otherwise it was essential to be stalwart.[70] Stevens, a gentlemanly

---

*Many Republican senators continued to be wary of McCarthy, who in January 1954 registered a Gallup support score of 50-29-21. Eisenhower's own January 1954 Gallup rating, reported later in the month, was 71-19-10—higher both than McCarthy's and his own December 1953 score.[69]

textile manufacturer, was no match for a political gutter fighter and proved to be highly pliable under investigation and susceptible to repeated attempts by Cohn and McCarthy to secure special favors from the army for Schine, who had never served his obligatory military service.

Schine was tapped by the Selective Service system in mid-1953. Beginning in July, Cohn, McCarthy, or staff aide Francis Carr, sought first to get Schine a commission; and when that failed, to have him assigned to Communist-detecting intelligence work; and when that too failed, to see that he had special privileges in basic training. Meanwhile, in September 1953, McCarthy told the press that he was in pursuit of subversion in the military. Then he closed in on the Army Signal Corps radar research laboratory at Fort Monmouth, N.J. He and Cohn continued investigating the army while at the same time exerting pressure in Schine's behalf, through January 1954.

Drawing on the testimony (or refusal to testify) of a number of people who had been associated with Monmouth in World War II, McCarthy extracted the admission of Army Secretary Robert Stevens that there might have been wartime spying at Monmouth. Simultaneously he issued charges—none of which held up—that numerous current employees at the fort were security risks. His short-run impact on Fort Monmouth morale was considerable. McCarthy's actions led a compliant Department of the Army to suspend thirty-three Fort Monmouth employees, most of whom were later restored to duty. There was no clearly discernible pattern to the news stories about Fort Monmouth during the autumn and winter, perhaps because much of the "real" agenda concerned private exchanges between the McCarthy staff and Stevens and his aides in connection with Schine.

On January 21, 1954, Stevens's principal intermediary with McCarthy, department counsel John Adams, sought help from Eisenhower's three top political strategists, Attorney General Brownell, United Nations Ambassador Lodge, and Sherman Adams. These four, accompanied by Gerald Morgan of General Persons's legislative liaison staff, met in Brownell's office. The army counsel wanted advice about how to respond to an action McCarthy was planning that would require the department to break its rule protecting the confidentiality of loyalty and security board members. McCarthy wanted to subpoena them, but on the Eisenhower strategists' advice, the army persuaded the Republicans on his committee to block this move.

The meeting with John Adams had far greater significance for Eisenhower's planners, however. John Adams regaled them with a detailed account of the influence-seeking on Schine's behalf that had begun the previous summer. The president's aides immediately recognized that the record of special favors sought for Schine was powerful ammunition. At Sherman Adams's suggestion, the army counsel set to work preparing a chronology itemizing influence attempts, a document that ignited the army-McCarthy hearings.*[71]

With his usual ingenuity in unearthing new issues, McCarthy found another by the end of January. He learned of a loyalty-security gaffe in Camp Kilmer, N.J. Irving Peress, a dentist who was inducted under the doctor's draft law, had refused to sign a loyalty oath but, nevertheless, was commissioned and promoted to major before all of his personnel records converged; his discharge was then ordered. McCarthy interrogated Peress just a day before his discharge, eliciting from him the familiar Fifth Amendment plea.

Who had promoted Peress? McCarthy called Camp Kilmer's commanding officer, General Ralph Zwicker, to testify. Confronting Zwicker in a one-man hearing, he commenced an abusive interrogation. He asked Zwicker whether the officers responsible for promoting Peress should be removed from the army. Zwicker replied that as base commander and neither a maker of policy nor a loyalty-security official, "That is not a question for me to decide." McCarthy retorted: "You are ordered to answer it, General. You are an employee of the people." Before the exchange was over, McCarthy, as the transcript he released after the hearing showed, had suggested that Zwicker who had been decorated for heroism on D-day, did not have "the brains of a five-year-old-child" and was "not fit to wear" his uniform.

Stevens ordered Zwicker not to testify further. "I am confident," he announced, "that the American people do not believe in unwar-

---

*Stevens was to testify on the basis of the chronology that there had been "more than 65 phone calls and 19 meetings between army and committee representatives on Schine. Requests on Schine's behalf included those for direct commission, special assignment, relief from duty such as KP, extra time off, and special visitor privileges. Schine got 15 passes between November 10, 1953, and January 16, 1954; most other inductees got 3."[72]

ranted abuse of our officers any more than I do." Most of the press treated Stevens's action sympathetically and played up McCarthy's bullying. But when McCarthy ordered Stevens himself to testify, the Republican members of the subcommittee plus Knowland and Nixon met with Stevens. They warned him that McCarthy would convert the issue from abuse of Zwicker to the army's faulty procedure on Peress. As one of them put it, "Joe will murder you."

Nevertheless, they made it possible for McCarthy to do just that. On February 23 Stevens lunched—he thought confidentially—in a Senate office with McCarthy and two members of his committee, Karl Mundt and Everett Dirksen, to arrange a compromise. Mundt drafted the resulting "Memorandum of Understanding" which included Stevens's agreement to reverse himself, permitting further testimony by Zwicker and agreeing to release "the names of everyone involved in the promotion and honorable discharge of Peress" and require them to testify.

On leaving the "secret" meeting, a dumbfounded Stevens encountered a corridor full of reporters ready to send out dispatches on his "surrender."* Further, since the reporters knew that Nixon was in the next office to the one in which Stevens had met with McCarthy, Mundt, and Dirksen, they presented the story in terms of a surrender by the administration, not just Stevens.[73] The *New York Times,* for example, headlined its story "Stevens Bows to McCarthy at Administration Behest. Will Yield Data on Peress." Deeply distressed, Stevens called Press Secretary Hagerty and offered to resign. Hagerty, who increasingly acted as Eisenhower's agent in a covert war with McCarthy, wrote in his diary for that day, "We were sure dumb. Someone let Stevens walk right into a bear trap and now I'll have to work like hell to get him out."[74]

There followed a flurry of remarkably successful activity by Eisenhower and his aides to salvage Stevens and remedy the damage caused by his signing of the "Memorandum of Understanding." On February 25 Eisenhower explained to Lucius Clay, who phoned from New York, that Stevens "in a state of hysteria and shock" had been deliberately misled by McCarthy. It was McCarthy, Eisenhower said, who now

*The reporters were primed by someone on the Hill. Whether it was the Committee Republicans or others (such as McCarthy) who informed them of the meeting has never been established.

needed to be "shocked."[75] The day before, he had instructed Lodge to convey suggestions to Stevens about how to deal with McCarthy.[76] To Hagerty, he fulminated, "This guy McCarthy is going to get in trouble over this. . . . My friends tell me it won't be long before McCarthy starts using my name instead of Stevens's. He wants to be President. He's the last guy in the world who'll ever get there if I have anything to say."[77]

Eisenhower set to work. He held one of his meetings with Everett Dirksen, who not only became Eisenhower's informal Senate Republican leader after Taft's death, but also was on the McCarthy Committee. They discussed substantive and procedural measures for salvaging the situation. One outcome of the meeting was Dirksen's agreement to seek a change in committee rules that would require a majority vote in order to issue subpoenas, depriving McCarthy of his capacity to run unannounced, one-man hearings.[78] Eisenhower also instructed General Persons and Jack Martin, a former Taft aide on Persons's staff, to devise a plan to persuade the subcommittee's Republicans to sign an expression of confidence in Stevens and an agreement that all army officers called to testify would be treated with respect.[79]

McCarthy refused to agree to sign the statement, but another course of action was available. A congressional-administration team, including Hagerty, Dirksen, Adams, Stevens, Nixon, Bernard Shanley, Roger Kyes, Fred Seaton, Persons, and Gerald Morgan drafted a statement for Stevens's delivery stressing that he had not surrendered to McCarthy and that he would defend army personnel. Eisenhower privately edited the statement, strengthening it. Then he had Stevens issue it from the White House for maximum impact.[80]

Stevens read to the press on February 25 the stout affirmation, "I shall never accede to the abuse of Army personnel [or to] them being brow-beaten or humiliated. From the assurances which I have received from members of the subcommittee, I am confident that they will not permit such conditions to develop in the future." He concluded by promising that in the event of abuses, "I shall once again take all steps at my disposal to protect the rights of individuals in this department."[81] Hagerty announced that Eisenhower had seen the statement and "he approves it one hundred percent." The next morning's *New York Times* headline read "President Backs Stevens, Who Bars Browbeating."

On the day of Stevens's statement the Republican Senate Policy Committee voted unanimously to initiate a study of investigating-committee guidelines. Press interpretations stressed that the study was aimed at requiring majority votes in issuing subpoenas, thus ending the kind of hearing in which McCarthy had interrogated Zwicker.[82] Signs of closer vigilance over McCarthy continued to appear. A February 28 *New York Times* story, for example, reported that Eisenhower had asked the Republicans on McCarthy's committee to attend hearings, even if they had other major business demands. The story began "Senator Joseph McCarthy's days as a one-man investigating committee appeared to be numbered today partly because of the intervention of President Eisenhower."

Many administration officials provided the press with material for background stories. On February 25, for example, Nixon, in an off-the-record interview told one of the capital's most influential journalists, Arthur Krock of the *New York Times,* about Cohn and McCarthy's influence-seeking activities, revealing to him the existence of a file "two inches thick" of reports on these activities. The plan, Nixon said, was to use this evidence to coerce McCarthy into ceasing his forays against the administration. Krock's interview provides an added key item of information. Nixon reported what Lodge, Brownell, and Adams were to remember in the 1980s—Eisenhower was well aware of the Cohn-Schine abuses and was countenancing the strategy of using them as the vehicle for attacking McCarthy.[83]

Eisenhower's Covert Anti-McCarthy Campaign: The Critical Month

On the morning of Monday, March 1, 1954, Eisenhower used the formal setting of his official meeting with the Legislative Leadership to launch a sequence of actions to respond to the indignities Stevens

187

and Zwicker had undergone and, more broadly, to lay the groundwork for a campaign against McCarthy. After reminding the leaders of the urgency of enacting the party program he turned to consider the major impediment to that effort, the army-McCarthy affair. Noting that the affair would prompt questions at his Wednesday press conference, he urged the leaders to "help the Administration get a better handling of things like this." Stevens, he pointed out, had apologized and made clear that promotions such as Peress's would not recur. Nevertheless the Republicans on the Hill had allowed Stevens to be drawn into the luncheon meeting, had persuaded him to sign the "Memorandum of Understanding," and had led him to believe the meeting would be off-the-record.

Eisenhower forewarned the congressmen that he would tell the press he recognized the right of Congress to investigate, but "we can't defeat Communism by destroying the things in which we believe." The leaders all appeared to agree with House Majority Leader Halleck's description of "the present controversy" as "a bad fight among Republicans"—one that, worse yet, had the potential of unraveling into a "televised fight between Republicans." Knowland said he was appalled that the army had permitted the Peress slipup, but that he and other Republican senators "were trying to protect Secretary Stevens from a bad situation" and "were interested in protecting the party just as were those now sitting at the Cabinet table."[84]

Eisenhower met again with Knowland the following day and received further assurances that the leadership would seek to curb the kind of investigating practices on which McCarthy thrived. But he was unpersuaded that Knowland would follow through. As he put it to Hagerty, "What's the use of trying to work with guys that aren't for you and are never going to be for you?"*[85] On that day, Tuesday, March 2, further signals began to emerge indicating that the adminis-

---

*The entire Eisenhower-McCarthy conflict was conditioned both by a general aspect of American politics and by a specific circumstance. The general condition is that, apart from the veto, the president of the United States has no formal means for exercising control over legislators. Furthermore, informal political realities and traditions of institutional independence make the president's prime-ministerial role one of persuasion, not control. The specific circumstance was the death of Taft, a skilled, ideologically congenial Senate leader with whom Eisenhower could work effectively, and his replacement by Knowland. Further, as hard as Eisenhower worked to find other Senate allies in his party on the McCarthy issue, he was reluctantly forced to recognize limits on his strategy of "action based on personality." There simply were too few senior Republican senators with the ability and willingness to back him consistently and effectively.

tration was going on the offensive. Dulles announced that Scott Mc-
Leod's personnel powers would be eliminated and his work as a loyalty
officer would be supervised by departmental superiors, an action that
the press and the senator from Wisconsin correctly interpreted as anti-
McCarthy.[86] Republican National Chairman Leonard Hall, who a
short while before had been describing McCarthy as a party asset, declared he could not "go along" with him when he attacked "persons
who are fighting Communists just as conscientiously as he is."[87]

Eisenhower also began preparing his March 3 press conference.
After lunching with Hagerty, Nixon, Adams, and Persons to discuss
the continuing need to keep up the pressure on the congressional Republicans to back the administration, Eisenhower looked at a statement
drafted by Hagerty for delivery at the opening of the press conference.
Hagerty took as his point of departure the phrase Eisenhower had used
with the leaders on Monday—"We can't defeat Communism by destroying the things in which we believe." Eisenhower suggested revi-
sions in the text, gave it to Hagerty for further work, sharpened it himself that evening, and in the morning met with Hagerty and Gerald
Morgan of the congressional liaison staff to put a final gloss on his statement.[88] This was not to be an equivocal nonclarification as was the
follow-up to the Dartmouth speech the previous June. Eisenhower also
asked Hagerty to be sure to plant a question with a sympathetic reporter on Scott McLeod's reduction in status.

Following his standard caveat that a senator's comportment was not for
the chief executive to judge, he read the passage Hagerty had drafted:*

> I want to make a few comments about the Peress case. The Department
> of the Army made serious errors in handling the Peress case and the Secre-
> tary of the Army so stated publicly, almost a month ago. The Army is cor-
> recting its procedures to avoid such mistakes in the future. I am completely
> confident that Secretary Stevens will be successful in this effort.

Having thus followed his own advice to Stevens of confessing an
error and indicating the remedial practice, he obeyed his admonition
to stand firm. "Neither in this case, nor in any other," he continued,

---

*The statement was mimeographed and distributed to the journalists.

"has any person in the executive branch been authorized to suggest that any subordinate, for any reason whatsoever, violate his convictions or principles or submit to any kind of personal humiliation when testifying before congressional committees or elsewhere."

Of course, "we must be increasingly vigilant . . . to make certain there is no subversive penetration." Nevertheless, he continued, with a phrase similar to the one he had used in the Monday leadership meeting, "In opposing communism, we are defeating ourselves if either by design or through carelessness we use methods that do not conform to the American sense of justice and fair play." Still ignoring his adversary's name, Eisenhower delivered a tribute to the general whom McCarthy had maligned:

> All of us know that our military services and their leaders have always been completely loyal and dedicated public servants, singularly free of suspicion of disloyalty. Their courage and their devotion have been proved in peace as well as on the battlefields of war. In this tribute to the services I mean to include General Zwicker, who was decorated for gallantry in the field.

Pressing the point further, he made clear that Stevens was correct in ordering Zwicker not to testify further: "Officials in the executive branch of government will have my unqualified support in insisting that employees in the executive branch who appear before any kind of executive and congressional investigation body will be treated fairly." "Of course," he added, taking off from his conferences with Knowland and the other party leaders,

> I expect the Republican membership of the Congress to assume the primary responsibility in this respect, since they are the majority party and, therefore, control the committees. I am glad to state that Senator Knowland has reported to me that effective steps are already being taken by the Republican leadership to set up codes of fair procedure.

The statement concluded with a reiteration of his remarks to the leaders, deploring distractions and stressing the importance of passing the party's program which, he added, included legislation designed to insure "vigilance against any kind of subversion" while maintaining "the standards of fair play recognized by the American people."

Immediately after reading the statement he opened the question period, calling White House correspondent Merriman Smith:

SMITH: Senator McCarthy yesterday questioned the wisdom of Secretary Dulles having removed from Mr. McLeod the authority over personnel problems in the State Department. I wonder if you could tell us your feeling on that.

THE PRESIDENT: Well, the assignment to duty of any administrative officer in any department is the responsibility of that department, and no one else's whatsoever. I hold the head of the department responsible to me for proper operation of the department. He is, in turn, responsible for everything that goes on within it.[89]

The press treatments of Eisenhower's reply illustrate the technique he was perfecting. In a conversation with General Clay, Eisenhower said, "I put it in talk, principle and idea. They usually put it in headlines, 'The President spanks so and so.' "[90] He might have added that he and Hagerty fostered this translation. His statements of principle were unmistakably addressed to McCarthy, and, lest reporters miss the point, Hagerty primed them.[91] The next morning's *Washington Post* rendered Eisenhower's answer to Smith as, "President Eisenhower said yesterday the action stripping State Department Security Chief Scott McLeod of power to hire and fire was not the responsibility of Joseph R. McCarthy." And the *New York Times* headed its account of Eisenhower's prepared statement: "President Chides McCarthy on Fair Play at Hearings."

McCarthy, however, managed to blunt the effect of Eisenhower's carefully prepared statement by defiantly convening a televised committee meeting two hours after Eisenhower's press conference, thus insuring that the news stories reporting Eisenhower's implied criticism of him also included McCarthy's reply. McCarthy made it clear that he himself construed Eisenhower's abstract disquisition as a broadside at him. (The previous year he had denied that Eisenhower's Dartmouth remarks applied to him, since *he* had never burned a book.) He assured his national television audience that "if a stupid, arrogant or witless man in a position of power appears before our committee and is found aiding the Communist Party, he will be exposed. The fact that he might be a general places him in no special class as far as I am concerned."

To this he added a sardonic swipe at Eisenhower, saying "apparently the President and I now agree on the necessity of getting rid of Communists."[92] Later he drew attention to the "now" by publicly deleting it, in effect highlighting his readiness to reply to presidential criticism.*

The March 4 *New York Times* story concerning Eisenhower's prepared statement contained a subhead reading "Senator Defiant in Retort." And the *Washington Post* accompanied its story about Scott McLeod with another front-page account headed "McCarthy Blast Defies Ike." This coverage—and editorials lamenting that Eisenhower's attack on McCarthy was not more personal[94]—triggered the Eisenhower temper but did not lead him to adopt the *ad hominem* mode. Nor did it reduce the pace of his actions against McCarthy. For the moment, however, he shifted to his familiar hidden-hand approach.

Eisenhower had breakfast on March 4 with the man he had asked after Taft's death to be the "knight in armor" on Capital Hill, Everett Dirksen. In dictated notes, Eisenhower tersely summarized this meeting: "Discussion was to the effect that Senator Dirksen will try to influence Republican members on McCarthy's committee to observe proper procedure."[95] Before the day was over the senior committee Republican, Karl Mundt, asked that the body require majority votes for calling unscheduled out-of-town meetings of the sort at which McCarthy had belabored General Zwicker. In so doing, he was following through on the earlier Eisenhower-stimulated proposal by the Republican policy committee that this be general practice for committees. Meanwhile, stories initiated by Eisenhower's associates hit the papers.[96] Defense Secretary Wilson described McCarthy's claim that the army was not vigilant in warding off Communist infiltration as "damned tommyrot."[97] Party Chairman Hall gave an interview to Hagerty's own father, a veteran *New York Times* political reporter. The notion that McCarthy had split the party was "nonsense" said Hall, who went on to cite "cold facts on what has been done to stamp out Communism" in the Eisenhower Administration.[98]

---

*Nor was the ostentatious deletion lost on the White House. The original phrase, with the "now" underlined, appears in the briefing papers Hagerty provided for Eisenhower's press conference a week later, a reminder to his boss that combat with McCarthy was a serious business.[93]

Thus, in the span of a week, Eisenhower had used the formal setting of his Monday conference with the leaders to forewarn them of his intention to criticize McCarthy's methods, linking this to clearing the way to pass the legislative program in which he and they had an interest. He had held or taken advantage of a number of informal meetings aimed at weakening McCarthy's support. He had made (in spite of McCarthy's clever counterattack) a strong statement in his Wednesday press conference, defending the army and condemning McCarthy's procedures. And the polemical work of directly attacking McCarthy had been delegated to Hall and Wilson and had been carried out.

One might imagine that by Friday, March 5, Eisenhower would use the regular cabinet meeting to discuss and further plan the assault. As usual, however, he barely mentioned the divisive McCarthy issue in the meeting. Instead he relied on preventative medicine, bringing in Leonard Hall to announce a plan for each cabinet member to establish liaisons with his congressional counterpart, preventing breaches from developing by using "positive publicity to replace rearguard actions." Later in the meeting Eisenhower explained what he meant by avoiding "rearguard actions." Remarking on the agenda item entitled "Emphasis on Administration Program," he briefly alluded to the week's events, noting that his own "statement in regard to Senator McCarthy and Secretary Stevens conformed to this idea."[*][99]

Eisenhower also took March 5 as an occasion to communicate to the cabinet in a different way. He dispatched a stern "Personal and Confidential" memorandum addressed to each department and agency head entitled "Treatment of Government Personnel." It contained the unequivocal admonition not to succumb to concessions of the sort Stevens had made.

> Each superior, including me, must remember the obligations he has to his own subordinates. These obligations comprise, among other things, the protection of those subordinates, through all legal and proper means available, against attacks of a character under which they might otherwise be helpless.

*Cabinet Secretary Maxwell Rabb's briefing memorandum to Eisenhower on this item "respectfully submitted" the observation that the Stevens affair had "the unfortunate result of diverting attention from the Administration's program, which is exactly the result desired by the opposition." Rallying the Cabinet, Rabb volunteered, would "get the situation once again into proper focus."[100]

> . . . No hope of any kind of political advantage, no threat from any source, should lead anyone to forsake these principles of organizational leadership.[101]

Before the week was over a new McCarthy skirmish threatened, one that could easily have produced the need for rearguard action. This time the instigation was not McCarthy's abuse of members of the executive branch, but rather a Democratic assault calculated to unite in the public mind what Eisenhower was seeking to differentiate—his program and McCarthy's freewheeling attempts to dominate the political scene. Adlai Stevenson, in a nationally televised speech on Saturday, March 6, depicted the Republican Party as "hopelessly, dismally, fatally torn and rent . . . divided against itself, half McCarthy and half Eisenhower."[102] McCarthy demanded time to reply. Eisenhower thwarted the demand before the networks could answer. At his Monday meeting with the leadership, after again pressing the leaders on the primacy of the party program, he insisted it was time to "stop this nonsense." Stevenson's attack, he argued, was on the party. Therefore the networks should ask the party chairman to designate who would reply. The leaders agreed to go along with Eisenhower, who then phoned Hall, instructing him to call the networks and request equal time for the National Committee, not McCarthy, adding that he would personally intervene and call the presidents of NBC and CBS if Hall encountered resistance.[103] Within the day Eisenhower enlisted a reluctant Richard Nixon (who was still straddling the McCarthy issue) to give the speech.[104]

When Hall's request was granted by the networks, McCarthy threatened to appeal the case to the Federal Communications Commission (FCC). Press Secretary James Hagerty recorded in his diary that Sherman Adams would "call FCC chairman and get that nailed down."[105] In his March 10 press conference, when asked if he thought the matter had been handled justly, Eisenhower made a remark which, while literally true, successfully veiled the administration's actions of the two previous days. "I am not going to make the decisions that, of course, the Federal Communications Commission makes, and that the networks make on their own responsibility. Personally, I think that the networks have certainly discharged their responsibility for being impartial."[106]

By this March 10 meeting with the press, Eisenhower's cause had been advanced not only by the decision to grant rebuttal time to the Republican National Committee, but also by a Senate Eisenhower republican, Vermont's Ralph Flanders, who accused "the junior Senator from Wisconsin" of "doing his best to shatter the party whose label he wears."[107] The FCC decision and Flanders's speech provided openings for the increasingly more pointed remarks ostensibly about political principles Eisenhower was now regularly feeding the newsmen, knowing they would inject McCarthy's name into their accounts.

His remark on the assignment of air time to the Republican National Committee was in response to one of ten successive questions about McCarthy that opened the conference. He answered easily and at times in a way that seemed intentionally to make light of McCarthy. The closest he came to mentioning the senator by name was in response to Robert Spivak's query about whether the choice of Nixon to reply to Stevenson meant that "Senator McCarthy will not be speaking for the party in the campaign." "You pose a question that I don't suppose anyone in the world can answer," Eisenhower replied, "I suppose when he speaks, he will say he is representing what he chooses. The Republican Chairman has made it quite clear in this instance who has been selected to speak for the party."

His responses to half a dozen of the questions enabled him to defend the choice of Nixon as party speaker and explain the inappropriateness of a McCarthy rejoinder. ("You know, suppose any one of you would make a speech, whatever party you belong to, and mention 20 names on the other side; now, does the network have to give 20 people the right to get up and answer, or is it a party thing?") When finally asked about Flanders's speech Eisenhower hit his stride, evoking friendly laughter. He alluded to the McCarthy phenomenon, praised the Vermont senator, and in the same reply initiated the practice that became standard of allowing Hagerty to release texts, recordings, and films of his exchanges with the press. It was the New York *Herald Tribune's* Roscoe Drummond who raised the question:

DRUMMOND: Mr. President, will you tell us what your reaction is to Senator Flanders's talk yesterday in the Senate?

195

THE PRESIDENT: Well, I was perfectly certain I wasn't going to get through this morning without getting that question. [laughter] And I thought about it in on the way out. [laughter] Now, certainly, I can agree with this part: the Republican Party is now the party of responsibility, charged by the people of the United States in the elective process. And when Senator Flanders points up the danger of us engaging in internecine warfare, and magnifying certain items of procedure and right and personal aggrandizement, and all such questions, to the point that we are endangering the program of action that all the leadership is agreed upon and we are trying to put across, then he is doing a service when he calls [attention to] the great danger to that kind of thing that is happening.

Asked if he would put his answer on the record, Eisenhower called forth more good humor:

I will tell you what you can do. I believe they keep a transcript; after the meeting is over, Mr. Hagerty can see how many errors of grammar, of which I was guilty, when I stated it—[laughter]—and if he thinks it is worthwhile stating it, or if it is all right, you can put it in.[108]

His praise of Flanders was interpreted as intended. The *Washington Post* story, which was headed "Ike Lauds Blast at McCarthy," was typical. Hagerty released the text. It was soon evident that he had found an effective vehicle for transmitting Eisenhower's messages and his appealing personality via radio, television, and newsreels.[109]

Eisenhower's private language and actions also revealed his mounting impulse to do battle with McCarthy, albeit from sheltered vantages. Immediately after the March 10 news conference he told General Persons: "If McCarthy wants to get recognized anymore, the only way he can do it is stand up and publicly say 'I was wrong in browbeating witnesses, wrong in saying the Army is coddling communists, and wrong in my attack on Stevens. I apologize.' That's the only way I'll ever welcome him back to the fold." That day Eisenhower had a conversation with Hagerty that led the press secretary to record they had "agreed I should sort of leak a story of McCarthy's actions . . . pointing out presidential press conference statement, McLeod answer, and Hall action taken with White House and leaders' agreement."[110] Hagerty's notes are a perfect outline of Roscoe Drummond's story on the front page of the March 11 *Herald Tribune* under the heading "Administration Plans New Curbs on McCarthy."

By March 13, when Nixon's reply to Stevenson was broadcast, the vice president's intention to act as a foot soldier in a skirmish defending the administration and criticizing McCarthy could scarcely have received a greater advance billing. Eisenhower had stressed in his news conference Nixon's appropriateness as a party spokesman. Nixon had told reporters "my talk will reflect the view of the Republican Party" and pointedly added, "particularly the view of the President, who is the leader of the Republican Party."

Nixon took a line of argument completely consistent with the one Eisenhower had been advocating. He devoted much of his speech to recounting administration accomplishments, including the loyalty and security program. He praised the defense policy, adding a point Eisenhower could scarcely have made himself—that Eisenhower was "one of the greatest military leaders in the world today." And he criticized McCarthy with the kind of superficially veiled indirection that by this time in the controversy had become an administration staple:

> The President, this Administration, the responsible leadership of the Republican Party, insist that . . . the procedures for dealing with the threat of Communism in the United States must be fair. . . . Now in recent weeks we've seen a striking example of the truth of the principles I've just enunciated. Men who have in the past done effective work exposing Communists in the country have, by reckless talk and questionable methods, made themselves the issue rather than the cause they believe in so deeply . . . and have allowed those whose primary objective is to defeat the Eisenhower Administration to divert attention from its great program to those individuals who follow these methods.

Nixon was happy to drive the point further home. When asked if his statement had been aimed at McCarthy, he came closer than Eisenhower would have to "personalities" by replying, "The speech speaks for itself, wherever the shoe fits."[111]

Nixon's speech, coming just five days after Stevenson's March 6 attack on "GOP McCarthyism," was the culmination of a week of daily, highly publicized criticism of McCarthy.* On March 11, the Depart-

*It also was the week of Edward R. Murrow's now legendary indictment of McCarthy's practices and career in his regular "See It Now" CBS telecast.

ment of the Army—ostensibly on its own but actually at White House instigation—set in motion what was to become a marathon televised exposure of McCarthy's uncivil comportment. Drawing on the chronology that by then had been prepared of attempts by McCarthy and his aides to secure special favors for Schine, the army sent a thirty-four-page report to each member of the Investigations Subcommittee. It charged that McCarthy had subjected the army to repeated threats in an effort to help Schine. When he read the chronology, Hagerty gleefully anticipated its impact. "It's a pip," he wrote. "Shows constant pressure by Cohn to get Schine soft Army job, with Joe in and out of threats, really bad report that could bust this thing wide open."[112] McCarthy reversed the army's charge, claiming that it had attempted to use Schine as blackmail to curb his investigations. Faced with charges and countercharges the Investigations Subcommittee needed an investigation of its own chairman.

The issue took shape as a conflict between the army and McCarthy. Eisenhower and staff appeared as peripheral actors. There were no hints in the press of what Adams later described as the "countless White House staff hours spent coaching Stevens."[113] In the White House staff meeting the morning after the report's release, Hagerty warned aides that they were not to give any sign that they had inside knowledge of it—their position should be that they "didn't know anything about request on Schine-Cohn-McCarthy."[114]

In his March 17 press conference, Eisenhower took care not to express himself on the substance of the charges. Nevertheless, when asked if he was disturbed by McCarthy's allegations about the secretary of the army, he replied:

> Now when you ask me whether I believe in Secretary Stevens, of course I do. If I didn't believe in him . . . he wouldn't be where he is; of course I believe in him. I don't say he can't be mistaken, I should make that clear. I don't know, there may be something he has been misinformed on; but as far as his integrity and honesty are concerned, I stand by him.[115]

The *New York Times* of March 18 made the now customary insertion of McCarthy's name in the headline of its report: "President Voices Faith in Stevens in McCarthy Fight."

The remainder of March was devoted to establishing a procedure for evaluating the claims of McCarthy and Stevens. At first Eisenhower seemed not to realize that an extended, public hearing would hurt McCarthy. He complained to a friend that conflict over McCarthy interfered with enacting the party's program: "We have sideshows and freaks where we ought to be in the main tent with our attention on the chariot race."[116] Initially Sherman Adams attempted to change the venue from the McCarthy Committee to the Senate Armed Forces Committee. Its chairman, Massachusetts Senator Leverett Saltonstall, was up for reelection in November and unwilling to preside over so threatening an issue. On March 16 the McCarthy Committee voted to do the job itself, substituting a special counsel for Cohn and replacing McCarthy with Mundt as the chairman.

On March 18 Eisenhower telephoned Mundt, stressing the urgency of completing the hearings in order to clear the boards for the legislative program. Mrs. Whitman's paraphrase of the conversation indicates that he asked Mundt:

> How rapidly he can drive through the job for which he was just appointed Chairman. Mundt said less than a week, once they get a staff. DDE can't think of anything that's hurting our position more, and looks to Mundt to settle it. Mundt looking for high-ranking counsel that the country will accept—in stature, objectivity and competence. Right now, he has call in for Earl Warren to see if he will lend a District Judge. DDE mentioned he'd like John W. Davis [one-time Solicitor Gen. of U.S.], one of the rudest and most dedicated old patriots he's ever known. . . . DDE's next question, confidentially and as a Republican: what would reaction be to having one committee man involved as deeply as the Senator? Mundt replied that McCarthy insists upon staying on as a member of the Subcommittee, but that they will insist that Army have right to cross-examine him. DDE advised that, since it isn't now only a Subcommittee, but a Republican Committee, Mundt and Dirksen and Charlie Potter must not let anything be put over on them. . . . DDE's 2 points: Push; and remember there's honor and decency at stake right now.[117]

Mundt's estimation that the hearings would take a week was wildly off. They began in April and continued to the second week of June. Eisenhower did not get John W. Davis as counsel. The committee's choice, Roy Jenkins, made rather modest contributions to the proceedings, but the army's special counsel, Joseph Welch, is still being memorialized a quarter century later for his art in inserting barbs into McCarthy's flesh.*

McCarthy's personal standing on the committee remained to be settled. Eisenhower called Knowland, who said he had stressed to Mundt and Potter that McCarthy should be barred from voting or questioning witnesses. "Everyone in America will approve what you said," Eisenhower replied.[119] McCarthy refused to give up his right to ask questions, although he agreed to have his ally, Idaho Senator Henry Dworshak, replace him as a voting member of the committee. Ironically, it was McCarthy's display of abrasively aggressive questioning and claims of "points of order" that made him so vulnerable to Welch's rejoinders and produced negative public impressions of him during the marathon televised hearings.

Before his ·March 24 press conference Eisenhower listened to his staff debate about whether he should comment on the issue of McCarthy's serving on the committee that was judging him. The "Easterners"—Jackson, Hagerty, and Cutler—thought that Eisenhower would be belabored by the press if he ducked it. The legislative liaison staff argued that he should treat it as a congressional issue, not for presidential comment.[120] Eisenhower cut short the exchange: "I know exactly what I'm going to say, I'm going to say that he can't sit as judge. . . . I've made up my mind you can't do business with Joe, and to hell with any attempt to compromise."[121]

He was slightly—but only slightly—less forthright when the question came up in the morning press conference. Beginning with a noncommittal sounding "Well I have no feelings at all about a particular situation or technicality of which I know nothing," he went on to say, "I am perfectly ready to put myself on record flatly, as I have before, that in America, if a man is a party to a dispute, directly or indirectly, he does not sit in judgment on his own case, and I don't believe that any leadership can escape responsibility for carrying on that tradition

*Welch was chosen at the suggestion of one of the first major Republican public officials to participate in the draft Eisenhower movement, New York Governor Thomas Dewey. In consultation with Sherman Adams and Attorney General Brownell, Dewey drew on his long experience with lawyers as a public prosecutor. Welch had a reputation as "a people's attorney—one who could appeal to the common man" (Adams's phrase, in a 1981 interview). He was a perfect choice for the prolonged sequence of televised hearings.[118]

and that practice."[122] The *New York Times* story transmuted this generalization into the headline, "President Opposes McCarthy as Judge in His Own Dispute."

Eisenhower's press conference remark coincided with the date that interviewing was completed for the Gallup poll reported to the press on April 4. The army-McCarthy hearings, commonly described as the arena in which McCarthy so clearly displayed his inadequacies that his support dropped drastically, had not yet begun. McCarthy's slide in popularity, however, *had* occurred. The previous Gallup survey released on March 15, based on interviews conducted between February 25 and March 2, still showed him riding high—46 percent of a national cross-section had expressed a generally favorable opinion of McCarthy, 36 percent an unfavorable impression, and 18 percent no opinion. That is to say, among those with opinions 60 percent approved of McCarthy. The April 4 Gallup press release, based on interviews conducted between March 19 and 24, reported a striking turnabout—38 percent approval, 46 percent disapproval, 19 percent no opinion. The percentage of people expressing opinions who favored McCarthy had dropped to 45 percent—he lingered at this plateau in the remaining surveys of the year. The decline occurred in the aftermath of McCarthy's assault on Zwicker; Eisenhower and Hagerty's shift to releasing press conference tapes; the media's framing of the issue as McCarthy versus the United States Army, McCarthy versus fair play, *and* (without Eisenhower's ever acknowledging his part in changing press coverage and public images), McCarthy versus an exceedingly popular president.*

The Army-McCarthy Hearings

The Army-McCarthy hearings finally commenced on April 22, 1954. Within the day McCarthy was already interjecting before the television audience his soon-to-be characteristic phrase "Point of order!" fol-

---

*Eisenhower's April 1954 Gallup rating was 68-21-11; that is, 76 percent approval among those with opinions. From inauguration to McCarthy's censure Eisenhower's support ranged between 57 percent and 75 percent approval.[123]

lowed by lengthy, abusive orations. McCarthy's demeanor in the hearings soon drew such widespread derision that at one of Eisenhower's news conferences that spring a member of the White House press corps evoked laughter by introducing a question with "Mr. President, point of order."[124] McCarthy's Gallup rating never declined further during or after the hearings, but it did not, as it had in the past, ever rise again either. The hearings probably kept him from recouping his support, since, among the many Americans who watched the televised hearings, the proportion telling Dr. Gallup's interviewers they favored Stevens over McCarthy was consistently two-to-one.[125]

As the hearings ground on, the emphasis shifted away from the McCarthy-Eisenhower conflict to prolonged trench warfare between McCarthy and the army. By May 10 Stevens had been on the stand for ten days, an endurance record that was solemnly recorded as the longest in the annals of the upper chamber.

At that point Dirksen proposed to cut short the spectacle that was dominating television screens by moving immediately to McCarthy's testimony and then holding the remaining hearings in closed session and issuing a summary after each. Stevens (who felt that all witnesses should be exposed to public cross-examination just as he had) and the committee Democrats (who by this time realized how damaging the prolonged hearing was to McCarthy) objected. So, too, in the privacy of his conversations with Hagerty, who carefully filled him in on each day's events, did Eisenhower. (Eisenhower also phoned Defense Secretary Wilson telling him to encourage Stevens to be steadfast about insisting on open hearings.)[126] This time when asked in press conference whether the hearings were blocking the business of the nation, he answered in the affirmative but declared they should be continued until they got to the bottom of the case.[127] Mundt accepted this, voted with the committee Democrats on Dirksen's proposal, and open hearings continued.

The next witness was army counselor John Adams, who closely narrated the events summarized in the army's chronology of abuses, beginning with an encounter he had with Schine on October 12, 1953. Adams methodically proceeded to recount chronologically the occasions when he had received inquiries in connection with Schine from McCarthy or a member of his staff, perfunctorily noting the January

21 meeting with Eisenhower's strategists that had led him to prepare the chronology. This was the first public reference to that strategy session.

Everyone recognized the likely significance of such a meeting. McCarthy's antagonist no longer seemed to be the army. Democratic Senator Stuart Symington asked army counselor Adams why Lodge, as ambassador to the United Nations and presumably removed from the management of political strategy, had attended the meeting. Joseph Welch immediately interjected, "This was a high-level discussion of the Executive Department." Adams, he continued, "has been instructed not to testify as to the interchange of views . . . at that meeting." At this point the hearing was adjourned—the day was Friday, May 14—and Adams was directed to come back Monday with signed instructions justifying his refusal to testify.[128]

The instructions with which Adams returned after the weekend were from none other than the president. Rather than explaining his January meeting with Eisenhower's strategists and its connection with the army-McCarthy hearings, however, the instructions contained a disquisition on constitutional doctrine. Eisenhower had dispatched a letter, dated May 17, to Defense Secretary Wilson instructing him that, although executive departments were required to furnish congressional committees with information within their jurisdictions, they were barred from disclosing "conversations, communications and documents" concerning the need for confidentiality in advisors' relationships "because it is essential to efficient and effective administration that employees of the Executive Branch be in a position to be completely candid with each other on official matters." Appended was a ten-page memorandum dated March 2 signed by Brownell, backing up this strict interpretation of the separation of powers doctrine with examples from the Washington to Roosevelt administrations of refusals by presidents to provide Congress with confidential executive branch communications.[129] As the two-month-old date of the Brownell memorandum suggests, Eisenhower had been ready for a congressional inquiry into the White House role in planning a confrontation between the army and McCarthy.* He had been prepared well before John

*Perhaps because they were so persuaded that Eisenhower was a bystander, contemporaries did not note the difference in dates between Eisenhower's letter and Brownell's brief. The *New*

Adams's testimony on the January 21 meeting to rely on executive privilege to dissociate himself from the appearance of being involved.

On March 2, the very date of Brownell's memorandum listing historical examples of presidential exercise of executive privilege, in the wake of the McCarthy-Zwicker exchange and Stevens's contretemps on Capitol Hill, Eisenhower had called Brownell to request a legal reading on his power to order subordinates not to testify. Reaching Deputy Attorney General Rogers (Brownell was out of town), the president commented, "One thing people keep talking about is the power of the president to protect people against McCarthy." But, he continued, "no one has ever suggested what kind of authority this is"—especially "when it comes to people down the line appointed to office. . . . I would like to have a brief memo on precedent." Eisenhower had framed the issue in terms of what his power would be if "I made up my mind that McCarthy is abusing someone in a Department," but Rogers transmitted a history of exercises of executive privilege and these precedents turned on preserving the confidentiality of executive branch discussions rather than protecting public servants from abuse.[130]

On May 3 and May 5 Eisenhower had elicited further Justice Department readings on his power to withhold confidential information from Congress.[131] And on May 7, Lodge informed Eisenhower that if asked to testify on his role in initiating the army-McCarthy affair, he would refuse to do so on the grounds that he was a presidential advisor. Eisenhower's reply was, "The position you propose to take is exactly correct. I would be astonished if any of my personal advisors would undertake to give testimony on intimate staff counsel and advice. The result would be to eliminate all such offices from the Presidential staff. In turn, this would mean paralysis."[132]

When army counsel Adams revealed the January 21 meeting, Eisenhower set a covey of aides to work to implement the executive privilege strategem. They included Hagerty, Brownell, Persons, Morgan, Martin, Shanley, and Sherman Adams. Eisenhower made clear that

---

York Times reprinted excerpts of both without indicating the two dates. The discrepency is evident in *The Public Papers of the President.* I have not been able to find the original news release to see whether the *New York Times* had received the texts of the letter to Wilson and the brief by Brownell with the two dates indicated.

Hagerty was to fend off reporters[133] until the official response with the letter to Wilson and the appended Brownell brief, was released.[134]

The advisory group breakfasted with Eisenhower on May 17, just before his Monday morning meeting with the Republican Legislative Leadership. After discussing with them how to break his stand to the leaders, Eisenhower took a familiar approach to avoiding debate with the lawmakers: he announced his decision as a fait accompli, stoked up his indignation, and defended it on principled grounds. "Pseudo-liberals all over the country have been urging me to raise hell," he grumbled to the leaders. "I have not done that, but I have issued instructions to the Secretary of Defense which order him to keep confidential any advisory discussions in the administrative side of this government. Any man who testifies as to the advice he gave me won't be working for me that night." Knowland said he sympathized with the president's viewpoint, although he was reluctant to see the administration seem to weaken congressional subpoena powers. Subpoenas were not mentioned in his statement, Eisenhower replied. Nevertheless, "Those people who have a position here in this government because of me, those people who are my confidential advisors are not going to be subpoenaed. . . . Governor Adams's official job is really a part of me and he's not going up on the Hill." Swept along by this onslaught, Knowland told the press that the congressional leaders recognized Eisenhower's decision as a legitimate exercise of presidential power.[135]

Other congressmen, however, including the committee members, were unwilling to ignore what had occurred in a meeting of such a distinctively influential set of Eisenhower advisors. McCarthy denounced the order, calling it an "iron curtain" and arguing that Eisenhower had been duped into signing it by officials who sought to cover up "what went on when they cooked up those charges against Mr. Cohn, Mr. Carr and myself." The committee then recessed for a week, instructing Mundt to seek a modification in Eisenhower's order.[136]

Eisenhower used the remainder of the week both to blunt the widespread impression that he was seeking to hide his hand and to shore up Stevens. Stevens, who in February was "nearly hysterical" and ready to resign, had already absorbed White House coaching and

205

had performed solidly before the committee. Eisenhower, having backed Stevens several times in press conferences now used a Tuesday, May 18, trip to a North Carolina observance of Armed Forces Day to demonstrate his support for the secretary more visibly. Taking Stevens with them, he and Hagerty went out of their way to arrange for several photographs of Eisenhower and Stevens together. He enhanced their news value in his speech, asserting, "We are still confident of our Armed Services from their secretaries and high commanders on down to the last private."[137] The next day's *New York Times* reproduced a three-column picture of the two men beaming and shaking hands on page one immediately below the masthead. The caption read "Reaffirms Faith in the Armed Forces," and the story immediately below was headed "Eisenhower Backs Stevens; Southern Crowd Hails Both."

That morning before flying to North Carolina, Eisenhower and Hagerty planned how Eisenhower should disassociate himself from the controversial January meeting when he met the press the following day. On the plane they brought Stevens into the conversation and arranged with him that after Eisenhower's statement Stevens would announce that he took full responsibility for the Schine investigation.[138]

On May 19 in his regular Wednesday press conference Eisenhower explained that he issued the executive privilege order to Wilson because he saw "an investigation going ahead where it appeared that there was going to be a long sidetrack established . . . and which in any event would directly and instantly raise the old question of the proper division of powers between the executive and the Legislature."*

When asked if it would be correct to assume that he had approved of the plans to release the chronology, his answer was succinct if inaccurate: "It would not." And when asked if he had known of the January 21 meeting before it occurred, he waffled and attributed shortcomings to his powers of recollection that have no resemblance to the many accounts of his excellent memory: "Well, I wouldn't answer it in any event because, after all, we do come to a place here where you can't

---

*Having become convinced that the extended series of hearings was sapping support for McCarthy, Eisenhower also stressed that although he hoped the hearings would conclude "as soon and expeditiously as possible," they should not do so until "the principals tell their stories openly and fully, and so the public can know the facts. . . . Let the chips fall where they may, and then let's go about this important business of government."

go into detail: but my memory wouldn't serve me anyway. I couldn't remember such a thing."[139] At any rate, he suggested, he was too busy with serious problems of executive leadership to review requests for information or testimony on consultations within the executive branch: "you can well know, ladies and gentlemen, I cannot stay too close to the details of this argument."[140]*

Hagerty phoned Stevens immediately after the press conference, to help the army secretary draft a statement that was promptly released: the January meeting and Stevens's actions thereafter were initiated "by the Army alone"; the meeting "was only for the purpose of obtaining [an] interpretation of existing directives"; no "meeting or confluence influenced my decision to protest and to fight attempts to obtain preferential treatment for a private in the Army by the use of the power and prestige of the Senate."[142]

Hagerty then reported what had transpired to Brownell, who was about to have lunch with Mundt. After lunch Brownell called back to say that Eisenhower's and Stevens's statements had been persuasive.[143] Mundt announced that Stevens's explanation "minimized the impact" of Eisenhower's order, thus signaling his willingness to resume the hearings. The issue rapidly died down, largely because Eisenhower's apolitical reputation was so thoroughly taken for granted, and the hearings again became defined in most interpretations as what they were originally thought to be—McCarthy versus the army, not the administration and much less Eisenhower.

McCarthy, himself, was less conciliatory than Mundt, however, inching closer and closer to directing his scathing figures of speech at Eisenhower personally. "This," he pronounced, "is the first time I've ever seen the executive branch of government take the fifth amendment."[144] Hagerty noted in his diary, "I hope he lets me burn McCarthy's ears off."[145] Instead Eisenhower refused to engage in "arguments with McCarthy from the White House," and Stassen, the most vocal McCarthy antagonist in the administration, was commis-

---

*On other occasions Hagerty issued reports indicating that Eisenhower was not watching the hearings,[141] and by implication that he had more important matters with which to deal. But, while Hagerty's diary, appointment lists, and a simple assessment of the other policy demands on Eisenhower support the impression that he was not part of the eight-hour-day television-viewing audience, Hagerty's account makes it clear that Eisenhower could not have been further from being inattentive. He listened eagerly to Hagerty's briefing on each day's events.

sioned to reply. Mentioning personalities freely, he accused McCarthy of "frantically searching for diversionary headlines after the sorry spectacle of his record in the recent hearings."[146]

As May progressed, Eisenhower's expressions of irritation at the failure of Senate Republicans to rally against McCarthy and in support of the administration's foreign and national security policy became a regular theme in Hagerty diary entries. On May 20, Eisenhower exploded: "The trouble with our so-called supporters in the Senate is that they haven't the guts to defend the Administration—Boy! We really need a few good hatchet men on our side up there!"[147] On May 25, his displeasure at Mundt's chairmanship of the subcommittee erupted: "I used to think he was just a weak man, but now it is obvious he is playing on McCarthy's side. Now I wish we had run Mrs. Gunderson* in the primaries. She could have beat him hands down."[148]

Eisenhower's ire again was stirred on May 26. The Republican majority of the subcommittee succeeded in a 4-3 vote to drop two matters scheduled for investigation—the Carr and Hensel cases. McCarthy aide Francis Carr had been accused by the army of participating in the efforts to help Schine, and McCarthy had accused Assistant Defense Secretary H. Struve Hensel of trying to stop investigations of the army so that the subcommittee would not look into dubious business practices Hensel had allegedly engaged in during World War II. Superficially the vote seemed to be an effort to hasten completion of the hearings by eliminating two minor protagonists. In fact, Carr was quite vulnerable and would have performed poorly on the stand. Hensel was a model of respectability who had been arbitrarily maligned by McCarthy and whose testimony would have further discredited him. The motion passed only because Dirksen misinformed Michigan Senator Potter that Eisenhower wanted the charges dropped.[150]

In this instance the hidden hand had slipped. A member of the liaison staff promptly was dispatched to extract an apology from Dirksen. "Think it is a good thing that those Senators on the committee realize we are checking closely on everything concerning the committee," Hagerty wrote. "It will also serve to warn them that they can't pull fast ones without our hearing about it."[151]

---

*Mrs. Barbara Gunderson, Republican National committeewoman from South Dakota[149]

On May 27 McCarthy made himself particularly vulnerable to criticism in an exchange with a committee Democrat who increasingly had begun tangling with him—Arkansas's acerbic John McClellan. McClellan suggested that McCarthy's practice of using his "underground" of government employees and in particular his release of a confidential FBI document during the hearings might well make "Senator McCarthy . . . guilty of a crime." McCarthy replied with a broadside rejecting the very notion that civil servants had obligations that should keep them from reporting confidential information to him. "I would like to notify [the] two million federal employees," he announced, "that I feel it's their duty to give us any information which they have about graft, corruption, Communists, treason, and that there is no loyalty to a superior officer which can tower above and beyond their loyalty to this country."[152]

The next day, after a meeting with his staff to consider what to do about the McCarthy challenge, Eisenhower strode back and forth in his office, displaying his wrath to Hagerty. "This amounts to nothing but a wholesale subversion of public service," he exclaimed.

McCarthy is making exactly the same plea of loyalty to him that Hitler made to the German people. Both tried to set up personal loyalty within the Government while both were using the pretense of fighting Communism. McCarthy is trying deliberately to subvert the people we have in government, the Constitution and their superior officers. I think this is the most disloyal act we have ever had by anyone in the Government of the United States.

The two of them considered how best to respond. Eisenhower's first thought was to have Hagerty plant a press conference question to which the president would reply: "If such an invitation is accepted by any employee of the Government and we find who that employee is, he will be fired on the spot if a civilian and court martialed on the spot if a military man." They then resolved on a measure that would have a more immediate impact, would be more consistent than Eisenhower's first impulse, and that had the familiar transcendent character of commenting on issues, but not on McCarthy.[153] Hagerty drafted a strong statement asserting that the executive branch has sole and fundamental responsibility to enforce laws and presidential orders. . . . That responsibility cannot be usurped by any individual who may seek to set himself above the laws of our land, or override orders of the President of the United States to federal employees of the executive branch of government.

The constitutional basis of this rejoinder to McCarthy's proposed "usurpation" was underscored by issuing the statement in Attorney General Brownell's name. Eisenhower's commitment to the position was stressed by releasing the statement from the White House with a Hagerty announcement that it had presidential endorsement.[154]

Eisenhower commissioned Hagerty to get to work with "certain key people that I know in radio, television, and the newspapers" in order to "build up public opinion." By the late afternoon Hagerty dropped by the White House lawn, where Eisenhower was taking a respite swinging a golf club, and told his boss to listen to that evening's Edward R. Murrow broadcast.[155]

In his broadcast, Murrow described the White House statement as a "considerable footnote in the turbulent history of our time." Noting that it was an "obvious and direct reference to McCarthy's statement of yesterday," he concluded that

the issue between the Eisenhower Administration and McCarthy has finally been joined. . . . In due course it will cause senators and citizens to be counted on whether or not there is to be an elaborate system of informers inside the government violating the law by providing to a senator documents and information which can only be described as stolen.[156]

Eisenhower launched one more public foray before the hearings sputtered to a close on June 17. He had long been scheduled to deliver a talk on May 31 at Columbia University's National Bicentennial Dinner and had already established that the theme would be the need to use responsible means to combat domestic subversion. In response to McCarthy's statement that government workers were obliged to be informants, he sharpened the text of the speech so that the allusions to McCarthy were unmistakable. In doing so, he asked his brother Milton to scan the text, identifying passages that might be construed as attacks on McCarthy. Making some more pointed, he kept the messages in the speech and inserted new ones such as a warning against confusing "honest dissent with disloyal subversion."[157] At the dinner, Hagerty counted twenty-five interruptions for applause. The line that received the most applause read, "Through knowledge and understanding, we will drive from the temple of freedom all those who seek to establish over us thought control—whether they be agents of a foreign state or demagogues thirsty for personal power and public notice."[158]

CBS President Paley, who sat next to the press secretary while Eisenhower delivered the speech, told Hagerty he would instruct the network's news department to give it extensive coverage.[159] The *New York Times* was one of the many papers that focused on Eisenhower's use of the word "demagogue." The head and subhead of its July story on the address read "Eisenhower Warns U.S. of Demagogues Hungry for Power: President, in an Allusion to McCarthy, Declares Thought Control Imperils Nation."

In his June 2 news conference, Eisenhower accentuated the positive. Briefly announcing a new report by Brownell of the current results of the administration's loyalty and security program and referring to the attorney general's earlier statement about the responsibilities of executive branch employees, he said that this would be his last word on the topic of the McCarthy proceedings. The need now was to secure passage of the legislative program.

By and large he was true to his word. When a reporter asked later in the conference whether the McCarthy hearings had delayed the domestic program, Eisenhower simply said, "Next question."[160] He did not comment on the dramatic episodes in the final two weeks of the hearings, the most well remembered and highly publicized of which was Joseph Welch's castigation of McCarthy on June 9 ("Senator. . . . Have you left no sense of decency?")[161] The day after the hearings closed, he met privately with Welch in the Oval Office and congratulated him on his prosecution of the army's case, agreeing with Welch's observation that the main effect of the hearings had been to exhibit McCarthy's tactics before a national television audience.[162]

The army-McCarthy hearings and, more particularly, the events that led up to them in March 1954 (the month when McCarthy's public approval underwent its sharp decline) mark the point of Eisenhower's most intense direct involvement in helping to facilitate the outcome

211

he plainly desired—a state of affairs in which the junior Wisconsin senator would no longer be able to "create trouble on the Hill with members of the party," to "irritate, frustrate and infuriate members of the
Executive Department," or by "going to the extremes in calling names
and making false accusations" to terrify "the ordinary European statesman."[163]

It was mainly in March that Eisenhower exercised consistent hidden-hand influence. His anti-McCarthy strategists had learned of
McCarthy's point of vulnerability in January; from then through early
March they built up the record against him. McCarthy meanwhile
overstepped himself in his wanton attack on representatives of the
army, a bastion of patriotic respectability. As a result Eisenhower could
obliquely castigate McCarthy by defending a highly respected institution—the army—and could privately work with the Republican congressional leaders to influence the ground rules for the hearings so that
McCarthy would not dominate them and in general contribute to the
campaign that sharply reduced McCarthy's public support, thus also
encouraging political leaders who might want to oppose him.

Aftermath of the Hearings

By the time the army-McCarthy hearings had adjourned, it was clear
that the April Gallup Poll release reporting the decline in McCarthy's
public approval rating since the March Poll was no aberration—in May
and June, Gallup reported the same negative findings, along with numerous others showing that substantially more citizens favored Stevens
than favored McCarthy and a striking finding in late April that more
than twice as many voters said they would vote against than for a candidate who had McCarthy's endorsement.[164] (McCarthy did little campaigning in 1954—a sharp contrast with 1950 and 1952. Eisenhower,
on the other hand, spent much time on the hustings.) Disapproval of
McCarthy was all the more politically significant because it was highest
among a segment of the public most likely to have the time and intel-

lectual resources to seek retribution against a pro-McCarthy official—college graduates with occupations in the business and professional worlds.

Eisenhower proclaimed in his 1954 campaign oratory that the Republican administration and Congress had been notably successful in getting approval of its "must" legislation—an 83 percent approval rate by his tabulation. By implication he argued that McCarthy's investigations were unnecessary because the administration had instituted and enforced its own loyalty and security program, one that periodically generated statistics on the number of "security risks" who had been separated from federal employment.* McCarthy's thunder was also stolen by the passage of the Communist Control Act of 1954, a law approved with only a handful of dissenting votes, that made the Communist party illegal. So strong was the bipartisan cold war consensus on this act that McCarthy could get no credit for it. And McCarthy's frequent hints that the United States had been insufficiently aggressive to the Soviet Union lacked credibility in the face of Eisenhower's ability to remind voters that he had brought about an honorable settlement of the Korean conflict and that during his period of stewardship (he avoided adding because of the Central Intelligence Agency's [CIA] intervention) "Communist leaning" governments in Iran and Guatemala had been eliminated.

The Politics of Censure: A Waiting Game

After the army-McCarthy hearings it was crucial that Eisenhower and his anti-McCarthy aides lie low—even to the extent of only rarely issuing the usual abstract statements of principle. The key was to encourage Senate action against McCarthy. Now the McCarthy affair

---

*During the course of 1954, partly at Eisenhower's insistence, the practice of listing security risks by categories, distinguishing loyalty cases from those based on sexual deviance and other moral criteria began. Very few of the "risks" proved to be ones of suspect loyalty. Most were in the new categories of personal unreliability.

was a deeply intramural matter of political privilege, partisanship, and senatorial institution maintenance. External influence, as Adams later put it, was likely to be "counter-productive."[165]

On June 15, two days before the army-McCarthy hearings adjourned, Senator Flanders introduced a resolution moving that McCarthy be deprived of his committee chairmanship. When it became clear that Flanders wanted to pursue the issue but had neither the strategic skills nor staff resources to do so, an alliance arose between the New England Republican and an informal caucus of liberals— mostly congressional staff aides—who had been coordinating the largely unsuccessful attacks on McCarthy from the left. This group raised money for Flanders's cause from a wealthy industrialist and long-time Eisenhower supporter, Studebaker Corporation Board Chairman Paul Hoffman. Hoffman visited Eisenhower on at least four occasions during the summer, and there are notes on one meeting showing that they discussed the McCarthy censure, but evidence of the precise nature of any influence Eisenhower might have exercised through Hoffman has never come to light.[166]

It soon became clear that Flanders would not succeed within the Senate with a motion depriving McCarthy of his chairmanship, because southern Democrats were not prepared to tamper with seniority. In mid-August Flanders moved that McCarthy simply be censured for activities that cast discredit on the Senate. A bitter debate in which McCarthy maligned Marshall provided one of the few occasions in this period when Eisenhower departed from ignoring McCarthy, indulging himself in a passionate defense of his former chief.[167]

On August 5, Utah's austere Arthur Watkins was chosen to chair a carefully selected committee of three members from each party. Each was noted for his judicious temperament and was from a state in which the McCarthy issue did not cut deeply; for example, Republican Francis Case of North Dakota and Democrat Sam Ervin of North Carolina. The Watkins Committee waited until after election day to render its report, a recommendation of censure. This was voted 67 to 22, on December 2.

Eisenhower's failure to intervene even through oblique language during the Watkins Committee hearings and censure debate paralleled Lyndon Johnson's strategy as Democratic minority leader. Johnson restrained Democratic liberals from speaking on the topic.[168] He knew that if the issue became a liberal-conservative fight, many southern Democrats and middle-of-the-road Republicans would not go along with them. So, he insisted that it should be one of individual conscience rather than of party, refusing to state his own view until the final day of debate.

Eisenhower faced the same requirement from his perspective at the other end of Pennsylvania Avenue. He was well aware of the backfire produced by Roosevelt's attempt in 1938 to purge congressmen who had not supported him.[169] And he recognized that one of his favorite persuasive instruments, appeal to the separation of powers, would be turned against him, if as president he took a position on whether a senator had been properly carrying out his duties.

He was far from indifferent to the affair after the army-McCarthy hearings. He consistently followed the maneuverings of congressional McCarthy politics. From time to time he readied himself for a threatened course of action by McCarthy. The senator proposed early in June, for example, to make the CIA his next target. By the end of the month Eisenhower had pre-empted a congressional investigation, establishing an Administrative Branch Commission, under the aegis of Herbert Hoover's study of government organization and headed by Eisenhower's old friend Mark Clark, explaining that the secret nature of the CIA precluded a congressional inquiry. He told Hagerty that he would gladly entice McCarthy into renewing the threat, if he could, since he was sure that McCarthy would have lost further popularity by threatening to poach on a national security agency whose activities and mission were classified.[170]

Hagerty's network remained active. Eisenhower knew in advance, for example, that reporter Eddie Folliard of the *Washington Post* would be asking a press conference question about the anti-Marshall statement McCarthy made during the debate that led to constitution of the Watkins Committee. Conservatives on the legislative liaison staff recommended that he not reply, but he brushed them aside, saying "I know just what I'm going to say on this one." He proceeded with his tribute to Marshall.[171]

Periodically Hagerty and the president discussed the effect that planned presidential statements would have on McCarthy and other critics.[172] They called a press conference for the very morning of the Senate censure vote, shifting to Thursday, December 2 from the usual Wednesday date. It began with extemporaneous—though in fact carefully rehearsed—remarks implicitly replying to a recent Knowland proposal (echoed by McCarthy) that Eisenhower declare a naval blockade of mainland China in response to the shooting down of an American plane in an area north of Japan bordering on Soviet territory.

The cold war was bound to be marked by tensions and explosive issues, Eisenhower submitted. Some would be so egregious that the natural temptation would be to strike out. But a blockade was an act of war. And anyone who, like him, had written thousands of letters to the wives and mothers of soldiers killed in battle would know that mature, balanced action, not potential acts of war, was the way to respond to provocative international incidents. News coverage and editorial comment on his "lecture" were favorable. In the same press conference he was asked whether he would comment "on the way the Senate vote is going thus far on the censure of Senator McCarthy." His reply was that he would not: "This is a matter of the Senate . . . determining what is required in the preservation of the dignity of the Senate; and no one else is in it."[173]

Eisenhower and Watkins: McCarthy's "Break" and Political Demise

On December 3, however, in the aftermath of the condemnation vote, Eisenhower called in Hagerty to discuss "the kicking around" Senator Watkins had received from McCarthy in the course of the debate the previous day. How might he give Watkins favorable recognition? Hagerty writes in his diary for Saturday, December 4: "He told me to have Watkins down for a conference and to give out the appointment to the press." Watkins and Eisenhower met for forty-five minutes that morning. Hagerty then introduced Watkins to the reporters and told them that Eisenhower had praised his handling of the hearings. Stories and photographs were prominently displayed in the Sunday papers.[174]

Monday morning, after a breakfast with Knowland and Dirksen, both of whom had voted against censure, Eisenhower called Hagerty in and asked how the story had come to be released, professing not to remember that he asked Hagerty to release it. Then he laughed and said, "That's all right, my boy, I thought the pictures looked good in the Sunday papers." Hagerty and Mrs. Whitman were puzzled by Eisenhower's query, but, Mrs. Whitman wrote, that "since the President had had breakfast with Knowland that morning," she inferred "he only talked to Jim for the record."[175]

Earlier in the year Eisenhower had not "trapped" McCarthy into the politically self-destructive act of proposing to investigate the CIA. But now, intentionally or not, Eisenhower's benediction of Watkins *did* bring McCarthy into the open, producing what the press dubbed as McCarthy's "break" with Eisenhower. McCarthy, after unsuccessfully attempting to get Mundt to read a statement he had prepared, rose on the floor of the Senate to "apologize to the American people for the unintentional deception" he had committed in the 1952 campaign, when he told them that the Eisenhower administration would engage in a "vigorous, forceful fight against Communists in government. . . . I was mistaken."

The "break" earned McCarthy the criticism of many of the senators who had voted against censure—notably conservatives such as Dirksen, Knowland, and Goldwater, who, rather than defending McCarthy, had argued against the precedent of censure, which they claimed could have the effect of inhibiting free debate in the Senate.[176] The White House response to McCarthy was a Hagerty statement reminding the press of Eisenhower's recent enunciation of his policy of balanced response to international crises (McCarthy had renewed his demand for a blockade of China) and stressing again that the administration had the "security problem" in hand by having new security-risk discharge statistics released.[177] Eisenhower himself had a single-sentence response when asked to comment on McCarthy's attack on him: "I do not indulge in personal vituperation."[178]

McCarthy's prominence virtually dissolved. He seemed personally demoralized and was under obvious stress as he announced his break. Other senators immediately fell into the traditional pattern of ostracism, refusing to talk to him or even answer his questions. His own impulse to win and build support and attention dropped sharply. And, as if in agreement, the press began paying less and less attention to him.[179]

Hagerty remarks on the dramatic change with obvious relish in a March 11, 1955, diary entry. That day McCarthy had written an abusive letter to Eisenhower criticizing him for not securing the immediate release of eleven American airmen held by Communist China. The letter simply was sent to the State Department for routine answer by an underling.[180] And, when on March 16, McCarthy attacked Milton Eisenhower in remarks in the Senate, calling him a member of his brother's "New Deal palace guard," the White House issued "no comment whatsoever." Of this strategy, Hagerty writes,

> All of us on the staff, including the President, will make it a point not to have a comment whatsoever on anything McCarthy says or does. We have him relegated to the back pages of the papers and he knows he is not news anymore. Consequently, he is desperately trying to get back on the front pages and is trying to stir up anything he can to cause him to become once again a controversial subject, particularly between himself and the White House.

Hagerty concludes the passage with almost the same words Eisenhower entered in his private diary entry in April 1953, enunciating a policy that Eisenhower had been obliged to supplement during the tumultuous period, but which was now fully appropriate.

> The best treatment for McCarthy is to ignore him. That is one thing he cannot stand and if we continue this sort of silent treatment, he will blow his top and still sink lower in political importance.[181]

In fact, McCarthy's physical existence barely exceeded his years of political influence. On May 2, 1957, he was dead.

The Eisenhower Style: A Trial Balance

What insights does the McCarthy case provide into the effectiveness of the various elements of Eisenhower's political style? Consider first the strategies, the five approaches to maintaining a covert prime ministership: hidden-hand leadership, instrumental use of language, refusal to "engage in personalities," action based on personality analysis, and delegation selectively practiced, plus the basic strategy of maintaining public support for the president and the presidency and hence for the chief of state side of the presidential role. Then consider his approach to organization—his flexible blend of formal and informal procedures.

An overall insight the case provides is that the elements of his style were complementary. Eisenhower's successful and unsuccessful use of each strategy and of organization often depended on his ability to complement one element with another. Refusal to "engage in personalities" was most successful when used with language as an instrument for obliquely making the points he chose not to make directly. And this pair of strategies often needed to be complemented by such hidden-hand techniques as planting questions at press conferences.

The case also shows that each of the elements could under some conditions be effective, under others, not. Sometimes success or failure stemmed from reasons relating to Eisenhower the man, other times from external circumstances over which he had no control, and sometimes for reasons intrinsic to the individual elements themselves. In striking a trial balance it is instructive to examine reasons for the success and failure of each element of his leadership style in the McCarthy affair, so far as possible choosing examples that were not predominantly influenced by personality and circumstances. More than a single example of the pros and cons of each element would be tiresome and would hardly move the analysis much further toward definitiveness. Then I will consider the effectiveness of Eisenhower's overall style as reflected in the final outcome of the episode.

Perhaps the single most effective use of hidden-hand leadership over the two years was the action Eisenhower took early in March 1954 following Stevenson's speech accusing his party of McCarthyism—his effort to insure that the networks allow Republican National Committee Chairman Leonard Hall to allocate air time for a response and deny a request by McCarthy. Eisenhower had used the interest he shared with the legislative leadership in establishing a record to win their concurrence, saying "Let's stop this nonsense—[and] get down to having the program passed." Having agreed with him, the leaders were in no position to question the authoritative sounding press reports that the request had been made on Hall's initiative. And Eisenhower had been disarming when asked about the matter in his press conference. His answer was so much of a piece with his professed inattention to detailed political strategy that there was no reason to view him as the instigator of the events that led Nixon to be an effective anti-McCarthy spokesman later in the week, by which time numerous other bombs intended to disable McCarthy were detonated.

There were occasions, however, when Eisenhower was unsuccessful because his insistence on hiding his hand barred him from directly conveying his wishes to another politician rather than concealing his involvement. Just as he failed in later years at hidden-hand efforts to influence Nixon (1956) and Adams (1958), he did not succeed when he wanted the army-McCarthy hearings to yield the maximum public exposure of testimony that would be averse to McCarthy in May 1954. Senator Dirksen, his "knight," had either not got the word or had been unpersuaded that Eisenhower took the matter seriously, when he both voted to drop the charges against McCarthy's weak witness, Carr, and the army's strong witness, Hensel, and misinformed Senator Potter about the White House position.

His instrumental use of language was especially instructive in the McCarthy case in connection with his press conference utterances. Most effective were the assertions he deliberately used to combat McCarthy without mentioning his name in March 1954. Two qualities marked these assertions: they were sharply focused and consisted of only thinly veiled allusions to specific McCarthy actions, virtually insuring (although Hagerty often hammered the meaning of the messages home in informal conversations with the journalists) that the press would translate from the abstract to the concrete, ignoring Eisenhower's feigned lack of concern with McCarthy in their reports, although the oblique language itself enabled Eisenhower to avoid a rupture with right wingers on Capitol Hill. The least successful of his efforts to condemn McCarthy without mentioning his name was in the press conference following his Dartmouth college book-burning remarks. Eisenhower's expansion of his remarks was *not* clearly focused and specific in alluding to concrete, recent McCarthy activities. By allowing himself to ramble on in a general way about the complexities of the issue of censorship, he expressed himself far too diffusely to convey a clear message. Diffuse expression was sometimes an Eisenhower weapon, but in this instance it was not in his interest to "just confuse" the reporters and the larger audience.

When he discussed McCarthy, Eisenhower was consistently true *in the letter of the word* to his precept of not even alluding in public to the shortcomings of others. In practice, however, his responses to queries about the senator sometimes approached the trajectory of direct fire. In the course of his career, "no personalities" sometimes was a genuine way of turning the other cheek in the interest of making a short-run adversary into a potential long-run ally. In the McCarthy case, however, especially when in 1954 McCarthy challenged his leadership directly in specific ways, the no-personalities strategy tended to become a dignified and therefore more effective variant on personal invective.

Eisenhower was better able to counter McCarthy's scurrilous language and outrageous acts by condemning an abstract demagogue than by seeming to take seriously the actual demagogue. There were, however, severe costs. At times in 1953 it was not clear that his intended indirect criticisms of McCarthy were meant seriously. And for the many loyal and secure members of the federal establishment, who looked to the president as a defender against McCarthy investigations, the absence of a spokesman—indeed the presence in office of a president who himself was using ambiguous criteria to eliminate "undesirable" federal employees—was scarcely reassuring.

The systematic attention that Eisenhower gave to the personalities of those with (and against) whom he worked ("action based on personality") marked the McCarthy case, as it did much of his other political activity. His use of this strategy is best considered together with his practice of selective delegation. Assessing colleagues' personalities is an inexact science, as Eisenhower showed in his overestimation of Army

Secretary Stevens's capacity to deal with McCarthy. The politically in-experienced Stevens was so poorly suited to defend the army's integrity from a McCarthy that he had to be restrained from resigning out of distress at his own performance. Eisenhower and his associates did do an extraordinary job of resurrecting Stevens's professional reputation and coaching him to perform solidly in the hearings. Once Eisenhower decided in 1954 that it was necessary to stop McCarthy and that McCarthy himself was now vulnerable to effective attack, he chose un-erringly from his White House and cabinet team men to assist him in this endeavor. (With congressmen he had to use the material at hand and neither Knowland nor the committee members participating in the army-McCarthy hearings were suited to be cooperative, effective Eisenhower agents.)*

In the case of his core strategists, those at the January 21, 1953, meeting and Hagerty, he worked with men whose values and other per-sonal qualities he knew intimately and with whom he had worked close-ly. If a key aide was personally averse to tangling with McCarthy—as was General Persons—Eisenhower simply left him out of the action or used him for ministerial duties such as specifically defined negotia-tions, or the drafting of statements. Even Stevens served one of the functions for which Eisenhower used delegation well—that of the lightning rod. Once Stevens had been encouraged, he did what was expected of him, unquestioningly accepting the role Eisenhower as-signed to him as the official responsible for the army's indictment of McCarthy. (Eisenhower expected this of him: in discussing what the army should have said in the Peress case, he remarked "It seems to me that Stevens is there to take the blame.")[182]

The press never stopped writing in terms of Eisenhower versus McCarthy. But as long as the direct attacks were not Eisenhower's, he could continue to insist to the conservatives who dominated the Republican congressional party that it was Stevens, not he, who was the aggrieved party, and the case was the Senate's, not his. He adhered to the dogma of strict separation of powers that he so strongly defended in other contexts, putting his suggestions for committee procedure in

---

*Eisenhower did do his best to encourage Flanders, however, and while he kept his distance from the censure hearings, his accolade to Watkins evidently forced McCarthy into his self-destructive "break."

terms of the need he and the party leaders shared to clear up the charges and move on to enactment of the legislative program.

For many McCarthy opponents, the most infuriating aspect of Eisenhower's comportment during the period from his entry into domestic political life through McCarthy's loss of political effectiveness was the impression Eisenhower left of being unwilling to confront McCarthy. No one doubted which of the two had the greater support. From March 1954 on, fewer citizens favored McCarthy than disapproved of him. Eisenhower, on the other hand, had great respect as a beloved chief of state. During his entire first two years in office, roughly seven out of every ten Gallup respondents who had an opinion about Eisenhower's performance approved of it. Here, many observers are bound to conclude, is an example of a major negative tradeoff implicit in the overall Eisenhower style of avoiding conflict. He deplored McCarthy's influence, but would not bolster those who shared his view by stating it forthrightly and directly.

Eisenhower the organizer complemented Eisenhower the strategist. The cabinet was an organ for promulgating the party's legislative program, including its loyalty and security component. Advancing the program linked Eisenhower to the Republican Senate leadership and otherwise contributed to pushing McCarthy and his preferred issue (the alleged continuing need to root subversives out of the government) to the wings. But Eisenhower did no more than signal his general position on McCarthy in formal cabinet meetings. The only time he drew on that "policy body" for a related purpose was to discuss overseas information service library policy, and the Babel of debate reflected his own unclear news conference after his Dartmouth speech. This was an issue on which he found it propitious to organize informally, selecting for delegation only his anti-McCarthy aides. On the matter of coordinating formal and informal organization and using selective delegation, it is difficult to fault Eisenhower's style or the skill with which he used it (except perhaps when he failed to anticipate Stevens's shortcomings).

Eisenhower's refusal to confront McCarthy directly by name was a strategy he felt had worked. In his memoirs he stressed not only that he had sought to avoid further magnifying the public and press belief that McCarthy was so personally important that his every charge deserved headlines. He also credited the no-personalities strategy for his

223

success in keeping the censure issue from being defined as "one of Executive versus Congressional prestige," arguing that "it is doubtful whether . . . [the censure] would have ever come about if I had adopted a practice of referring to McCarthy by name in press conferences."[183] His cautious wording reflects the reservation appropriate to any such hypothetical question about historical causation. Nevertheless, it is not hard to see ways in which an Eisenhower who truly "got into the gutter" with McCarthy could have stumbled. By using phrases such as Truman's "Kremlin's best asset" that gave the impression of one mudslinging politician in a feud with another, Eisenhower could have reduced his own support, strengthened McCarthy's, and lost the support of the many conservative guardians of Senate tradition who voted for censure.

Eisenhower never gave evidence that he recognized any costs resulting from not directly castigating McCarthy, or of instituting a government security program that exposed civil servants to a wave of administrative investigations in which they were open to discharge because of allegations about their personal habits as well as their political loyalties. Yet the new security program undoubtedly produced casualties similar to those Eisenhower attributed in his memoirs to McCarthy's depredations.* Considered only from the narrow perspective of fostering the morale and creative energy of the civil service and not in moral terms, the program had substantial costs. Most government insiders of the period remember it as having driven able people from government and fostered bureaucratic cautiousness rather than as a creative housecleaning.

The morale of civil servants also undoubtedly suffered adverse effects because Eisenhower, even though he was more popular than McCarthy, failed to confront him. Moreover, from the standpoint of fostering general public support for civil liberties, any citizen, bureaucrat or not, might feel that this failure was more directly costly in terms of not promoting a policy in which freedom of discussion would prevail in the spirit of Eisenhower's Dartmouth speech.

---

*"McCarthyism," Eisenhower wrote in 1963, "took its toll on many individuals and on the nation. . . . Innocent people accused of Communist associations or party membership have not to this day been able to clear their names fully. . . . The cost was often tragic, both emotionally and occupationally.[184]

Whether Eisenhower could have used the presidency as a pulpit to preach civil liberties by attacking McCarthy in that era is dubious. Certainly the one study of public reactions to the army-McCarthy hearings that was designed with sufficient subtlety to elicit citizens' spontaneous perceptions of the hearings, without framing the issue in terms of pollsters' multiple-choice questions, suggests this. G. D. Weibe used open-ended market research techniques to find out how the viewers themselves were interpreting that daily television fare. He found that antagonism to McCarthy arose from his incivility and abrasiveness—he came across as a stereotypical "bad guy"—and was not grounded in general principles, much less in the belief that investigation of communism in government had gone too far.

Weibe found this out by intensive questioning of a small sample of people in a single locality.[185] A major study of public attitudes on these matters, based on a well-designed national survey, provides further evidence that Eisenhower's instincts were correct about the limits on what he could have accomplished by personally challenging McCarthy and by deprecating the "Communist menace" in government. Harvard sociologist Samuel Stouffer carried out this research—in his classic study, *Communism, Conformity and Civil Liberties* [186]—during and just after the army-McCarthy hearings. Eisenhower had no knowledge of the Stouffer study, and Stouffer never reported his data concerning public perceptions of the presence of Communists in government and whether these perceptions could have been changed by Eisenhower, or by a hypothetical investigating committee chairman. But the raw data are available for tabulation.*

When asked if they thought there were Communists in government at the time, only 7 percent of Stouffer's 5,000 respondents said "no," whereas 79 percent said "yes," although only 6 percent estimated the number of Communists in government to be as great as in the thousands. Only 2 percent said that if there were Communists in government their presence would not hurt the country. Forty-two percent said they would present a great danger, 41 percent said "some danger,"

---

*I am indebted to John Geer for tabulating the percentages I discuss from Stouffer's original data, which are available in the archives of the University of Michigan Inter-University Consortium for Political Research.

and only 14 percent said "not much." In short, the prevailing view was that there were some Communists in government and their presence was dangerous.

So much for perception of menace. But, Stouffer asked, what if Eisenhower were to say that the menace had been eliminated? He then added as a follow-up question the further twist (obviously alluding to McCarthy): suppose "the chairman of a congressional committee investigating Communism said there was still a great danger from Communists within the government, would you still believe President Eisenhower was right, or not?" When asked if they would believe Eisenhower, 49 percent of the sample said they would if he said the danger was gone, 40 percent said they would not, and the other 11 percent had no opinion. By Eisenhower's standards, 49 percent would have been a far from ideal credibility rating. Responses to a follow-up question suggest that his credibility would have declined further if his conclusion were challenged by a committee chairman. In that event only 30 percent said they would believe the president.

Eisenhower's strong suit then would not seem to have been tackling McCarthy on the civil liberties-national security issue. And of course his chosen style—calling for undermining rather than attacking McCarthy, partly by using his prime ministerial strategic repertoire of avoiding the appearance of being an antagonist, and partly by maintaining his esteem as chief of state—helped provide the contrast that led many citizens to begin to view McCarthy as the "heavy" and Eisenhower and his associates as the "good guys."

A measure of Eisenhower's success in this role is reflected in James Reston's August 11, 1954, *New York Times* column, written in the midst of the Watkins Committee hearings. Reston, who often had deprecated Eisenhower's effectiveness, entitled his piece "A General Stands at Ease" and lauded the assurance and good humor with which Eisenhower met the press. "His overall effect," Reston wrote, "was of a sincere man thinking out loud with a company of associates." As long as he could convey that effect—and as long as things were going well, Eisenhower had a good chance of outlasting a demagogic competitor—especially one with a heavy-handed manner who eventually was backed into the position of personally attacking such an unassailably sincere-seeming president.

In his memoirs Eisenhower does not make the outright claim that by refusing to exchange invective he had terminated McCarthy's effective career. However, it is difficult to see how, at least for the purposes of defusing McCarthy, another technique would have worked faster and more decisively in the context of the time. Eisenhower's memoirs do not allude to his secret prime ministerial interventions, but the memoirs of strategist Henry Cabot Lodge discuss both the political and the nominally politically transcendent sides of the approach Eisenhower and his staff used to end McCarthy's influence. Lodge's memoirs offer an interpretation that the private Eisenhower (who was not given to euphemism) surely would have accepted:

The January 21 meeting was Eisenhower's first move. It led to thirty-six days of televised hearings, collapsed McCarthy's campaign, and ended in the adoption by the Senate of the motion of censure presented by Senator Flanders of Vermont. These wholesome things would not have happened if Eisenhower had magnified McCarthy by confronting him face to face.[187]

6

LESSONS FOR
OTHER
PRESIDENTS

HOW FEASIBLE or profitable would it be for other presidents to draw on Eisenhower's political style? Before the question can be addressed, a reminder is necessary. My analysis has been of his *mode* of leadership, not of the *merits* of his policy aims.

His policies, of course, could also be viewed in terms of their virtue in his time and of their present applicability. An obvious area for reexamination in the 1980s would be the approach he took to balancing three potentially conflicting goals: a strong military, détente with the Soviet Union, and a federal budget held to a noninflationary level. Another (far less likely to elicit enthusiasm) would be his use of covertly managed coups, such as those in Iran and Guatemala, as weapons of cold war counterrevolution. Such policy evaluations, however, would have to be built on foundations quite different from those of this study of political operating procedures. Here it is appropriate only to ask what lessons can be derived from Eisenhower's leadership style.

In order to identify the potential uses for other presidents of the Eisenhower style, we have to take account of factors apart from the style itself that influenced his leadership. One is the political climate and context in which he operated. Would his style be effective in a different political environment? An obvious second factor is the man. Could Eisenhower's style of leadership be employed by a president who lacks Eisenhower's personal qualities? In addition, although my concern is not with the *content* of his policies, their *scope* must be considered in assessing the transferability of his style. Since Eisenhower was not seeking sharp departures from existing policies, it is plausible that a style that fit his incrementalist goals would not be useable by a president bent on effecting major policy change.

The matter of scope can be dealt with most briefly. Many of the modern presidents from Roosevelt to Reagan have proclaimed their desire to institute major change, but all have been restrained much of the time by the official and unofficial checks and balances of American politics, and some have been restrained all of the time. Thus, modest change of the sort Eisenhower favored has been the rule rather than the exception in presidential politics. On three occasions, however, major political change has resulted from modern presidential initiatives. Roosevelt presented Congress with a sweeping legislative program that resulted in a sequence of massive policy innovations which continued until the conservative coalition took control of Congress in his second term. Johnson led the way to enactment of a profusion of Great Society programs after his 1964 landslide election. Reagan successfully sponsored unprecedented budget and tax cuts in 1981.

The Roosevelt case at its initial stage illustrates the most likely circumstance in which Eisenhower-style leadership could be adapted to a presidential program calling for comprehensive change. A number of the enactments in Roosevelt's historic "100 Days" immediately after his 1933 inauguration had extensive bipartisan support and were *not* accompanied by publicized presidential wheeling and dealing. Later on, Roosevelt's willingness to take the lead in politicking with Congress became publicly evident—at least until Pearl Harbor when he announced that "Dr. New Deal" had become "Dr. Win the War" and emphasized the chief of state side of his leadership. In March 1933, however, social and economic conditions were so grievous that he could lead the way to major innovations without being visibly manipulative or highly controversial. For the moment, leaders of both parties were willing to treat normally divisive presidential proposals as if they were the appropriate initiatives of a nonpartisan head of state. Eisenhower's style could have been equally successful in producing major innovations at such a time.* But except in such a period of crisis, Eisenhower's leadership style is not suited to effecting major political change, though we should note that other approaches normally do not succeed either.

Eisenhower's leadership style also would have been unsuitable for enacting Johnson's Great Society programs and the 1981 Reaganomics policies. Both of these decision-making sequences were marked by publicized presidential political pressure which was precisely what Eisenhower sought to avoid.

This does not mean that Eisenhower avoided exercising *un*publicized influence or that his style was ill-suited for bringing about less than sweeping change. Initiation of the long stalemated St. Lawrence Seaway project and of the complex, far-reaching interstate highway construction program and passage of the first civil rights legislation since Reconstruction were among the outcomes of his approach. His style also enabled him to exercise leadership by preventing outcomes he opposed. The bipartisan bloc of conservatives who dominated his first three Congresses did not succeed in "rolling back" the basic New Deal reforms. The liberals who were strong in his final Congress did not succeed in instituting substantial welfare-state innovations. In each case, his aim was to hold the line and he got what he wanted, as he did over the eight years in resisting pressures to increase defense spend-

---

*Roosevelt's procedure during the 100 Days was particularly consistent with Eisenhower's leadership style in the legislative session's first enactment, the Emergency Banking Act. He cleared the way for action by vividly and effectivly establishing himself as an inspirational chief of state through his inaugural address. On March 9, 1933, "the bill passed the House without a record vote, received approval of the Senate four hours later, and was promulgated by the chief executive the same evening." The Senate Republican leader's often quoted remarks to his colleagues urging support of Roosevelt are a perfect illustration of how leaders respond to a president at times when they view him as worthy of support by virtue of his status as head of state: "The House is burning down," he said, "and the President of the United States says this is the way to put out the fire." There was resistance to a number of measures passed in that brief, extraordinary legislative session and Roosevelt did serve as principal de facto strategist, but by and large he saw to it that his congressional allies engaged in the bargaining and confined himself to announcements that emphasized his role as a broad-based leader responding to a national emergency.[1]

ing. His style, then, is suitable for producing incremental change and otherwise exercising influence, but not for sparking major sequences of change, except in emergencies such as the virtual national economic collapse at the time when Roosevelt took office.

What about the political climate and context of Eisenhower's time in office? Were these necessary for his style to work? And were they without parallel in the political settings future presidents will face?

Eisenhower's times, it may be argued, were so static and politically uneventful that his approach of subordinating the visible side of political leadership could work then (at least to the extent of enabling him to remain so popular), but the approach would have no applicability to the tumultuous years which followed the 1950s. Eisenhower's critics commonly have argued that the success of his presidency was due to the serenity of the period. If this view were valid, there would be no profit in looking to his leadership for lessons.

A few broadly stated reminders refute the notion that Eisenhower led the country during an intrinsically uneventful time. The 1950s were as potentially tense and vexed as the 1960s. Eisenhower took office in the midst of a stalemated, unpopular war. One reason for the tranquility of the times was that his administration achieved a truce within six months of the inaugural ceremonies. Another was that he refused to become enmeshed in further military conflicts, as in 1954 when a number of his associates urged that the United States commit its military strength to Indo-China to retrieve the fast collapsing French resistance to Ho Chi Minh's forces. Moreover, it is largely in retrospect that his presidency is remembered as conflict-free in the realm of foreign policy. There were sharp disagreements within and between the parties over whether the nation's foreign policy should be basically internationalist and over how aggressively the cold war should be prosecuted.

The domestic political context of Eisenhower's presidency appears gentle partly because McCarthy's condemnation reduced public preoccupation with American subversives and with American policymakers' responsibility for the growth of Soviet power after World War II. And there were major domestic political conflicts over such issues as civil rights, education, welfare, and regulatory policy, just as there were foreign policy conflicts.

Such conflicts were less prone to produce a *sense* of eventfulness during Eisenhower's incumbency than they would have under another president because Eisenhower successfully implemented his hold-the-line domestic policies,* and because he kept intact a bipartisan internationalist foreign policy coalition and avoided allowing the cold war to reheat into military encounters and confrontations. Eventfulness is equated with change and attempts at change, rather than effort expended to prevent undesired change. Apart from putting much of his energies into curbing outcomes he wanted to avoid, he invested continuing effort in fostering a *sense* of calm by quietly dealing with likely sources of controversy and by adopting a crisis-minimizing demeanor in volatile situations.

In short, the Eisenhower years were not so uniquely uncontroversial in the potentiality they offered for eventfulness that a presidential style which worked then would be irrelevant to other periods. Eisenhower, moreover, experienced one problem common to chief executives in all but a few of the years since presidential responsibilities grew so substantially in the Roosevelt era—congressional intractability. His internationalist foreign policies consistently received more Democratic than Republican congressional support, and his basically conservative domestic programs required him to rely on coalitions of Republicans and conservative Democrats.† In Eisenhower's time a president was better able to use party leaders to build coalitions than presidents have been in the past decade with the increased autonomy of individual legislators. At the same time, however, high seniority committee chairmen had more power to block presidential initiatives than in recent Congresses. Overall, congressional intractability to presidential leadership is likely to be similar in degree, if different in form, in the final decades of this century as it was in the 1950s.[3]

The conclusion that Eisenhower's leadership style was not so bound to his times and goals as to be irrelevant to today's presidents, brings

---

*Eisenhower, of course, did not inherit the troubled economy of the early 1980s. It is beyond the scope of plausible "what ifs" to attempt within the compass of this analysis to reason intelligently about what Eisenhower (or for that matter any president) could do to counter the "stagflation" of recent years.

†Eisenhower remarked in 1953 to a supporter who wondered why the first Republican president in twenty years was not being more partisanly assertive, "Every measure we deem essential to the progress and welfare of America normally requires Democratic support in varying degrees."[2]

us to the elusive issue of man and style. Will this style be able to be used by other presidents, since they inevitably will not have Eisenhower's personal qualities?

The most unique of these was a *result* of the combination of his personality and life experiences, but it had its immediate source in public reactions to him—his status as a national hero for almost a decade before taking office. During much of that time leaders of both major parties viewed him as a man they wanted to see in the White House. Eisenhower also had less obvious qualities that were highly distinctive. Few presidents are likely to have his talent for compartmentalizing their private and public sides while conveying a sense of spontaneity. No do-it-yourself book can teach a leader to manage to be vague and folksy in public yet precise and analytic in private, to exude an apolitical aura while constantly devising political strategies and accurately appraising political personalities and practices, to view his immediate associates and other political actors with analytic detachment while conveying easy openness in working with them, and to pour intense energy into his efforts while appearing in public to be reasonably relaxed.

Since such apparent dichotomies underpinned Eisenhower's ability to blend political with chief of state leadership and formal with informal organization, it is unlikely that we will see many other presidents capable of adopting the full Eisenhower style.

Therefore the question must be not whether other presidents can *adopt* Eisenhower's style, but rather, if they are so disposed, whether they can *adapt* aspects of it to their own capacities and needs. The lessons any president's style can have for a successor are best viewed in the spirit of de Tocqueville, who in commending American political ways to Europeans, took for granted that other nations neither could nor would want simply to imitate the United States, but rather might come to understand the principles underlying American governance by drawing selectively on them and making modifications consistent with their own nation's traditions and properties.[4]

Eisenhower's political strategies provide a convenient starting place for considering the degree to which elements of his leadership style could be adapted to the needs of other presidents. I have noted the five strategies he used in handling the prime ministerial side of his job—hidden-hand leadership, instrumental use of language, refusal to engage in personal attacks on other political actors, combined with close private attention to the personalities of other political actors, and a selective approach to his acts of delegation. These played directly into his continuing efforts to enhance the chief of state role by encouraging public support for the president and the presidency.

Presidents of the future will not be able to hide their involvement in political maneuver so thoroughly that their very connection with the details of day-to-day leadership eludes many of their contemporaries. Eisenhower had a combination of attributes that are unprecedented and would seem to be unrepeatable in the annals of the presidency: electability, a credible public reputation as a nonpolitician, and well-developed political skills.

Even another Eisenhower would be ill-advised to *ground* a presidency on hidden-hand leadership. There were risks in at least some of his concealed politicking. While the transcript of Eisenhower's conversation with Republican Chairman Hall on removing Nixon from candidacy in 1956 does not have the repugnant quality of the transcripts of Nixon's Oval Office conversations, the release of the content of the Eisenhower-Hall discussion (apart from whether it became known that it was recorded) would inevitably have hurt Eisenhower's esteem precisely because this was the kind of conversation he was supposed not to have.

Eisenhower's leadership, however, was not "grounded" on hidden activity. There could be no hand hiding in connection with much of the political side of presidential leadership—for example, his legislative proposals, his vetoes, and his speeches at campaign rallies and party fund-raising events. It would be more correct to say that he managed to minimize the visibility of the political side of his role and play up his chief of state status.

Future presidents will be less able to emphasize the chief of state role to the extent that Eisenhower could. Nevertheless, the option exists to move in the same direction. In order to do so, a president necessarily will have to forego one source of influence that has its classic description in Richard Neustadt's authoritative commentary on how presidents can be effective leaders. Chapter four of *Presidential Power* is devoted to "professional reputation," the belief on the part of significant other political actors that the president is an able politician, who consistently rewards allies and punishes enemies. Neustadt is undoubtedly correct in arguing that Eisenhower's political effectiveness sometimes suffered because he lacked such a reputation. But there can be advantages to the lack of professional reputation as long as the actual performance of the political system and society satisfies the electorate. By conveying the sense of being more than a mere politician, the president can add to his store of what Neustadt properly identifies as another of the major resources for presidential influence, prestige with the general public.[5]

Eisenhower's instrumental use of language is even less suitable to use by other presidents than his hidden-hand leadership, because it was closely tied to his unusual range of verbal capacities. The precept a future president might take from Eisenhower's instrumental use of language, whether or not he had Eisenhower's rhetorical versatility, is to avoid, at least in public, the luxury of using his articulations as ends in themselves rather than as means of securing results. Rhetoric periodically has served the needs of presidents to vent their feelings rather than as a tool of leadership. Nixon and Carter, for example, gave evidence in various of their speeches and press conferences of seeking to propitiate their own sense (in Carter's phrase) of "malaise" rather than using language to advance their political and policy goals.

Eisenhower's no-personalities formula was a subset of his more general insistence on adapting his public discourse to the requirements of effective leadership. The principle behind the formula was more important for his leadership style than was his refusal to speak critically of other individuals. The principle is captured in his observation to Paul Helms that "a leader's job is to get others to go along with him in the promotion of something. To do this he needs their good will. To destroy good will, it is only necessary to criticize publicly."[6]

Eisenhower had a remarkable capacity to hold his tongue. He maintained amicable relations with Field Marshall Bernard Montgomery although he was offended by Montgomery's public deprecation of his military skill. Why was that self-restraint desirable? A rupture between Eisenhower and Montgomery would have damaged Anglo-American relations. Needless to say many politicians, some of them presidents, seem incapable of avoiding deeply personal conflicts with political enemies; some even seem to reach out to make enemies, as for example

Lyndon Johnson with Robert Kennedy. For such an individual the no-personalities rule, even if adopted, would be of no avail in its fundamental purpose of maintaining sufficiently cordial relations that today's adversary can be tomorrow's ally. Such a president could mechanically use Eisenhower's formula, but it would be hollow.

On the other hand, antagonistic personal exchanges that leave no lasting wounds are standard in the dramaturgy of professional party politics. Eisenhower did not find it comfortable or consistent with his sense of personal comportment to engage in such exchanges. Another president, one gifted at light polemic and able to direct his barbs only at adversaries accustomed to playing the same game, might successfully achieve Eisenhower's aim without literally adhering to the rule. Thus, those presidents with the capacity to follow the spirit (but not necessarily the letter) of the no-personalities rule can enhance their effectiveness, especially in keeping options open for future alliances.

Eisenhower's preoccupation with noting the qualities of other political actors and adjusting his actions to their "personal equations" can be commended to any leader. Clearly there is no guarantee that a president will have the psychological acuity to gauge his own political choices on the basis of judgments of the personal qualities of the people with whom he works and deals. Eisenhower's extensive experience exercising command over large organizations and in managing or helping manage the headquarters of organizations sensitized him to "personnel psychology." From the start of his career, he showed a gift for organizational leadership, including choosing people who were well suited for their jobs, or finding jobs to match their qualities.

In Eisenhower's case the ability to make judgments about who did or did not fit where and how best to use associates seemed rooted in a constellation of personal qualities. These included his capacity for practical abstraction—that is for stripping down policy problems to their major components and conceptualizing the variables composing them—as well as his sensitivity to the fact that a major variable in analyzing and acting on a problem almost inevitably is the personal qualities of the individuals involved. And, while he exuded impressive personal warmth to associates, he had the capacity to put psychological space between himself and them, unemotionally analyzing their strengths and weaknesses.

Although Eisenhower's personnel-assessment skills were unusually well developed, many politicians are shrewd at gauging personality. Once in the White House, however, a president may fail to make a regular point of thinking about how to factor the personal qualities of the people with whom he works and deals into his own leadership. A president, for example, might not want his White House national security assistant to be his principal channel of foreign policy information and advice, but might neglect to take pains to choose a secretary of state with a forceful personality and a record for making himself heard in bureaucratic decision making.

A particularly important presidential personnel-management quality, judging from the several presidencies in which the president employed advisers who reinforced his own weaknesses or shortcomings, is the capacity to choose subordinates who compensate for one's own weaknesses. This calls for a high degree of self-awareness on the part of the president, as well as a better capacity to make personality assessments than some recent presidents have exhibited. For those presidents (by some accounts Carter was one) who are themselves not good judges of associates' strengths and weaknesses, the better part of intelligent action based on personality will be to find trustworthy aides who are gifted at making such evaluations.

Just as the instrumental-use-of-language and no-personalities strategies overlap and complement each other, so do those of action based on personality and delegation selectively practiced. Much of Eisenhower's selectivity in what he would and would not entrust to an associate was a result of his observation of the subordinate's aptitudes. His willingness to make broad delegations in relatively lower priority policy areas has become increasingly germane to presidential leadership, as the number of responsibilities assigned to the executive branch increases.

Of the six presidents since Eisenhower, the one who has projected the strongest impression of being devoted to delegation both in theory and practice is Ronald Reagan. Without engaging in instant history of the Reagan administration, it is possible to say that published accounts of conflicts within the Reagan administration exceed not only the 1950s journalism about the Eisenhower administration, but also the later archival and oral history record.

237

At some distant time a Ronald Reagan presidential library may release records comparable to the Eisenhower Library's Whitman papers, and it will be possible to confirm or discredit a seeming difference between the two men's approach to delegation. In Eisenhower's case we know that he consistently applied himself to the task of committing cabinet members to the notion that they were a team, giving them a strong sense of participation in framing an overall administration program, and insisting that differences be hammered out within the administration after which all members could form a common front. On the face of it Reagan has been less able to mold solidarity, though his difficulties have largely been in foreign policy, and seemed certain to diminish with the replacement of Alexander Haig with George Shultz as secretary of state.

As long as Eisenhower had established general guidelines within which departments were to operate he was prepared to leave many specifics to the department secretary. More than one former cabinet member was surprised at how much leeway Eisenhower gave him, but remembers that Eisenhower told him, in effect, "You'll be hearing from me if I disapprove of your actions." Knowing that a president who attempted to do everything would wind up accomplishing nothing, Eisenhower made substantial delegations in some areas in order to have a maximum impact in others. Part of his style which should be adaptable by other presidents was assessing who could be left to operate reasonably independently and who should be monitored or even supervised. Another part was to delegate without abdicating by promulgating clear general guidelines and by fostering in colleagues a strong sense that they *should* pull together.

I have emphasized Eisenhower's use of the lightning-rod effect of delegation. In this era when presidents are so vulnerable to losing public support, future presidents have much to gain from allowing associates to promulgate and take responsibility for some of the less popular administration decisions.*

---

*Jimmy Carter, for example, had in his first HEW secretary, Joseph Califano, a public figure with a sufficiently independent reputation and personal disposition to be effective as a deflector. Califano might, for example, have been prepared to take responsibility for painful retrenchments in welfare programs that seemed increasingly necessary in the economic environment of the late 1970s. As it turned out, however, Califano instead became one of the casualties of Carter's July 1979 cabinet purge, an action that probably contributed to Carter's eroding public support.

Interestingly, during the Reagan administration, with its many publicized procedures that parallel 1950s accounts of Eisenhower's operations, the term "lightning rod" has come into general use.[7] Office of Management and Budget Director David Stockman has been prototypical of a Reagan aide said to be used in this manner. An aide viewed as a lightning rod, however, will not keep bolts from striking the president. This is especially true if the president is a visible co-implementer of the policies with which the controversial subordinate is associated.

Reagan in his first presidential year was more Neustadtian than Eisenhowerian. He allowed himself to be publicized telephoning congressmen to enlist their support for the budget cuts that Stockman had defended in congressional hearings. His public addresses were designed to add further to the pressure on the legislators. He and his staff made no secret of their vigorous efforts to stimulate constituency pressures for what was explicitly labeled a presidential policy. Legislative action of far greater than ordinary scope emerged from this process during his first year in office, but not lightning-rod protection. Clearly, Eisenhower's style of leadership was not suitable for this kind of approach to policy enactment. Eisenhower, by the same token, would not have been drawn to a style that led to the rapid erosion in support Reagan had experienced by his second year in office.

Eisenhower's high level of support and its broad base was central to his strategy of publicly emphasizing the chief of state over the prime-ministerial component of the presidency. Although future presidents are unlikely to take office with the initial capital of being a national hero, they may be able to draw on Eisenhower's low profile, anti-conflictual approach to politicking in ways that maintain their national esteem. By hiding their part in day-to-day machinations, they can avoid being viewed as controversialists. By using even their partisan language (as did Eisenhower) in ways that stress the common interests and equal loyalty of the parties (contrast McCarthy on "the party of treason"), they can further stresss commitment to the nation as a whole. Thus, departing from the tendency of many Republicans to impugn the loyalty of the Democrats, Eisenhower practiced a precept he once enunciated to Mrs. Whitman: "Always leave a line of retreat open to your antagonist, and the most important . . . is never to challenge his motives."[8]

Even the way he used the linked strategies of no personalities and action based on personality helped build his image as a national unifier. The first persistently put him on the record as a man who would not stoop to personal animosity. The second helped him maintain warm personal relations with many individual Democrats, including the Democratic leaders of the two houses of Congress. At the very least, the heat-deflecting aspect of his delegation practices increased his capacity to maintain broad public backing.

Another general source of his widely diffused support was his presentation of self. We know that he had been aware of the importance of a leader's demeanor for rallying followers in his wartime capacity as Supreme Commander in Europe, resolving to "meet everyone from general to private with a smile, a pat on the back, and a definite interest in his problems," saving his worries for his pillow.[9] Eisenhower explained to Henry Luce, who sent him an October 1960 *Life* editorial reflecting on whether Eisenhower's leadership had been too gentle, that as president he acted with a view to "maintaining a respectable image of American life before the world. Among the qualities the American government must exhibit is dignity. In turn the principal governmental spokesman must strive to display it. In war and in peace I've had no respect for the desk-pounder and have despised the loud and slick talker."[10]

Seeking to communicate a sense of balance, stability, and responsibility to the world, he simultaneously conveyed to his countrymen that their president was worthy of respect. In the 1950s, public confidence in and respect for the presidency was widespread. The research literature of the time accepted as fixed the great support people expressed for the chief executive—a level of support that Eisenhower helped produce and that since has seriously declined.[11]

No formula exists for conveying the impression of a respect-worthy chief of state. Eisenhower indulged in remarkably little obvious presidential "mystification." He would probably have considered Nixon's introduction of uniformed White House guards and Reagan's display of ruffles and flourishes to be mere pompousness. But we have seen the efforts he took to compose an inauguration speech that would reach the Kansas ditchdigger, yet carry conviction at the Quai d' Orsay. And we know that he drew on the homely resources of his Kansas boyhood and alluded to his wartime experience, never seeming to brag, but still reinforcing the public images that had originally made him so attractive as a presidential candidate. Reserving his angular side for his friends, he projected to the public the image of a quintessential American.

The personal raw materials he employed to convey his ecumenical commitment to all categories of Americans are of course not available to every other president. Although other presidents claimed some similar elements in their backgrounds and experiences, including down-to-earth qualities that people found appealing in Eisenhower, they were less successful in employing them to achieve public esteem. Being a farmboy did not win Truman great contemporary prestige, nor did Ford's references to his football days seem to make much difference in the public's esteem for him. To the degree that there are lessons in Eisenhower's self-presentation, they are to establish links across the nation's party and social divisions.

Eisenhower's organizational leadership would seem on the surface to be the most easily transferable part of his political style. If as an organizer he had simply been the formalist he was once thought to be, his organizational leadership would be simple to copy. But the formal side of his leadership, as highly developed as it was, succeeded because it was intertwined with informal procedures and practices. Nevertheless, because many of the forms did have functions in and of themselves, they also are suitable for employment by presidents in the years to come. Obvious possibilities for emulation are the cabinet as a collegial body, the National Security Council and its accompanying "policy hill," the use of a chief of staff as a deputy. Taking his use of these structures and procedures as a point of departure, we can briefly review formal procedure and weave in the informal in quest of further lessons.

In the case of the cabinet, when Eisenhower told his secretaries-elect that he was going to constitute them as a "policy body," he surely knew that the cabinet would not make policy, but he nevertheless foresaw that cabinet meetings would play a significant part in his leadership. Their major functions were general policy clarification and, especially, team building, consolidation, and conveying the policy line, so that extensive delegation was possible. The existence of the secretariat helped make cabinet members take their collegial commitment seriously, and the Policy Planning Board did this even more effectively in the case of the NSC.

That carefully planned group consultation can contribute to clarifying policy goals and finding effective means of attaining them is suggested by some of the unhappy experiences encountered during the highly informal, brief presidency of Eisenhower's successor, John F. Kennedy. Kennedy's great faith in informal organization and distrust of staff procedures were influenced by the criticism he helped promulgate in the late 1950s of "overorganization" in the Eisenhower presidency.

In retrospect, it can be seen that a number of Kennedy decisions might have profited from more formal analysis. The obvious example is the Bay of Pigs episode. Eisenhower might not have dealt with such a sensitive operation in the NSC, but he would have subjected it to extensive staff work. Less obvious and less evident in its effect is the Apollo project. The manned moon expedition was far more costly, a good many scientists argue, and yielded fewer scientific results than did the unmanned space exploration that has since taken place. It is not clear whether the project ever received a disciplined analysis in terms of tradeoffs. Evidently not, judging from Kennedy's chief aide Theodore Sorenson's remark in his Kennedy Library Oral History that the project was undertaken because the administration was in need of a dramatic action to maintain its appearance of forward motion.[12] While it may be true that the impact of the moon landing on "world opinion" was worth the expense and allocation of resources, programs of Project Apollo's magnitude should be stiffly debated beforehand. In the domestic sphere, Kennedy might plausibly have made contingency plans for responding to possible steel price increases in 1962 which did not call for so powerful an assault on the steel industry that the administration's relations with business would be strained thereafter.[13]

Eisenhower's use of collegial bodies for team building also is potentially adaptable to other presidents' needs and abilities. Certainly the results helped him, just as the absence of collective commitment by key associates tended to hurt other presidents. Eisenhower never had such contentious breaks with cabinet secretaries as did Truman with Harold Ickes, Henry Wallace, and James Byrnes or Carter with Joseph Califano. There were no lamentations from Eisenhower's cabinet members that they never saw the president or received a hearing as occurred during Nixon's presidency when Interior Secretary Walter Hickel resigned after being unable to see the president for many months. Nor was there the public acrimony within and between the White House staff and cabinet that has been prevalent in several recent presidencies.

Eisenhower's regular cabinet meetings and even more regular (and longer) NSC meetings were time-consuming. This practice of routinized, prestaffed committee discussion called for a president who was prepared to meet regularly with his top aides and press through a closely packed agenda. When supplemented by the requirement that implementation planning be undertaken for all decisions, the process indicated to everyone concerned that they were in an administration with recognizable standards and policies. As William Bundy, who served in the CIA in the Eisenhower years and as assistant secretary of state for Southeast Asia affairs during the Johnson years, put it, the Eisenhower NSC process clarified foreign policy and made at least its broad policy assumptions explicit so that they could be collectively understood and reasoned about by the chief policy makers. It was less necessary for the president's colleagues to make inferences about what he would or would not support. Bundy was both a member of Eisenhower's Policy Planning Board and a participant in Johnson's highly informal "Tuesday Luncheons" where much Vietnam policy was made. He commented:

[Johnson] was very difficult to pin down on where he *had* come down on a thing. I think his style generally carried lack of system and structure way too far; I lived through the Eisenhower period when there was too much of it, but there was just a lot too little of it for the effectiveness and the sense of working together of senior people. . . . What *really* do we think our bombing's doing? What *really* do we think our forces add up to?[14]

Eisenhower's use of a staff chief as a deputy also has much to commend it. The Sherman Adams role had come under so much fire in the 1950s that Kennedy and Johnson underplayed and even refused to elucidate the degree to which certain aides were chief coordinators (especially Sorenson under Kennedy). The presumption was that a president who did not personally draw together the staff's endeavors would

243

be fed a bland diet consisting of only the information and proposals the staff chief wanted to bring to his attention.

Eisenhower's "invisible White House"—his extensive informal communications network—helped preserve him from this danger, as did the limited jurisdiction of his chief of staff, who was completely out of foreign policy and only one of several aides with direct access to the president. Adams's most important function for Eisenhower was as a deputy—in the language of science fiction genetics, a policy clone. Rather than restraining the president by cutting him off from decisions, Adams had the responsibility of magnifying Eisenhower's influence by learning, partly through osmosis and trial and error, partly by direct consultation, precisely what his general policies were and acting for him on lesser issues. If a chief of staff can act reliably for a president, enabling him to delegate lesser chores but maintain overall perspective and control over White House policies and decisions, that president stands some chance of mustering his energies around major issues that demand his close attention.

Nixon was the next president after Eisenhower to employ a de facto chief of staff, namely, H.R. Haldeman. Like Adams, Haldeman was confined to domestic affairs. (Henry Kissinger, of course, was Nixon's preeminent foreign affairs advisor, roughly paralleling the role Dulles played for Eisenhower, though doing so from the White House rather than the State Department.) Under Nixon, however, centralized staff procedures appear in fact to have reinforced the president's reclusiveness and to have had certain of the isolating consequences that were inaccurately attributed to Eisenhower's staff organization.[15] Ford and Carter began without staff chiefs, but found it necessary to institute them. Reagan carried over his use of a pyramidal staff from his governorship.

Indeed, by the 1980s the National Academy of Public Administration issued a new report with the new conventional wisdom that there *should* be a White House chief of staff.[16] The Eisenhower lesson therefore becomes less one of whether to institute such a position than of how to make it work as Eisenhower's did, neither making de facto policy decisions that the president merely ratifies, nor confining him to a single stream of information.

Eisenhower's capacity to think organizationally—to conceive policy problems in terms of the formal and informal group processes through which they could best be clarified and implemented—is, of course, far less transferable than the specific instruments and arrangements he employed. This faculty would have been less well developed, if Eisenhower's organizational experience had not been vast. The military practice of making organizational arrangements explicit and debating over and experimenting with different approaches to command also conditioned him, above and beyond what might be expected of other categories of public servants, to think in the abstract about organization. In addition, the ubiquitous need for effective military administrators to understand how to work "outside channels" surely helps account for his continuing disposition to blend the rhythm of formal structure with the melody of creative use of informal organization.

Eisenhower's personal equation clearly influenced his style of group leadership. Military procedures often are consistent with the stereotype of rigidity, overreliance on hierarchy and channels, and order for its own sake. Eisenhower may have avoided this because he was singularly free of the need to impose systems on his subordinates out of a compulsion to show he was "in charge" rather than to accomplish practical ends. He had a temper, but remarkably little sign of feelings of personal inadequacy.

The writer responsible for the most thoughtful, research-based contemporary account of Eisenhower's World War II leadership, Kenneth C. Davis, concluded that because of the efficiency of his command, journalists at Eisenhower's wartime headquarters frequently underestimated his military skills and his ability unobtrusively to exercise decisive leadership over his many strong-willed subordinates. He never seemed to be dressing people down or otherwise demonstrating that he was on top. Davis concluded that Eisenhower's image fell short of reality on this score because "what he did in the military sphere seemed so easily, almost casually, done that it was easily under-rated." In his copy of Davis's book, Eisenhower wrote at the margin of this passage "If this is true it is the highest possible praise—all C.O.'s should strive for it."[17]

Leaders who strain to be formalists—Eisenhower called them marti-

245

nets—are the heavies in his anecdotal memoir about his early years and military career.[18] His manner as a West Point cadet who received an above average quota of demerits for violating the academy rules governing superficial aspects of students' personal comportment prefigures the career soldier who regularly obeyed the letter of rules but found ways of solving problems informally when ritualistic conformity would have stalled or halted him in attaining his goals. In establishing formal-cum-informal organizations, such capacities as analytical precision in evaluating relationships and purposes and an aptitude for assessing how to suit personalities to specific responsibilities accounted for Eisenhower's success.

As president, Eisenhower's use of formal and informal organization is only hinted at by the examples in chapter 4. He regularly put people together in ad hoc or standing groups, seeking reports from them, encouraging them to develop the personal ties necessary for successful cooperation, and making creative use of a proposition social psychologists of organizations have repeatedly found persuasive—decisions are likely to be of better quality if they have been reflected upon by more than one mind. Kennedy and Roosevelt used multiple advisors to insure that decisions were not based on limited information or reflection, but Eisenhower was far more concerned than either of them to build into his routines the requirement that policies be exposed to "multiple advocacy"[19]— that policy making and policy advising should not be adventitious or unbalanced. He forcefully stated his view of how to gather advice and information in group settings in his 1967 Columbia University Oral History interview:

> I have been forced to make decisions, some of them of a critical character, for a good many years. And I know of only one way in which you can be sure you've done your best to make a wise decision. That is to get all of the people who have partial and definable responsibility in this particular field, whatever it be. Get them with their different viewpoints in front of you, and listen to them debate. I do not believe in bringing them in one at a time, and therefore being more impressed by the most recent one you hear than the earlier ones. You must get courageous men, men of strong views, and let them debate and argue with each other. You listen, and you see if there's anything been brought up, an idea that changes your own view or enriches your view or adds to it. Sometimes the case be-

comes so simple that you can make a decision right then. Or you may go back and wait two or three weeks, if time isn't of the essence. But you make it.[20]

Eisenhower's keenness as an organizer of the advice he received was rooted in his makeup and experience. Transferability of his procedures probably cannot be dealt with much more rigorously than with the tautological formula that given Eisenhower's skills and a desire to follow his procedures, a president can do so. At a minimum his formal procedures can be imitated and warrant study by future presidents. Rigorous staff work and systematic institutional back-up for policy making is persistently lacking in modern presidencies, as is the teamwork that is an informal offshoot of this procedure. Eisenhower's capacity to use informal organization was more idiosyncratic. Nevertheless, once understood, aspects of his informal leadership also may be available to future presidents, though here, as in his strategies, some presidential personalities will accommodate to the Eisenhower style, some will not, and some presidents may find it profitable to draw on aides to help them surmount their personal inability to take advantage of aspects of Eisenhower's style that would advance their leadership.

Above and beyond detailed strategies and organization styles, Eisenhower's approach to presidential leadership reflects a broad bias for a kind of politics that need not be confined to the presidency. The converse of a politics of setting the nation's sights by bringing controversial issues to a head is a politics of unobtrusive guidance. Eisenhower did not subscribe to the idea that problems automatically go away. He believed that they should be attacked, but not necessarily with publicity. Undoubtedly, his long experience with the bureaucracies of the interwar army helped shape his belief, as did perhaps his parental tradition of religiously based pacifism. In its mature manifestations, this predilection is reflected in Eisenhower's remark to Paul Helms that making enemies is inconsistent with leadership. Thus he preferred a compromise agreement to a public fight. An ex-boxer and competitive sportsman, his conciliatory impulse does not seem to have stemmed from fear of conflict. Rather, he thought in terms of feasibility and concluded that fights often cost more than they yield.

His concern with problem solving was linked to a perception that

247

many people with whom he had to work did not share his own rationality, but rather tended to use politics as an emotional outlet. In his 1945 correspondence with Mark Clark about the inadvisability of answering Congressman Rankin's charges, Eisenhower acutely observed that, if he did, everyone who sought attention or nursed grudges would come forth and testify.[21]

If one believes that political conflict commonly has irrational roots, it follows that the task of politics often will be, as political psychologist Harold Lasswell puts it, less to solve problems than to prevent them.[22] This calls for a politics of seeking agreement and minimizing discordant open debate. Eisenhower's preoccupation on this score may have been excessive and may have been based on an underestimation of the harmless, not to speak of the positive, functions of conflict. Yet even presidents who favor sharp public debate may nevertheless agree that, at least in the case of especially emotion-arousing political issues, prevention may succeed where cure cannot. Presidents who make judicious use of preventive politics may be more likely to sustain stable public support, mitigating the make-and-then-break pattern of most modern presidencies.

Although Eisenhower was a far more effective leader than many critics realized, he was not a political genius. His style may have left a greater legacy than his use of it. He failed in some of his most heartfelt goals, such as a Nixon victory in 1960 and progress toward easing East-West tension. Furthermore, the style has obvious shortcomings, including some that were identified in the standard 1950s critiques, in addition to its strengths.

What is most important about the Eisenhower leadership for the 1980s is understanding that a distinct and until recently unstudied leadership style was employed in the 1950s, that the style existed and worked much of the time for fostering the nation's last two-term presidency. The study of how Eisenhower managed his leadership has only just begun. It behooves Americans who are concerned about the future of their institutions to continue to dig and to learn more about this unexpectedly fascinating presidency. In doing so we are sure to gain insight into the potential for successful leadership in a complex society with a political system that often seems unmanageable and poses truly formidable obstacles to achieving intelligent direction.

Key to Primary Sources and Abbreviations

COHC   Columbia Oral History Collection
      (Permission to quote has been granted by the Trustees of Columbia University or by all living participants or their executors.)

PDDE   *The Papers of Dwight David Eisenhower: The War Years, I-V,* ed. Alfred D. Chandler, Jr., (Baltimore: The Johns Hopkins University Press, 1970); and *The Papers of Dwight David Eisenhower: The Chief of Staff, VI–IX,* ed. Louis Galambos (Baltimore: The Johns Hopkins University Press, 1978).

PPOP   *Public Papers of the Presidents: Dwight D. Eisenhower, 1953–1961,* (Washington, D.C.: U.S. Government Printing Office).

Eisenhower Library Material

OF   Records as President, White House Central Files, 1953–61, (Official File).

HD   James C. Hagerty Diary

PD   Dwight D. Eisenhower Diaries 1935–38, 1942, 1948–53, 1966, 1968, 1969. I also include in the classification PD so-called diary entries from the presidential period 1953–61, which can be located in the Ann Whitman File, DDE Diary Series (WF-DDE). The bulk of these diary items for 1935–67 have also been published by Robert H. Ferrell as *The Eisenhower Diaries* (New York: Norton, 1981). Ferrell has also taken items from WF-DDE, and to be consistent with his published text I cite these as PD.

WF   Dwight D. Eisenhower, Papers as President of the United States, 1953–61 (Ann Whitman File); Divided into the following series:

WF-A   Administration Series

WF-AWD   Ann Whitman Diary Series
WF-C   Cabinet Series
WF-DDE   DDE Diary Series
WF-DH   Dulles Herter Series
WF-I   International Series
WF-IM   International Meeting Series
WF-L   Legislative Meeting Series
WF-N   Name Series
WF-PC   Press Conference Series
WF-PT   Presidential Transition Series
WF-S   Speech Series
WF-SD   Stag Dinner Series

Other primary materials (including Eisenhower Library materials) will be cited in full.

NOTES

Prologue and Acknowledgments

1. Murray Kempton, "The Underestimation of Dwight D. Eisenhower," *Esquire*, September 1967:108.

2. Garry Wills, *Nixon Agonistes* (Boston: Houghton Mifflin, 1970).

Chapter 1

1. Of all survey organizations, the Gallup Poll [American Institute of Public Opinion (AIPO)] has conducted the longest sequence of inquiries into public approval of incumbent presidents. Beginning early in the 1940s AIPO interviewers regularly asked random samples of Americans "Generally speaking how do you think President X is doing his job?" Basic sources for Gallup statistics are *The Gallup Poll: Public Opinion 1935–1971*, 3 vols. (New York: Random House, 1972); *The Gallup Poll: Public Opinion 1972–1977*, 2 vols. (Wilmington, Del.: Scholarly Resources, Inc., 1978 and annual volumes thereafter). From time to time AIPO summarizes its full record of presidential popularity ratings in *Gallup Opinion Index*. See, for example, Report no. 125, November-December, 1975. On Reagan's year-end popularity see AIPO Release, January 10, 1982.

2. There have been two waves of scholarship documenting and reappraising Eisenhower's policies, actions, and to a lesser extent leadership style. The first, based on documents that became available in the early 1970s, includes Herbert S. Parmet, *Eisenhower and the American Crusades* (New York: Macmillan, 1972); Peter Lyon, *Eisenhower: The Portrait of a Hero* (Boston: Little, Brown, 1974); Charles C. Alexander, *Holding the Line: The Eisenhower Era, 1953–1961* (Bloomington: Indiana University Press, 1975); and Elmo Richardson, *The Presidency of Dwight D. Eisenhower* (Lawrence, Kans.: The Regents Press of Kansas, 1979). For valuable reviews of these and related writings see Vincent P. De Santis, "Eisenhower Revisionism," *Review of Politics* 38 (1976): 190–207; and Gary W. Reichard, "Eisenhower as President: The Changing View," *South Atlantic Quarterly* 77 (1978): 265–81. The second, drawing on substantial additional material released in the mid-1970s, includes Robert A. Divine, *Eisenhower and the Cold War* (New York: Oxford University Press, 1981); Blanche Wiesen Cook, *The Declassified Eisenhower: A Divided Legacy* (Garden City, N.Y.: Doubleday, 1981); William Bragg Ewald, Jr., *Eisenhower the President: Crucial Days 1951–1960* (Englewood Cliffs, N.J.: Prentice Hall, 1981); Stephen E. Ambrose, *Ike's Spies: Eisenhower and the Espionage Establishment* (Garden City, N.Y.: Doubleday, 1981); and Robert H. Ferrell, ed., *The Eisenhower Diaries* (New York: Norton, 1981), which, in addition to including hitherto unpublished writings by Eisenhower, has valuable notes.

3. For an expansion of these observations see Fred I. Greenstein, "Change and Continuity in the Modern Presidency," in *The New American Political System*, ed. Anthony King (Washington, D.C.: American Enterprise Institute, 1978), pp. 45–86.

4. Compare Cronin's comments on Americans' expectations that the president be both "national unifier" and "national divider." "Our nation is one of the few that calls upon its chief executive to serve also as its symbolic, ceremonial head of state . . . [W]e call on our presidents and our presidency to serve as a unifying force in our lives . . . We have designed a presidential job description, however, that impels our contemporary presidents to act as national dividers. A president, as a creative chief executive, cannot help but offend certain interests." Thomas E. Cronin, *The State of the Presidency*, 2nd ed. (Boston: Little, Brown, 1980), p. 14. Clinton Rossiter, in his once standard, idealized account of *The American Presidency*, rev. ed. (New York: Harcourt, Brace and World, 1960), chap. 1, views the president's status as "king and prime minister rolled into one," as a political asset contributing to the ability of presidents to exercise effective influence over domestic and international affairs. Rossiter may have been rendered insensitive to the potential conflict between these facets of the presidential role by the lack of controversy over the presidency as an institution at the time of his study and the unusually high popularity of the then incumbent president—Eisenhower. There is wide diversity in different writers' views of the roles played by the president and in whether or not they claim that contradictions among roles are not inherent in his job. In bifurcating the presidency into the two roles of chief of state and prime minister, I am making an analytic distinction that captures what Americans seem implicitly to expect of the institution and its incumbent. I do not posit (and public opinion poll research undoubtedly would not support) that the bulk of citizens verbalize this distinction. Nor should it be assumed that the condition Rossiter thought of as general (one in which the chief of state and roles of the president reinforce each other) *never* obtains. I give examples of circumstances during Franklin Roosevelt's administration in which both roles were clearly complementary in chapter 6, pp. 229–30.

5. Richard E. Neustadt, *Presidential Power: The Politics of Leadership* (New York: Wiley, 1960). The most recent edition of this highly influential work, subtitled *The Politics of Influence from FDR to Carter*, was published in 1980.

6. Richard H. Rovere, *Affairs of State: The Eisenhower Years* (New York: Farrar, Straus and Cudahy, 1956), pp. 6, 17, 353.

7. Arthur M. Schlesinger, Sr., "Our Presidents: A Rating by 74 Historians," *New York Times Magazine*, July 29, 1962, pp. 12*ff*. The statistics Schlesinger based his account on are presented in full by Samuel Rosenman and Dorothy Rosenman, *Presidential Style* (New York: Harper and Row, 1976), pp. 551–52.

8. An example of nostalgic celebration of innocent Ike and his era is Vic Gold's "Bury My Heart at Burning Tree: A Fond Remembrance of the Eisenhower Years," *Washingtonian* 14 (May 1979): 142–49.

9. On Guatemala see Richard Immerman, "Guatemala as Cold War History," *Political Science Quarterly* 95 (Winter 1980–81): 629–53 and his *The CIA in Guatemala: The Foreign Policy of Intervention* (Austin: University of Texas Press, 1982). On Iran see Richard Cottom, *Nationalism in Iran* (Pittsburgh: University of Pittsburgh Press, 1964); Barry Rubin, *Paved with Good Intentions: The American Experience in Iran* (New York: Oxford University Press, 1980); and Kermit Roosevelt, *Countercoup: The Struggle for the Control of Iran* (New York: McGraw-Hill, 1979).

10. An outstanding example of the reassessment of Eisenhower as a leader is Gary Reichard's systematically documented, carefully reasoned study of Eisenhower administration strategy and tactics in the first congressional session after he took office, *The Reaffirmation of Republicanism: Eisenhower and the Eighty-third Congress* (Knoxville: University of Tennessee Press, 1975). This "first wave" study, which stresses the skill of the new administration in its congressional relations, is amply supported by the documents that became available shortly after Reichard's book was published—for example, the minutes of Eisenhower's cabinet meetings and meetings with members of Congress. Other accounts of Eisenhower as a political practitioner include, Fred I. Greenstein, "Eisenhower as an Activist President: A Look at New Evidence," *Political Science Quarterly* 94 (Winter 1979–80): 575–99; Richard Immerman, "Eisenhower and Dulles: Who Made the

Notes

Decisions?" *Political Psychology* 1 (1979): 21–38; Douglas Kinnard, *President Eisenhower and Strategy Management: A Study in Defense Politics* (Lexington: University Press of Kentucky, 1977), and "President Eisenhower and the Defense Budget," *Journal of Politics* 39 (1977): 596–623. Historian Mary S. McAuliffe, in a review of "second wave" scholarship on Eisenhower, "Commentary: Eisenhower, The President," *The Journal of American History* 68 (1981): 625–32, observes that "however one considers him . . . Eisenhower is emerging as one of the most important presidents of this century (p. 632)."

11. Rovere, *Affairs of State*, pp. 355–67; quotation on p. 367.

12. Arthur Krock, "Impressions of the President—and the Man," *New York Times Magazine* (June 23, 1957): 5 *ff*.

13. Murray Kempton, "The Underestimation of Dwight D. Eisenhower," *Esquire*, (September 1967): 108 *ff*. Cf. Richard Rovere's rejoinder "Eisenhower Revisited A Political Genius?" *New York Times Magazine* (February 7, 1971): 14.

14. Eisenhower writes in *The White House Years: Waging Peace, 1956–1961* (Garden City,: N.Y. Doubleday, 1965).

> A final important characteristic of the plane was its fragile construction. This led to the assumption insisted upon by the CIA (and the Joint Chiefs) that in the event of mishap the plane would virtually disintegrate. It would be impossible, if things should go wrong, they said, for the Soviets to come in possession of the equipment intact—or, unfortunately, of the pilot. This was a cruel assumption, but I was assured that the young pilots undertaking these missions were doing so with their eyes wide open and motivated by a high degree of a patriotism, a swashbuckling bravado, and certain material inducements. (p. 546).

15. Richard M. Nixon, *Six Crises* (Garden City: Doubleday, 1962), p. 161.

16. The phrase is from a letter Eisenhower wrote to a family friend who had remarked on the spate of news stories about his personality and background after he became commander of the North African invasion in the fall of 1942.

> While I have seen only a very few of the articles and notices involving me that have appeared in the United States, I hear there have been quite a number considering the fact that the authors had only a Kansas farmerboy to start on in the first place. . . .
>
> When I have time to think about the matter at all, I merely wonder what kind of a fanciful picture of my very ordinary characteristics all this publicity is building up in the popular mind.

Eisenhower to Ethel Mae Megginson Wyman, December 13, 1942, PDDE, Vol. 2, p. 835.

17. Among the primary sources and works rich in primary source material for the account that follows are: Dwight D. Eisenhower, *At Ease: Stories I Tell to Friends* (Garden City, N.Y.: Doubleday, 1967); and his *Crusade in Europe* (Garden City, N.Y.: Doubleday, 1948); Bela Kornitizer, *The Great American Heritage: The Story of the Five Eisenhower Brothers* (New York: Farrar, Straus and Cudahy, 1955); Stephen Ambrose, *The Supreme Commander: The War Years of General Dwight D. Eisenhower* (Garden City, N.Y.: Doubleday, 1970). The most thorough journalist's account, completed shortly before the end of World War II on the basis of two years of thorough research, is Kenneth S. Davis, *Soldier of Democracy: A Biography of Dwight Eisenhower* (Garden City, N.Y.: Doubleday, 1945). A copy of this book, annotated by Eisenhower, noting assertions he considered especially to the point, indicating inaccuracies, and adding supplementary observations, is in the Rare Book Room of the Ellis Slater Library, Eisenhower College, Seneca Falls, N.Y. I am indebted to Milton Eisenhower for background conversation on his brother's early years and prepresidential career. My principal documentary primary sources and their abbreviations are listed on pp. 249–50.

18. PD, January 21, 1953.

19. Eisenhower, *At Ease*, p. 213.

20. Lucius B. Clay, COHC.

21. Eisenhower, *Crusade in Europe*, p. 22.

22. *New York Times*, February 20, 1942, p. 3.

23. Ambrose, *The Supreme Commander*.

Notes

Chapter 2

1. Theodore H. White, *In Search of History: A Personal Adventure* (New York: Harper & Row, 1978), p. 347.

2. Richard Fenno interview with Stuyvesant Wainwright, 1961; confirmed and cleared for publication by Wainwright in 1980 interview with Richard Immerman.

3. Henry Kissinger, *The White House Years* (Boston: Little, Brown, 1979), p. 43.

4. Ibid., pp. 451–52.

5. There is an intrinsic difficulty in carrying off this chapter's mission and that of chapters 3 and 4. It is circular to explain a leadership style in terms of the leader's personal characteristics and to infer those characteristics from the fact that he employed the leadership style. Yet since I must take much of the evidence of the personal qualities Eisenhower brought to the presidency from examples of his leadership, I inevitably reveal elements of his leadership style in this chapter, just as the man is periodically visible in chapters three and four. Edward J. Thomas, in what is probably the most systematic discussion of the requirements of analyzing the relationship between personality and role, makes clear that criteria for making the analytic distinction between the two have not been well developed by behavioral scientists. His own analysis, which draws illustratively on representative studies, moreover, deals exclusively with quantitative studies in which psychometric criteria have been used to measure personality and in which personality characteristics are being correlated with performance of rather standardized roles. Eisenhower is not available for psychological testing, even if the technology for quantitative personality assessment were adequate for adumbrating the politically consequential traits of a leader.

Further, while all presidents (at least in the modern era) do face somewhat similar role requirements, it is in fact the distinctive aspect of the way Eisenhower carried out the presidential role that I seek to explain. My "solution" has been to *emphasize* dispositions (and their biographical antecedents) in this chapter and to *emphasize* role performance (including examples of his political style before entering the White House) in chapters 3 and 4, recognizing that some of the illustrations and episodes in this chapter and in the two that follow can be interpreted in terms of personality or in terms of role depending on which of their facets the reader notes.

On general issues of role and personality see Thomas's essay, "Role Theory, Personality and the Individual," in *Handbook of Personality Theory and Research*, ed. Edgar F. Borgatta and William W. Lambert (Chicago: Rand McNally, 1968), pp. 691–727; Ralph H. Turner, "The Role and the Person," *American Journal of Sociology* 84 (1978): 1–23; and Alexander George, "Assessing Presidential Character," *World Politics* 26 (1974): 248–82. For suggestions as to how more traditionally rigorous standards for social science hypothesis testing than are appropriate for this analysis can be applied to the study of individual political actors, see Fred I. Greenstein, *Personality and Politics: Problems of Evidence, Inference and Conceptualization*, rev. ed. (New York: Norton, 1975), chap. 3; and Greenstein, *"Personality and Politics,"* in *Handbook of Political Science: Micropolitical Theory II* ed. Greenstein and Nelson W. Polsby, (Reading, Mass.: Addison-Wesley, 1975), esp. pp. 32–43 and the literature cited therein.

6. The Eisenhower Library holds the original Signal Corps recordings of his press conferences as well as an extensive film collection.

7. Eisenhower to Henry Luce, August 8, 1960, WF-DDE.

8. Dwight D. Eisenhower, *The White House Years: Mandate for Change 1953–1956* (Garden City, N.Y.: Doubleday, 1963), pp. 232–33.

9. A biographical note makes Eisenhower's powers of reasoning and exposition less surprising. Although his overall academic rank among the 164 graduates of the West Point class of 1951 was 61st (and his rank in deportment 95th), he was 10th in his class in English composition. His classmates report that the essays with which he won this recognition typically were written rapidly, a few minutes before class. Clear reasoning presumably generated clear writing. In Abilene High School, where he also failed to distinguish himself generally as a scholar, he nevertheless had stellar grades—A+ equivalents—in subject matter calling for clear sequences of deductive reasoning, namely plane geometry. His abilities at writing and reading contributed to his top-ranking performance in the 1925 Command and General Staff College graduating class and were extensively used by the army in the prewar years, notably in his work for MacArthur in the 1930s which involved preparing documents, including War Department annual

reports, for MacArthur's signature and writing MacArthur's speeches. When Marshall brought Eisenhower to the Planning Division of the War Department immediately after Pearl Harbor, he asked John J. McCloy to size up the new man. McCloy was immediately impressed by Eisenhower's ability to lay bare the essentials of complex problems, putting his conclusions on paper systematically and lucidly.

This biographical information was culled from Dwight D. Eisenhower *At Ease: Stories I Tell to Friends* (Garden City: N.Y. Doubleday, 1967), and Kenneth S. Davis, *Soldier of Democracy: A Biography of Dwight Eisenhower* (Garden City: N.Y.: Doubleday, 1945). I am indebted to the superintendent of the United States Military Academy, West Point, N.Y., for a copy of Eisenhower's cadet grades and class standing and to John J. McCloy for his account. Edgar F. Puryear, Jr., *Nineteen Stars* (Washington, D.C.: Coiner Publications, 1971) draws on interviews with Eisenhower's classmates, including one describing his essay-writing speed and ability.

10. Eisenhower to Alfred M. Gruenther, February 1, 1955, WF-A (Gruenther). See also Bennett C. Rushkoff, "Eisenhower, Dulles, and the Quemoy-Matsu Crisis, 1954–55," *Political Science Quarterly* 96 (1981): 465–80.

11. Eisenhower to George Catlett Marshall, December 3, 1944, PDDE, vol. 2, p. 789.

12. Andrew J. Goodpaster, COHC and personal communication.

13. PD, April 1, 1968.

14. William E. Robinson Diary, July 18–25, 1960, Eisenhower Library.

15. Arthur Krock Papers, "Approx. May 5, 1965," Mudd Library, Princeton University. Also see Arthur Krock, *Memoirs* (New York: Funk and Wagnalls, 1968), pp. 398–99.

16. PDDE, vol. 7, p. 776n.

17. Eisenhower to Mark Wayne Clark, April 4, 1945, PDDE, VII, p. 982.

18. PDDE, vol. 7, p. 983n.

19. Eisenhower to Mark Wayne Clark, July 3, 1946, PDDE, Vol. 7, p. 1172.

20. Stephen Ambrose, *The Supreme Commander: The War Years of General Dwight D. Eisenhower* (Garden City, N.Y.: Doubleday, 1970), p. 214.

21. Personal interview, Arthur Minnich.

22. Robert Bowie, COHC.

23. From a letter from Lieutenant Edward C. Thayer to his mother from Leavenworth, January 1918. Enclosed in January 1958, WF-AWD.

24. Stephen Hess, *Organizing the Presidency* (Washington: The Brookings Institution, 1976) p. 60.

25. Emmet John Hughes, *The Ordeal of Power* (New York: Atheneum, 1963) p. 135.

26. Ibid.

27. Robert Bowie, COHC.

28. Walter Bedell Smith to General Maxwell D. Taylor, February 1, 1956, Walter Bedell Smith Papers, Eisenhower Library.

29. "Notes on Ike," January 4, 1954, C. D. Jackson Papers, Eisenhower Library. Portions of these notes, but not the passage quoted here, are interspersed in the text of a January 18, 1954 laudatory *Time* word and photographic feature on Eisenhower's personality that appeared shortly before Jackson left the White House staff.

30. Robert K. Gray, *Eighteen Acres Under Glass* (Garden City, N.Y.: Doubleday, 1962), p. 172.

31. Eisenhower to James Vincent Forrestal, February 7, 1948, PDDE, vol. 9, p. 2250.

32. Ibid.

33. Eisenhower to John S.D. Eisenhower, June 19, 1945, PDDE, vol. 2, p. 1198.

34. Herbert Hyman and Paul B. Sheatsley, "The Political Appeal of President Eisenhower," *Public Opinion Quarterly* 17 (Winter 1953–1954): 443–60.

35. Eisenhower, *Crusade in Europe* manuscript, "Introduction not in Book," n.d., p. 4, Eisenhower Library.

36. Eisenhower, *Mandate for Change*, p. 60.

37. John Osborne, "White House Watch: Gabbing with [Bryce] Harlow," *New Republic* (May 13, 1978): 12–14.

38. For example, Eisenhower to Milton Eisenhower, August 10, 1943, PDDE, vol. 2, p. 1330.

39. Ambrose, *The Supreme Commander*, p. 320.

40. Eisenhower, *At Ease*, p. 354.

41. Ibid., p. 355.

42. PD, February 7, 1950.

43. Remarks such as the following are scattered throughout the book written by Clifford Roberts, Eisenhower's friend, golf and bridge companion, fundraiser, and investment counselor, *The Story of the Augusta National Golf Club* (Garden City, N.Y.: Doubleday, 1976):

> The President never liked to sit down, even at a meeting. He had to get up and walk about as he thought or talked. He had to work or play constantly, unless he was completely tired out. More than once after eighteen holes of golf I've wanted badly to stretch out and rest, only to have Sergeant Moaney [Eisenhower's valet] come and tell me as I stepped out of the shower, "The Boss is ready to play bridge!" (p. 165).

Eisenhower's accounts of bridge games resemble his assessments of political and military situations and actors. For example, Eisenhower to Paul Alfred Hodgson, November 28, 1947, PDDE, Vol. 9, pp. 2086–87:

> The other evening I played a game with Al Gruenther, Averell Harriman and Ely Culbertson. I was the only loser. Mr. Culbertson plays aggressively and quickly. He has a nice personality and is perfectly willing to play for any size stake, including the smallest. Al is likewise a top-notch player—a bit on the deliberate side. Averell loves the game but seems to me to be a bit unsure of himself. On the other hand his seeming hesitance may be nothing but a continuing revision of his analyses to assure he makes no mistakes. I often wish I were a bit more deliberate myself.

The letter goes on to detail "the only hand of any real interest" and reconstruct how he and his partner Culbertson would have carried the evening if Eisenhower had more clearly signaled the strength of his hand.

44. See the suggestion that Eisenhower be photographed less on the golf course and more in the pursuit of official duties in Henry Cabot Lodge's unsigned memo entitled "Grass Roots Report from California," September 30, 1953, WF-DDE.

45. See, for example the poll released June 26, 1953: "In your opinion do you think President Eisenhower is taking too much time off to play golf or not?" Yes: 17 percent; No: 73 percent; No opinion: 10 percent. *The Gallup Poll: Public Opinion 1935–1971*, 3 vols. (New York: Random House, 1972).

46. Dillon Anderson, COHC.

47. "Confidential notes on visit with General Dwight D. Eisenhower," Oct. 17, 1947, W.E. Robinson Diary, Eisenhower Library.

48. These schedules, consisting of ex post facto listings of the president's official day, are contained in WF-AWD. My supplementary observations about his actions in the unofficial portions of the day are derived from interviews, notably with Milton Eisenhower. Appointment Files, Eisenhower Library.

49. Eisenhower to Captain Everett ("Swede") Hazlett, January 23, 1956, WF-N (Hazlett).

50. "Text of Harlow's Keynote Address at Nashville Symposium," *Center House Bulletin* 4 (Winter 1974): 7. (This is the parent publication of *Presidential Studies Quarterly*).

51. Bryce N. Harlow, John Foster Dulles Oral History Project, Princeton University Library. Quoted with permission.

52. When asked by reporters if his parents had been pacifists, Eisenhower said that while his mother had joined a sect with pacifist tenets, "I think it would be enough to say about my father's belligerency that he was Pennsylvania Dutch and he had the temper of a Pennsylvania Dutchman and there was nothing pacifistic about him." July 7, 1954 News Conference, PPOP, 1954, p. 624. And in *At Ease* (p. 304) he says of his father, "His temper would blaze with frightening suddenness." Other references in *At Ease* to David Eisenhower portray the father as a stern, old-fashioned disciplinarian. In describing his mother he stresses her gentleness of temperament and her instinct for mediation. For example: "Father had quick judicial instincts. Mother had, like a psychologist, insight into the fact that each son was a unique personality and she adapted her methods to each (p. 33)."

53. Special Counsel Bernard Shanley, Shanley Diary, Preface, Eisenhower Library.

54. CBS Special, "Five Presidents on the Presidency," a production of CBS News, 1973, Producer Peter Poor, Executive Producer, Perry Wolff.

55. Such psychological inferences are inevitably tentative. For an expansion and defense of my assertion about Nixon, see Greenstein, "A President is Forced to Resign: Watergate, White

House Organization and Nixon's Personality," in *American Politics in the 1970s,* ed. Allan Sindler (Boston: Little, Brown, 1977), pp. 50–98.

56. CBS, "Five Presidents on the Presidency."

57. See the entries in the index of Ambrose, *The Supreme Commander* under Montgomery for "Eisenhower" and "Eisenhower Showdown," p. 724.

58. Eisenhower to George Catlett Marshall, August 24, 1943, PDDE, vol. 2, p. 1354.

59. Vernon A. Walters, *Silent Missions* (Garden City, N.Y.: Doubleday, 1978) p. 226.

60. James David Barber, *The Presidential Character,* 2nd. ed., (Englewood Cliffs, N.J.: Prentice-Hall, 1977), pp. 156–73, esp. pp. 172–73.

61. See Eisenhower's preface to Stephen Ambrose,*Duty, Honor, Country: A History of West Point* (Baltimore: The Johns Hopkins University Press, 1966).

62. Eisenhower, *At Ease,* p. 118.

63. See especially PD, January 1, 1950. I do not mean to suggest that these remarks about duty plumb the depths of his motivations. He also was ambitious, concerned about his historical reputation, from time to time self-righteous and, as anyone is, activated by motives he himself probably barely sensed. Nevertheless, his feelings were so secure (or as some psychologists might conclude, his defenses so intact) that he does not lend himself to as easy psychodiagnosis as do people who conspicuously parade their inner strains.

64. "Resume of Conversation with Lucius Clay," November 18, 1954, WF-DDE.

65. Milton Eisenhower in a personally typed letter to his brother, dated September 15, 1955, WF-N (Eisenhower, Milton) pointed out that Vice-President Nixon had been seeking to lock Dwight into a second-term commitment by telling journalists that he personally was convinced the president would run again. Milton offered to leak, "in complete confidence" to members of the party who were known to be loquacious, the information that, while he had no positive information, as the man with the best sense of his brother's thinking and motivation he was sure that Dwight meant *not* to seek a second term. This information, Milton submitted, would rapidly spread and soon create a field of contenders, increasing Dwight's own flexibility about whether or not to run again and if not how best to make his influence felt in the choice of the next nominee.

The letter probably arrived in Denver after Dwight's September 24 heart attack. Dwight began attending to certain official responsibilities remarkably soon after the heart attack, but his physicians deliberately insulated him from newspaper and radio news (and by extension issues likely to provoke his pique or anger) for five weeks and he then operated on a limited schedule until late in the year. On March 26, 1956, in a letter to Everett Hazlett, (WF-N Hazlett) he said that of the "vast combination" of "delicately balanced factors that had led him to run again, one "—and this has been mentioned to one one else—had to do with a guilty feeling on my own part that I had failed to bring forward and establish a logical successor for myself." The time "lost" in the final months of 1955 would have been a crucial period for him to do this.

66. "Conversation between the President and Senator Styles Bridges, 5/21/57," WF-DDE.

67. "Eisenhower to Richard L. Simon, Simon and Schuster, Inc., April 14, 1956," WF-DDE:
I have spent my life in the study of military strength as a deterrent to war, and the character of military armaments necessary to win at war. The study of the first of these questions is still profitable, but we are rapidly coming to the point that no war can be *won.* War implies a contest: when you get to the point where contest is no longer involved and that the outlook comes close to destruction of the enemy and suicide for ourselves—an outlook that neither side can ignore—and arguments as to the exact amount of available strength as compared to somebody else's are no longer the vital issues. When we get to the point, as some day we will, that both sides know that in any outbreak of general hostilities, regardless of the element of surprise, destruction will be both reciprocal and complete, possibly we will have sense enough to meet at the conference table with the understanding that the era of armaments has ended and the human race must conform its actions to this truth or die.

68. PD, January 17, 1949. Also see Samuel F. Wells, Jr., "The Origins of Massive Retaliation," *Political Science Quarterly* 96 (1981): 31–52, esp. pp. 40–41.

69. For a brief account by Eisenhower, see *At Ease,* pp. 370–72. The episode is described from Senator Taft's perspective by his biographer, James T. Patterson, in *Mr. Republican: A Biog-*

raphy of Robert A. Taft (Boston: Houghton Mifflin, 1972), pp. 483–84. I am indebted to Brigadier General Robert Schultz for an eyewitness account of this episode.

70. Dwight D. Eisenhower, COHC.
71. Eisenhower to Clarence J. Brown, June 12, 1957, OF, III-C-7.
72. PD, January 18, 1954.
73. PD, January 4, 1950.
74. Eisenhower to Edgar Eisenhower, November 8, 1954, WF-N (Eisenhower, Edgar).
75. "MEMORANDUM FOR THE DIRECTOR OF THE BUREAU OF THE BUDGET," December 22, 1953, WF-DDE.
76. "MEMORANDUM TO THE DIRECTOR OF THE BUREAU OF THE BUDGET," November 5, 1953, WF-DDE.
77. Eisenhower to Nelson Rockefeller, May 5, 1960, WF-DDE. Eisenhower's predilection for compromise was imbedded in a view of society that rejected the necessity for and desirability of social class and other conflicts among the major groups in the body politic. See Robert Griffith, "Dwight D. Eisenhower and the Corporate Commonwealth," *American Historical Review* 87 (1982): 87–122.
78. Harry C. Butcher, *My Three Years with Eisenhower* (New York: Simon and Schuster, 1946) p. 438.

Chapter 3

1. Grant McConnell, *Steel and the Presidency* (New York: Norton, 1963).
2. See the detailed reconstruction by John D. Pomfret in the *New York Times*, April 27, 1954.
3. See, for example, *Time*, October 2, 1978.
4. This point is well discussed by Erwin C. Hargrove, who points out that many commentators on American politics confuse advocacy of policy innovation by a leader with the issue of whether the leader himself attacks his work actively. "Presidential Personality and Revisionist Views of the Presidency," *American Journal of Political Science* 17 (1973): 819–35.
5. Phone Calls, March 19, 1954, WF-DDE.
6. Alfred Steinberg, *Sam Rayburn* (New York: Hawthorn Books, 1975), p. 240.
7. Robert B. Anderson, Lyndon Baines Johnson Library, Oral History Collection.
8. Henry Cabot Lodge, *As It Was* (New York: Norton, 1976), pp. 55–57.
9. Henry Cabot Lodge to Eisenhower, October 21, 1957, WF-A (Lodge); and Eisenhower to Robert B. Anderson, November 7, 1957, WF-A (Anderson).
10. Eisenhower to Governor James F. Byrnes, August 14, 1953, WF-N (Byrnes).
11. "Memorandum for Mr. Rabb," August 12, 1953, WF-DDE.
12. Minutes of NSC meeting, February 11, 1953, WF-NSC.
13. Dwight D. Eisenhower, *The White House Years: Mandate for Change 1953–1956* (Garden City, N.Y.: Doubleday, 1963), p. 181. (The phrase after the first ellipsis in the quoted passage appears in the previous sentence in the original text.)
14. See chap. 1, n. 9.
15. Conversation with Leonard Hall, "Diary," February 9, 1956, WF-AWD.
16. Conversation with Fred Seaton, "Diary," March 13, 1956, WF-AWD.
17. Conversation with Leonard Hall, "Diary," February 9, 1956, WF-AWD.
18. "Notes dictated by the Vice President after his discussion with Governor Adams, July 15, 1958, at 5:00 P.M.," July 15, 1958, WF-AWD.
19. "Diary," September 17, 1958, WF-AWD.
20. Sherman Adams, *Firsthand Report: The Story of the Eisenhower Administration* (New York: Harper and Bros. 1961), p. 447.
21. "Notes by the President on State of Union Speech, Draft No. 1," December 16, 1953, WF-DDE.
22. Ibid.
23. *New York Times*, June 25, 1942.

24. Eisenhower to George Smith Patton, Jr., February 4, 1943, PDDE, vol. 2, p. 939.

25. Pre-press Conference Briefing, July 21, 1957, WF-PC.

26. Ibid.

27. "The President's News Conference," July 17, 1957, PPOP.

28. Sissela Bok, *Lying: Moral Choice in Public and Private Life* (New York: Pantheon, 1978).

29. Eisenhower, *The White House Years: Mandate for Change 1953–1956* (Garden City, N.Y.: Doubleday, 1963), p. 478.

30. "The President's News Conference," March 23, 1955, PPOP. Eisenhower made a similar response the very next week to another question by Harsch on defending Formosa:

I think that the attitude and the calculations of this Government were pretty well laid out before the Senate and the House at the time of the passage of the recent resolution asking for authority to act under given situations.

However, I would say this: a terrific burden would depend upon the forces and the people occupying Formosa as to the possibility of its defense.

You have to have forces there who are of high morale, who have something in which to believe if they are going to fight well, as that is the only way men fight. They don't fight just to get out and shoot each other, so they must believe in something. And we must be careful not to destroy their morale. That is a factor that you must always calculate when you talk about surrendering this place or that place or doing anything else.

Now, as I say again, even for me, I don't think there is much to be gained by speculation in this field. But I do want you to see this one factor that is terrifically important if you are going to make a successful military defense of any area.

"The President's News Conference," March 30, 1955, PPOP.

31. "Note on Legislative Leadership Meeting," April 30, 1953, WF-L.

32. *"Top Secret.* One copy only of this memorandum made. Notes destroyed." May 1, 1953, WF-DDE.

33. "Note on Legislative Leadership Meeting," May 12, 1953, WF-L.

34. Legislative Leadership Meeting, Supplementary Notes," July 9, 1957, WF-L.

35. *25th Anniversary Reunion of the Staff of President Dwight D. Eisenhower,* processed booklet, 1979, p. 11.

36. Eisenhower to Maxwell Davenport Taylor, January 2, 1946, PDDE, VI, p. 710.

37. "To The Men and Women of the Allied Expeditionary Force: Victory Order of The Day, May 8, 1945," PDDE, vol. 6, pp. 16–17.

38. Eisenhower to Douglas Black, October 9, 1959, WF-DDE.

39. Eisenhower to Paul Helms, March 9, 1954, WF-N (Helms).

40. Senator Robert A. Taft, May 26, 1953, *Facts on File,* p. 165.

41. PD, July 1, 1953.

42. Senator Robert A. Taft, May 26, 1953, *Facts on File,* p. 165.

43. May 28, 1953, WF-PC.

44. "The President's News Conference," May 28, 1953, PPOP.

45. Walter Bedell Smith to Maxwell D. Taylor, February 1, 1946, Walter Bedell Papers, Dwight D. Eisenhower Library.

46. Eisenhower to George Catlett Marshall, September 20, 1943, PDDE, vol. 3, pp. 1439–40.

47. Eisenhower to George Catlett Marshall, March 3, 1943, PDDE, vol. 2, p. 1006.

48. HD, January 5, 1955.

49. See p. 63.

50. Eisenhower to John Foster Dulles, March 23, 1955, WF-DDE.

51. PD, January 18, 1954.

52. Eisenhower to Alfred M. Gruenther, July 2, 1954, WF-DDE.

53. William F. Knowland, COHC.

54. Report by Eisenhower of breakfast with Dirksen, July 23, 1953, WF-DDE. Consciously designating a lower level officer as the "real" leader of an organization was scarcely new to Eisenhower. In a December 10, 1942, note he dictated to Butcher, who kept his wartime diary, Eisenhower made this observation on the problem of choosing the most able person as a commander.

Occasionally, because of governmental practices and difficulties as to rank, he cannot place them [the "real" commanders] in actual command, but he can frequently bolster up an otherwise weak situation by getting one of these men into a position where, by personality and ability, he is the actual though not the nominal leader. (To Harry Cecil Butcher, PDDE, vol. 2, p. 824.)

55. PD, May 14, 1953.

56. Ibid.

57. Ibid.

58. Eisenhower, *Crusade in Europe* (Garden City, N.Y.: Doubleday, 1948), p. 35.

59. PD, June 25, 1942.

60. Eisenhower to Henry Luce, August 8, 1960, WF-DDE.

61. "Memorandum for the Director of the Bureau of the Budget," November 5, 1953, WF-A (Dodge).

62. Robert B. Anderson, Lyndon Baines Johnson Library Oral History Collection.

63. PD, May 14, 1953.

64. E. Bruce Gellhoed, *Charles E. Wilson and Controversy at the Pentagon, 1953–1956* (Detroit: Wayne State University Press, 1979), p. 19.

65. "Memorandum for the Secretary of Defense," November 30, 1953, WF-DDE.

66. "Memorandum for the Secretary of Defense," December 21, 1955, WF-DDE.

67. "Memorandum for General Cutler," October 21, 1953, WF-DDE.

68. Eisenhower to Brownell, January 25, 1954, WF-DDE.

69. Eisenhower requested the brief from Solicitor General Sobeloff and made changes which were included in the final brief. His edited version may be found in the Simon Sobeloff Papers, Manuscript Division, Library of Congress.

70. Eisenhower to Brownell, April 25, 1956, WF-DDE.

71. These interpretations are captured in a quantitative analysis of historians' judgments of the two men by Lloyd Etheridge, who has carefully reduced the standard secondary sources and memoirs of the period into statistical indexes. He finds the secretary of state to be exceedingly high on a scale of "personality dominance" (9.18 on a scale of 10) and Eisenhower to be extraordinarily low (a mere 2.33). Having reduced the public impressions of the day into quantitative indicators, Etheridge then turns the circle by concluding that his data support—"the traditional historians' judgments that . . . Eisenhower often took a back seat." Lloyd Etheridge, *A World of Men: The Private Sources of American Foreign Policy* (Cambridge: M.I.T. Press, 1978), pp. 79 and 92.

72. Richard Immerman, "Eisenhower and Dulles: Who Made the Decisions?" *Political Psychology* 1 (1979): 21–38. Immerman's analysis is anticipated by Richard Neustadt, who examined Dulles's appointment diaries during the Suez Crisis in order to establish that Eisenhower not Dulles was calling the signals in that episode. See his *Alliance Politics* (New York: Columbia University Press, 1970), pp. 103–7.

73. Telephone conversation, July 1, 1954, WF-DDE.

74. Dulles's press secretary, Carl McCardle, has provided an illuminating account of the details of how Dulles and Eisenhower kept steadily in touch and how Dulles's pronouncements were cleared with Eisenhower. Carl McCardle, COHC.

75. PD, February 13, 1953.

76. Eisenhower to John Foster Dulles, March 26, 1958, WF-DDE.

77. "Memorandum of a conference with the President, February 17, 1959," February 18, 1959, WF-DDE.

78. Stephen Hess, *Organizing The Presidency* (Washington, D.C.: The Brookings Institution, 1976), p. 65.

79. President Reagan's use of acerbic-seeming associates—for example, his Office of Management and Budget Director David A. Stockman—to promulgate in detail his controversial proposals for substantially reduced federal activity was widely viewed in the press as a self-conscious adoption (perhaps in deliberate departure from Jimmy Carter's tendency to absorb blame for all that befall his administration) of a policy of using delegation as a lightning rod to protect him from political blame. See Steven R. Weisman, "Reagan Dissipates Heat by Delegating Authority," *New York Times*, October 11, 1981, p. 4. On Reagan and Eisenhower, see Fred I. Greenstein and Robert Wright, "Reagan . . . Another Ike?" *Public Opinion* 3 (December/January 1981): 51–55 and my remarks in chapter six on the applicability of Eisenhower leadership style to other presidents.

Notes

80. Photostated copies of Eisenhower marginalia in Arthur Krock, *Memoirs* (New York: Funk & Wagnalls, 1968), p. 384, from Arthur Krock Papers, Mudd Library, Princeton University.

81. Gordon Hoxie, ed., *The White House: Organization and Operations* (New York: Center for the Study of the Presidency, 1971), p. 4.

82. For sources, see chap. 1, n.1.

83. Angus Campbell, Philip E. Converse, Warren E. Miller and Donald E. Stokes, *The American Voter* (New York: John Wiley & Sons, 1960), chap. 3.

84. Marquis Childs, *Eisenhower: Captive Hero* (New York: Harcourt, Brace, 1958).

85. Stanley Kelley, Jr., *Political Campaigning* (Washington, D.C.: The Brookings Institution, 1960).

86. *Time*, November 16, 1942.

87. For example, Raymond Daniell, " 'He is our Eisen and This is our Hour,' " *New York Times Magazine*, November 1, 1942, p. 9; Hanson W. Baldwin, "Men of Destiny—Leaders in North Africa"; *New York Times Magazine*, June 20, 1932, p. 5; Drew Middleton, "Eisenhower Plans Minutely, Then Strikes," *New York Times Magazine*, July 25, 1943, p. 3; Milton Bracken, "Our Hard-Hitting Invasion Chief," *New York Times Magazine*, January 2, 1944, p. 5.

88. Eisenhower to Edgar Newton Eisenhower, September 26, 1944, PPDE, vol. 4, pp. 2192–93.

89. Eisenhower to Charles Douglas Herron, June 11, 1945, PDDE, vol. 2, pp. 1186–87. Editor's note 1 refers to Butcher's draftsmanship.

90. See Stanley Kelley, Jr., *Professional Public Relations and Political Power* (Baltimore: The Johns Hopkins University Press, 1956), chaps. 4–5, and Robert Griffith, "Dwight D. Eisenhower and the Corporate Commonwealth," *American Historical Review* 87 (1982): 93–95.

91. Robert K. Merton, *An Inventory of Communications Addressed to General Eisenhower in the Spring of 1948: A Summary and Digest* (New York: Columbia University Bureau of Applied Social Research, September 1949), copy provided to me by Professor Merton. I thank him also for discussing the study with me and for his report of the experience of briefing Eisenhower.

92. "Radio and Television Address to the American People on the State of the Nation," April 5, 1954, PPOP.

93. Campbell et al., *The American Voter*, chap. 3.

94. "The President's News Conference," November 23, 1954, PPOP.

95. "Eisenhower to Emmet Hughes," December 10, 1953, WF-DDE.

Chapter 4

1. See Peter Blau, *The Dynamics of Bureaucracy* (Chicago: University of Chicago Press, 1955); Philip Selznick, *Leadership in Administration* (New York: Harper & Row, 1957); Peter Blau and W. Richard Scott, *Formal Organizations: A Comparative Approach* (San Francisco: Chandler, 1962); and Charles Perrow, *Complex Organizations* (Glenview, Ill.: Scott, Foresman, 1979), chap. 1.

2. Richard Tanner Johnson, *Managing the White House* (New York: Harper & Row, 1974), and his "Presidential Style," in *Perspectives on the Presidency* ed. Aaron Wildavsky (Boston: Little, Brown, 1979), pp. 262–300. Johnson uses the somewhat pejorative suffix "-ic" to identify presidential organizational procedures that emphasize official channels. He contrasts "formalistic" presidential organization with two types of informally organized advising systems—the "collegial" in which advisors have equal status and interact flexibly with the president on an amiable basis and the "competitive" in which the advisors vie for influence and attention. Johnson classifies the Eisenhower and Nixon arrangements as formalistic, those of Roosevelt as competitive, and those of the other modern presidents he discusses—Truman, Kennedy, and Johnson—as collegial. Alexander L. George suggests ways that formal and informal organization of advisors can be combined in a single president's operating procedures in *Presidential Decisionmaking in Foreign Policy: The Effective Use of Information and Advice* (Boulder, Colo.: Westview Press, 1980), pp. 164–69.

3. Longtime White House Chief Clerk William J. Hopkins provides a good description in his John F. Kennedy Library oral history. See also Fred I. Greenstein, "Change and Continuity

Notes

in the Presidency," in *The New American Political System* ed. Anthony King (Washington, D. C.: American Enterprise Institute, 1978), pp. 45–85.

4. Dwight D. Eisenhower, *The White House Years: Mandate for Change, 1953–1956* (Garden City, N.Y.: Doubleday, 1963), p. 87.

5. Eisenhower, *Mandate for Change*, p. 114.

6. To take one of the great many examples see Charles J. V. Murphy, "Eisenhower's White House," *Fortune*, July 1953, 75.

7. See the account of the informal approaches to operating the presidency of Roosevelt and Truman by Richard E. Neustadt, *Presidential Power: The Politics of Leadership from FDR to Carter* (New York: Norton, 1980), chap. 7, "Men in Office," which originally appeared in the 1960 edition of this classic work.

8. All quotations from the Hotel Commodore meeting are from the verbatim transcript of it, January 12–13, 1953, WF-C.

9. Carter Burgess, COHC; and Bradley H. Patterson, Jr., "The President's Cabinet: Issues and Answers," Special Publication, American Society for Public Administration, May 1976, pp. 106–11.

10. Bradley Patterson, "The President's Cabinet," p. 108.

11. Ibid., p. 110.

12. Ibid., p. 112.

13. Ann Whitman to Milton Eisenhower, August 28, 1956, WF-N (Eisenhower, Milton).

14. C. Douglas Dillon quoted by Arthur Schlesinger, Jr., *A Thousand Days* (Boston: Houghton Mifflin, 1965), p. 136.

15. Patterson, "The President's Cabinet," p. 109.

16. PD January 18, 1954.

17. Eisenhower to James V. Forrestal, February 7, 1948, PDDE, vol. 9, pp. 2242–56.

18. On Burns winning out over Humphrey see the Vanderbilt University collection of oral histories of former heads of the Council of Economic Advisors, publication forthcoming. I am indebted to Professor Erwin Hargrove for making this available to me.

19. John Bricker, COHC.

20. Eisenhower to Milton Eisenhower, November 23, 1954, WF-N (Eisenhower, Milton).

21. Milton Eisenhower to Eisenhower, "Monday" (no further date), WF-N (Eisenhower, Milton).

22. Cabinet Meeting, January 9, 1957, WF-C.

23. See Nathan R. Howard, ed., *The Basic Papers of George M. Humphrey as Secretary of the Treasury* (Cleveland: Western Reserve Historical Society, 1965) for the text of Humphrey's statement and a transcript of his news conference—"Remarks concerning the President's 1958 Budget," January 15, 1957, pp. 236–52. Also see Ellis Slater, *The Ike I Knew* (Published privately by the Ellis Slater Trust, 1980), p. 50.

24. Howard, *The Basic Papers of George M. Humphrey*, "Remarks Concerning the President's 1958 Budget," January 15, 1957, pp. 236–52.

25. *New York Times*, January 17, 1957. The request to the stenotypist is reproduced on p. 252 of Howard, *The Basic Papers of George M. Humphrey*.

26. Richard Neustadt, *Presidential Power*, chapter 6.

27. Patterson, "The President's Cabinet," p. 109.

28. "Excerpt of Cabinet Discussion," "Minutes of the Cabinet Meeting," January 16, 1959, WF-C.

29. Gordon Gray to Eisenhower, January 13, 1961, WF-N (G. Gray).

30. National Security Act of 1947 (61 Stat. 496; 50 U.S.C. 402).

31. For a study showing major continuities between NSC practices initiated during Truman's presidency and elaborated and formalized under Eisenhower, see Anna Kasten Nelson, "National Security I: Inventing a Process (1945–1960)," in *The Illusion of Presidential Government*, ed. Hugh Heclo and Lester M. Salamon (Boulder, Colo.: Westview Press, 1981), pp. 203–28. On later NSC developments, see I.M. Destler, "National Security II: The Rise of the Assistant (1961–1981)," in the same volume, pp. 203–28.

32. For this and other quotations by Cutler and much of the source for my description of detailed aspects of the workings of the NSC and the Planning and Operations Coordinating Boards, see Cutler's closed session testimony before Senator Jackson's subcommittee on May 24, 1960,

Notes

found in the subcommittee report of the U.S. Senate's (Jackson) Subcommittee on National Policy Machinery of the Committee on Government Operations, United States Senate *Organizing for National Security*, 3 vols. (Washington, D.C.: Government Printing Office, 1961). Cutler's testimony appears in volume 1, pp. 577–608. In volume 2 also see reprints of the following articles: Dillon Anderson, "The President and National Security," *Atlantic Monthly* (January 1956): 42–46; Robert Cutler, "The Development of the National Security Council," *Foreign Affairs* 34 (1956): 441–58; Gordon Gray, "Role of the National Security Council in the Formulation of National Policy," paper delivered at the Annual Meeting of the American Political Science Association, September 1959, pp. 180–91.

33. Representative contemporary critiques of the Eisenhower national security machinery are: ' Hans J. Morgenthau, "Can We Entrust Defense to a Committee?" *New York Times Magazine*, October 11, 1959, p. 9; and Paul Y. Hammond, *Organizing for Defense: The American Military Establishment in the Twentieth Century* (Princeton: Princeton University Press, 1961).

34. "The National Security Council—Official Description," Jackson Subcommittee Report, vol. 2, p. 131.

35. In addition to appearing in the official subcommittee documents cited in note 32, the Cutler testimony on which this and related documents are available in a commercially published volume: Henry M. Jackson, ed., *The National Security Council: Jackson Subcommittee Papers on Policy Making at the Presidential Level* (New York: Praeger, 1965).

36. "Memorandum of Discussion," August 30, 1956, WF-NSC.

37. For Dulles aide Bowie's comments on Eisenhower's readiness to resolve disputes and the common sense Bowie felt he displayed in his decisions, see chap. 2, pp. 46–47.

38. Elmer Staats, COHC.

39. The foreign policy community's awareness that many OCB-generated papers did not eventuate in actions fed the 1959–1960 debate about "government by committee" that stimulated and in turn was stimulated by the Jackson Committee Hearings. The OCB acquired a particularly poor reputation among the limited circle of Americans who attended to national security policy machinery and the still more limited circle of veteran foreign policy advisors associated with the Democratic party. Stigmatized as a mere "paper mill," it was dispatched unceremoniously by President Kennedy. Eisenhower himself comments in his memoirs that he was not fully satisfied with the OCB operations and thought they needed modification. But he was seeking a more effective way of planning for policy implementation—he did not favor doing without procedures to anticipate the requirements of putting policy plans into action. Dwight D. Eisenhower, *The White House Years: Waging Peace, [1956–1961]* (Garden City, N.Y.: Doubleday, 1965), p. 634.

In the view of Elmer Staats, the veteran civil servant who had been deeply involved both in Eisenhower's OCB and the Truman administration Psychological Strategy Board, much of the criticism misses the mark by overemphasizing the OCB paperwork. The busy policy-implementing top executives who served on the OCB began their Wednesday afternoons with a luncheon—an informal occasion for discussing the fundamental issues of who would do what and why in carrying out policy. Staats's view of this informal nexus is unequivocal:

> The OCB functioned, in my opinion, best when it was functioning most informally. The board members met at lunch, weekly, and at the luncheon no one was present except the members of the board, plus myself. This was an opportunity for free discussion on any matter which might be of concern, and each member usually came with some problems or some news to bring people up to date. . . .
>
> The second informal benefit that I saw grow up from this was the improvement of communication among agencies at the staff level. Now, this was a hard thing to measure. People got acquainted with their counterparts, in ways in which they never had to get acquainted before. The coordination took place between Individual A and Individual B simply because they had worked together in an OCB context, and therefore were able to go to lunch together, or to get on the telephone together, and relate their efforts. (Elmer Staats COHC).

40. Ann Whitman to Milton Eisenhower, August 28, 1956, WF-N.

41. Douglas Kinnard, "President Eisenhower and the Defense Budget," *Journal of Politics* 39 (1977): 598–623, quotation on p. 621. Also Douglas Kinnard, *President Eisenhower and Strategy Management: A Study in Defense Politics* (Lexington: University Press of Kentucky, 1977).

Notes

42. Personal communications with John S.D. Eisenhower and Andrew J. Goodpaster. See I.M. Destler, *Presidents, Bureaucrats and Foreign Politics of Organizational Reform* (Princeton, N.J.: Princeton University Press, 1972) and Destler's "National Security Management: What Have Presidents Wrought," *Political Science Quarterly* 95 (Winter, 1980–81): 573–88).

43. "Memorandum for the Secretary of Defense," June 3, 1959, WF-DDE.

44. Ann Whitman to Milton Eisenhower, August 28, 1956, WF-N.

45. "Memorandum for the Record," January 30, 1958, WF-DDE.

46. Telephone Conversation, Eisenhower with General Walter Bedell Smith, April 27, 1954, WF-DDE.

47. Stephen Ambrose, *The Supreme Commander: The War Years of General Dwight D. Eisenhower* (Garden City, N.Y.: Doubleday, 1970), p. 55.

48. Eisenhower, *Mandate for Change*, p. 89.

49. Sherman Adams, *Firsthand Reports: The Story of the Eisenhower Administration* (New York: Harper & Row, 1961), p. 50.

50. Statement by Adlai Stevenson, February 22, 1958, *Facts On File*, p. 64.

51. Marion D. Irish, "The Organization Man in the Presidency," *Journal of Politics* 20 (1958): 269.

52. Eisenhower to James V. Forrestal, February 7, 1948, PDDE, vol. 9, p. 2244.

53. Eisenhower to Walter Bedell Smith, November 14, 1942, PDDE, vol. 2, p. 712.

54. Photostated copies of Eisenhower marginal comments in Arthur Krock, *Memoirs* (New York: Funk & Wagnalls 1968), p. 306, from Arthur Krock Papers, Mudd Library, Princeton University.

55. Eisenhower to Forrestal, February 7, 1948, PDDE, Vol. 9, p. 2244.

56. Dwight D. Eisenhower, *Crusade in Europe* (Garden City, N.Y.: Doubleday, 1948), pp. 18–20. Also see Eisenhower's brief characterization of Marshall's general views of organization in leadership (p. 35)—they are identical in all respects to precepts Eisenhower frequently voiced. On the role of "mentors" in adult personality development (a category into which first Fox Conner and then Marshall fit in Eisenhower's career), see Daniel Levenson, *The Seasons of a Man's Life* (New York: Knopf, 1978).

57. Numerous sketches of Adams's public image have been written. Patrick Anderson summarizes the highlights of them in the Eisenhower chapter of his *The President's Men: White House Assistants of Franklin D. Roosevelt, Harry S. Truman, Dwight D. Eisenhower, John F. Kennedy, Lyndon B. Johnson* (Garden City N.Y.: Doubleday, 1969), Chap. 4. On Adams as an organizer see Carter Burgess, COHC.

58. "Memorandum of Conference with the President," March 23, 1959 (George V. Allen and Major John S.D. Eisenhower attending), WF-DDE.

59. Andrew J. Goodpaster, COHC.

60. Milton Eisenhower to Eisenhower, March 16, 1953, WF-N (Eisenhower, Milton).

61. Author's Personal communication with Sherman Adams.

62. "Notes taken during President's conversation with Governor Adams," October 12, 1955, WF-AWD.

63. Teletype, Eisenhower to Adams, September 25, 1954, WF-DDE. Eisenhower's passion for system clearly did not always bear results. His instructions of six months earlier had not been acted on, showing that he was not immune from the kinds of delays that led Jonathan Daniels to remark:

> Half of a President's suggestions, which theoretically carry the weight of orders, can be safely forgotten by a Cabinet member. And if a President asks about a suggestion a second time, he can safely be told that it is being investigated. If he asks a third time, a wise Cabinet officer will give him at least part of what he suggests. But only occasionally, except on the most important matters, do presidents ever get around to asking three times,

Frontier on the Potomac (New York: Macmillan, 1946), pp. 31–32.

64. "O.K., S.A." *Time*, January 9, 1956, pp. 18–22.

65. *United States Government Organization Manual 1951–52* (Washington, D.C.: Government Printing Office, 1951), pp. 55–58 and *United States Government Organization Manual 1957–58* (Washington, D.C.: Government Printing Office, 1957), p. 58.

66. Anderson, *The President's Men*, chap. 3, and personal interview, John Steelman.

Notes

67. Stephen Hess, *Organizing the Presidency* (Washington, D.C.: The Brookings Institution, 1976), p. 68.

68. "O.K., S.A." *Time*, January 9, 1956, p. 19.

69. Elmer Staats, COHC.

70. Wilton B. Persons, COHC. There is an overabundance of theories purporting to explain "the new Eisenhower"—that is, the notion that Eisenhower suddenly became an active president in 1959 and 1960. Both Adams and Dulles were gone. Staats (COHC, personal communications) was convinced that after Dulles had been replaced by Herter, Eisenhower "was more familiar with cables, reports and detailed departments" and more active in NSC meetings. He also noted the greater access subordinates had to discuss details with Eisenhower after Persons replaced Adams. But the NSC change may have been more in the division of verbal labor— Eisenhower had more need to carry the burden of exposition on specifics of foreign policy in Dulles's absence—than in the president's information level as far as foreign policy is concerned.

There was also a change in 1959 to a new, more aggressive Republican congressional leadership team. House Leader Joseph Martin was deposed of by his colleagues and replaced by Charles Halleck. Senate Leader William Knowland had been replaced by Everett Dirksen. Domestically, Eisenhower did get deeper into legislative affairs, evidently out of sheer delight in the new Republican leadership. But there was a third reason for his behavior to seem to be more that of an "activist." He was framing partisan issues for the 1960 campaign and combating a welfare-policy oriented, heavily Democratic Eighty-sixth Congress. In short, his style seemed new, but a substantial part of the newness resulted from surface responses to situational change and media preoccupation with the news value of a "new Eisenhower."

71. Richard M. Nixon, *Six Crises* (New York: Doubleday, 1962), p. 169 (paperback).

72. My sources include interviews with Milton Eisenhower, concerning his letters to his brother, WF-N (Eisenhower, Milton), and with Bernard Stanley and Thomas Stephens concerning their respective tenure as appointments secretary.

Chapter 5

1. Cf: Harry Eckstein, "Case Study and Theory in Political Science," in *The Handbook of Political Science VII*, ed. Fred I. Greenstein and Nelson W. Polsby (Reading, Mass.: Addison Wesley, 1975).

2. Robert Griffith, *The Politics of Fear: Joe McCarthy and the Senate* (Rochelle Park, N.J.: Hayden Book Co., 1970), p. 199. A similar view of Eisenhower's part in the McCarthy affair is taken in the other major "second stratum" monograph, Richard Fried's *Men against McCarthy* (New York: Columbia University Press, 1976). For the basic exposition of this episode, my sources when not cited are these works plus the *New York Times* and *Facts on File*. When I quote newspaper accounts and date them in the text, I do not also cite them in notes. I use citations to document all new information I present that is neither in the Griffith and Fried works nor in the newspaper articles identified in the text. The best "first stratum" account is Richard Rovere's *Senator Joe McCarthy* (New York: Harcourt, Brace, 1959). Two unpublished sources upon which I also rely heavily are Robert Wright, "Ike and Joe: Eisenhower's White House and the Demise of Joseph McCarthy" (Senior thesis, Princeton University, 1979), and Guenther Bischof, "Before the Break: The Relationship between Eisenhower and McCarthy" (Master's thesis, University of New Orleans, 1980). Also see Thomas C. Reeves, *The Life and Times of Joe McCarthy: A Biography* (Briarcliff Manor, N.Y.: Stein and Day, 1982). This work draws on a handful of the more recently released sources from the Eisenhower Library, but essentially is a study of McCarthy the man.

3. On press coverage of McCarthy's rise see Edwin R. Bayley, *Joe McCarthy and the Press* (Madison: University of Wisconsin Press, 1981).

4. "The President's News Conference," February 16, 1950, PPOP (Truman).

5. "The President's News Conference," March 30, 1950, PPOP (Truman).

6. *The Gallup Poll: Public Opinion, 1935–1971*, 3 vols. (New York: Random House, 1972), May 21, 1950, McCarthy survey, vol. 2, p. 911.

7. For persuasive arguments that McCarthy was not responsible for the electoral defeats of his opponents see Louis Bean, *Influence in the 1954 Mid-Term Elections* (Washington, D.C.:

Public Affairs Institute 1954); and Nelson W. Polsby, "Towards An Explanation of McCarthyism," *Political Studies* 8 (1960): pp. 250–71.

8. PD, April 27, 1950.

9. PD, April 5, 1950.

10. For valuable perspective on Eisenhower's thinking from 1950 through 1952 see the Personal Diary entries for this period printed in Robert H. Ferrell, ed., *The Eisenhower Diaries* (New York: Norton, 1981) and the editor's illuminating annotations.

11. PD, October 28, 1950.

12. PD, March 13, 1951.

13. On this speech see Robert Griffith, *The Politics of Fear*, pp. 143–46.

14. PD, June 14, 1951.

15. *New York Times,* June 6, 1952.

16. *New York Times,* August 23, 1952.

17. This episode has been reconstructed best by William Ewald in his *Eisenhower the President* (Englewood Cliffs, N.J.: Prentice-Hall, 1981), pp. 58–63. Ewald unfortunately does not employ citations. His synthesis, however, accords with the most reliable primary documents and oral histories and is further substantiated by his own interviews. As recently as October 28, 1981, Richard Strout in his *New Republic,* "T.R.B." column comments that it is an incident "I remember when revisionist historians try to upgrade the amiable Ike."

18. *Facts on File, 1953,* p. 83 (quotation from a February 27, 1953, Dulles statement).

19. "The President's News Conference," March 5, 1953, PPOP.

20. "The President's News Conference," March 5, 1953, PPOP.

21. See p. 105–13.

22. Minutes of Cabinet Meeting January 23, 1953, WF-C.

23. Martin Merson, *The Private Diary of a Public Servant* (New York: Macmillan, 1955).

24. Personal interviews with Sherman Adams, Herbert Brownell, Jr., and Bryce Harlow.

25. See, for example, C.D. Jackson, Logs for November 30, December 1–3, 1953, in Jackson Papers, Eisenhower Library; and Robert J. Donovan, *Eisenhower: The Inside Story* (New York: Harper and Bros, 1956), p. 248.

26. McCarthy to Eisenhower, February 3, 1953, WF-N (McCarthy).

27. Memorandum for Stephens from Persons, February 4, 1953, WF-N (McCarthy).

28. See James N. Rosenau, "The Nomination of 'Chip' Bohlen," *Case Studies in Practical Politics* (New York: Henry Holt, 1958).

29. Telephone conversations between Dulles and Adams, Hagerty, and Lourie, March 20, 1953, Dulles Papers, Princeton University Library.

30. "The President's News Conference," March 26, 1953, PPOP.

31. "Diary," April 1, 1953, WF-DDE.

32. *Facts on File, 1953,* p. 101 (McCarthy statement of March 27, 1953).

33. "The President's News Conference," April 2, 1953, PPOP.

34. For example see *New York Times* subheadline "Loss for Stassen is Seen," April 3, 1953; the Don Irwin article in the New York *Herald Tribune* of the same date; and the April 4, 1953 *Washington Post* comment that "Both sides said yesterday they were happy over the outcome . . . but from all indications the jubilance in the McCarthy camp appeared far the greater of the two."

35. PD, April 1, 1953.

36. Personal interview with Milton Eisenhower.

37. Eisenhower to Everett Hazlett, July 21, 1953, WF-N (Hazlett).

38. Eisenhower to Philip D. Reed, June 17, 1953, WF-DDE.

39. Eisenhower to Harry Bullis, May 18, 1953, OF-99-8.

40. "Minutes of the Cabinet Meeting," January 23, 1953, WF-C.

41. "Memorandum on Legislative Leaders Meeting," January 26, 1953, WF-L.

42. *Facts on File,* April 27, 1953, p. 131.

43. Among the standard sources on the Eisenhower and Truman security programs are: Athan Theoharis, "The Rhetoric of Politics: Foreign Policy, Internal Security, and Domestic Politics in the Truman Era, 1945–1950," in *Politics and Policies of the Truman Era,* B. Bernstein, ed.

(Chicago: Quadrangle, 1970); Alan Harper, *The Politics of Loyalty: The White House and the Communist Issue* (Westport, Conn.: Greenwood Press, 1970); and Earl Latham, *The Communist Controversy in Washington* (Cambridge: Harvard University Press, 1966).

44. Minutes of Cabinet Meetings for 1953: January 23, January 30, February 2, February 12, February 25, March 27, April 24, May 8, May 22, June 19, June 26, July 31, August 27, September 25, October 2, October 9, October 22, October 30, November 20, December 9, December 11, December 15, WF-C.

45. On the general topic of framing a presidential legislative program in that period see Richard Neustadt "Presidency and Legislation: The Growth of Central Clearance," *The American Political Science Review* 48 (1954): 641–47, and "Presidency and Legislation: Planning the President's Program," *The American Political Science Review* 49 (1955): 980–1021; and Larry Berman, *The Office of Management and Budget and the Presidency, 1921–79* (Princeton: Princeton University Press, 1979), esp. chap. 3.

46. "Minutes of Cabinet Meeting," March 27, 1953, WF-C.

47. In addition to the accounts given in the works cited in note 2 of this chapter, Kaghan's own summary of his experiences can be found in his "McCarthyization of Theodore Kaghan," *The Reporter*, July 21, 1953, pp. 17–25.

48. "Minutes of Cabinet Meeting," July 10, 1953, WF-C.

49. Merson, *The Private Diary of a Public Servant*, p. 16.

50. *New York Times*, June 11, 1953.

51. "Remarks at the Dartmouth College Exercises, Hanover, New Hampshire," June 14, 1953, PPOP.

52. "Address at the Annual Convention of the National Young Republican Organization, Mount Rushmore National Monument, South Dakota," June 11, 1953, PPOP.

53. "The President's News Conference," June 17, 1953, PPOP.

54. *Facts on File*, November 24, 1953, p. 392.

55. Emmet John Hughes, *The Ordeal of Power* (New York: Atheneum, 1963) pp. 94–96.

56. *Facts on File*, November 16, 1953, p. 384.

57. Personal interview with Herbert Brownell, Jr.; also see Warren Olney's Oral history, California Regional Oral History Program, Bancroft Library, University of California at Berkeley.

58. Sherman Adams, *Firsthand Report* (New York: Harper, 1961), p. 137.

59. Personal interview with Herbert Brownell, Jr.

60. Ibid.

61. "The President's News Conference," November 11, 1953, PPOP.

62. "Wednesday, November 11, 1953—called Herb Brownell in N.Y. (7:15 A.M.)" WF–DDE.

63. *Facts on File*, November 16, 1953, pp. 383–84.

64. *Facts on File*, November 24, 1953, pp. 393–94.

65. Dulles Press Conference of December 1, 1953. *Facts on File*, p. 404.

66. "The President's News Conference," December 2, 1953, PPOP.

67. Arthur Krock, *New York Times*, December 10, 1953.

68. *Gallup Opinion Index*, Report No. 125, November and December, 1975, p. 30.

69. *The Gallup Poll: Public Opinion*, 1935–1971, January 8, 1954, "Eisenhower Popularity Survey," vol. 2, p. 1200.

70. "Interview with Senator Watkins," December 4, 1954, WF-DDE.

71. Adams, *Firsthand Report*, pp. 143–45; and personal interviews with Sherman Adams, Herbert Brownell, Jr., and Henry Cabot Lodge.

72. Secretary Stevens' remarks before proceedings of Senate Permanent Subcommittee on Investigations (Army-McCarthy Hearings), April 22, 1954, *Facts on File*, p. 137.

73. This and the three previous paragraphs are solidly documented by Griffith in *The Politics of Fear*, pp. 246–48; Fried, in *Men against McCarthy*, pp. 279–80, and *Facts on File*, February 18–24, 1954, pp. 63–64.

74. HD, February 24, 1954.

75. Phone call to General Lucius Clay, February 25, 1954, WF–DDE.

76. Diary entry "Asked Ambassador Lodge to talk to Sec. Army Stevens re his suggestions McCarthy hearings," February 24, 1954, WF-AWD.

77. HD, February 25, 1954.

78. Ibid.

79. Ibid.

80. Ibid.; Adams, *Firsthand Report*, p. 147; Shanley Diary, Eisenhower's Library.

81. Stevens statement, *Facts on File*, February 25, 1954, p. 61; *New York Times*, February 26, 1954, and Shanley Diary, February 25, 1954, Eisenhower Library.

82. *New York Times*, February 27, 1954.

83. "Private Interview with Vice President Nixon, 4 p.m. February 26, 1954," Arthur Krock Papers, Princeton University Library; and private interviews by the author with Herbert Brownell, Jr., Henry Cabot Lodge, and Sherman Adams.

84. "Supplementary Notes, Legislative Leadership Meeting," March 1, 1954, WF-L.

85. HD, March 2, 1954; and phone call to Senator Knowland, March 3, 1954 (regarding previous evening's meeting). WF-DDE.

86. *Facts on File*, March 1 and 2, 1954, pp. 68–69.

87. *New York Times*, March 3, 1954; and Griffith, *The Politics of Fear*, p. 248.

88. HD, March 2 and 3, 1954.

89. "The President's News Conference," March 3, 1954, PPOP.

90. Phone call to General Lucius Clay, February 25, 1954, WF-DDE.

91. See, for example HD, March 3, 1954, March 8, 1954, and on May 28, 1954.

92. McCarthy's televised reply to Eisenhower, March 3, 1954, *Facts on File*, p. 68.

93. Press Conference Materials, May 10, 1953, WF-PC.

94. See, for example, James Reston's column the following morning entitled "Other Cheek is Struck—Eisenhower Would Turn It to McCarthy and the Senator, He Just Up and Obliged," *New York Times*, March 4, 1954.

95. Notes dictated on March 5, 1954, re March 4 breakfast meeting with Senator Dirksen, WF-DDE.

96. *New York Times*, March 5, 1954.

97. Ibid.

98. Ibid.

99. "Minutes of Cabinet Meeting," March 5, 1954, WF-C.

100. Memorandum to the President from Maxwell Rabb, March 5, 1954, WF-C.

101. "Personal and Confidential" Memorandum to Cabinet, "Treatment of Governmental Personnel," WF-DDE, March 5, 1954.

102. Adlai Stevenson, March 6, 1954, *Facts on File*, p. 76.

103. HD, March 8, 1954.

104. Phone Calls, March 8, 1954 WF–DDE.

105. HD, March 9, 1954.

106. PPOP, March 10, 1954.

107. Senate speech by Senator Ralph E. Flanders, March 9, 1954, *Facts on File*, p. 77.

108. "The President's News Conference," March 10, 1954, PPOP.

109. HD, May 20, 1954.

110. HD, March 10, 1954.

111. Nixon television broadcast, March 13, 1954, *Facts on File*, p. 84.

112. HD. March 11, 1954.

113. Personal interview with Sherman Adams.

114. HD, March 12, 1954.

115. "The President's News Conference," March 17, 1954, PPOP.

116. Eisenhower to William E. Robinson, May 12, 1954, WF-DDE.

117. Phone call to Senator Karl Mundt, March 18, 1954, WF-DDE.

118. Personal interviews by the author with Sherman Adams and Herbert Brownell.

119. Phone call to Senator Knowland, March 20, 1954, WF-DDE.

120. HD, March 24, 1954.

121. Ibid.

122. "The President's News Conference," March 24, 1954, PPOP.

Notes

123. All of these figures are taken from *The Gallup Poll: Public Opinion, 1935–1971*, March 15 McCarthy Survey, vol. 2, p. 1220; April 15 McCarthy Survey, vol. 2, p. 1225; Eisenhower data are from *The Gallup Opinion Index*, Report No. 125 (November–December, 1975), p. 30.

124. The question was by reporter Edward J. Milne of the *Providence Evening Bulletin*, "The President's News Conference," May 5, 1954, PPOP.

125. *The Gallup Poll: Public Opinion, 1935–1971*, surveys of April 21, vol. 2, p. 1229; May 1, vol. 2, pp. 1231–32; May 14, vol. 2, p. 1235; June 11, vol. 2, p. 1242.

126. Phone conversation, Secretary Wilson, May 11, 1954, WF-DDF.

127. "The President's News Conference," May 5, 1954, PPOP.

128. *Facts on File*, May 14, 1954, pp. 155–59.

129. "Letter to the Secretary of Defense Directing Him to Withhold Certain Information from the Senate Committee on Government Operations," May 17, 1954, PPOP; and Eisenhower to Wilson, May 17, 1954, WF-DDE.

130. Phone call to William Rogers, March 2, 1954, WF-DDE.

131. Phone call to Brownell, May 5, 1954, WF-DDE; and Brownell to Adams, May 3, 1954, WF-A.

132. Henry Cabot Lodge, *As It Was* (New York: Norton, 1976), p. 135.

133. HD, May 13, 1954.

134. HD, May 15, 1954.

135. HD, May 17, 1954.

136. *Facts on File*, May 17, 1954, p. 166.

137. HD, May 18, 1954.

138. Ibid.

139. "The President's News Conference," May 19, 1954.

140. "The President's News Conference," May 17, 1954, PPOP.

141. *New York Times*, April 12, 1954; and HD, May 21, 1954.

142. Stevens statement of May 19, 1954, *Facts on File*, p. 163; and HD, May 19, 1954.

143. HD, May 19, 1954.

144. McCarthy statement, May 20, 1954, *Facts on File*, p. 171.

145. HD, May 20, 1954.

146. *New York Times*, May 22, 1954.

147. HD, May 20, 1954.

148. HD, May 25, 1954. The Gunderson suggestion indicates deeper Eisenhower penetration in party affairs than is generally assumed.

149. I am indebted to Professor Cornelius Cotter of the University of Wisconsin-Milwaukee for this information.

150. Griffith, *The Politics of Fear*, pp. 262–63.

151. HD, May 27, 1954, and May 28, 1954.

152. Senate Subcommittee Hearings, May 27, 1954, *Facts on File*, p. 183.

153. HD, May 28, 1954.

154. Wright, "Ike and Joe," p. 87.

155. HD, May 28, 1954.

156. Edward R. Murrow broadcast text, in Edward Bliss, Jr., ed., *In Search of Light* (New York: Knopf, 1967), pp. 255–56.

157. Memo "From Ann Whitman to President Re Milton Eisenhower speech suggestions," May 27, 1954, WF-AWD.

158. "Address at the Columbia University National Bicentennial Dinner, New York City," May 31, 1954, PPOP.

159. HD, May 31, 1954.

160. "The President's News Conference," June 2, 1954, PPOP.

161. Welch statement to subcommittee, June 9, 1954, *Facts on File*, p. 199.

162. HD, June 18, 1954.

163. PD, April 1, 1953.

164. *The Gallup Poll, 1935–1971*, vol. 2, p. 1232.

165. Personal interview.

166. Hoffman met with Eisenhower throughout 1953 and 1954, generally once a month. During the period after the army-McCarthy hearings up to censure he met with Eisenhower on June 17, July 14, August 10, October 22, and December 1. (Dwight D. Eisenhower, records on President, Daily Appointments, Eisenhower Library). A transcribed recording of one of their meetings picked up Eisenhower's voice (but unfortunately not Hoffman's) and it records that McCarthy was among the topics discussed; August 10, 1954, WF-AWD. Also see Griffith, *The Politics of Fear*, pp. 271–81.

167. "The President's News Conference," August 4, 1954, PPOP.

168. Griffith, *The Politics of Fear*, pp. 307, 309.

169. To Indiana Governor George Craig, who urged Eisenhower to "discipline" McCarthy (and other "recalcitrants"), the president replied: "To attempt this, publicly, could react adversely on the legislative program, for the American people do not seem to like 'purges.' " Eisenhower to George N. Craig, March 26, 1954, WF-DDE.

170. HD, June 8, 1954.

171. HD, August 4, 1954 and "The President's News Conference," August 4, 1954, PPOP.

172. See, for example, HD, March 30, May 14, 18, 20, 21, 28, and 30, 1954.

173. "The President's News Conference," December 2, 1954, PPOP.

174. HD, December 4, 1954.

175. HD, December 6, 1954, and "Events leading up to break made by Senator McCarthy with President," December 7, 1954, WF-AWD.

176. Griffith, *The Politics of Fear*, p. 316.

177. White House Statement, December 7, 1954, *Facts on File*, p. 407.

178. "The President's News Conference," December 8, 1954, PPOP.

179. On McCarthy's postcensure ostracism, see Griffith, *The Politics of Fear*, pp. 316–19; and Rovere, *Senator Joe McCarthy*, pp. 237–39.

180. HD, March 11, 1955.

181. HD, March 16, 1955.

182. Telephone conversation with Secretary Wilson, May 11, 1954, WF-DDE.

183. Dwight D. Eisenhower, *The White House Years: Mandate for Change 1953–1956* (Garden City, N.Y.: Doubleday, 1963), p. 330.

184. Eisenhower, *Mandate for Change*, p. 331.

185. G. D. Wiebe, "The Army-McCarthy Hearings and the Public Conscience," *Public Opinion Quarterly*, 22 (Winter 1958–59): pp. 490–502.

186. Samuel A. Stouffer, *Communism, Conformity, and Civil Liberties* (Garden City, N.Y.: Doubleday, 1955).

187. Henry Cabot Lodge, *As It Was* (New York: Norton, 1976), p. 137.

Chapter 6

1. Pendleton Herring, *Presidential Leadership: The Political Relations of Congress and the Chief Executive* (New York: Rinehart, 1940), esp. pp. 57–58. Frank Freidel, *Franklin D. Roosevelt: Launching the New Deal* (Boston: Little, Brown, 1973).

2. Eisenhower to William Phillips, June 5, 1953, WF-N.

3. Cf. Anthony King, "The American Polity in the Late 1970's: Building Coalitions in the Sand," in *The New American Political System*, ed. Anthony King, (Washington, DC: American Enterprise Institute, 1978), pp. 371–197.

4. Alexis de Toqueville, "Author's Preface to the Twelfth Edition (1848)," *Democracy in America* (New York: Harper & Row, 1966): "Let us not turn to America in order slavishly to copy the institutions she has fashioned for herself; let us look there for instruction rather than models; let us adopt the principles rather than the details of her laws."

5. Richard E. Neustadt, *Presidential Power: The Politics of Leadership* (New York: John Wiley & Sons, 1960). The most recent edition of this highly influential work was published in 1980.

6. See p. 74.

Notes

7. Steven Weisman, "Reagan Dissipates Heat by Delegating Authority," *New York Times*, October 11, 1981, p. 4.

8. April 7, 1956, WF-AWD.

9. See p. 37.

10. Eisenhower to Henry Luce, August 8, 1960, WF-DDE.

11. On this matter compare Fred I. Greenstein, "The Benevolent Leader: Children's Images of Political Authority," *American Political Science Review* 54 (December 1960): 934–43 with Greenstein, "What the President Means to America: Presidential 'Choice' Between Elections," in *Choosing the President*, ed., James David Barber, (Englewood Cliffs, N.J.: Prentice Hall, 1974), pp. 121–47.

12. Theodore Sorenson, Oral History, John F. Kennedy Library. One person who was convinced that the manned moon landing program was ill-planned and ill-advised was Dr. T. Keith Glennan, Eisenhower's National Aeronautics and Space Administration head. When Kennedy announced the moon landing program on May 26, 1961, Glennan added this postscript to the diary he had kept while in office: "This single speech is designed to cost the people of this nation at least an extra 20 billion dollars and probably much more to race an uncertain opponent on an uncertain course toward an uncertain goal." Glennan Diary, Dwight D. Eisenhower Library.

13. J.F. Heath, *John F. Kennedy and the Business Community* (Chicago: University of Chicago Press, 1969).

14. William P. Bundy, Oral History, Lyndon B. Johnson Library.

15. On Nixon's use of Haldeman, see this case study and the sources on which it draws: Fred I. Greenstein, "A President is Forced to Resign: Watergate, White House Organization and Nixon's Personality," in *American Politics in the 1970's*, ed. Allan Sindler (Boston: Little, Brown 1977), pp. 56–88.

16. *A Presidency for the 1980's: A Report on Presidential Management by a Panel of the National Academy of Public Administration* (Washington, D.C.: National Academy of Public Administration, 1980), reprinted in Hugh Heclo and Lester M. Salamon, eds., *The Illusion of Presidential Government* (Boulder, Colo.: Westview Press, 1981), pp. 299–345.

17. Kenneth C. Davis, *Eisenhower: Soldier of Democracy* (Garden City, N.Y.: Doubleday, 1945), p. 401. Eisenhower's annotated copy is in the Rare Book Room of the Ellis Slater Library, Eisenhower College, Seneca Falls, N.Y.

18. Dwight D. Eisenhower, *At Ease: Stories I Tell My Friends* (Garden City, N.Y.: Doubleday, 1967).

19. On the general issue of the importance of multiple advocacy in policy making, see Alexander George, *Presidential Decisionmaking in Foreign Policy: The Effective Use of Information and Advice* (Boulder, Colo.: Westview Press, 1980) and the sources cited therein.

20. Dwight D. Eisenhower, COHC.

21. See pp. 40–41.

22. Harold D. Lasswell, *Psychopathology and Politics* (Chicago: University of Chicago Press, 1930). I do not mean to suggest that Eisenhower had read Lasswell or subscribed to Lasswell's utopian scheme for employing social science knowledge to bring about a major reordering of "human nature" and social structure.

INDEX

accommodation toward McCarthy, 164–65
activism, covert, 58–59; *see also* hidden-hand leadership
Adams, John (army counselor), and army-McCarthy hearings, 183–84, 186, 203
Adams, Sherman (Chief of Staff), 82, 91, 107, 138, 139, 144; ad hoc committees, use of, 245–46; Administrative Branch Commission, 215, and anti-McCarthy campaign, 178, 179, 186, 187, 189, 194, 205; and army-McCarthy hearings, 198, 199, 200n, 204, 205; as Assistant to the President, 106; on Commodore transcript, 112; deputy function of, 138, 140–43 passim, 146, 147, 244; Eisenhower good-guy image, 147; failed hidden-hand strategy, 63, 64–65, 220; in McCarthy censure, 214; and media image of, 138, 139; and NSC, 142n; papers of, 10n; personality equation of, 141; Persons on staff of, 146; public image of 144–45, 147; resignation of, 147; and soil bank program, 143–44; and Status of Actions report, 114; *Time* "O.K., S.A." image of, 144–45
advisors, 34, 40, 115–16, 205; and Kennedy use of, 246; Truman unofficial use of, 104
agriculture, 50; and soil bank program, 143–44; *see also* Benson, Ezra Taft
Agriculture, Department of, Milton Eisenhower at, 12, 102
aid to education, 49n, 122–24, 231
allies, McCarthy attitude toward, 181, *see also* Western Alliance
ambiguity, use of, 67, 69, 178, 219, 259n30
Ambrose, Stephen, 31; *Supreme Commander, The*, 13
american airmen in PRC, 181, 216, 218
American Communist Party, 163, 213

Americans for Democratic Action, 177
analytic reasoning, 18, 26, 27, 71, 233; and military background, 26, 30, 149n, 244–45, 254–44n9
Anderson, Robert (Secretary of the Treasury), 60, 61, 63, 82, 123
anti-McCarthy campaign: business community, and explanation of, 170–71; and Congress, 173, 189, 192; and emphasis on administration programs, 170, 173, 193, 197, 223; FCC role in, 194, 195; Hagerty's role in, 164, 187, 189, 191, 196–97, 205, 206, 210, 215–16, 222; hidden-hand style, 173, 188–201 passim, 212, 220, 221; and instrumental use of language, 221; and Legislative Leadership meeting, 188; and Nixon rebuttal of Stevenson, 194, 195, 197–98, 220; post-censure strategy, 217, 218; and press conference, 195–96, 197; and press statements by intermediaries, 193; and role of Rogers, 178, 204; and role of Stevens, 207; strategy for, 179, 191, 197, 223, 226, 227; strategy meeting on, 205, 206; and use of selective delegations, 224; *see also* army-McCarthy hearings
Anti-McCarthy sermons, 177
Apollo project, 242, 271n12
appearance, 37, 38
appointment calenders, 41, 42
Arbenz government (Guatemala), CIA, in overthrow of, 6, 62, 137, 213, 228
Armed Forces Day Speech, 206
army-McCarthy hearings, 173, 202–12; and attempted change of venue, 199; and Eisenhower's covert involvement in, 198, 199, 200, 204, 205, 212; and failures of hidden-hand style, 198, 199, 208–9, 220–21; and Hoffman-Eisenhower meetings on censure, 269n166; influence seeking as reason for, 184; Jenkins as subcommittee council,

Index

200; and McCarthy's popularity, 201, 212; members of committee for opening of, 209; and press conference on role of McCarthy during, 200; public attitude toward proceedings, 225–26; and public reaction to McCarthy, 200, 225;
army personnel, McCarthy attacks on, 183, 184, 185;
Assistant to the President, 106, 126
At Ease (Eisenhower), 45
Atomic Energy Commission, in NSC, 125–26
Atoms for Peace, 52, 90, 181–82
Augustine, and Eisenhower strategy, 69*n*
Australia, Eisenhower's WW II strategy, 12
authority: maintainance of, 82

Baker Library, Sherman Adams papers, 10*n*
Baltic States, and trade policy, 109–10
Benson, Ezra Taft (Secretary of Agriculture), 78, 123, 144
Berlin, and McCarthy's criticisms, 160
blame, coping with, 91–92, 260*n*79
Bohlen, Charles E. "Chip" (Ambassador to USSR), 165–67
book censorship, 174, 175–77
Bowie, Robert, 31, 33–34, 132
Bradley (General), charisma of, 36
Bricker, (Ohio Senator), 120, 167
Bricker Ammendment, 86, 120
bridge playing, 26, 39, 256*n*43
Bridges, Styles (Rep. Senator), on military policy, 47, 137
briefings on army-McCarthy hearings, 202, 207; bipartisan, 137; for cabinet meetings, 113; on intelligence, 134; on Korean truce negotiations press conference, 76
Brown, Clarence (Ohio Congressman), 49*n*, 110–11
Brownell, Herbert (Attorney General), 108, 207; and advice to Army Counsel on McCarthy, 183–87; Bricker Ammendment, 86; and delegation of authority, 85–87; on Eisenhower's interest in Republican politics, 159*n;* and government informers, 210; implementing executive privilege, 203–4, 204*n*, 205; as political operative, 86; on security in Truman administration, 178, 179; Truman reply to, 180; and Welch as choice for counsel in McCarthy hearings, 200*n*
budget, 6, 51, 121, 169, 228; and Wilson's defense spending, 83; *see also* Bureau of the Budget; Humphrey
Bundy, Wm. (Policy Planning Board), 243
Bureau of Applied Social Research, (Columbia Univ.), 96
Bureau of the Budget: and access of director to Eisenhower, 146; Roosevelt's organization of, 102; Stans, as director of, 123; Staats as Deputy director of, 147; Truman's reorganization of, 102; *see also* Dodge, Joseph
Burgess-Patterson study, on White House organization, 113
Burma, policy on, 130, 132
Burns, Arthur (Chairman of Council of Economic Advisors), 120

businessmen; 121, 149; and McCarthy problem, 170–71, 213; attitude toward McCarthy, 170–71
Butcher, Harry and publicity of Eisenhower's military career, 95
Byrnes, James, 61, 242

cabinet, 104, 193; as advisory body, 115–16; divergent views in, 122; formal/informal nature of, 108–9; leaks, 116; organization of, 113–24, 241 (*see also* cabinet secretariat); as policy council, 113–18, 241; *see also* cabinet meetings; cabinet members
cabinet meetings, 104, 105, 113–17; and aid to education, 122–24; and attitude toward McCarthy, 164; debate on function of, 122; of Eisenhower and other presidents compared, 104, 113, 116; formal nature of, 105, 124; and NSC compared, 124, 126; and overseas information library policy, 174–75, 223; and policy toward McCarthy, 171, 173–74; and Record of Actions, 114; role of assistant to president, 126; *see also* Hotel Commodore meeting
cabinet members, 32, 91, 108, 140; and direct access to Eisenhower, 146; and liaison with Congress, 193; McCarthy, and attitude of, 164; organizational management of, 103–4
cabinet secretariat, 113–14, 126, 132, 241
Califano, Joseph (Carter HEW Secretary), and relationship with Carter, 238, 242
Campbell, Angus, 92, 93
Camp Kilmer, and McCarthy attack on, 184
candidate popularity study, 92, 93
Carr, Francis, and army-McCarthy hearings, 205, 208, 220–21
Carroll, Paul (General), 142
Carter, James "Jimmy" and staff staff chief, 244; cabinet/White House Staff relationship compared to Eisenhower, 243; as judge of character, 237; public perception of effectiveness of, 3; and publicized activism, 58, 242; and taking blame, 260*n*79; use of rhetoric 235; and the Washington game, 61
Case, Francis (Rep. N. Dakota Senator), on Watkins Committee, 215
CBS: and Butcher as Naval aide, 95; and Eisenhower interview, 43, 44, 45
Central Intelligence Agency (CIA); McCarthy attacks against, 217; and overthrow of Communist-leaning governments, (*see* Guatemala; Iran)
centralized staff procedures of Nixon, 244
chain-smoking, 38, 39
charismatic leadership, 36, 96
checks and balances, and effect on policy change, 4, 229
Chiang Kai-shek, 20; *see also* offshore islands controversy
Chicago Executives Club, and Brownell's exposure of White-Truman case, 180
Chief of Staff: Eisenhower's involvement with, 135–36; and Eisenhower organization of, 103, 141; need for, 140, 244; pre-presidential experience as, 102, 118, 141; role of, 138, 142, 243; use of as

273

deputy, 241, 243, 244; *see also* Adams Sherman; Persons Wilton B.
Chief of State, and dichotomy in presidency, 252*n* 4; Eisenhower's role as, 5, 7–8, 92, 93, 234; and professionalism, 234–235; Roosevelt leadership style, compared to Eisenhower, 229–30
childhood, 43, 45
Childs, Marquis (columist) on Eisenhower's "captive hero" image, 93
China, *see* Nationalist China; People's Republic of China
China blockade proposal, 181, 216, 218
Christian Science Monitor, and press conference coverage, 69
Churchill, Winston, 11, 13
CIA, *see* Central Intelligence Agency
civil liberties, and Eisenhower image, due to silence on McCarthy, 227
civil servants, morale during McCarthy era, 224–25
clarity, use of language for, 66
Clark, Mark (General), 247–48; and Eisenhower diplomacy, 29–30; as head of Administrative Branch Commission, 215
Clay, Lucius (General), 41, 46, 150, Eisenhower's explanation of anti-McCarthy strategy to, 191; and Eisenhower's explanation of "Memorandum of Understanding," 186; on Eisenhower's political experience in Philippines, 12
clergymen, 149; Matthews accusations against, 177
Cohn, Roy (McCarthy aide), 164, 187, 199, 205; and influence seeking for Schine, 198; and Information Service Libraries investigation, 174; role of, in McCarthy's army investigations, 183
cold war, 231, 232, 248
collective security, 47, 48, 124, 137
Columbia University: Eisenhower's public appeal, 96; Eisenhower as president of, 14, 49, 159
Columbia Univ. Oral History, 10*n*, 246
Command and General Staff College, 11, 254*n*9
Commanding General, European Theater of Operations, *see* World War II
Committee on Government Operations, 162
committee meetings, organization of, 104–5
communication capabilities, 66; via telephone, 147, 149, 254–55*n*9
Communism: avoidance of, as campaign issue, 181; Eisenhower attitude toward, 50, 97; policy for eradication of, in U. S., 197; and press conferences, 176–77; public perception of, in government, 225, 226; threat of, and defense spending, 70
Communist Control Act of 1954, 213
Communist Party, *see* American Communist Party
Communists: and congressional approval of military action, 131; image as agents of USSR, 172; jail sentences for, 177; and McCarthy's accusations against State Department, 158; and McCarthy's attacks on educational community, 165; McCarthy's search for, in executive branch, 162; Nixon's attitude toward, 164; and territorial expansion, 124, 132; White as, 179
Communist satellite countries, attitude toward trade with, 109–10
Communist sympathizers, and liberals, 163
complexity of personality, 9, 9*n*, 15

Conant, James B. (U.S. High Commissioner to Germany), and accommodationist policy toward McCarthy, 164–65
conciliation, 89–90
condemnation of methods, indirect attack on McCarthy, 170–71
confidence, 37, 98
"confidence in Stevens" paper, 186
confidentiality rule, 158, 203, 204
conflict-avoidance, 29–30, 76, 110–11, 223, 247, 248
conformist bureaucrat, image as, 139
confusion, at press conference, 176–77
Congress: and approval of military action against Communists, 131; Eisenhower attitude toward working with, 24, 111, 112; Eisenhower hidden-hand relationship with, 60–61, 107, 193; McCarthy's effect on, 169; PACGO relationship with, 110; Persons as liaison with, 146, 148; and role of, in anti-McCarthy campaign, 173, 189 (*see also* Republican congressional leadership); presidential administrations and, 204; and strategic role of personality assessment, 78–80
congressional committees, and executive privilege, 203, 204, 205
congressional intractability, 232
congressional liaison program, 193, 214, 216
congressional relations unit, 107
conservatism, 48, 49, 49*n*, 50, 58
Constitution: and presidency, 5, and creation of NSC, 124–25
constitutional monarch image, 137
constitutional principles, defense, of, 11
consultation leadership style, 115–16
controversy, Eisenhower's handling of, 92
Cooper, John Sherman (Ambassador to India), 78
coordination: and group leadership, 116, 133; of White House staff, 142
correspondence, 10, 147
Council of Economic Advisors: under Eisenhower, 146; under Truman, 102
covert activism, 6, 58–59, 228, 234; *see also* hidden-hand leadership style; hidden-hand strategy
Cowles publications, 75
Craig, George (Indiana Gov.), 169, 270*n*
credibility, 158, 226
criticism, Eisenhower's use of, 74
Cutler, Robert (Special Assistant for National Security), 85, 106, 107, 106–7*n*, 125, 127, 134
Czechoslovakia, and U.S. trade policy, 109–10

daily routine, 38, 41, 42, 202, 207; and meetings with Dulles, 134; as supreme commander, 38
Dartmouth College speech, 175–76
Davis, John W., 199, 200
debate: use of, 128, 246 (*see also* cabinet meetings)
decision making, 129, 132, 133–36 passim; criterion for 24, 25; and emergencies, 42–43
Defense Department, involvement in, 87, 144
Defense Department Research and Development Board, use of, 118
defense spending, 6, 48, 48*n*, 70, 83, 85
de Gaulle, Charles, 11, 33

Index

delegation of authority, 80–92, 238; and media image of Eisenhower, 139; and Roberts's resignation, 143; use of, to attack McCarthy, 192–93; *see also* selective delegation

Democratic congressmen, Eisenhower relationship with, 93, 232, 232*n*, 239, 240, and pressure for active opposition to McCarthy, 169

Democratic Eighty-sixth Congress, 122, 123*n*; and Eisenhower's activism, 265*n*70

Democratic National Chairman, and criticism of Brownell's McCarthyism, 179

Democratic Party: defeat of anti-McCarthy candidates, from, 159*n*; and draft Eisenhower movement, 50, 92, 159; on Republican disunity, 194; and support of foreign policy, 232; and support of open army-McCarthy hearings, 202–3

deputy function, 82, 140, 241;

despondency, coping with, 36–37

détente, 47; gestures toward, 52, 90; and policy goals, 228, 248

de Tocqueville, and European government, 233

Dewey, Thomas E. (N.Y. Gov.): and choice for army counsel, 200*n*; and draft Eisenhower movement, 50, 159; staff of, in Eisenhower White House, 107, 108, 164

diary,

dichotomies: in personality, 53–54; and organizational leadership, 101–5; in presidency, 18, 67, 68, 150–51

Dien Bien Phu, and Indo-China, 136

Dillon, Douglas (Undersecretary of State), on cabinet meetings, 117

diplomacy, 29–30, 78, 248; and Gifford incident, 89

direct intervention, 83–85

Dirksen, Everett (Illinois Senator), 79, 186, 259–60 *n*54, 265*n*70; and army-McCarthy hearings, 199, 202, 203, 209, 220–21; and McCarthy censure vote, 217, 218; and Memorandum of Understanding, 186; role of, on McCarthy Committee, 185, 186; use of, in anti-McCarthy conflict, 192

disarmament, 47–48, 257*n*67

Dodge, Joseph (Budget Bureau Director), 51, 107, 146, 173; and defusing potential conflict on PACGO, 111; on deputy approach to delegation of authority, 82; and social program directives to, 115; at tense meetings, 72

domestic conservatism, 50, 50*n*, 51; and defense spending, 48; Taft and Eisenhower compared, 49, 49*n*

domestic policy, 124; congressional support for, 170–71, 232; and covert activism, 58–59; and effect on McCarthy, 173; and Eisenhower's conservatism, 48, 49, 49*n*, 58; and White House Cabinet, 113–14, 123

domino theory, 136–37

Drummond, Roscoe *(Herald Tribune)*, on anti-McCarthy campaign, 196, 197

Dulles, John Foster (Secretary of State), 87–92; and administrative responsibilities, 141–42, 142*n*; on aid to S. E. Asia, 130–31; on elimination of McLeod's loyalty duties, 189; and Gifford incident, 88–89; and Greek shipping treaty incident, 168; and loyalty certification of Bohlen, 165–66; on McCarthy's demand for coercion of allies, 181; and McCarthy's demands for Information Services

vices Libraries, 174–75; personality assessment of, 80, 90; and relationship with Eisenhower, 68, 78, 134, 147; on the security program, 172–73; and USSR, 52, 90

Dulles Collection, *see* John Foster Dulles Collection

duty, 38, 45, 161

Dwight D. Eisenhower Library, *see* Eisenhower Library

Dworshak, Henry (Iowa Senator), role of, in army-McCarthy hearings, 200

dynamism, 38–46

East-West relationship, 48, 248; *see also* cold war; foreign policy

economic aid, to Southeast Asia, 130

economic conservatism, 14, 120

Eden, Anthony (Prime Minister of England), as British Foreign Secretary, 88, 89, 136–37

effectiveness: of Adams, as staff chief, 141; of anti-McCarthy campaign, 219–27; of Eisenhower's organizational management, 138–50; and perception of Carter and Ford, 3; and public support, 3; *see also* leadership style

Eighty-sixth Congress, *see* Democratic Eighty-sixth Congress

Eightieth Congress, *see* Republican Congress

Eisenhower, David (father), 43, 256*n*52

Eisenhower, Dwight David: and age at inauguration, 39; attitude toward presidency, 5; childhood of, 43, 45, 254*n*9; election of (*see* presidential candidacy); personal equation of, 43–44, 245; presidential motto of, 57; recreation of, 8, 26, 39, 256*n*43

Eisenhower, Dwight D., works of: *At Ease*, 45; *Crusade in Europe*, 36, 74, 81; *Mandate for Change*, 37; *Papers of Dwight D. Eisenhower, The*, 10–11

Eisenhower, Edgar (brother), 50, 94–95, 95*n*

Eisenhower, Ida (mother), 256*n*52

Eisenhower, John (brother), 134

Eisenhower, Milton (brother), 41, 46, 117, 135, 143, 149; and Department of Agriculture, 12, 102; on Humphrey's views, 120–21; and influence on anti-McCarthy activism, 169, 210; McCarthy attack on, 218; on PACGO panel, 110; on second-term candidacy, 257*n*65; and speech writing, 210

Eisenhower administration: major issues of, 231–32; organizational meeting for, 105–13; priorities of, 47, 85, 124

Eisenhower-Hall discussion, on Nixon second-term vice-presidency, 63, 234

Eisenhower Library, contents of, 10, 10*n*, 20, 36, 84–85, 146, 238

Eisenhower-McCarthy conflict, 188–201

elimination of troublemakers, 93–94

Emergency Banking Act, passage of, 203*n*

emergency decisions, 42–43

emotional control, 39

emotional opposition, coping with, 72

Emphasis on Administration Program, 193

energy level, 38–41, 43, 233

England, *see* Great Britain

Ervin, Sam, on Watkins Committee, 215

Europe, *see* Western Alliance; World War II

evasive use of language, 67, 68–69

executive branch, McCarthy intrusion into, 162, 165, 168, 169
Executive Department, McCarthy's effect on, 169
Executive Office of the President (EOP), 102, 107, 146
executive privilege, 190, 204, 205
extremism: and McCarthy's credibility, 158; Eisenhower strategy, against, 173

Federal Communications Commission (FCC), role of, in McCarthy case, 194–95, 220
Federal Trade Commission (FTC), and Goldfine/Adams incident, 64
Ferguson, Homer (Michigan Senator), and Hoover II conflict, 110–11
Fifth Amendment Communists, 163, 175, 184
Flanders, Ralph (Rep. Vermont Senator), 195, 222n; and McCarthy censure resolution, 214, 227
Flemming, Arthur (HEW Secy): and education bond proposal, 122–23, 123n; and PACGO panel, 110
Folliard, Eddie *(Washington Post)*, 216
Folsom, Marion, and aid to education, 122
Ford, Gerald, 3, 244, 273
foreign policy, O16, 49, 71, 87–90; 107, 124, 228, 243; and Atoms for Peace, 52, 90, 181–82; and balanced response to international crisis, 216, 218; and collective security, 137; Democratic support for, 232; and disarmament, 47–48; and effect on McCarthy, 170, 174, 213; Eisenhower control of decisions in, 87, 130–32 passim, 134–36, 208; and Eisenhower's political convictions, 47, 48; and foreign aid, 69, 120; and Hainan incident, 87–88; implementation of (*see* Dulles, John Foster); on Indo-China, 136–37, 231; on missiles, 85, 85n; and selective security, 47, 48, 124, 137; short-term goals, 47; in Southeast Asia, 71, 129–31, 132; Soviet Union 89–90, 213 (*see also* Soviet Union); and Taft isolationism, 49; on trade with Communist countries, 109–10; *see also* defense spending; détente; Dulles, John Foster; military policy; NSC; offshore islands controversy; USSR
foreign policy-making machinery, 16, 243
foreign policy professionals opinion of OCB, 263n 39
foreign political climate, 47, 231, 248
formal/informal organizational blend, 108–9, 245, 246; and Eisenhower's effectiveness, 138–50, 241; and national security policy making, 124–38
formal organization, 100, 241–42; and anti-McCarthy strategy, 171, 188; and domestic policy, 113–14
formal procedure: and adaptability of Eisenhower style, 247; and Eisenhower organizational style, 101, 104–5; as tool against McCarthy, 192
Formosa, *see* Nationalist China
Formosa Straits, and hidden-hand strategy for ending Korean conflict, 62
Forrestal, James V. (Secy of Defense), 48n; advice on organizational management to, 35, 118, 119, 140, 141
Fort Monmouth, and McCarthy accusations, 183, 184

France: and Indo-China, 136, 137, 231
Freedom of Information Act, 129
friendships, and team functioning, 119
friendships: in business community, and influence on candidacy, 46; personal, 8, 41
friends in politics: Macmillan, 33; and Eisenhower/ Taft relationship, 167
functional professionalism, and White House staff, 146

Gallup Poll, 3, 4; and Eisenhower's popularity, 4, 92, 182, 182n, 223; and Eisenhower popularity compared to Truman, 159; and Eisenhower public image, preceding army-McCarthy hearings, 201; of McCarthy's popularity, 182n, 201, 202; and McCarthy public approval rating, 212–13; on public approval of presidents, 251n1; and public attitude toward Eisenhower's golf playing, 40; on public awareness of McCarthy's charges, 159; and Stevens's approval rating, 202, 212
gastrointestinal disorder, 38–39
General Motors, and Wilson background, 83
"General Stands at Ease, A" (Reston), 227
Germany: Eisenhower as governor of, 31–32; *see also* Berlin
Gifford, Walter (Ambassador to Britain), and diplomatic error, 88–89
Glennan, Keith T. (National Aeronautics and Space Administration), 271n12
goals: for economy, 51; of McCarthy and Eisenhower compared, 171–72
Goldfine, Bernard, 64–65
Goldwater, Barry, 167, 218
golf playing, 39, 40, 256n43
Goodpaster, Andrew J. (Staff Secretary), 90, 146; on Eisenhower's analytic thinking, 26, 27; on Eisenhower's interest in command process, 35; "Memoranda of Conferences with the President," 133–34; and organizational coordination of White House Staff, 142; and records of Eisenhower's operational decisions, 129n; role of, compared to Cutler, 134; *Times* image of, 144
government, 33, 176; and criticism of Eisenhower's organizational management, 104; image of, 42, 93; and McCarthy's confidential underground, 209; and public perception of Communists in, 225, 226
government informers, 162, 209, 210
government security program, 172–73, 224–25;
grammar, and Eisenhower press conferences, 8, 19, 20, 196
Gray, Robert, 35, 113
Great Britain: and Gifford retirement incident, 88–89; and Indo-China policy, 136–37; and opinion of Montgomery, 44
Great Society, 229; and Eisenhower's social programs compared, 6
Greece: and Eisenhower IRBM policy, 134–35; and shipping treaty incident, 167–68
group leadership, 116, 133
Gruenther, Alfred (NATO Commander), 20–25, 70, 136, 256n43
Guatemala, 213; *see also* Arbenz Government
Gunderson, Barbara 208, 208n

Index

Hagerty, James (Press Secretary): and anti-McCarthy campaign, 187, 189, 191, 198, 206, 210; and blame taking, 91–92; and briefings of Eisenhower on army-McCarthy hearings, 202, 207; and briefing for press conference on Korean truce negotiations, 76; and Brownell statement against government informers, 210; in Dewey organization, 107, 108; and Eisenhower's concern for Stevens, 189; on Eisenhower's reaction to Republican non-support, 208; and press release of Eisenhower-Watkins breakfast, 217; and planned presidential statements, 216; and reaction to McCarthy's anti-Eisenhower statements, 208; and relationship to Eisenhower, 146, 147, 148; and release of press conference transcripts, 195, 196; role of, in McCarthy case, 164, 196–97, 205, 215–16, 218, 221, 222; and Stevens's denial of surrender to McCarthy, 186, 187; and Stevens's press release on army prosecution of McCarthy, 207; on White House silence on army-McCarthy hearings, 198
Hainan incident, 87–88
Hall, Leonard (RNC chairman), 193; and covert strategy in RNC rebuttal of Stevenson speech, 197–98, 220; on Eisenhower's hidden-hand attempt eliminating Nixon as running mate, 63; and opinion of McCarthy, 189; and television response to Stevenson, 194, 197–98
Halleck, Charles (House Majority Leader), 80, 188, 265n70
Hanna Steel, 119, 120
Harlow, Bryce (legislative liaison), 42–43, 73, 108
Harsch, Joseph (news correspondent), 69, 259n30
Harvard University, McCarthy on, 165
Hauge, Gabriel (economist), 146, 147
Hazlett, "Swede," 41, 170, 257n65
headlines, McCarthy creation of, 158–59
health, 16; and ileitis, 38–39, 40; see also heart attack
heart attack, 40, 46, 257n65; Adams's responsibilities following, Eisenhower's, 143
Helms, Paul, 74, 235, 247
Hensel, H. Struve (Assistant Defense Secretary), 208–9, 220–21
Herter (Secretary of State), 265n70
Hess, Stephen, 90–91, 145–46
Hickel, Walter resignation of, 242–43
hidden-hand leadership, style, 233; and elimination of troublemakers, 93–94; non-transferability of, 235; and relationship to Johnson, 59, 60; and unpublicized activism, 58–65 (see also covert activism); and planted questions at press conferences, 219; problems with, during army-McCarthy hearings, 208–9, 220–21; targeting, 61; and use of intermediaries, 59 (see also intermediaries); see also delegation of authority; hidden-hand strategy
hidden-hand strategy: and Adam's resignation, 63, 64–65, 220; and anti-McCarthy campaign, 173, 188–201, 212, 221; for army-McCarthy hearings, 198, 208–9, 220–21; and CIA aided coups, 6, 62, 137, 213, 228; and covert politicking, 60, 61, 234; for ending Korean conflict, 62; failure of, 63–65, 209, 220–21; and instrumental use of language, 67; and leadership style, 58–65; and McCarthy firing of Matthews, 178; and maintaining public support, 93–94, 239; and use of media, 62; see also hidden-hand leadership style

Hobby, Oveta Culp (HEW Secretary), 50, 51, 122
Hoffman, Paul (Studebaker Corp.), and role in McCarthy censure, 214, 269n166
hold-the-line domestic policy, 232
Hoover, Herbert, 102, 111, 215
Hoover, J. Edgar (FBI Director), and White's Communist connections, 179
Hoover Commission, 111
Hoover Commission II, avoidance of conflict through team leadership, 110–11
Hotel Commodore meeting, 105–13;
House Armed Services Committee, 108
House Un-American Activities Committee, and White-Truman incident, 178, 180
Howard, Roy (newspaper publisher), on soil bank program, 143–44
Hughes, Emmet (Time/Life writer), 146; and anti-McCarthy action, 178; on leadership of cabinet members, 33; as writer of inaugural address, 109
humanitarian image, 90, 96
Humphrey, George (Treasury Secretary), 119–21 passim; as moderating influence, 72; use of as intermediary, 59
Hunt, H. L., on New Deal programs, 50

idealism, 53–54
image: importance of, 19; public/private dichotomy, 53, 67, 68; see also public image
impulse, control of, 45
inaugural address, 105, 109–10, 240–41
inauguration, 39
India: and NSC aid debate, 130; and role in ending Korean conflict, 62;
indirect approach, technique, 161
Indo-China, 136–37, 231; see also S. E. Asia
inflation, attitude toward, 6
informal advisory channels, 41, 150
informal leadership style, 148–49, 247; with NSC members, 130–33 passim; use of in McCarthy case, 224
informal organization, 100–1, 193, 243–44; and policy making, 114, 133–34; of White House, 146–50
information gathering, 144, 148, 150, 246
Information Services Libraries investigation, 174, 175
informers, Eisenhower's position against, 209–10;
instrumental use of language: and ambiguity, 67, 69, 178, 219, 259n30; and apolitical profile, 239; and clarity, 66; for evasiveness, 67, 68–69; ineffectiveness of, following Dartmouth speech, 221; as leadership tool, 66–73, 233; non-transferability of, 235; in press conferences involving McCarthy case, 160, 219, 221–22; and role of homilies, 97; see also ambiguity
intelligence reports, 41, 134
intensity, 39
intercontinental ballistic missiles, 85, 85n
intermediaries: use of Anderson as, in covert politicking, 60, 61; use of, in anti-McCarthy campaign, 193; and use of Dulles to control McLeod, 166; use of, in hidden-hand leadership, 59
Intermediate range ballistic missiles, 85n; Eisenhower policy on, 85, 134–35

277

Index

internal security, 7; *see also* security program; security risk

international politics, 47, 168, 216

International Information Agency (IIA), 162, 163, 164

International Monetary Fund (IMF), and Brownell on Truman security, 178

Investigations Subcommittee, *see*, McCarthy Committee

invisible White House, 243–44

Iran, 213; *see also* Mossadegh government

Irish, Marion, 139, 144; "Organization Man in the Presidency, The," 139

isolationism, attitude toward, 49

Jackson, C. D. (Time Inc. executive), 34–35; and opposition to McCarthy, 164

Jackson, Henry (Senator), *see* Jackson Committee Hearings

Jackson Committee Hearings, 127–28, 263n39

Japan: Status of Forces Treaty, 12; trial incident, 72

John Foster Dulles Collection at Princeton, and unpublished material, 10, 10n

Johnson, Lyndon Baines: craftiness, 156; delegation of authority, 82–83; Eisenhower's analysis of motives of, 27–29; Eisenhower's hidden-hand relationship to, 59, 60; Eisenhower's personal opinion of, 28; foreign policy mechanism under, 16, 27, 243; Great Society program, 229; and insulation from blame, 91; and opinion of Eisenhower, 29; organizational style of, and Eisenhower compared, 243; public image of, 3; and publicized presidential activism, 58; and public support, 92; and rejection of second-term nomination, 27; and relation to problems of office, 91; and relationship to Robert Kennedy, 235–36; role of chief of staff under, 243; and role in Watkins Committee hearings, 215; as Senate Leader, 42, 59, 215; temper, of, 43; and Tuesday Luncheons, 243

Joint Chiefs of Staff, 125–26, 130–32, 136

journalists, 94, 169, 174; *see also* press

Journal of Politics, The, essay on image of Eisenhower (by Irish), 139

Justice Department: and files on White, 179; and interpretation of executive privilege, 204; *see also* Brownell, Herbert

Kaghan, Theodore (Information Services Library), resignation of, 174

Kennedy, John Fitzgerald, 242; and abolition of OCB, 263n39; cabinet meetings of, and Eisenhower's compared, 113; foreign policy-making machinery under, 16; and moon landing program, 242, 271n12; popularity of, 3, 4; and publicized presidential activism, 58; and relationship to Robert, compared to Eisenhower's relationship with Milton, 149n; role of Sorenson compared to Eisenhower's chief of staff, 243; role of special assistant Bundy to, 134; and steel industry conflict, 242; use of multiple advisors, 246

Kennedy, Robert, 149n, 235–36

Kennedy Library Oral History, 242

Kissinger, Henry (Nixon Secretary of State), 16–17, 18, 244

Knowland, William F. (Senate Republican Leader), 79, 191, 265n70; and Bricker Amendment, 86; and China blockade proposal, 216; and Eisenhower's coping with emotional opposition of, 72; on Eisenhower use of executive privilege, 205; and McCarthy censure, 200, 217, 218; and protecting Stevens from McCarthy, 185, 188

Korea: and Eisenhower's pre-presidential role, 108, 159

Korean conflict: Eisenhower administration and, 6, 169; Eisenhower, and end to, 61–62, 213, 231; and Taft's policy toward, 75; and Truman NSC, 125

Korean truce negotiations: and Eisenhower's covert intervention, 61–62, 93; press conference briefing on, 76

Krock, Arthur *(New York Times):* and article on Eisenhower, 7–8; on effect of Atoms for Peace speech on McCarthy, 181; and Johnson's opinion of Eisenhower, 29; on Johnson's loss of public support, 92; and McCarthy influence-seeking story, 187

Kyes, Roger, and Stevens's denial of surrender to McCarthy, 186

language: capability in use of, 66; *see also* instrumental use of language

Lasswell, Harold (political psychologist), on Eisenhower politics of agreement, 248

Latin America, aid policy for, 120–21

leaders, 259–60n54

leadership in conference, 31–35

leadership qualities, 7, 33–34, 35, 37, 44, 119, 235; leadership style, 10–11, 229–30, 233–34, 248; and coping with opposition, 72; and covert intervention *(see* delegation of authority; hidden-hand strategy; intermediaries); and crisis-mimimizing approach to problems, 232; and effectiveness in McCarthy case, 219–27; and effectiveness of no-personalities strategy, 233–35 passim; and face-to-face discussions, 31–35; formal/informal blend in, 233; hero image, and effect on, 233; and hidden-hand strategy, 58–65; and insulation from blame, 90–92; military influence on, 245; minimization of feuds, 116, 118; and practical abstraction, 236; role of guidance in, 247; and World War II *(see* military career); *see also* hidden-hand leadership style; informal leadership style; team leadership style

legal procedure, use of to weaken McCarthy, 170, 171

legislative leadership, 220, 239, 265n70

Legislative Leadership meeting: McCarthy campaign, 188; and budget analysis, 70; and executive privilege, 205; on Flemming proposal, 123; security over loyalty emphasis at, 171–72

legislative programs: cabinet promotion of, in McCarthy case, 223; campaign emphasis on successes in, 213; and recent presedential powers, 4

278

liberals: and Communist sympathizers, 163; as critics of Eisenhower administration, 5; and opposition to McCarthy, 214; and pressure for active anti-McCarthy presidential position, 169, 205; Taft attacks on, 50

librarians, and book censorship, 175

lightning-rod effect, 223, 238–39, 260n79

Lodge, Henry Cabot (U.N. Ambassador), 60, 138; anti-McCarthy strategy meeting, 203; on guidelines for congressional relations, 61; role of, in McCarthy case, 183–84, 204, 227

Long, Huey, analysis of success of, 170

loyalty, 34, 81–82, 91, 177; and Bohlen certification, 165–66; McCarthy request for files, 158; under Truman, 171

loyalty-security blunder, and McCarthy attack on army personnel, 184

loyalty and security program, and RNC reply to Stevenson, 191; see also McLeod

loyal underground, and McCarthy, 162

MacArthur, Douglas (General), 36; Eisenhower as aide to, 11–12, 254–55n9

McCarthy, Joseph R. (Wisconsin Senator), 156–227; abusive manner of, 204; accommodationist policy toward, 164–65; and accusations against, 177; on American Communist Party, 163; and Army personnel, 183–85; Atoms for Peace, and effect on, 181; and attitude toward allies, 181; and Bohlen nomination, 165–67; cabinet members' attitude toward, 164; and cabinet meetings, 115; as campaign issue, 13, 160–61; as chairman of Senate committee, 162; on China blockade, 216, 218; on CIA, 215, 217; and Cohn-Schine influence-seeking story, 183, 184n, 187, 203; on college graduates' attitude toward, 213; Congress, and effect of, 169; on Conant's appointment, 164–65; and credibility, 158, 226; and defeat of opposition candidates, 159 n; and demand for coercion of allies, 181; on educational community, 165; on Eisenhower (Milton), 218; on Eisenhower administration, 165; Eisenhower's ambiguous press conference on, 178; Eisenhower's analysis of, 169; Eisenhower's covert interventionism, and public support, 93; Eisenhower's domestic policy, and effect on, 173; Eisenhower's early assessment of, 157; Eisenhower's effectiveness against, 219–27; and Eisenhower's foreign policy, 170, 174, 181, 213, 218; and Eisenhower's no personalities strategy, 224; and Eisenhower's objectives, 212; Eisenhower's policy toward, 173; Eisenhower's pre-presidential observation of, 159, 160; Eisenhower's reaction to attacks from, 208; and Eisenhower support of senatorial candidacy, 161; on Eisenhower's WW II leadership, 160; and encroachment on executive branch powers, 162, 165, 168, 169, 223; and executive branch investigation, 162; and executive privilege, 205; and Fifth Amendment Communists, 163, 175, 184; goals of, and Eisenhower compared, 171–72; and government informants, 162, 209–10; and Greek shipping treaty incident, 167–68; hidden-hand techniques used against, 188–201, 220–

21, 227; on IIA, 163; and internal security controversy, 7; and investigation of Information Services Libraries, 174–75; on liberals, 163; key issue of, 223; on Marshall, 160, 214; Matthews incident, 177, 178; media, and rise of, 158–59; and "Memorandum of Understanding," 185, 186; morale, and effect of, 164, 183, 224–25; New York Times on, 158, 163–64, 185, 187, 192, 193, 201, 227; Nixon criticism of, in reply to Stevenson, 197–98; as object of investigation, 173; and opponents' view of Eisenhower, 223; and opposition of liberal congressional staff aides, 214; and political climate, 321; popularity of, 182n, 223; post-censure strategy for coping with, 219; and presidential advisors, 205; pressure for active opposition to, 169; and public image (see Gallup Poll); public opinion, and Eisenhower's action toward, 169, 270n; rebuttal of Eisenhower condemnation of, 191–92 (see also press conference); relationship with Eisenhower, 93–94, 217–19, 222n; Republican Party, and effect of, 188, 193, 195; and Schine incident, 198; and security files, 166; on security programs on Eisenhower and Truman, 172; on State Department, 158; strategy against, 169–71 passim, 203, 210, 227 (see also anti-McCarthy campaign); and televised committee meeting, 191–92; and Truman, 162, 180; on Voice of America, 163–64; and Wheeling speech, 158; see also McCarthy censure; McCarthy Committee

McCarthy "break," 217–19, 222n

McCarthy censure, 156, 214–17, 218, 224, 269n166; see also Watkins Committee

McCarthy Committee, 162, 198, 199; Army charges against McCarthy, 198 (see also army-McCarthy hearings); attitude of Cabinet toward, 164; and "confidence in Stevens" paper, 186; and Democratic support of open hearings, 202–3; Dirksen's role on, 185, 186; Eisenhower's attempt to restrict testimony, 190; Eisenhower press statements on investigations of, 163, 164; and executive privilege, 204; guidelines for, 187; and Matthews' attack on Protestant clergy, 177–78; methodology of, 162; rules for, 186; use of legal procedure to weaken investigations, 170, 171

McCarthyism, long-range effect of, 224–25n

McClellan, John (Dem. Ark), on army-McCarthy Committee, 209

McClendon, Sarah (journalist), 76

McCloy, John, J., 254–55

McLeod, Scott (Loyalty and Security Officer), 165, 166; press conference on, 191, 197; removal of, from security duties, 189; Washington Post on, 192

MacMillan, Harold (Prime Minister of Great Britain), 33

Mandate for Change (Eisenhower), 37

Marshall, George C. (General), 77, 161, 254–55n9, 264n56; charisma of Eisenhower compared to, 36; Cutler as aide to, 106; and delegation of authority, 81; Eisenhower as assistant to, 12–13; and Eisenhower as Chief of Staff, 141; McCarthy attacks on, 160, 214

Martin, Jack (Person's aide), and "Memorandum of Understanding," 186

Martin, Joseph (House Leader), 80, 205, 265*n*70;
Matsu, *see* offshore islands controversy
Matthews, J.B., and accusations against Protestant
  clergy, 177–78
media: Eisenhower's attitude toward McCarthy's
  seeking of, 169; and Eisenhower-press exchanges,
  195–96; on Eisenhower's relationship with
  McCarthy, 160; and Eisenhower's World War II
  military career, 13; and image of Adams's influence, 138, 139; and image of Eisenhower, 139; and
  rise of McCarthy, 158–59; use of, in hidden-hand
  strategy, 62;
memoirs, 9, 224
"Memoranda of Conferences with the President"
  (Goodpaster), 133–34
Memorandum of Understanding, 185–88 passim
Michigan, University of, and candidate popularity
  survey, 92, 93
military action, and congressional approval, 131
military aid: to Southeast Asia, 130, 131–32; to Indo-
  China, 136, 137
military career, 8, 11–14, 31, 38–39; as advisor on
  national security, 125 (*see also* national security);
  as Army Chief of Staff, 13, 118, 125; under Con-
  nor, 26; and delgation of authority, 80–81; and
  diplomacy, 29–30; and duty, 45; and influence on
  presidency, 14; and influence on thinking methodology, 26, 30, 149*n*, 244–45; and leadership, 197,
  245; and organizational experience, 101, 102, 103,
  138, 245; in Panama, 26; and source materials on
  Eisenhower, 10; and use of "personnel psychology," 236; and policy council, structure, 118; and
  public image of Eisenhower's organizational management, 103–4; publicity of, 13, 95; and public
  relations, 94
military hero: Eisenhower as, 96, 97
military policy, 197, 228, 231; and Congress, 131,
  137; and Eisenhower's involvement in, 83–85,
  135–36; on dependents overseas, 98; and disarmament, 47–48, 257*n*67; on Indo-China, 136–37,
  231; on intervention in Southeast Asia, 130, 131–
  32; on officers, 84; *see also* defense spending; foreign policy; military aid; missiles
missiles, 85, 85*n*, 134–35
Montgomery, Bernard (WW II field marshall), Eisenhower's relationship with, 44, 235
Montgomery, Robert, as coach, 96, 146
morale: importance of, in war, 259*n*30; McCarthy's
  effect on, 164, 183, 224–25; security program, and
  effect on, 172–73
Morgan, Gerald (liaison staff), and access to Eisenhower, 146; advisory role to army during
  McCarthy Committee era, 184, 186; and implementing executive privilege, 205
Mossadegh government (Iran): role of CIA in overthrow of, 6, 62, 137, 213, 228
Mundt, Karl (McCarthy Committee), 199, 208, 217;
  and army-McCarthy hearings, 207; and attempt to
  limit executive privilege, 206; and "Memorandum
  of Understanding," 185; and rule changes on
  McCarthy Committee, 192; and support of open
  army-McCarthy hearings, 203
Murrow, Edward R.: on Eisenhower-McCarthy conflict over informers, 210; and "See It Now" indictment of McCarthy, 198*n*

National Academy of Public Administration, on
  need for Chief of Staff, 244
National Conference of Christians and Jews, 178
Nationalist China, 20, 21, 72, 175; *see also* offshore
  islands controversy
national security, 33, 68, 85, 124–38; and budget,
  48*n*, 83; Eisenhower's role in Truman administration, 125, 159; and Jackson's role in, 34–35;
National Security Council, 106, 124–25, 265*n*70;
  Adams role in, 142*n*; adaptability of formal organization of, 241; and advice to Nixon and Kissinger, 17; and danger of leaks, 17; and debate on
  congressional approval of military action, 131; Eisenhower's attitude toward role of, 127; foreign
  policy role of, 114; implementation of policy decisions by OCB, 132; and informal policy making,
  133–34; Eisenhower's intervention in policy making, 85, 129; and Eisenhower leadership style,
  130–33 passim; members of, 125–26; and operational decisions, 133; organization of, under Truman, 102; planning process, 134 (*see also* Operations Coordinating Board); relation to NSC
  planning Board, 126–28; Tafts views of, 71
National Security Council meetings, 104, 128, 129–
  31, 133; and cabinet meetings compared, 124, 126;
  debates in, 127; Eisenhowers role at, 40; and Record of Actions, 132; and team building, 133
National Security Council Planning Board, 126–28;
  Cutler's role in, 125; and formal organizational
  style, 241–42
national security policy: classified documents on,
  129, 129*n*; and formal/informal organization role,
  124–38; McCarthy as deterrant to, 160; lack of
  Republican support for, 208
NATO (North Atlantic Treaty Organization: and
  Carroll as Eisenhower aide, 142; Eisenhower as
  commander of, 14, 125, 160, 165; and evasiveness
  on nuclear weapons for, 68; and hidden-hand termination of Korean conflict, 62; and organizational management, 101; Persons's role in, 107,
  146; resignation from, 160; and strategy conferences, 35; and U.S. missile policy, 134–35
Neustadt, Richard: *Presidential Power*, 234–35; on
  professionalism in presidency, 5, 121
neutralization, ineffectiveness of, 182
New Deal policies, public attitude, 50
New Eisenhower, in post-Adams era, 147–48
New Look defense policy, 48*n*, 70, 85
newspapers, use of, 41, 134, 147; *see also* press
New York *Herald Tribune* 96, 177, 196, 197
New York Times 13, 16, 68; and Brownell memorandum, 204*n*; coverage of McCarthy, 158, 163–64,
  185, 187, 192, 193, 201, 207; on Eisenhower's plea
  for congressional fair play, 191; on Eisenhower
  support of Stevens and army, 187, 206; and Eisenhower statements on McCarthy committee hearings, 163; on "Memorandum of Understanding,"
  185; and misquoting of Humphrey statement,
  121; and NSC proceedings leaks, 17; on
  McCarthy's role in army-McCarthy hearings, 201;
  see also Krock, Arthur; Reston, James
Nixon, Richard Milhaus (Vice-president): and accommodationist attitude toward McCarthy, 164;
  on aid to education, 123; as anti-McCarthy spokesman for Eisenhower, 189, 220; attempted removal

of, as running mate, 220, 234; on Eisenhower anti-Communism policy, 197; on Eisenhower's conversations with subordinates, 148–49; and Eisenhower failed goals, 248; on Eisenhower's hidden-hand failures, 64–65, 220, 234; on Eisenhower as military leader, 197; on Eisenhower's second-term candidacy, 257n65; Eisenhower's use of personality analysis, 78; and Hickel resignation, 242–43; as intermediary in Sherman Adams incident, 64–65; Oval Office Transcripts of, 234; as president, 3, 9, 9n, 17, 43, 44, 235, 240, 242–44; and press interest in McCarthy's influence seeking, 187; and rebuttal to Stevenson, 194, 195, 197–98; and second-term vice-presidency, 234; and Stevens, 185, 186; supporters of, 64

no personalities policy, 28, 29; adaptability of, 236; drawbacks of, in McCarthy case, 222, 224; and Eisenhower image, 239–40; and leadership style, 73–76, 233–34, 235; use of, with McCarthy, 160–61, 219, 221–22, 224; use of press conferences, 75–76, 160

non-professional presidential image, 121

Normandy invasion, 133

North African campaign, 25, 37, 42, 94

NSC 5612, and U.S. Policy in Mainland Southeast Asia, 129–31

Nuclear war: Eisenhower's attitude on, 33, 47–48; policy against, 96–97

nuclear weapons and strategy of evasiveness, 68

Office of Civil and Defense Mobilization, and NSC, 125

Office of Defense Mobilization, 146

Office of Management and Budget, *see* Bureau of the Budget

offshore islands controversy, 20–25, 69, 259n30

"O.K., S.A." (Time), on Adams, 144–45

"100 Days," and Roosevelt's leadership style compared to Eisenhower, 229, 230n

Open Skies foreign policy, 52, 90

operational decisions, records of, 129n

Operations Coordinating Board (OCB), 132–34, 263 n39; Staats as executive secretary of, 147

opposition, coping with, 70–73, 239

optimism, as leadership quality, 37, 38

organizational chart, and *Time*, 146

organizational innovations, 110

organizational leadership: dichotomies in 101–5; facility for, 236; and strategy against McCarthy, 171 (*see* leadership style); styles in modern presidencies, 242, 243, 261n2, 262n7

Organizational Man, The (Whyte), 139

"Organization Man in the Presidency" the (Irish), 139

organizational management, 101, 103–5, 110, 138; and advice to Secretary of Defense, 35, 118, 119, 140, 141; and coordination of White House staff, 142; and effectiveness of, 138–50; informal style, 114, 113–34, 146–50; of Roosevelt, 102, 261n2, 262n7; transferability of, 241–47 passim; *see also* team leadership

organizational structure, of White House, 105–13

organizational study, 113

organizational thinking, 244–45

Oval Office, recordings of meetings, 47

overseas information libraries, McCarthy investigation of, 162–63

overseas information service, 223–24

Pacciardi, (Italian Defense Minister), 44–45

PACGO, *see* President's Advisory Commission for Governmental Organization

painting, as hobby, 39

Panmunjom, and ending Korean conflict, 63

Papers of Dwight D. Eisenhower, The, 10

parochialism attitude toward, 118

party leaders, at stag dinners, 149

Patterson, Bradley (State Dept. Secretariat), 116–17, 122–24

Patton, George S., Jr. (General), 68, 77

peacemaker, image as, 96, 97

Pearson, Drew (journalist), 160

Pennsylvania State University, Milton Eisenhower as president of, 149

Pentagon, Eisenhower as advisor to, 125

People's Republic of China: and blockade proposal, 181, 216, 218; and Chinese Civil War, 20, 21; and hidden-hand strategy for Korean negotiations, 61–62; Knowland's reaction to, 79, 216; and McCarthy's attitudes, 160, 181, 218; and McCarthy treaty with Greek shippers, 167; and offshore island controversy, 20–25; and policy on Japan's trade with, 124; and press conference on policies toward, 70; Republican attitude toward, 69; and shooting of American planes, 216

Peress, Irving (Army Major), *see* Peress incident

Peress incident, 184, 188, 190, 223

Permanent Investigations Subcommittee, *see* McCarthy Committee

personality, 7–8, 15–18, 53, 54, 96, 97; *see also* personal qualities

personality assessment: and appointment of officials, 118–19; and delegation of authority, 80; of Dulles, 90; Eisenhower facility for, 236; of Fredendall, 78; of Halleck, 80; as leadership tool, 77–80, 234, 237; and McCarthy, 157, 222; of Nehru, 78; and tailoring of job descriptions, 77, 141, 142

personality conflicts, *see* no personalities policy

personality equations 27; of Adams, 41; of Eisenhower, 43–44, 245; use of, 236; *see also* personality assessment

personality management, 73–76

personal qualities, 257n63; and charisma, 36; and complexity, 9, 9n, 15; desirable in subordinates, 237; and energy, 38–41, 43, 233; and Eisenhower leadership style 233, 234, 236; and humanitarian image, 89; and intensity, 39

personal support, importance of, 99

personal unreliability, and security risks, 213n

personnel psychology, use of, 236, 237

Persons, Wilton B. (General): and attitude toward McCarthy, 164, 222; as Chief of staff, 147–48; as congressional liaison, 146, 148; on Eisenhower's request for McCarthy apology, 196; and implementing executive privilege, 205; on "the new Eisenhower," 265n70; and meeting on anti-

McCarthy congressional support, 189; and relationship with Eisenhower, 146, 147; role of, in Eisenhower's hidden-hand maneuvering, 61; and selection of Harlow, 108; on staff of Sherman Adams, 146; and Stevens, 186; and White House congressional relations unit, 107

persuasion: and analytic reasoning, 70–71; aptitude for, 53; presidency, and power of, 117; techniques of, 118

Pescadores, 20, 21

Philippines, military service in, 12, 13, 38–39

physical appearance, 7–8, 35

physical fittness, 32, 39

Pickett (General), at Gettysburg, 30

Planning Board, see National Security Council Planning Board

poker, 26

Poland, policy on trade with, 109–10

policy: changes in, 4, 229; see also cabinet; domestic policy; foreign policy; National Security Council

policy, and political convictions compared, 53

policy decisions, and Eisenhower's role, 85, 114–15, 129

policy goals of Eisenhower administration, 228

policy making, 114–15; for national security, 85, 124–38; in National Security Council 85, 129, 133–34; public and covert activism, 58–59 (see also hidden-hand leadership); and role of multiple advocacy, 246; and team leadership style, 109–12

policy papers and role of Adams, 147

political activism, 159, 265n70; see also hidden-hand leadership style

political climate, 229, 231, 248

political convictions, 46–52, 79, 116; and public policy compared, 53

political executive, Eisenhower's as, 5

political experience, in the army, 11–14

political leader, president as, 5

political motives, Eisenhower analysis of, 25; see also personality assessment

political psychology, 18, 24, 26, 45, 248

political skills, and leadership style, 234

political strategy, 233–34; see also delegation of authority; hidden-hand leadership; instrumental use of language; no personalities policy; personality assessment; public support

politicans: attitude toward, 8, 38; and Eisenhower's public/private image, 53; relationship with, 18, 28, 29, 46

politicking: and hidden-hand leadership, 60, 61, 234; military and presidential compared, 10–11; and Roosevelt leadership style, 229

politics: in military career, 11–14; public attitude toward, 25

Popular Front, censoring books on, 175

popularity: of Eisenhower, 4, 5–6; of Kennedy, 3, 4; of McCarthy, 202; see also Gallup Poll; Michigan, University of

positive program emphasis and anti-McCarthy strategy, 170, 173–74, 193

Potter, Charles (Rep. Michigan Senator), role of, in army-McCarthy hearings, 199, 209, 221

preinauguration cabinet meeting, 105–13

pre-presidential years, 14, 43, 45, 101; as Columbia University President, 14, 49, 159; see also military career

presidency, 3–5, 252n4; attitude toward, 11; military career and influence on, 12; suitability for, 54, 101

presidential campaign, 13, 96, 125, 181, 213

presidential candidacy: Democratic movement for, 159; and effect of NATO commandership, 160; and influence of foreign political climate, 47, 124; and position on McCarthy, 160–61, 213; Republican movement for, 14, 92, 159, 160; for second-term, 213, 257n65; support for, 46, 95–96; Taft's isolationalism as influence on, 49

presidential deportment, 240

presidential professionalism, 234–35

presidential treaty-making power, see Bricker Amendment

President's Advisory Commission for Governmental Organization, 110, 111

press: and Cohn influence-seeking story, 187; and coverage of Cabinet member's anti-McCarthy statements, 193; Eisenhower's attention to, 134; and image of Adams, 138; and interpretation of McLeod's removal 189; on McCarthy Committee, 163, 164, 185, 187; and reaction to Eisenhower's vague anti-McCarthy statements, 221; and Steven's denial of surrender, 186–87; "Memorandum of Understanding," 185; and underestimation of Eisenhower as WW II commander, 245; see also New York Times; Washington Post

press conference, 9, 19, 70, 97–98, 219; and anti-censorship position, 176–77; and anti-Communist position, 176–77, 189–90, 191; and anti-McCarthy position, 189–90, 193; on army-McCarthy hearings, 189–90, 200–1, 202–3; on Bohlen nomination, 166; on book censorship issue, 223; as candidate on McCarthy investigations, 160–61; on China blockade proposal, 216; on congressional fair play in committees, 191; and creation of confusion, 168, 176–77, 223; in defense of army, 189–90, 193; and Eisenhower's credibility, 148; and Eisenhower grammar, 8, 19, 20, 196; on Eisenhower-McCarthy conflict, 189–90; and Emphasis on Administration Program, 193; on executive privilege, 206–7; on Flander's speech, 196; on Formosa, 259n30; on Greek shipping treaty incident, 168; and Humphrey's apparent breach of unity on budget, 121; and image of Eisenhower's organizational management, 103, 104; and instrumental use of language, 67, 68, 75, 160, 161, 168, 176–77, 178, 206–7, 221, 259n30; on Korean truce negotiation, 76; on McCarthy, 160, 176, 178, 221; on McCarthy censure vote, 216; on McLeod demotion, 191; on management of foreign policy questions, 88; on network impartiality, 194–95; and no personalities policy, 75–76, 160; on Peress incident, 190; and planted questions, 219; and praise of Marshall, 161, 216; release of tape and transcripts, 195, 196, 201; and statements of political principle, 195; and support of Stevens 198–99; and Truman on McCarthy charges, 158–59; on Watkins Committee hearings, 227 (see also McCarthy censure); on White-

Truman incident, 179–80; *see also* Tuesday press conferences
press secretary, 41; *see* Hagerty, James
preventive politics, 248
principle: an executive privilege, 205; as anti-McCarthy strategy, 191
principles of leadership, 118–19, 194
priorities, 47, 85, 124
Protestant clergy, accusations against, 177–78
Psychological Strategy Board, 125, 132
psychology, and subordinates' selection, 119
public affairs, knowledge of, 16
public appeal, 96, 97, 241
public image, 96–97, 156, 182n, 239, 240; of Adams, 144–45, 147; of administrative ability, 42, 101, 103–4, 139 (*see also* organizational management); of cabinet members and Eisenhower compared, 91; of Communists, as agents of USSR, 172; of Dulles's authority in foreign policy, 88; and effect on leadership style, 233; of Eisenhower, 93, 96, 98, 137, 139, 147, 240; and Eisenhower compared to Roosevelt and Johnson, 156; of Eisenhower and McCarthy compared, 223; of Eisenhower and Dulles compared, 90, 91; of Eisenhower's management of McCarthy, 156, 161, 168, 201, 223, 225, 226; of Eisenhower's WW II military career, 94, 245; of Johnson, 3; and lack of activism, 58; of McCarthy, 182n, 200, 201, 206n, 225 (*see also* Gallup Poll); and media, 94, 139; of pre-presidential Eisenhower as liberal, 50; and press conference style, 70; and strategic use of language, 69; White-Truman incident, and Eisenhower's, 179–80; *see also* Gallup Poll; public opinion
publicity: of anti-censorship speech at Dartmouth, 176; and anti-McCarthy strategy, 170; attitudes toward, 94–95, 95n; and formal policy machine, 100; of McCarthy's investigations, 174; of presidential activism, 58; *see also* public relations
public opinion: of Eisenhower, 4, 15–16; of OCB, 263n39; influence of, on Eisenhower's handling of McCarthy, 270n169; on McCarthy's charges, 159
public/private dichotomy, 15–18, 53, 233
public relations, 94, 96; Hagerty use of, against McCarthy, 210
public relations professionals, and support of Eisenhower candidacy, 95–96
public speaking, effectiveness with, 19; rhetoric, 89
public support, 24, 71, 92–99; gaining, 18, 35, 36–38; and Eisenhower charisma, 36, 96; of offshore islands controversy, 20–25 passim; of post-FDR presidents, 3–4; maintenance of, 234
public works programs, 115

Quemoy, see offshore island controversy; question channeling for press conferences, 67
Quezo, Manuel (President of Philippines), and Eisenhower's military career, 12

Rabb, Maxwell (Cabinet Secretary), 113; role in "Emphasis on Administration Program," 193

racial integration, executive order on, 61
Radford, Arthur (Admiral, JCS), 130–31
radio commercials, use of in presidential campaign, 96
Rankin, John (Congressman), and Eisenhower diplomacy, 29–30, 247–48
Rapido River crossing incident, 29–30
Rayburn, Sam, (Democratic House Leader), 42
Reagan, Ronald: and declining public support, 3, 239; legislative leadership style compared to Eisenhower, 239; and major policy change, 229; pyramidal staff organization, 244; and use of lightning rod technique, 238–39, 260n79; and use of selective delegation, compared to Eisenhower, 237–38; and White House ambiance, 240
regulatory policy, and political climate, 231
reasoning, 9, 9n, 20, 21, 24; *see also* analytical reasoning
reassignment of duties, and organizational flexibility, 142
record keeping, 10; of operational decisions, 129n
Record of Action, 114, 132
recreation, 8, 26, 39, 256n43
Reed, Philip (General Electric), and Eisenhower explanation of anti-McCarthy Strategy, 170–71
Republican(s), 67, 70; and Adams resignation, 65; and domestic policy, 50, 50n, 51, 232; and movement to draft Eisenhower for president, 14, 92, 159, 160; on offshore islands controversy, 21–23 passim, 69; political philosophies, 122; and support for MacArthur, 36
Republican Congress: and appointment of McCarthy to committees, 162; and conflict over McCarthy, 188; and creation of NSC, 124–25; Eisenhower, 111–12; and foreign policy, 208
Republican congressional-administration team, and Stevens's denial of surrender statement, 186–87
Republican congressional leaders: changes in, 265n70; Eisenhower's relationship with, 104, 105, 112; Indo-China, and Peress incident, 188; on military policy, 137; and support of domestic program, 170–71
Republican congressmen: on disarmament, 47; and Eisenhower's team leadership style, 109–12; and legislative influence, 111; regarding McCarthy case, 189, 209
Republican conservatives: on disarmament, 47; Eisenhower's relationship with, 167
Republican convention, party unity, 161
Republican McCarthy Committee members: and advice to Stevens, 185; and "confidence in Stevens" paper, 186
Republican National Chairman, see Hall; Roberts
Republican National Committee, and Nixon's rebuttal to Stevenson, 194, 195, 197–98, 220
Republican Party, 50, 67; and draft Eisenhower movement, 14, 92, 159; and early McCarthy era, 158; Eisenhower's objectives for, 51–52; Eisenhower's relations with, 70, 159, 159n, 269n148; McCarthy's effect on, 188, 193, 195; Nixon as spokesman for, 194, 195, 197–98
Republican Senate Policy Committee, and McCarthy Committee guidelines, 187

respectability, image of, 240
responsibility, attitude toward, 45
Reston, James *(New York Times)*, "General Stands at Ease, A," 227
rhetoric, as strategic tool, 235
Roberts, Wesley (Republican National Chairman), and Adams's resignation, 143
Robertson, Reuben (Undersecretary of Defense), on aid to S. E. Asia, 130–31
Robinson, William E. (public relations), 95–96; on Eisenhower, 28, 41–42, 150
Rogers, William (Deputy Attorney General), and anti-McCarthy action, 178, 204
Roosevelt, Franklin D., 11; Bohlen role under, 165; Bureau of the Budget under, 102; cabinet meetings of, and Eisenhower's compared, 104; craftiness of, compared to Eisenhower, 156; and Eisenhower's military career, 13; and Emergency Banking Act, 203*n*; expansion of presidency, 232; face-to-face conversations compared to Eisenhower administration, 148; and leadership style compared to Eisenhower, 229–30; and major policy change, 229; organizational management style, 102, 262*n*2, 262*n*7; and political role of president, 4; and purge of unfriendly congressmen, 215; use of multiple advisors, 246; use of staff compared to Truman and Eisenhower, 145–46
Rovere, Richard, on Eisenhower, 5–6, 7, 21

Saltonstall, Leverett (Mass. Senator), and army McCarthy hearings, 199
Schine, G. David (McCarthy aide), 164; army assignment of, 183; and charges against McCarthy, 187, 198, 203; and Information Libraries investigation, 174; McCarthy's use of, for influence seeking, 183, 184, 184*n*, 203; Stevens's responsibility for investigation of, 206
Schine-Cohn-McCarthy request, and White House position of ignorance, 198
Schlesinger, Arthur, Sr., opinion poll on Eisenhower, 6
Seaton, Fred, and Stevens's denial of surrender, 186
second-term campaign, and emphasis on program achievements, 213
second-term candidacy, reasons for, 257*n*65
security files, limits on access to, 166
security-loyalty destinction, 171
security program, 7, 171–73
security risk, 171, 213, 213*n*; and McCarthy accusations against army, 183
Secretary of Defense: Eisenhower as, de facto, 136; as statutory member of NSC, 125; *see also* Forrestal, James V.
Secretary of State: as statutory member of NSC, 125; *see also* Dulles, John Foster
Secretary of the Treasury: as nonstatutory member of NSC, 126; *see also* Anderson; Humphrey
selective delegation, 222, 234, 238; and Eisenhower/Dulles foreign policy collaboration, 87–90; of Eisenhower and Reagan compared, 237–38; *see also* delegation of authority
self-assurance, 257*n*63
self-control, 43–45, 235

Senate, and McCarthy censure, 214
Senate Armed Services Committee, 199
seniority, 214, 232
separation of powers, 21; and Greek shipping incident, 168; and McCarthy case, 214, 223
Shanley, Bernard (Special Counsel), 146, 186, 205
silence, as strategic tool, 68, 227
sincerity, effect of, 92, 96, 97
sleep, and Eisenhower's routine, 38, 41
Smith, Merriman (Associated Press), 176, 191
Smith, Walter Bedell (Undersecretary of State): on Eisenhower's analysis of personalities, 77; on Eisenhower's consultation leadership, 115; on Eisenhower's gaining of subordinates, 34; and Eisenhower's policy making for Indo-China, 136–37; responsibilities of, 140; on use of Wilson as executive tool, 83–85
Snyder, Howard, (physician), and Eisenhower's health routine, 39
socialism, attitude toward, 50; and Eisenhower's attitude toward, 50
social programs, 6, 51, 115; and congressional approval of military action, 131
social security, 50, 51
Sorensen, Theodore: and reasons for Apollo project, 242; role of under Kennedy, compared to Eisenhower chiefs of staff, 243
source material, 9, 10, 10*n*
Southeast Asia: foreign policy toward, 71, 130–31; NSC meeting on, 129–31; under Johnson, 27, 243; *see also* Indo-China
Southeast Asia Treaty Organization, 130
Soviet Union: and Atoms for Peace, 181; and Eisenhower goal of détente, 228, 248; and Eisenhower's WW II strategy, 13; image of Communists as agents of, 172; on IRBM deployment to Greece, 134–35; and McCarthy's attacks on liberal sympathizers, 163; and U.S. foreign policy, 24, 71, 89–90, 213; and U-2 incident, 9
Sparkman, John: and Bohlen's files, 166; on Taft/Eisenhower Korean policy, 75; differences, 75
speaking style, 97
Special Assistant to the President for National Security, *see* Cutler, Robert
speech writers, Eisenhower as, 11, 16
Spivak, Robert, (journalist), and question on Nixon's defense of Republican Party, 195
spontaneity, and leadership style, 233
Staats, Elmer, 147–48; on OCB, 263*n*39
staff conferences, Eisenhower at, 40
staff procedure, formal organization of, 113; drawbacks of, 8
staffwork, and Eisenhower style compared to recent administrations, 247
Stassen, Harold (State Dept. Mutual Security Administration Chief): clash and Greek shipping treaty incident, 167–68; Stassen on Information Libraries, 174–75; and reply to McCarthy's anti-Eisenhower statements, 208
State Department, 158, 164, 174
State of the Union 1954, and instrumental use of language, 66
State, War and Navy Department, and military career, 102

Status of Actions reports, 114
Status of Forces Treaty, 12
Steel industry, Kennedy conflict with, and hypothetical Eisenhower approach compared, 242
Stephens, Thomas (appointments secretary), 108, 164, 165
Stevens, Robert (Army Secretary), 182–88 passim, 193–94, 222; and army-McCarthy hearings, 198, 202, 212; Eisenhower press conferences on, 190, 198–99; Eisenhower support of, 190, 198–99, 206; and Gallup Poll ratings, 202, 212; and "Memorandum of Understanding," 185, 186, 188; and press release on prosecution of McCarthy, 207; and Republican's "Confidence in Stevens" paper, 186; use of as lightning rod, 223
Stevenson, Adlai, 96, 97, 139, 220; as cause of Eisenhower-McCarthy confrontation, 194; and GOP McCarthyism speech, 198; Nixon rebuttal of campaign speech by, 197–98
Stockman, David (OMB Director), as lightning rod for Reagan, 238–39, 260n79
Stouffer, Samuel *Communism, Conformity and Civil Liberties*, 225–26
strategy, and coping with McCarthy, (see McCarthy, strategy against); and pretense of ignorance, 67
Strauss, Lewis (Secretary of Commerce), 123; ideological opposition to education, 123
structure of the presidency, 4–5
subordinates, 90–91, 193; Eisenhower relationship to, 34, 81–82, 91, 148–49; and gaff taking, 90–92; and lightning rod effect, 238; manipulation of, 44; protection of, 193–94; selection of, 77; and selective delegation, 238; and tailored job descriptions, 140–41
subpoenas: and John Adams's response to, *from* McCarthy, 183–84, 203; *see also* executive privilege
subversive books, 174–75
support, 18, 31–35, 97; sources of, 61, 71, 239–40; *see also* public support
Supreme Commander Allied Forces Europe, 13, 31, 73, 94, 101, 138, 240, 245
Supreme Headquarters Allied Powers Europe (SHAPE), 88

Taft, Robert A., 49, 49n, 50, 72, 189n; and Bohlen supporter, 166, 167, 169; death of, and effect on Congress, 186; Eisenhower's private criticisms of, 75; personality assessment of, 78–79; reaction to Eisenhower's defense/economy balancing, 70–71; and relationship with Eisenhower, 167; and support of Eisenhower programs, 71
talkativeness, and security risks, 171
taxes, Eisenhower's attitudes toward, 48
team building, 119–20, 122; Eisenhower and Reagan's capability for, 238; and NSC meetings, 133
team leadership, 105–13, 119, 241, 242, 247
techniques of leadership, see delegation of authority; hidden-hand leadership; instrumental use of language, no personalities policy; personality assessment; public support

television: as anti-McCarthy strategy, 220; use of, to combat Stevenson's speech, 194, 197; use of in presidential campaign, 96; use of, for public support, 19
temper, 16, 18, 38, 43–45, 254
Thailand, as SEATO member, 130
Third Army, Eisenhower as chief of staff of, 11
Time "O.K., S.A.," and Adams's image, 94, 144–45, 146
tradeoffs, and conflict avoidance in McCarthy case, 223
transferability, of leadership qualities, 35
treaties: and Greek shipping incidents, 167–68; Status of Forces treaty, 12; *see also* NATO; SEATO
"Treatment of Government Personnel", 193
troublemakers, covert elimination of, 93–94
Truman, Harry S, 11, 139; and accusations of McCarthyism in Eisenhower administration, 180; and Big Four conferences, 112; and Brownell criticism of security, 178, 179, 180; Bureau of the Budget under, 102; and cabinet of, 104, 242; coping with McCarthy, 158–59, 169; and Council of Economic Advisors, 146; Cutler as NSC advisor to, 106; Eisenhower advisory role to, 125, 159; and Eisenhower NATO appointment, 160; Eisenhower as chief of staff to, 102; Eisenhower's postwar relationship with, 13; and formation of EOP, 102; and Gallup poll, 159; and Hoover Commission, 110; and loyalty, 171; McCarthy's attacks on, 162, 180, 182; and NSC under, 102, 106, 125; organizational style, 261n2, 262n7; and outgoing budget, 70, 107; and Psychological Strategy Board, 132; security program of, 172; Steelman as assistant to, 145n; and *United States Organizational Manual*, 145; White House organization under, 102, 145–46
"Tuesday Luncheons," 243
Tuesday press conferences, 88
Two-term presidents, 4; Eisenhower as, 4

United Nations General Assembly, and Eisenhower's Atoms for Peace, 181
United States Army: and charges against McCarthy (see army-McCarthy hearings); Eisenhower support of, 206; McCarthy attack on, 182–87; *see also* Peress incident; Stevens; Zwicker
United States Information Agency (USIA), 142
United States Organizational Manual, 145, 146
United States Policy in the Event of Renewal of Agression in Vietnam, NSC meeting on, 129–31
United States Policy in Mainland Southeast Asia, NSC meeting on, 129–31
United States Presidency, changing character of, 3–5, 102
United States President, as statutory member of NSC, 125
unity, breach of, in Cabinet, 121
University of Michigan Survey Research Center, on effect of speaking style on election, 97
unpublished documents, 9, 10, 10n, 36
U-2 incident, 9, 253n14

VE-Day Victory Order, to avoid personal criticisms, 74
verbal strategies, 66–73, *see also* instrumental use of language
Vice-President, as statutory member of NSC, 125
Vice president elect at Hotel Commodore meeting, 105
Vichy France, 13, 25
Vietnam policy of Johnson, 27, 243
voice, commanding nature of, 17
voice of America, (VOA), McCarthy's investigation of, 162

Wainwright, Stuyvesant (Congressman) opinion of Eisenhower, 16, 18
Wake Island meeting, and team leadership, 108
Walters, Vernon A. ("Dick") (Translator) on temper as strategic tool, 44–45
War: attitude toward, 48, 257n67 (*see also* nuclear war)
War Department congressional liaison, persons as, 107
War Department, Planning Division, 12, 13, 254–55 n9
warmth: and public appeal, 96, 97; and public support, 92
Warren, Earl, 199
wartime newstreets, Eisenhower's support for, 36
Washington, D.C., military service in, 12, 13, 102, 103, 254–55n9
Washington Post: and Eisenhower's praise of Flanders, 196; and Eisenhower statements principle, 191; and Folliard's questions on McCarthy, 216; and McCarthy on Eisenhower's oppositional remarks, 192
Watkins, Arthur (Utah Sen.): Eisenhower praise for, 222n; *see also* Watkins Committee
Watkins Committee, 215, 216; *see also* McCarthy censure
Weitee, G.D. and public reaction to army-McCarthy hearings, 225
Welch, Joseph (army special counsel), 203; and army-McCarthy hearings, 200, 200n
Welfare program, 6, 115, 231
welfare state, attitude toward, 49, 50
Western Alliance, 21, 31, 71; and collective security policy, 47; Eisenhower leadership of, 13–14, 31; *see also* allies
Western Hemisphere meeting, 120
West Point: Eisenhower at, 32, 245–46, 254n9; motto of, 45; need for psychology at, 73
Wheeling speech, against Communism, 158
White, Harry Dexter (Truman aide), Brownell's Communist spy charges against, 178–80 passim
White, Theodore, on Eisenhower, 15–16, 18
White House, 42–43, 138, 146; during Hoover and Roosevelt administrations, compared, 102; infor-
mal style of, 146–150; organizational coordination of, 142; organizational structure of, 105–13, 138; role of, in army-McCarthy hearings, 198, 204, 221; and role in Stevens's denial of surrender statement, 186–87
White House aides, 144–46 passim, and Hotel Commodore meeting, 105; interaction among, 148; Roosevelt use of, 102; strengthened role of, 106; *see also* White House staff
White House Legislative Leadership Meeting, 70, 123, 171–72, 188, 205
White House Office, 102, 107
White House Staff, 8, 106, 139–41 passim, 146–47; *see also* White House aides
Whitman, Ann (confidential secretary), 10, 32, 238; cabinet meeting agendas, 117; Dirksen-Knowland postcenture meeting, 217; on Eisenhower query to Mundt regarding McCarthy hearings, 199; and notes on hidden-hand strategy, 59, 64–65; notes on, in military policy planning, 135
Wilson, Charles (Defense Secretary), 83, 84–85; and attitude toward trade with communist satellites, 109–10; and defense spending, 83; and Eisenhower's directives regarding McCarthy, 202–6 passim; on Information libraries problem, 174; personality assessment of, 80; statements, 193
Wilson, Richard (journalist), and Eisenhower's no personalities strategy, 75
Wisconsin, and Eisenhower/McCarthy candidacies, 161
working relationships and Eisenhower/McCarthy interaction, 87–92
World War II: and Eisenhower's dealings with Vichy France, 13, 25; Eisenhower's public image, 94, 245; Eisenhower's role in, 12–14, 31, 245; and Eisenhower's self-control, 44; Eisenhower's strategy, 12; Eisenhower as Supreme Commanding General, European Theater of Operations, 13, 31, 38, 73, 94, 101, 240, 245; and personality assessment, 77–78; and McCarthy criticisms of Eisenhower in Berlin, 160; and Normandy invasion, 133; North African campaign, 25, 37, 42, 94; and organizational management, 101, 138; and strategy in the Philippines, 13; and *Supreme Commander, The* (Ambrose), 13
writing skills, 86, 254–55n9

Yalta, Bohlen's role at, 165
Young Republican convention, 176

Zwicker, Ralph (Camp Kilmer), 201, 204; Eisenhower support of, 190; McCarthy interrogation on Peress case, 184–85, 188